Technopopulism

Technopopulism

The New Logic of Democratic Politics

CHRISTOPHER J. BICKERTON
AND
CARLO INVERNIZZI ACCETTI

OXFORD
UNIVERSITY PRESS

Great Clarendon Street, Oxford, OX2 6DP,
United Kingdom

Oxford University Press is a department of the University of Oxford.
It furthers the University's objective of excellence in research, scholarship,
and education by publishing worldwide. Oxford is a registered trade mark of
Oxford University Press in the UK and in certain other countries

© Christopher J. Bickerton and Carlo Invernizzi Accetti 2021

The moral rights of the authors have been asserted

First Edition published in 2021

Impression: 5

All rights reserved. No part of this publication may be reproduced, stored in
a retrieval system, or transmitted, in any form or by any means, without the
prior permission in writing of Oxford University Press, or as expressly permitted
by law, by licence or under terms agreed with the appropriate reprographics
rights organization. Enquiries concerning reproduction outside the scope of the
above should be sent to the Rights Department, Oxford University Press, at the
address above

You must not circulate this work in any other form
and you must impose this same condition on any acquirer

Published in the United States of America by Oxford University Press
198 Madison Avenue, New York, NY 10016, United States of America

British Library Cataloguing in Publication Data
Data available

Library of Congress Control Number: 2020951571

ISBN 978-0-19-880776-6

DOI: 10.1093/oso/9780198807766.001.0001

Printed and bound by
CPI Group (UK) Ltd, Croydon, CR0 4YY

Links to third party websites are provided by Oxford in good faith and
for information only. Oxford disclaims any responsibility for the materials
contained in any third party website referenced in this work.

Pour Ema et Mati

A mia madre,
Se' tanto grande e tanto vali
Che qual vuol grazia e a te non ricorre,
Sua disianza vuol volar senz'ali.

Acknowledgements

This book has been a long time in the making. It began as a series of conversations between us in 2012. We were both living in Paris at the time and our shared interest in the relationship between technocracy and populism was explored in the cafés and bars that lie between the Institut d'Etudes Politiques and the Saint-Sulpice Church. The conversation evolved into an intellectual project and eventually a book. The bulk of the work has been done once we had left Paris, one of us to New York and the other to Cambridge.

It is customary in shared writing projects of this kind to divide up the work and to think in terms of 'my' chapters and 'your' chapters. This is not the way we have written this book. The contents were worked out in long days of intensive discussions, once in Cambridge and a few times in New York. The job of drafting one or another chapter was divided up, but subsequent revisions have made it impossible to really identify any part of the book as 'mine' or 'yours'. This experience of thinking and writing together has been exhilarating. Our first and principal acknowledgement is to each other and to our shared willingness to push the limits of our thinking. We have aspired above all to reach what we felt was the right argument, wherever that might lead us.

We would like to thank Dominic Byatt at Oxford University Press, who has been an exemplary editor. He moved quickly at the beginning to give us the encouragement we needed. He then gave us the time to develop our ideas, pushing gently and eventually letting us move along at our own pace. The book would not have been possible had it not been for his support and (near infinite) patience over the years.

The ideas in this book have been articulated by us in a number of different settings. At times we presented them together, at other times separately. We would like to thank the following colleagues and institutions: a conference at the London School of Economics, organized by Lea Ypi and Jonthan White, where we presented the earliest version of our argument; the Centre for European Studies at Sciences Po, Paris, and their invitation to present our ideas at the Centre's general seminar, where we received stern but encouraging comments from Colin Hay; the Department of Politics and International Studies (POLIS) at the University of Cambridge, where the book's main argument was presented as part of the departmental seminar series; the Hertie School of Government in Berlin and Claus Offe and Ira Katznelson for their invitation there; the Moynihan Institute of Global Affairs at Syracuse University and Glyn Morgan for his invitation; the Executive Vice-Rectorship of the University of Guadalajara and

Melissa Amezcua Yepiz for her invitation; the Yale University Political Theory Workshop and Giulia Oskian for her invitation; the Rifkind Center for the Humanities and the Arts at The City College of New York and Mikhal Dekel and Andreas Killen for their invitation; the Thomae Smithi Academae meeting at Queens' College, Cambridge; and the European politics seminar at the Centre for European Studies, Harvard University, and Art Goldhammer in particular for his invitation.

We are very fortunate to have a group of generous colleagues and friends who accepted to participate in a manuscript workshop organized at The City College of New York in February 2020. This workshop was a remarkable experience of intellectual exchange which served to iron out a great number of imperfections in the manuscript. It remains far from perfect, but the workshop was crucial in helping us refine and more clearly articulate our claims. We would like to thank Sheri Berman, Pablo Bustinduy Amador, Sandipto Dasgupta, Nicolas Guilhot, Rajan Menon, Jonathan White, and Ian Zuckerman for their participation in that workshop. We would also like to thank a group of scholars who came together in May 2019, once again at City College, to discuss our first conceptual chapter, alongside their own work on related themes. These are Carlos de la Torre, Lisa Disch, Giulia Oskian, Maria Paula Saffon, and Nadia Urbinati.

Finally, as with any book, we have each incurred a long list of personal debts. I (Christopher Bickerton) would like to thank Philip Cunliffe, Alex Gourevitch, Lee Jones, and Peter Ramsay for their intellectual input into the ideas developed in this book. I would also like to thank my brilliant group of doctoral students, some of whom have been there since the writing on this book began. Jose Piquer, Daniel Smith, and Anton Jäger have been a great source of support, and it has been a delight to observe the development of their own projects which intersect in various ways with some of the themes of this book. I would like to thank Richard Nickl for introducing me to *The Lime Works* by Thomas Bernard, which proved the best antidote to writer's block, and to Daniel Beer, for the conversations towards the end of the writing process.

The book itself was finished during the Coronavirus lockdown in the spring of 2020. Finishing books are painful at the best times. This one was finished through bouts of writing in the early morning, before anyone was awake. Amidst all the worry and anxiety, my abiding memory of these days are the long walks with Mati through the empty city of Cambridge, animated by stories of treasure hunts and fairies that would last for hours, and the sound of Ema and Mati conducting science experiments in the back garden, as their laughter was joined by the sounds of the birds in the park beyond. My greatest debt is to my wife, Ema, and daughter Mati, for the never-ending joy they bring to my life.

I (Carlo Invernizzi Accetti) would first of all like to thank my department colleagues at The City College of New York for being the best thing that happened to me since the beginning of my professional career; and in particular Richard

Bernstein for being a true friend, as well as a great colleague and neighbour, for sharing his love of books with me, and being always willing to engage in any Pindaric flight of fancy, in his simultaneously playful and serious way; Bruce Cronin for his infectious good humour and for being the backbone of our department, with his elastic bands and questionable jokes; Rajan Menon for being a mentor as well as a colleague, his enduring support and wisdom, as well as probing comments on an earlier version of the manuscript, which helped clarify it in decisive ways; and Dan DiSalvo for being a great Chair, as well as a good friend, a constant source of inspiration and advice, and a model in the art of living. Other colleagues and friends I owe an enduring debt of gratitude to, for sharing their ideas with me and for constant support and advice, include: Sheri Berman, François Carrel Billiard, Lisa Disch, Nicolas Guilhot, Florence Haegel, Lavie Margolin, Jan-Werner Müller, Nadia Urbinati, and Jonathan White.

Amongst my personal friends, I would like to thank Pablo Bustinduy Amador, Joshua Craze, Sandipto Dasgupta, Luca Falciola, Zelia Gallo, Alex Gourevitch, Amana Fontanella-Khan, James Fontanella-Khan, Clara Mattei, Giulia Oskian, Federico Poggianti, Francesco Ronchi, Tom Theuns, and Fabio Wolkenstein for the infinite conversations which are the true ground and intellectual lifeblood of all the ideas I have contributed to this book. I would also like to thank both my parents, Emanuele Invernizzi and Consuelo Accetti, for their undying love and guidance, which is more than a compass and a drive: it feels like a set of wings, as Dante explains much better in the verse I lifted from him to dedicate the book to my mother. Finally, I thank Brittany Huckabee, the woman I love, for sharing virtually every moment in the writing of this book with me, for contributing decisively to many of its ideas, but also for the warmth and joy you have brought to my life, and the promise of more.

Christopher J. Bickerton
Cambridge, UK

Carlo Invernizzi Accetti
New York

Contents

Introduction	1
1. The Concept of Technopopulism	17
2. Varieties of Technopopulism	39
3. The Origins of Technopopulism	88
4. The Consequences of Technopopulism	144
5. Normative Reflections on Technopopulism	169
Conclusion: Beyond Technopopulism?	198
Bibliography	219
Index	243

Introduction

We shall never understand politics until we know what the struggle is about.

Schattschneider (1960: vii)

You have a new dimension in politics today... It is not as easy as when you hasd a left-right scale on which you could plot political choices. It is not necessarily a chaotic system, but a new political landscape is taking shape... We are going to see it for many years.

Hans Wallmark, centre-right Swedish MP,
quoted in Hall (2019)

Making Sense of the Present

What's wrong with contemporary democracy? That something is going on should be evident to all. Many long-established parties are in terminal decline. Others have disappeared altogether. Party systems are being transformed beyond recognition as new political actors and party types emerge. The lines of conflict and struggle that structured political competition appear increasingly blurred. Doubts proliferate about whether existing democratic regimes are able to sustain their basic values. Citizens are becoming increasingly dissatisfied, not just with specific political actors and organizations, but also with the democratic order itself.

The idea that democracy is somehow in 'crisis' has become commonplace. However, the categories used to describe and interpret this crisis have so far remained primarily *negative*, in that they focus on what is fading away or being actively undermined. We have been told that we live in a 'post-democratic' age (Crouch 2003), that 'the age of party democracy has passed' (Mair 2013), and that representative democracy is being 'disfigured' (Urbinati 2014). According to some, democracy may even be 'dying' (Levitsky and Ziblatt 2018) or close to its 'end' (Runciman 2018).

If a crisis signals the transition from one state of affairs to another, then it necessarily means leaving something behind. This proliferation of negative images is therefore understandable and highlights a number of important tendencies at work in contemporary democratic regimes. What remains is the challenge of delineating the contours of the new type of politics that is replacing what is being left behind. This book's ambition is to develop a set of *positive* conceptual categories for understanding the present crisis of democracy. We do not mean positive in the sense of 'good' rather than 'bad' but in the sense of describing and explaining what does exist and how it works.

What we are observing is neither the 'end' nor the 'death' of democracy but rather a transformation in the logic of political competition *within* existing democratic regimes. By and large, democratic orders have proved more resilient than some of the direst predictions made over the past few years would have had it. This is true at least in the minimal sense that elections and basic rights remain mostly in place, and it seems possible to replace incumbents by constitutionally guaranteed means. Nevertheless, the way in which political actors operate within these constitutional frameworks, and the sorts of outcomes generated by our political systems, have been profoundly transformed.

For most of the history of modern democracy, political competition was structured primarily by the left/right ideological divide. This meant that candidates for office competed with one another by proposing alternative visions of the way in which society ought to be governed, which encapsulated different value systems and rival interests within it. Although this mode of political competition has not entirely disappeared, it has been overlain—and to some extent replaced—by a new logic, whereby candidates for office compete primarily in terms of rival claims to embody the 'people' as a whole and to possess the necessary competence for translating its will into policy. Populism and technocracy have therefore become the main structuring poles of contemporary democratic politics.

The relationship between populism and technocracy is not the same as that between left and right. Since the latter are rooted in conflicting value systems and interest groups within society, they are substantively at odds with one another. In contrast, because they abstract from substantive interests and policy commitments, populism and technocracy are better understood as *modes of political action*, which can be combined with one another in multiple and creative ways. Many contemporary political actors and organizations turn out to display the characteristic features of both. This suggests that the most salient differences between the main protagonists on the contemporary political scene do not lie in their substantive ideological profiles but rather in the specific way in which they *combine* both populist and technocratic traits with one another.

Two aspects of this overarching thesis are worth highlighting, since they imply significant transformations in the way contemporary democratic politics—and especially the role of populism and technocracy within it—are understood. First, we are suggesting that populism and technocracy should not be seen merely as characteristic features of a specific category of actors, which can be separated from and held in opposition to 'mainstream' politicians. Instead, they have become constitutive elements of a new political grammar—or logic—that affects the behaviour of *all* political actors in contemporary democratic regimes. As we will see with reference to many specific examples, even political actors who claim to want to stand against populism or technocracy (or both), ultimately end up assuming some of their characteristic features. This is because of the complex system of political incentives and constraints they are now faced with.

The second important point is that, within this new political logic, populism and technocracy do not function merely as opposites of one another. Even though appeals to the popular will and to competence are often rhetorically deployed against each other, there is also a deep affinity between them, which consists in the fact that they are both unmoored from the representation of specific values and interests within society and therefore advance an *unmediated conception of the common good*, in the form either of a monolithic conception of the 'popular will' or the specific conception of political 'truth' technocrats claim to have access to. This sets both populism and technocracy at odds with the traditional conception of party democracy as a system of 'regulated rivalry' between competing social interests and values that are all in principle equally legitimate (Rosenblum 2008).

The concept we propose to capture this set of developments is that of *technopopulism*, defined as a new logic of political action based on the combination of populist and technocratic traits. By this we mean that contemporary political actors face a new system of incentives and constraints which pushes them to adopt both populist and technocratic modes of discourse and organization, at the same time as they become increasingly unmoored from the representation of particular interests and values within society. While this doesn't necessarily spell the 'end' of democracy as such—since formal democratic procedures remain largely in place—it profoundly alters their *modus operandi*, as well as the political outcomes they lead to.

This book traces the contours of the technopopulist logic, but also sets itself the task of examining its historical origins, likely consequences, and normative implications. It provides the first comprehensive theory of technopopulism as the new structuring logic of contemporary democratic politics.

Combining Populism and Technocracy

We substantiate the overarching theses above with reference to a few illustrative examples. A political logic as we propose to define it—that is, a system of political incentives and constraints—is visible principally through its effects. For this reason, we focus on the discursive patterns and organizational forms adopted by a number of political actors in our primary area of focus, which is Western Europe. We also discuss the way in which some of the most long-standing political parties—such as the British Labour Party—have adapted and changed discursively and organizationally, in line with the technopopulist political logic. However, the main focus is on a number of new political parties that are currently in power in

France, Italy, and Spain. The advantage of focusing on relatively new political parties is that they display the structural conditions that shape contemporary political action in a purer—and therefore starker—way.

The Italian Five Star Movement (M5S) is a case in point. Founded in 2009 by the popular Italian blogger and comedian Beppe Grillo, together with the lesser known media strategist and internet guru, Gianroberto Casaleggio, it quickly asserted itself as one of the mainstays of contemporary Italian politics. By 2013 it had already obtained the largest share of votes compared to any other national party, and since 2018 it has consistently participated in government coalitions as a senior partner—first with the far-right *Lega Nord* and then with the centre-left *Partito Democratico*. From the start, it has been evident to commentators that the M5S constitutes a novel political phenomenon, which is difficult to characterize in terms of the traditional left/right divide. It explicitly challenges the relevance of those conceptual categories, claiming to stand 'above and beyond' the left/right distinction. Both its substantive policy commitments and sociological bases of support constitute an 'eclectic mix' which 'cuts across traditional ideological divisions' (Tronconi 2015).

The label that has been most often employed to describe it is that of 'populism', since the M5S does indeed display many characteristic features of the way this notion is ordinarily defined—from the antagonistic rhetoric opposing 'the people' to an evil and corrupt 'elite' up to the concentration of power within a leadership figure claiming a direct relationship of embodiment with ordinary voters that bypasses ordinary bodies (Mudde 2004; Müller 2016; Urbinati 2019). Yet, another set of distinctive features that is at the root of the M5S's recent political success has so far received less attention, namely its distinctively technocratic conception of politics. This is manifested by its claim to offer more competent and effective government than traditional political parties, in virtue of the 'collective intelligence' it is able to harness through its online decision-making tools. Differently from traditional political parties, the M5S is not held together by a specific set of contestable values, nor does it claim to represent the interests of any clearly identifiable social group. Instead, it presents itself as an instrument for improving the quality of public policy by relying on the organizational power of the World Wide Web as a way of pooling the diffuse competence of ordinary citizens (Bordignon and Ceccarini 2013; Bickerton and Invernizzi Accetti 2018).

For this reason, we suggest that the M5S is best understood as manifesting a particular combination of both populist and technocratic features, which we describe as amounting to a form of 'technopopulism from below'. In this particular manifestation of technopopulism, ordinary citizens are not apprehended as bearers of subjective interests or values, but rather as carriers of a specific competence or expertise, which can be put in the service of the rest of society through the means of the web. It is primarily as individual 'experts', capable of collectively formulating better policy, that the people are opposed to a political elite, represented as either incompetent or in the service of special interests. In turn, this formula's success demonstrates the powerful appeal of a political offer based on the combination of populist and technocratic elements in the present political landscape.

Another salient example is Emmanuel Macron's *La République En Marche* (LREM). Although this political movement has both sought to present itself and often been interpreted as a political nemesis—and indeed a bulwark—against populist movements such as the Italian M5S, on closer inspection it turns out to display many of the same characteristic features. LREM was originally created in March 2016 after its future leader (who had previously served as a Minister in François Hollande's Socialist government) launched a 'Great March' across France. This was essentially a 'fact-finding mission', through which a tightly knit group of policy specialists and public opinion experts sought to establish what the French electorate wanted most. In Macron's own telling, the two main findings of this endeavour were that French citizens were deeply dissatisfied with the 'political establishment' and that they were more interested in a set of 'consensual policy goals'—such as 'improving living standards' and 'preserving public order and security'—than in pursuing any ideologically connoted political projects (Macron 2016).

LREM was created as a self-conscious attempt to respond to these two specific sets of demands. As such, its populist and technocratic traits were constitutive features of LREM. The populist component is evident in Macron's claim to run against the French 'political establishment', even though, like many other populist leaders, he is in reality a member of that same establishment. We also see it in the high degree of personalization and concentration of power around the figure of Macron himself. As numerous commentators immediately pointed out, it was no coincidence that the acronym for LREM's first incarnation as *En Marche!* also corresponded to the initials of its founder and undisputed leader, Emmanuel Macron. At the same time, Macron has cultivated a characteristically technocratic image of himself as a competent and effective caretaker of the common interest, who is capable of 'achieving results', uninhibited by any ideological preconceptions.

LREM's synthesis between populist and technocratic traits occurs in a rather different way compared to the Italian M5S. In the latter case, populism and technocracy are fused together by the goal of harnessing 'collective intelligence' through the World Wide Web. In the case of LREM, the synthesis occurs in the person of Macron himself, who is presented as an embodiment of the French people's aspiration for political change while also construed as a competent and effective 'doer', possessing the necessary dynamism and expertise to deliver good policies. For this reason, we suggest that LREM is best understood as manifesting a form of 'technopopulism from above', which revolves around the leadership figure of Macron himself, rather than the M5S's notion of the 'citizen-expert'.

Nevertheless, the simultaneous electoral success of these two political forces in Italy and France clearly demonstrates a broader structural tendency for contemporary political actors to adopt some combination of both populist and technocratic features, at the expense of more substantive ideological orientations along the traditional left/right axis.

A third illustrative example is offered by Spain's *Podemos*. This is a more complex case than the other two we have considered because *Podemos* has a marked ideological profile on the left/right spectrum. Both its leadership and the vast majority of its electorate issue from an explicitly left-leaning political history. Its pattern of alliances—both within the European Parliament and the Spanish national assembly—confirm its left-leaning orientation. And yet, it is impossible to understand *Podemos's* rise to political prominence since 2014, and its transformative impact upon the Spanish party system, without taking into account the strength of its appeal on grounds other than its substantive ideological commitments.

The party was founded on what its leaders described as a 'populist hypothesis'. According to this hypothesis, 'the traditional ideological categories of "left" and "right" have become historically exhausted' and a new dimension of political confrontation ought to be created between 'the people' or 'democracy', on one hand, and 'elites' or '*la casta*' on the other (Errejon 2014). This discursive strategy was redoubled by a characteristically populist mode of organization, which revolves around 'a leadership figure with a high recognition factor', in Pablo Iglesias's own self-description (Iglesias 2015). At the same time, *Podemos* has also always cultivated a distinctively technocratic image of itself as a '*partido de profesores*' offering competent and pragmatic solutions to Spain's political problems (De Azua 2014). This dimension has been manifested most clearly in the party's recurrent insistence that its policy proposals are ultimately rooted in 'common sense'. *Podemos* went as far as modelling one of its electoral manifesto programmes on an Ikea catalogue, the message being that the party was in touch with the habits of 'ordinary voters' whilst also offering policies that were as self-evident as the instructions provided to put a piece of Ikea furniture together. In its other manifestoes, *Podemos* emphasized its appeal to competence by asking neutral 'independent experts' to validate them (Bickerton and Invernizzi-Accetti 2018).

For this reason, we suggest that *Podemos* is best understood as a 'hybrid' case of technopopulism, manifesting both a left-leaning political identity and a particular combination of populist and technocratic elements. In a private communication, one of the founders of this political movement—the former European political coordinator and member of the Spanish Parliament, Pablo Bustinduy Amador—suggested that both these features—i.e. its populist and technocratic traits—were self-consciously adopted by the party's leadership because they were thought to be necessary to stand a chance of gaining political power and therefore implementing its substantively left-leaning political agenda.

Precisely because of its hybridity, *Podemos* offers a powerful illustration of the concrete effects of what we have called the technopopulist logic on the public discourse and mode of political organization of contemporary contenders for power. Even a party with the intention of advancing an ideologically connoted political agenda faces a powerful set of incentives to adopt some combination of populist and technocratic forms of discourse and modes of political organization. That is precisely what we mean when we claim that populism and technocracy have become the constitutive elements of a new political logic, which is in part replacing and in part superimposing itself on the traditional left/right divide.

The Novelty of Technopopulism

An objection that might be raised at this point is that the phenomenon we are claiming to uncover is not that novel or surprising. After all, haven't all contenders for elected office in the history of modern democracy always claimed to represent the interests of the 'people' as a whole and to possess the necessary competence for translating its will into policy? Our response is that the apparent ubiquity of the technopopulist political logic in the present political landscape should not obscure its historical specificity. If we compare the instances of technopopulism we have mentioned above with the more traditional ideological parties that populated the West European political landscape throughout most of the twentieth century, significant differences emerge.

To begin with, it is worth noting that not all political parties have always appealed to the 'people' as a ground for political legitimacy and electoral support. Both families of mainstream political parties that dominated the West European political landscape in the aftermath of the Second World War—i.e. Social Democrats on the centre-left and Christian Democrats on the centre-right—construed themselves as the political exponents of a specific *part* of society: the working class in the case of Social Democrats and Christians in the case of Christian Democrats. Both of these party families did sometimes argue that the particular interests and values of the specific class or group they claimed to represent also corresponded to the general interest of society as a whole, but this yielded a very different conception of the general interest compared to the notion of the 'popular will' implicit in populist claims to represent the people as a whole. As Maurice Duverger noted in his classic discussion of modern mass parties, they offered a 'particular interpretation of the common good', rooted in a specific set of values and interests, which involves a recognition of the legitimacy of other competing interpretations (Duverger 1954). In contrast, a hallmark of populist discourse is the claim to 'exclusive representation' of the popular will, which leaves little or no space for the recognition of the legitimacy of political opponents (Müller 2016).

Something similar can be said of the currently pervasive appeals to competence or expertise as grounds for political legitimacy. During the early and middle parts of the twentieth century, such appeals were far less prominent in political discourse than they are today. This was because of the substantive ideological conflict that existed between traditional mass parties. In a situation in which there is deep disagreement over the *ends* of political action, it makes little sense to present oneself as competent at achieving results or delivering on 'good' public policy. What is at stake, and what is being debated, is precisely what constitutes 'good' public policy in the first place. Thus, for a large part of the history of the twentieth century, claims to competence and expertise only really had traction in intra-party or coalition struggles, where the main substantive political questions could be assumed to have been already settled. In appealing to voters at large, candidates for office tended to present themselves as champions of particular interests and value systems, and far less as ideologically neutral purveyors of 'good' public policy.

The current political salience of claims to competence and expertise is possible only because of the gradual closure—or at least shrinking—of the ideological horizon, as fundamental disagreements over the way in which society ought to be ran have been increasingly marginalized. Like the populist appeals to the 'people' as a whole, technocratic claims to competence or expertise as grounds for political legitimacy could only really become as dominant as they are today to the extent that ideologically driven conflicts of interest and value receded into the background.

What we call the technopopulist political logic is therefore a historically specific phenomenon. In principle, there might always have been an incentive for democratic political actors to present themselves as representatives of the 'people' as a whole, and to claim to have the necessary competence for translating its will into policy, but the historical record indicates that this was not the case. When electoral competition was structured primarily around ideological confrontation, populism and technocracy were far less salient as modes of political action. What requires explanation is that today these modes of action have become so omnipresent that it has become difficult to imagine a time when they were not so. That is precisely what this book sets out to do.

The Separation of Society and Politics

The explanation we provide for the rise of technopopulism as the main structuring logic of contemporary democratic politics focuses on the complex evolution of the relationship between societal divisions and partisan politics over the course of the past century or so. During the first few decades of the twentieth century—that is, at the height of what we propose to call the 'era of the ideological political logic'—society and politics were tied to one another by a variety of powerful instances of mediation between them, such as mass parties, but also trade unions, civic associations, religious organizations, and the information and opinion media. This was reflected in what Seymour Martin Lispet and Stein Rokkan have famously called the 'cleavage structure' of mid-century European politics: political parties were effectively the expression of underlying social groups, defined by differences of interest and value (Lipset and Rokkan 1967).

Over the course of the ensuing decades, this tight relationship of correspondence between societal divisions and partisan politics progressively broke down. One reason for this was the erosion of the social formations and groups that were the basis for the established sociopolitical cleavages. This erosion occurred because of *transformations in the economic structure* (which undermined the traditional class distinction between 'proletariat' and 'bourgeoisie'), an overarching process of *secularization* (which diminished the salience of the distinction between religious and non-religious citizens), and a generalized process of *cognitive mobilization* (which tended to produce more homogenous national cultures, across previously distinct localities and socio-economic groups).

The translation of this erosion of social group formations into politics was slow, uneven, and indirect. Party systems originating in the ideological divisions of the first few decades of the twentieth century remained 'frozen' in place long after the societies over which they governed had changed profoundly (Lipset and Rokkan 1967: 50). The result of this overarching process of separation between society and politics was a hollowing out of the existing mechanisms of intermediation between them. As Richard Katz and Peter Mair famously observed, political parties responded to their progressive loss of foothold in society by retreating into the state, colluding rather than competing with one another to share the benefits of public office (Katz and Mair 1995). Trade unions, religious organizations, and other civic associations retreated into the private sphere, defending particular interests and values, but shedding their broader orientation towards the common good (Putnam 2000). Even though these instances of political mediation remained, they were increasingly disconnected from each other, exacerbating the existing chasm between society and politics.

These broad sociopolitical transformations had an important effect on the incentives and constraints faced by political actors. In the absence of the social groups and communities defined by their distinctive worldviews, electoral contenders for public office were encouraged to tone down ideological distinctions and conflicts of value, focusing instead on their capacity to govern 'responsibly'. Political parties that do not compete with one another for specific sectors of the electorate, but rather collude with each other to share the benefits of public office, are more likely to appear legitimate in the eyes of the electorate if they can claim to deliver 'good' policies. By the same token, however, this process of 'cartelization' opened a window of opportunity for political outsiders to gain electoral advantage by challenging the collusion of mainstream political parties itself through a claim to representation of the 'people' as a whole, set against the self-serving political elites in office (Katz and Mair 2018).

The germs of the technopopulist logic were therefore present once the distinctive social formations corresponding to ideologically polarized forms of politics had given way to societies characterized by high levels of individualization, atomization, and the decline of those organized interests that could mediate the relationship between individual voters and the exercise of political power. Two further historical developments nonetheless proved necessary to break the empty carapace of ideologically driven partisan politics, which had remained 'frozen' in place since the 1920s. The first was the collapse of the Soviet Union and the ensuing end of the Cold War, which substantiated the idea that 'There Is No Alternative' to a market-based economy and a liberal-democratic political system (Séville 2017a, 2017b). This also deprived many of the Conservative and Christian Democratic parties of the *raison d'être* that had effectively converted them into anti-Communist coalitions during the Cold War (Invernizzi-Accetti 2019). The second critical juncture was the Great Recession of 2008–11. This elicited a distinctively technocratic response from the political and economic establishment, which fed into a broader 'populist backlash' by those perceived themselves as having been taken advantage of in the process (Tooze 2018). The effect of the Great Recession was to catalyse the technopopulist political logic, providing new opportunities for mobilization for actors and movements that had no direct connection to the social world of ideological politics that had been long gone.

The emergence of technopopulism is thus the result of a complex and far-reaching historical process, which ties together a number of different societal and political dynamics. In a nutshell, our argument is that technopopulism stems from an overarching process of separation between society and politics, which has undermined the mechanisms of intermediation between them. This has led to a far greater salience of unmediated conceptions of the common good—such as the populist idea of a unified and monolithic 'popular will' and the technocratic idea that there is an objective political 'truth'. These are very different claims about the public or collective interest that prevailed when ideologically driven political parties structured electoral competition along the lines of conflicting values and interests within society.

The Unbearable Lightness of Politics

The consequences of this deep political reorganization are equally wide-ranging. In this book, we focus on four in particular: two that affect the nature of electoral competition itself and two that concern the relationship between the political system and society at large. To begin with, we suggest that politicians claiming to stand for an unmediated conception of the common good are less likely to recognize the democratic legitimacy of their opponents, compared to politicians claiming to represent a particular interpretation of it. If one claims to have direct access to the ultimate ground of political legitimacy, then anybody who happens to disagree or advance a different interpretation of how society ought to be governed can only appear to be either mistaken about what the common good actually consists in, or in the service of special—and therefore illegitimate—interests. As purveyors of these unmediated conceptions of the common good, political actors whose appeal rests upon a synthesis of populism and technocracy are therefore more likely to dismiss their political opponents as politically ignorant or malicious.

The implication is that the rise of technopopulism can be expected to be accompanied by an *increasing conflictuality* within political life. Rival contenders for office increasingly misrecognize each other's democratic legitimacy and therefore attack each other personally, challenging one another's motivations, grounds of support, and moral probity. Political rivalry becomes more and more like all-out enmity. This is a phenomenon that has already been widely observed in contemporary democratic regimes in terms of rising levels of 'affective polarization' (see, for instance: Iyengar and Westwood 2015; Hobolt et al. 2018), increasing 'toxicity' of political language and strategy (Ignatieff 2017; Beckett 2018), and a generalized 'breakdown of traditional forms of cooperation and mutual respect' between partisan opponents (Drutman 2017).

A second parallel consequence of the rise of technopopulism stems from the fact that neither populist nor technocratic appeals are in principle tied to any specific policy agenda. Unmoored from the representation of particular interests or values within society, they are compatible with all kinds of substantive sets of policies. This is manifested not only by the fact that recent and contemporary populists and technocrats have been located on just about any point of the traditional left/right spectrum, but also (more importantly) by the fact that technopopulist political actors and organizations have shown themselves to be markedly more rapid in *changing* their substantive policy commitments compared to traditional ideologically driven politicians. Emmanuel Macron, for instance, began his political career as a Minister in François Hollande's Socialist government, ran his electoral campaign as a 'radical centrist', but has since been pursuing a political agenda that most closely approximates that of the centre-right. The Italian M5S has swung wildly in its substantive policy commitments, as testified by its successive coalition alliances with the far-right *Lega Nord* and the centre-left *Partito Democratico*.

As populism and technocracy become the main structuring poles of contemporary democratic politics, substantive policy commitments are losing the centrality they previously had in electoral competition. Instead, what matters more is the specific *way* in which candidates for office present themselves to the public, staking out simultaneous claims to competence and popular appeal. A consequence of technopopulism is therefore that seemingly trivial matters, such as the candidates' personal qualities, their skill in using the modern means of mass communication, as well as their track record of 'success' in whatever activity they engaged in before entering into politics, tend to assume centre stage, at the expense of substantive ideological and policy disputes. This development has been amply documented in writing on the 'personalization' and 'spectacularization' of politics (e.g. Mazzoleni and Schulz 1999; McAllister 2007). The limit point of this logic is what, following Ilvo Diamanti, we call the 'politics of doing'; that is, a politics that ceases to be about *what* is to be done, and instead becomes more and more about *who* does it, *how* it is done, and ultimately that *something* is being done, whatever that 'something' may be (Diamanti 2010).

Taking these first two consequences together, one obtains a picture of a politics that is at once deeply confrontational but also insubstantial, confirming a widespread impression that all the 'sound and fury' of contemporary electoral competition ultimately doesn't amount to much in the way of substantive political alternatives being presented to the electorate. The idea of an 'unbearable lightness' of contemporary democratic politics—first advanced by Tony Judt (2010), paraphrasing the title of a famous novel by Milan Kundera—captures this overall effect of the rise of technopopulism on the nature of contemporary electoral competition.

This description also gives an indication of what we take to be the third main consequence of the rise of technopopulism, which concerns the perception of the political system by society at large. It might seem a paradox that precisely as politicians claim to represent the interests of the 'people' as a whole and to have the necessary competence for translating its will into policy, electors appear to be increasingly distrustful of them, and more and more dissatisfied with their work. Yet, it is another widely documented fact that levels of trust in politicians and of satisfaction with the quality of democratic representation have been declining markedly over the past couple of decades—i.e. over the same time span during which populism and technocracy have emerged as the main structuring poles of contemporary democratic politics (e.g. Foa and Mounk 2016; Foa et al. 2020).

One way of interpreting these findings is to suppose that seething democratic discontent is a *cause* of the rise of populism and technocracy as the main structuring poles of contemporary democratic politics. However, there is also reason to believe that the rise of technopopulism may contribute in further *exacerbating* the widespread sense of political dissatisfaction. This generates a feedback loop whereby, instead of abetting or contrasting the crisis of confidence in politicians, technopopulism ultimately proves to deepen it further. The reason has to do with an important—though underappreciated—insight from democratic theory, which is another key component of our analysis of the present crisis of democracy. Namely, that instances of political mediation between society and the state—such as political parties, but also trade unions, religious organizations, and other civic associations, as well the information and opinion media—play an essential role in giving individual citizens the sense that they are being adequately represented. The disproportion between individual interests and values, on one hand, and those of the collectivity as a whole, on the other, is such that the former can only get a sense that they are adequately represented within the latter if they band together in intermediary bodies to act politically upon it. To the extent that both populism and technocracy stem from and further exacerbate a generalized crisis of these intermediary bodies, they therefore feed back into the widespread sense of democratic discontent, of which they are at least in part also an expression.

From this, we identify a final consequence of technopopulism. To the extent that technopopulism undermines the sense of effective democratic representation of the citizenry at large, it affects the ultimate grounds of political legitimacy of the state. To the extent that the latter is unable to rely on this kind of legitimacy to secure compliance from its citizens, it is likely to become more 'Hobbesian'; that is, to rely on physically repressive means for doing so. This too is a development that has been widely observed by recent political commentators, in connection with phenomena such as 'mass incarceration', increasing levels of surveillance and policing, and the rise of the so-called 'security state' (Garland 2001; Wacquant 2009; NRC 2014).

While a variety of different explanations for these phenomena have already been put forward, the connection with the nature and quality of democratic representation is a relatively new avenue of research (e.g. Ramsay 2016; Gallo 2018). The rise of technopopulism may offer further grounds to substantiate this connection, inasmuch as the growing democratic discontent it both stems from and further exacerbates may be plausibly supposed to contribute to the state's growing need to rely on physical repression to secure compliance from its citizens. The relatively uninhibited—and in some cases openly flaunted—use of the coercive apparatus of the state by technopopulist political actors who succeed in coming to power (such as Macron's handling the '*gilets jaunes*' protest movement) provides further evidence for this claim. The rise of technopopulism as the new structuring logic of contemporary democratic politics can therefore be said to contribute in bolstering a new form of authoritarianism, which compensates for its perceived deficit of democratic legitimacy with increasingly repressive means of social control.

Ways Out

After having examined the nature, origins, and likely consequences of the rise of technopopulism, the last chapter of this book takes a step back and develops some normative reflections upon it. Though we do not take it to spell the 'end' or 'death' of democracy as a set of institutionalized procedures, we do argue that the rise of technopopulism constitutes something *bad* for the quality of existing democratic regimes. The reason is rooted in our analysis of its consequences: to the extent that technopopulism increases the conflictuality of democratic competition, while at the same time depriving it of substance, it shrinks the range of available avenues for political change. And, to the extent that it exacerbates the separation of society from politics, while compensating for it with an increased use of the repressive apparatus of the state, it diminishes the extent of the democratic legitimacy of the political system as a whole.

For this reason, the book ends by considering some possible remedies—or ways out—from technopopulism. The discussion begins by noting that in the existing academic literature on populism and technocracy, these two political forms are frequently portrayed as possible *remedies for one another*. Populism is often justified as a reaction to—and therefore corrective for—the confiscation of popular sovereignty by unelected technocratic bodies and elites (e.g. Mouffe 2018). Technocracy is frequently defended as a bulwark against the threat of populist takeover of certain key areas of policy (e.g. Monti and Goulard 2012). This has led some commentators to suggest that populism and technocracy may need to be balanced with one another, in order for contemporary democratic regimes to obtain a healthy 'equilibrium' between responsive and responsible government; that is effective democratic representation and good policy outcomes (e.g. Rosenfeld 2019).

Our contention is that this is a misguided way of thinking because it depends on the assumption that the relationship between populism and technocracy is merely 'zero sum', in the sense that more of one implies less of the other and vice versa. A key thesis running throughout our book is that this is not so: beyond their outer elements of opposition, there is also an important dimension of affinity—and indeed complementarity—between populism and technocracy, which implies that they can go hand in hand and be combined with one another. This, in turn, implies that populism and technocracy cannot function as antidotes for one another, but can rather only be contrasted *together*, as part of the same overarching political logic.

In order to do that, we suggest, it is necessary to address the main underlying cause for the rise of the technopopulist political logic to begin with; that is, the crisis of traditional mechanisms of mediation between society and politics, which had historically exercised the function of articulating the particular interests and values present within society in rival conceptions of the common good, competing with one another for electoral support, while recognizing each other's democratic legitimacy. This is another way of saying that a possible way of contrasting both populism and technocracy lies in a revitalization of the mechanisms of *party democracy* which previously ensured the connection between society and politics.

Instead of calls for a more 'direct' representation of the popular will and for more 'competence' in government, we recommend more interest intermediation, ideological diversification, and partisan competition as an antidote for both.

Revitalizing the dimension of interest- and value-driven partisanship will be difficult, not least because the rise of populism and technocracy as the main structuring poles of contemporary democratic politics stems in large part from a crisis of the instances of political mediation in the first place. However, we maintain that it is necessary to draw a distinction between the dimension of interest- and value-driven partisanship *itself* and the specific organization *forms* through which it has been historically instantiated so far. While it may well be the case that the traditional organizational forms of ideologically driven mass parties, trade unions, religious organizations, and other civic associations have now become obsolete because of the deep-seated social and political transformations we began discussing above, the dimension of partisanship itself—construed as a way of articulating particular interests and values with one another in order to have them weigh politically at the level of the whole—does not appear any less relevant than it ever was. As long as there are conflicts of interest and value, individuals will have to band together with one another in order to have theirs affect the political direction of society as a whole.

A revival of the dimension of interest- and value-driven partisanship may therefore be possible through a transformation of its main organizational forms. Whereas the mass parties, trade unions, religious organizations, and civic associations of yore were by and large deeply hierarchical and bureaucratic organizations, more internally democratic modes of political organization may be able to better meet the demand for political participation expressed by today's more individualized and cognitively mobilized electorate. More democracy in the way in which forms of political mediation are organized may thus be a way to make political engagement more attractive for greater sectors of the population and therefore enable a wider range of conflicting social interests and values to recolonize the domain of electoral competition. Of course, many new technopopulist movements themselves claim to stand for the democratization of political life. Our argument about greater democracy is made as part of a call for a more *mediated* relationship between citizens and political power, not as a critique of the very idea of mediation, as we find in the M5S and other forms of technopopulism.

None of these suggestions should be understood as a 'golden bullet' capable of solving all the problems we take to be connected with the rise of technopopulism. As we hope to show through our analysis, technopopulism is the result of an extremely wide-ranging and deeply rooted set of sociological and political processes. It would be implausible to expect any simple and straightforward fix for it. Attempting to do so without also considering how to close the gap between society and politics is unlikely to succeed. We recognize that what ultimately matters is that politics is grounded in 'goal differentiation' (Kircheimer 1966), meaning that competing political actors stand for different views about to what ends do they wish to exercise political power. The democratization of the existing channels of political participation can contribute to this and should be considered as a *component* of any broader solution to the set of problems we have identified in this book.

1
The Concept of Technopopulism

Introduction

This chapter offers a formal definition of the concept of technopopulism, which is intended both as a theoretical basis for the more empirical chapters to follow and as an independent contribution to the broader field of interpretive political science. By this we mean that branch of the study of politics that is primarily concerned with developing adequate concepts for making sense of the political reality. This approach is sometimes opposed to explanatory political science, whose goal is said to be the study of causal relations between different political phenomena (Finlayson 2004). Our contention is that the two approaches are not mutually exclusive but complementary, since proper explanation supposes an adequate conceptualization of the relevant phenomena, just as adequate interpretation cannot abstract from genetic processes. The definitional exercise we undertake in this chapter should therefore be seen as preliminary to the broader discussion of the varieties, origins, and consequences of technopopulism contained in the ensuing chapters of the book.

We begin by surveying the various ways in which the concept of technopopulism has already been employed in the existing academic literature. Since we identify several layers of confusion in this domain, we propose to systematize the concept of technopopulism by defining it as an organizing logic of electoral competition based on the combination of populist and technocratic discursive tropes and modes of political organization. To clarify what we mean by this, we first explain what we take an organizing logic of electoral competition to be. We then offer formal definitions of the two main modes of political action that characterize the technopopulist political logic; i.e. populism and technocracy. Finally, we contrast the technopopulist political logic with what we take to be its main historical antecedent and contemporary rival; that is what we call the ideological political logic.

Jean-Jacques Rousseau once famously stated that: 'My ideas all fit together; but I cannot present them all at once' (Rousseau 1762: 65). In a similar vein, we develop our understanding of technopopulism in this chapter in way that is analytical, abstract, and focused above all on the task of concept formation. We then move into more empirical and historical discussions in the chapters that follow.

Technopopulism: The New Logic of Democratic Politics. Christopher J. Bickerton and Carlo Invernizzi Accetti, Oxford University Press (2021). © Christopher J. Bickerton and Carlo Invernizzi Accetti.
DOI: 10.1093/oso/9780198807766.003.0002

The Meanings of Technopopulism

Technopopulism is a relatively new concept. The term was first coined by Arthur Lipow and Patrick Seyd in a 1995 article entitled 'Political Parties and the Challenge to Democracy: From Steam Engines to Technopopulism'. Since then, but especially over the course of the past decade or so, the term has been appropriated—and sometimes reinvented—by a variety of authors, to describe a broad range of different phenomena and dynamics. Although it has by now become impossible to survey all the specific uses of this term, we identify two broad sets of confusions in the way in which it is generally employed.

The first set of confusions concerns the meaning and role assigned to the prefix 'techno-' in the concept of technopopulism. In Lipow and Seyd's original article, this referred rather explicitly to the notion of *technology*. This is why they use the notion of technopopulism almost interchangeably with that of 'tele-democracy', while opposing both to the mode of political organization they took to be dominant at the time of the 'steam engine', i.e. political parties (Lipow and Seyd 1995). More recently, the prefix 'techno-' has tended to be used to refer to the notion of *technocracy*, rather than technology. Lorenzo Castellani has proposed a definition of technopopulism as a 'political regime' characterized by 'an interaction between global capitalism, technocratic institutions, and new polarizing/populist political movements' (Castellani 2018). Others have continued to oscillate rather confusingly between these two uses. Emiliana De Blasio and Michele Sorice define technopopulism as 'the belief that government of the people, by the people and for the people is achievable by means of information communications technology' (De Blasio and Sorice 2018). However, they also later add that: 'Both technopopulism and technocratic approaches in neoliberal populism find common ground in considering technology as a framework and not simply a tool.'

In light of this confusion, it is important to make clear from the start that what we are interested in exploring in this book is not the relationship between technology and populism, but rather that between technocracy and populism. Following the more recent and prevalent uses of the term, we therefore assume the prefix 'techno-' to refer to the notion of *technocracy*. Of course, with this we do not mean to deny that recent technological developments have played an important role in the emergence of what we will be calling technopopulism. However, we are interested in the role of technology to the extent that it helps explain how populism and technocracy are related to one another in the contemporary political landscape.

Another important area of confusion related to the prefix 'techno-' in the concept of technopopulism concerns its way of relating to the other constitutive element in the construct; that is, the notion of populism. As Anders Esmark has pointed out, one of the results of the recent explosion in research on populism has been a proliferation of qualifying adjectives that aim to better specify the precise meaning of this notion—from 'agrarian' to 'right wing' and 'left wing', to 'media', 'economic', et cetera (see Esmark 2020). To the extent that it is interpreted in this way, the prefix 'techno-' has the effect of demoting the technocratic dimension to second class status, a variant of populism rather than a phenomenon in its own right. Carlos de la Torre has for instance used the notion of technopopulism to describe the specific 'type of populism' he claims to have been manifested by the former Ecuadorean president, Rafael Correa. 'Under Correa' he writes 'populism has turned into elitism...Technocratic reason—with its claim to be true and scientific—replaces the give-and-take of democratic debate over proposals' (De la Torre 2013: 39).

This way of defining technopopulism contrasts with the ones that construe technocracy as a separate and equally significant component notion, alongside (rather than merely qualifying) that of populism. One example is Castellani's definition of technopopulism we cited above; another is Bordignon's description of the Italian Five Star Movement as a 'technopopulist party' that 'combines populism and technocracy' (Castellani 2018; Bordignon 2016). In this book, we are interested in exploring the relationship between populism and technocracy, meaning that we will not be treating technopopulism as a specific type (i.e. subcategory) of populism but rather as the name for a broader political logic that puts them in relation with one another. In so doing, we follow Jan-Werner Müller (2016) and Daniele Caramani (2017), assuming that populism and technocracy constitute two 'parallel', but also in many ways 'specular' modes of political action or representation, and as such can be combined as well as contrasted with one another (see also Bickerton and Invernizzi Accetti 2015, 2017).

The second set of confusions in recent academic uses of the concept of technopopulism concerns the specific kind of phenomenon it is supposed to describe; that is, the *genus* of which it is a type. As we have already in part seen, some authors have used the concept of technopopulism to define a particular type of political *actor*, whereas others use it to describe a type of political *regime*. De la Torre and Bordignon focus on Rafael Correa and the Italian Five Star Movement, respectively. Similarly, Alexandros Kioupkiolis and Francisco Perez have used the concept of 'reflexive technopopulism' to describe Spain's *Podemos* (Kioupkiolis and Perez 2019), whereas for Lenka Buštíková and Petra Guasti the Czech ANO party amounts to a form of 'technocratic populism' (Buštíková and Guasti 2019). In contrast, Lorenzo Castellani explicitly suggests that technopopulism is best understood as a type of 'political regime'; or, as he also puts it, a 'mode of organization of political power' (Castellani 2018). Similarly, Mary Graham treats technopopulism as a 'new mode of governance', whose characteristic feature is the use of 'transparency regulation' to steer individual and collective behaviour (Graham 2002).

Somewhere in between the idea that technopopulism constitutes a type of political actor and a type of political regime lies Lipow and Seyd's original use of the term to describe a type of *discourse* or 'ideology'. In their article, the notion of technopopulism is not associated with any particular actor or set of actors, but also falls short of amounting to an entirely new set of institutions or system of relations between political actors. Instead, it is treated as a 'way of thinking' that can be manifested—to a greater to a lesser degree—by a variety of different actors. Similarly, in their discussion of technopopulism, De Blasio and Sorice maintain that: '[i]f we consider technopopulism as an emerging discourse, or a "discursive ideology", we should also consider the possibility of finding elements and dimensions of technopopulism even in parties not clearly definable as techno-populist' (De Blasio and Sorice 2018).

Our proposed definition of the term has in common with Lipow and Seyd's, and De Blasio and Sorice's, the idea that technopopulism cannot be reduced merely to a category of political actors—since it also concerns the relationships *amongst* political actors. Nor do we define it as an entirely new political regime since it is a phenomenon that takes place *within* existing democratic regimes. Differently from these authors, however, we do not think that the notions of discourse or ideology are adequate to capture the specific phenomenon we are interested in exploring, for at least two reasons.

The first is that the notions of discourse and ideology suffer from an intellectualist bias manifested by Lipow and Seyd's claim that technopopulism ultimately boils down to a 'way of thinking'. While we of course agree that ideas matter in determining political action, we also maintain that there is an important material—and especially organizational—dimension to technopopulism, which is missed by the notions of discourse and ideology. As well as determining how political actors 'think', technopopulism also affects the concrete ways in which they organize and act. For this reason, it cannot be reduced merely to a discourse or ideology.

Secondly, treating technopopulism as an ideology is also awkward because (as we will discuss in more detail in what follows) one of the defining features of this political logic is precisely the rejection of the traditional ideological categories of 'left' and 'right'. There is therefore a distinctively *anti-* or at least *post-*ideological dimension to technopopulism, which is obscured by the idea that it constitutes an ideology in itself. For this reason, we maintain that technopopulism is better understood as an organizing *logic* of political competition, characterized by a set of incentives and constraints that result in contemporary political actors increasingly adopting both populist and technocratic forms of discourse and modes of political organization, at the expense of more substantive ideological orientations.

What Is a Political Logic?

Our definition of technopopulism is predicated on the assumption that the behaviour of electoral contenders for office in democratic regimes is not determined exclusively by their preferences or goals. It is also structured by a set of incentives and constraints deriving from the broader social and political context, which have the effect of giving a certain shape and regularity to the behaviour of all political actors within it.

In the most general sense, we can say that the logic of all political competition in electoral democracies consists in the fact that rival contenders for public office compete for votes, and therefore ultimately political power, with one another. Of course, electoral victory and political power may not be the final goal of all these political actors. Politicians may be motivated by the desire to achieve certain substantive policy goals, as well as by power and prestige for their own sake. However, the point is that all electoral contenders for public office must have a proximate goal of obtaining as many votes as possible, at least in the long run. Otherwise they wouldn't engage in the electoral process to begin with.

Beyond this general logic, we maintain that there also exists a more specific political logic in electoral democracies, which concerns the *way* in which rival contenders for public office compete with one another for votes. This consists in the set of incentives and constraints that politicians face in a given social and political context. For instance, in a situation of high societal polarization, where political resources are scarce, all electoral contenders for office have an incentive to focus on mobilizing the support of specific groups within society, on the basis of their shared interests and values. Conversely, in a highly fragmented society, with plentiful and effective means of political mobilization, politicians may have a greater incentive to spread their electoral basis of support as thinly and widely as possible, to maximize their chances of winning.

The effect of these more specific sets of incentives and constraints is to impose a certain regularity on the patterns of action employed by competing candidates for office. Inasmuch as they concern the specific way of competing for electoral support, these regularities abstract from the substantive policy and personal goals of individual politicians. A political logic—in the sense in which we claim that technopopulism is the new structuring logic of contemporary democratic politics—is therefore a contextually and historically specific set of incentives and constraints, which affects the way in which rival contenders for public office compete with one another in the electoral sphere, independently of their substantive policy goals.

The closest approximation to this idea we were able to find in the existing academic literature is Eric Schattschneider's claim that electoral competition is always 'about' something, in the sense that it is governed by an overarching conflict and the attendant set of categories and distinctions (Schattschneider 1960). This idea was elucidated by Peter Mair when he wrote that:

> Party competition—and democratic politics more generally—is usually dominated by a particular overriding choice, to which other considerations are subordinated. This is not just a matter of what one party does or another party does. Rather, it is something around which the party system as a whole, or at least the core of that system revolves. Much as rival cigarette manufacturers have a mutual interest in the promotion of smoking, however competitive they may be vis-à-vis one another as far as the marketing of their particular brand may be concerned, the established parties in a party system have a mutual interest in the survival of their particular conflict as an axis of political competition... Party systems are therefore 'about' something in the sense that they center around a particular structure of competition (Mair 1997: 13–14).

What Mair is here calling the 'particular structure' of electoral competition is very close to what we proposed to call its organizing logic, inasmuch as both determine what electoral competition is ultimately *about*—i.e. the specific form it takes in a given historical and political context.

There remains, however, an important difference. Both Schattschneider and Mair assume that electoral competition must ultimately be a about a substantive social and therefore political 'conflict'. They therefore assume that the logic of electoral competition is necessarily *oppositional* in the sense that competing candidates for office stake out different substantive positions with respect to that overarching conflict, and then struggle to win votes on that basis. We maintain that the contemporary salience of both populist and technocratic modes of representation reveals the possibility of a different kind of political logic, which remains competitive but without being oppositional.

The difference between political 'competition' and 'opposition' was originally drawn by Otto Kircheimer (Kircheimer 1966). The former, for him, exists as long as 'political jobs are filled by selection from candidates whose number is in excess of the places to be filled' (1966: 237). In contrast, the latter supposes a measure of substantive 'goal differentiation' between available candidates, meaning substantive disagreement over the ultimate goals of political action. Thus understood, Kircheimer argues that: '[a]ny form of political opposition necessarily involves some kind of competition. But the reverse does not hold true: political competition does not necessarily involve opposition' (1966: 237). The implication is that politicians can still compete with one another for scarce offices, even if there is no goal differentiation. Under such circumstances, political competition appears 'more in the nature of a collision between people obliged to squeeze through the same narrow thoroughfare to punch the clock before 8:45am' (1966: 251).

The idea of political competition *without* substantive opposition alluded to by Kirchheimer is a central feature of the way in which we understand the way in which the technopopulist logic works in contemporary democracies. It is not accurate to suppose that political competition is necessarily structured around a substantive social and political conflict. While determining what electoral competition is 'about', a political logic can set the terms of electoral competition—i.e. offer a set of incentives and constraints that shapes *how* politicians compete with one another—without necessarily involving any substantive conflict over ultimate ends. This is significant because the distinctive feature of the technopopulist political logic we focus on in this book is precisely that it encourages all competing contenders for electoral office to adopt both populist and technocratic forms of discourse and modes of political organization, independently of their substantive policy goals.

To say that technopopulism has become the main organizing logic of contemporary democratic politics is therefore to argue that politics is increasingly about competing claims to represent the 'people' as a whole and to possess the necessary 'competence' for translating its will into policy. More substantive ideological conflicts recede into the background or are articulated in ways that are also bound up with the types of appeals and claims that are generated by the technopopulist logic.

The Technopopulist Logic

To further clarify the definition we have proposed, we propose to explore the different ways in which claims to represent the 'people' as a whole and appeals to competence or expertise can be combined with one another. In the existing academic literature, but also in recent political discourse itself, populism and technocracy are frequently *opposed* to each other. For instance, in the 2013 Italian political elections, when the insurgent Five Star Movement first fielded candidates against the incumbent government led by Mario Monti, it was common for observers and participants in the elections to frame them as a 'contest between populism and technocracy'. Similarly, the second round of the 2017 French presidential election, which saw a run-off between Marine Le Pen and Emmanuel Macron, was construed as pitting 'anti-establishment populism' against a 'technocratic defense of the established order'. In this case too, the participants themselves played along with these presumptive roles: Macron condemned Le Pen's populism whilst Le Pen railed at Macron's incarnation of the technocratic establishment.

Opposing populism to technocracy in this way is only one way of relating them to each other. Between the two extremes of claiming to be a populist standing against technocracy and vice versa, there is a whole range of possible ways of combining them with one another, which may turn out to be more politically profitable than simply opposing them to each other. In fact, we argue that in spite of their claims to the contrary, both the political forces we cited above ended up winning their respective electoral contests not simply by employing populist modes of action and representation *against* technocratic ones or vice versa, but also and more importantly by providing some synthesis of the two.

All political actors in contemporary democracies can reap political advantages by combining populist and technocratic forms of discourse and modes of political organization, though their ability to do so is conditioned by a variety of factors, including a party's ideological legacies, the specific issues that can arise in the course of campaigns and the relational quality of the positions taken by political actors in a campaign, meaning that one actor can be constrained by what another says or does. Thus, when we say that technopopulism has become the organizing logic of contemporary democratic politics, we mean that all political actors face a set of incentives and constraints that encourages them to assume the distinctive features of both populism *and* technocracy, independently of their substantive policy goals. In this sense, electoral competition is becoming increasingly 'about' populism and technocracy, since electoral contenders for public office compete primarily in terms of rival claims to embody the 'people' as a whole and to possess the necessary competence for translating its will into policy.

An implication of this logic is that what distinguishes competing candidates for office and determines their chances of electoral success is first and foremost the specific *way* in which they combine both populist claims to popularity and technocratic claims to expertise, rather than the particular sets of interests and values that are served by their substantive policy commitments. That is, they are distinguished by the specific *type* of technopopulism they manifest. This is certainly not the only logic that determines political outcomes in contemporary democracies. Technopopulist syntheses are made in response to political events, and whilst political logics shape the response to events, political outcomes are themselves heavily dependent upon crises or unexpected developments and not reducible to the logics themselves. At the same time, the technopopulist political logic has not entirely replaced the previously dominant logic of partisan competition, based on substantive ideological confrontation, meaning that we have to take in account the complex interaction between these two different, but also simultaneously operative, political logics.

We discuss the differences between the technopopulist and ideological political logics in the last section of this chapter. Before that, it is necessary to offer further clarity as to the specific ways in which we propose to define the notions of populism and technocracy themselves, since our definitions correspond in some ways with existing scholarship but also challenge this scholarship in a number of respects.

The Definition of Populism

The notion of populism has recently been the topic of much attention—and disagreement. No doubt because many sense that it captures something important about contemporary democratic politics, there has been a veritable explosion of research on this topic. At the same time, the very fact that the notion has been so widely employed has led to a proliferation of different meanings and connotations being attached to the term (for an overview, see Rovira Kaltwasser et al. 2017). We adopt an ecumenical approach to its definition. By this we mean that we do not seek to intervene in the ongoing disputes over the most appropriate way of defining populism but rather try to synthetize a variety of different approaches in a way that is best suited to our own task of concept formation. We are not seeking to make yet another 'distinctive' contribution to the existing academic literature on this topic but only to clarify the way in which we use the term for the purpose of building our broader concept of technopopulism.

Most existing studies of populism agree in defining it as a particular *mode of political action*; that is, not as a substantive set of policy or value commitments, but rather as a particular way of acting politically that inflects or transforms one's substantive policy goals, without determining them entirely. Jan-Werner Müller writes explicitly that 'populism isn't about policy content', but rather about 'making a certain kind of moral claim', the content of which can come from 'any particular ideology' (Müller 2016: 160). Similarly, Kurt Weyland maintains that:

> The driving force behind populism is political, not ideological. Prototypical populist movements are practically impossible to define in ideological terms. Argentine Peronism for decades spanned the full arch from fascist right to radical left. And who could define the Bolivarianism of Hugo Chavez, who took advice from reactionary Norberto Ceserolese as well as Marxist Heinz Dietrich? (Weyland 2017: 54).

Beyond this broad area of agreement, the existing academic literature on populism appears to be deeply divided over what, precisely, constitute the distinctive features of this particular mode of political action. 'Ideational' approaches to populism stress the use of a certain kind of language, or discourse, centring around the opposition between people and elite. 'Organizational' approaches focus on a distinctive mode of political organization, involving a direct appeal by a personalized leader to a disorganized electorate, which bypasses intermediary bodies. A few illustrative examples will serve to substantiate this point.

Cas Mudde defines populism in terms of the idea that 'society is ultimately separated in two homogeneous and antagonistic groups: the pure people vs the corrupt elite' (Mudde 2004: 543). This definition harks back to Ernesto Laclau's seminal characterization of populism as a 'political discourse' opposing a 'unitary popular identity' to a 'constitutive other' (Laclau 1977, 2005a, 2005b). However, Mudde adds the important qualification that populism involves a moralization of the opposition between the people and elites:

> Several ideologies—he writes—are based on a fundamental opposition between the people and the elite. However, whereas in socialism this opposition is based on the concept of class and in nationalism on the concept of the nation, in populism the opposition is based on the concept of morality... The essence of the people is therefore assumed to be their purity, in the sense that they are 'authentic', whereas the elite is 'corrupt' (Mudde 2017: 29).

This 'ideational' definition of populism was further elaborated upon by Jan-Werner Müller in his 2016 book on *What Is Populism?*, which argues that: 'It is a necessary but not a sufficient condition to be critical of elites in order to be a populist' (Müller 2016: 2). 'In addition to being anti-elitist' Müller writes 'populists are also always anti-pluralist' (2016: 3), in the sense that they 'hanker after what political theorist Nancy Rosenblum has called "holism": the notion that the polity should no longer be split and the idea that it's possible for the people to be one and—all of them—to have one true representative' (2016: 20). As such, Müller adds: 'Populism revolves around a *pars pro toto* logic and a claim to exclusive representation' whereby 'they, *and they alone*' are said to adequately represent 'the people'.

The 'organizational' approach to the study of populism emphasizes different features. Kurt Weyland has defined populism as 'a political strategy through which a personalistic leader seeks or exercises government based on direct and unmediated support from a large number of unorganized followers' (Weyland 2001: 14). For Weyland, populism falls within an overarching typology of 'political strategies' constituted by two key variables: the 'type of political actor that seeks and exercises political power' and the 'principal power capability which that actor mobilizes as a support basis' (Weyland 2017: 55). A 'personal leader' appealing directly to a 'disorganized mass' becomes the key organizational feature of populism.

Along very similar lines, Robert Barr has proposed a broadly organizational definition of populism, emphasizing the centrality of 'plebiscitarian linkages' between the populist leadership and its base of support within the population. 'Whereas party structures (and participatory linkages more generally) grant citizens substantial control' he contends 'plebiscites offer them a "take it or leave it" choice' (Barr 2009: 34). For Barr, 'rather than offering citizens the chance to make their own decisions, this form of linkage asks citizens to judge whether their rulers are doing a good job for them: policymakers present a choice to the voters, who may accept or reject it'. In this way, populism 'vests a single individual with the task of representing "the people", replacing traditional forms of political participation, and in particular political parties and other intermediary bodies, in that role' (2009: 36).

Nadia Urbinati's recent work on the concept of populism can also be categorized as falling within this broadly 'organizational' approach. In her view, populism is best understood as a distortion or 'disfigurement' of democratic procedures, which both 'simplifies' and 'reifies' them in the service of a 'power concentration plan' (Urbinati 2017: 572–8). With respect to the key democratic procedure of majority rule, for instance, she writes that: 'Populism reifies a given majority as it promotes policies that translate the interests of winners immediately into law, with no patience for mediation and compromise or institutional checks and balances' (2017: 580). For this reason, Urbinati argues that: 'Populism is parasitic on representative democracy because it challenges it in the name of an exclusive and undivided representation of the people, thereby challenging the identification of democracy with pluralistic political representation and the constitutional limitation of the power of the majority' (2017: 575).

Despite the numerous important insights offered by both ideational and organizational approaches to the study of populism, a striking feature that runs across both is the assumption that they must somehow be *alternative* to one another. We suggest this is not necessarily the case. Both the approaches we have considered construe populism as a mode of political action, implying that they both assume that there is a strategic dimension to populism, oriented towards the pursuit of power. It is surely possible, though perhaps not necessary, to employ *both* ideational and organizational means to achieve that end. Populism does not have to be only about what political actors 'say' or think, as opposed to what they 'do' or how they do it, but can rather be seen as a combination of the two.

We see this in the way that the defining features identified by the 'ideational' approach are related to the elements focused upon by the 'organizational' one and indeed are likely to occur in conjunction with one another. If you assume that there exists an internally homogenous and morally pure people, whose substantive will is being held back by a corrupt elite, there remains the question of who can speak for this collective body. The figure of a personal leader directly embodying the people's demands seems particularly apt for the purpose, since it reflects the putative unity of the people's will, while at the same time bypassing all the intermediary bodies and procedures, which populists portray as wiles of the corrupt elite. Conversely, a personal leader seeking direct legitimation from a disorganized mass seems likely to develop a discourse that opposes the people as a whole to a corrupt elite within it, while claiming that s/he and only s/he adequately represents it, because that enables him or her to bypass all forms of intermediation with the disorganized mass or individuals he or she claims to represent, promoting a more direct form of identification between them.

The upshot is that many of the features focused upon by the 'ideational' approach more or less imply those focused upon by the 'organizational' approach and vice versa. For this reason, we conceptualize populism as involving both ideational and organizational components. Our two-fold definition of populism for the purposes of the present analysis is as follows: *populism is a mode of political action that involves: (i) an ideational component, which construes society as divided in a 'pure people' and a 'corrupt elite', while maintaining that the latter has a right to govern itself in the name of a voluntaristic conception of popular sovereignty; (ii) an organizational component, consisting in a claim to exclusive representation of the people by a personal leader, validated through plebiscitarian means by a direct appeal to a disorganized mass, which bypasses intermediary bodies.*[1]

The Definition of Technocracy

Clarifying the way in which we will be using the notion of technocracy in this book requires a more complex discussion because the existing academic literature is more limited and our proposed definition diverges more significantly from the dominant uses of the term. By and large, in ordinary academic and political discourse, the notion of technocracy appears to be used to refer either to a type of political *regime* (which is usually opposed to democracy) or to a category of political *actor* (which is usually set against the figure of the professional politician).

The origins of the concept can be traced as far back as the political philosophy of Plato, which contains a radical critique of democracy based on the ancient Greek notion of *techne*, roughly translatable as competence or skill (Plato 2000). Since the majority, by definition, lack the competence or skill for government, Plato maintained, political power ought to be entrusted to the few who have it. This was notoriously supposed to result in a form of 'rule by the philosophers', which can be seen as amounting to a form of technocracy, since the distinctive feature of philosophers, for Plato, was precisely that they possessed the necessary *techne*—i.e. competence or skill—for governing (Wolin 2004).

---

[1] The main point we have sought to advance in this section is that these two separate component elements are likely to occur in conjunction. For this reason, we maintain that it is only possible to speak of populism in a 'full' sense when both are present. However, we also recognize that certain aspects of the populist discourse and mode of organization can sometimes occur without the others being present too. In these cases, it seems more appropriate to describe the phenomenon in question as having populist traits, without necessarily being populist in a full sense. Far from being a problem for our definition, we take the possibility this offers of distinguishing between different *degrees* to which a given phenomenon can be described as populist as one of its strengths. The reason is that, for us, populism is not a discrete category, in the sense that one either is or isn't a populist, but rather an ideal-type which concrete political actors can approximate to a greater or lesser extent.

It is in this sense that the notion of technocracy was first used by the so-called 'Technocracy Inc.' movement of the early part of the twentieth century in the United States, which coined the term itself (Akin and Akin 1977). Faced with the growing complexity of governing a modern industrial society, the members of this movement argued that ordinary citizens were becoming incapable of collectively pursuing their own best interests. Differently from Plato, however, these first explicit defenders of technocracy did not assume that those with the necessary competence for governing were philosophers, but engineers.[2] It is therefore at this time that the notion of technocracy became associated with specifically technical—i.e. pragmatically oriented—knowledge, as opposed to the broader idea of competence or skill in general. More generally, however, we can say that in its first explicit usage the notion of technocracy referred to a type of political regime defined in large part by opposition to democracy: whereas the latter literally means 'rule by the people', the former was taken to refer to a form of 'rule by experts' (Fischer 1990).

As democracy progressively became the 'only game in town' over the second half of the twentieth century (Linz 1996), the notion of technocracy was redefined as the name of for a particular category of actor *within* democratic regimes. The constitutive opposition was no longer between democracy and technocracy but between democratically elected politicians and independent technocratic institutions. Technocrats were now understood as those political actors entrusted with making specific policy decisions, by virtue of their competence or expertise and not because of their popular partisan support. This involved drawing a distinction between different areas of policymaking on the basis of their relevant criteria of legitimacy: some decisions were assumed to be 'inherently political' and therefore better left in the hands of elected politicians; whereas others were assumed to be 'purely technical' and therefore legitimately entrusted to competent experts (Bickerton and Invernizzi Accetti 2020).

It is in this sense that independent central banks and other presumptively neutral regulatory agencies are commonly referred to as 'technocratic institutions', even though they operate within an overarching political framework that is supposed to be democratic (e.g. Rosanvallon 2011). This point was already highlighted by Jean Meynaud in his classic 1969 treaties on *Technocracy*, which maintained that:

> On the plane of doctrinal reasoning and formal planning it is not difficult to imagine a perfect technocratic system in which power is held by virtue of

---

[2] The idea that societies should be governed by those with expertise was also a long-standing feature of industrial society, where the specialized quality of knowledge emerging out of an increasingly complex division of labour called for a shift away from democracy towards a society of 'planners' and experts. For a good account of the 'idea' of technocracy and its development in line with various phases of industrial society, see Esmark 2020.

competence alone. At the present time, however, there is no political system, and there has probably never been, which works entirely on this basis. The ability to acquire leadership because of technical knowledge or skill is a corruption of a political regime based, in practice or intention, on different principles... Sometimes, the right of choice or lawmaking is officially transferred to the technocrat in a specific policy domain. These are cases of open dispossession and they approach pure technocracy, although in a restricted area of policy-making. But, *in most cases, the technocrat's intervention is limited to acting or exerting influence upon the official holder of power*. When the former succeeds, there is an effective shift of power from the latter. The politician retains an appearance of power, but loses, to some degree, the substance of it. In actual fact, technocratic intervention is thus a process which relies *more on influence than on the explicit issuing of orders* (Meynaud 1969: 29–30; italics added).

It is this second, more recent definition of technocracy (as the name for a particular category of political actors *within* democratic regimes) which accounts for its association with the notion of 'depoliticization'. In an abstract sense, technocracy as it was originally defined was far from being something anti- or even apolitical, since it was always a deeply contentious—and therefore inherently political—claim that experts should rule instead of the people. However, within a firmly consolidated democratic context, it is more plausible to assume that politics is coextensive with electoral competition. The idea that empowering technocrats amounts to a form of 'depoliticization' can therefore be understood as implying that specific areas of government ought to be removed from the domain over which democratically elected politicians have direct authority. The conceptual opposition between democracy and technocracy remains a constitutive feature in this more recent definition of technocracy, even though the latter refers to a particular category of actors within democratic regimes.

We propose a different definition of technocracy because we are interested in studying a rather different set of phenomena. We do not discuss the challenge to democracy represented by the (complete or partial) transfer of political power to a set of unelected experts, but rather focus on the way in which electoral contenders for office use the legitimizing resource of claims to 'competence' or 'expertise' in their struggle for votes with one another. In other words, what interests us is not the sense in which technocracy amounts to a form of 'depoliticization' but rather the way in which it amounts to a *politicization of expertise*, one that can be used as a legitimizing resource for the purpose of succeeding within the electoral game itself. One of the important implications of this is that the politicization of expertise that comes with the rise of the technopopulist logic can result in a conflict with the expansion of technocratic power associated with depoliticization. When a political actor appeals to expertise in his or her attempt to win political power, or governs on this basis of politicized expertise, a conflict emerges between rival claims to *techne*: that of independent institutions or the skills of established state bureaucracies, challenged by claims to competence made by politicized experts—in the form of the M5S's 'citizen-experts' or the 'assorted weirdos' recruited by Dominic Cummings in the UK in his efforts to radically overhaul the British civil service (Cummings 2020).[3]

Two further features of our proposed definition of technocracy can be introduced with reference to other existing accounts that come closer to it. To begin with, our proposed definition has something in common with Miguel Centeno's suggestion that technocracy can be understood as a 'type of political legitimacy' in Weber's sense, whose distinctive feature is that it is assumed to derive from 'adherence to the dictates of a "Book"—whether that document contains the word of God, a theory of history, or the econometric functions that describe equilibria' (Centeno 1993: 313). The specific aspect of this definition we find particularly compelling is that it is purely *formal*, in the sense that it does not imply a necessary connection with any substantive set of policies or category of agents. For Centeno, any political actor can be considered a technocrat, to the extent that he or she claims legitimacy for what they are doing on the basis of an appeal to competence or expertise, independently of the nature of that competence and its objective validity.

One can therefore qualify as a technocrat (or, more precisely, be said to be acting in a technocratic way) simply by making a particular kind of *claim*. Just as the populist claims to directly embody the 'people' as a whole, the technocrat claims to possess a specific kind of 'competence' or expertise, which entitles him or her to govern others. Whether or not these claims are indeed true—or even objectively verifiable—is beside the point. Just as it is possible to distinguish between different variants of populism on the basis of what they take the substantive content of the popular will to be, it must also be possible to distinguish between different variants of technocracy, on the basis of what they take the substantive content of competence or expertise to be. This is alluded to by Centeno in his article when he points out that 'the Soviet Union had its own (socialist) technocrats', just as modern day democracies have their (presumptively capitalist) ones (1993: 308).

The main difference between our definition of technocracy and Centeno's is that his account remains wedded to the idea that technocrats constitute a separate category of political *actors*, which is clearly distinguishable from—and in fact conceptually opposed to—democratically elected politicians. This emerges when Centeno writes that: 'In imposing the domination by an instrumental rationale and scientific method technocrats are similar to theocrats or states that have

---

[3] Our thanks to Art Goldhammer for pushing us to consider this explosion in claims to competence and the rivalry that can exist between them.

explicit, dominant political ideologies' since 'in all these cases, legitimacy comes not from the barrel of a gun or from the ballot box', but rather from 'the application of instrumentally rational techniques' (1993: 313–14). The difficulty here is that by maintaining this distinction between technocrats and electoral politics so starkly, Centeno effectively disbars himself from even considering the possibility that electoral candidates for political office might also appeal to what he calls the technocratic 'type of legitimacy' in their struggle for votes—which is precisely the phenomenon we're interested in exploring in this book.

Another influential definition of technocracy which partially overlaps with ours is that proposed by Daniele Caramani, as a 'form of political representation' based on a 'trustee' rather than 'delegate' type of relationship between the representative and their constituency (Caramani 2017). This definition has in common with ours the recognition that technocracy can be a mode of action employed by electoral contenders for public office, meaning that it is not necessarily at odds with the organizing logic of democracy itself. There remains, however, an important difference between Caramani's approach and ours, which stems from the fact that he builds his definition of technocracy almost entirely by opposition to the notion of populism (which, for him, is based on a 'delegative' model of political representation), whereas we maintain that there is a more complex and complementary relationship between them.

In addition, Caramani also ignores the 'organizational' dimension of technocracy, which overlaps in many significant ways with that of populism. In fact, even within Caramani's account, we can find some notion of how this organizational dimension works. Caramani's own definition of technocracy as a form of political representation based on 'trusteeship' carries with it the implication that—since trust is by definition personal—an unmediated relationship exists between those who offer it and those who enjoy it. Moreover, to the extent that the basis of this trust is supposed to be the representative's possession of a specific kind of 'competence' or 'expertise', it follows that the represented cannot be assumed to be competent enough to establish whether their representative actually has the competence in question. Thus, the basis for trusting a technocratic representative must necessarily lie in his or her personal qualities and qualifications, rather than in any institutionalized procedure of validation.

The implication is that, like populism, technocracy has an 'organizational' dimension alongside its 'ideational' one, which consists in the establishment of a direct link of trust between a personal figure who claims to have a particular kind of competence or expertise and the people he or she aims to govern in this way. This yields a two-fold definition of technocracy, which matches our definition of populism, as: *a mode of political action involving (i) an ideational component, which consists in the claim to a particular type of competence or expertise that presumptively entitles its successor to legitimately rule over others; and (ii) an organizational component which involves a direct relationship of trust between the possessor of this competence and those he or she is supposed to rule over in this way.*[4]

Comparison between the Technopopulist and the Ideological Political Logics

On the basis of the definitions we have proposed, we can now move on to clarify the distinction between the technopopulist and the ideological political logics. This will hopefully serve to underscore both the conceptual distinctiveness and the historical novelty of the former, while also laying the ground for an examination of its complex relationship with the latter in contemporary democratic regimes. We first discuss the issue analytically in this chapter, whereas chapter 3 approaches the question of the relationship between these logics from a historical point of view.

The way in which electoral competition functioned at the height of what we propose to call the era of the ideological political logic was analysed by Seymour Martin Lipset and Stein Rokkan in their seminal 1967 essay on 'Cleavage Structures, Party Systems and Voter Alignments'. They argued that throughout the early and mid-parts of the twentieth century, societies were divided along a number of structuring 'cleavages', such as class (which opposed workers to business owners), religion (which opposed believers to non-believers), and region (which opposed urban centres to rural peripheries). In this context, electoral contenders for public office competed with one another by staking out 'packages' of political proposals—which is how Lipset and Rokkan conceive of 'partisan ideologies'—that were meant to appeal to the particular interests and values of specific social groups. During this period, political parties were essentially 'expressions' of underlying social cleavages. As Lipset and Rokkan put it:

> Political parties...help to crystallize and make explicit the conflicting interests, the latent strains and contrasts, in the existing social structure, while forcing subjects and citizens to ally themselves across structural cleavage lines and to set up priorities amongst their commitments (Lipset and Rokkan 1967: 5).

A significant implication that follows from this mode of electoral competition is that ideological political parties did not really compete for one another's electorates. Instead, the goal of vote maximization was served by trying to maximize as

---

[4] Like our definition of populism, this definition of technocracy is meant to function as an 'ideal-type' in a Weberian sense. This implies that it is not necessary for a mode of political action to fully display all of its constitutive features in order to qualify as technocratic. Instead, we suggest that any given mode of political action can be considered *more or less* technocratic, depending on the degree to which it approximates these characteristic features.

many voters as possible from *within* the specific social formation that one's ideology was meant to appeal to. As Maurice Duverger emphasized in his classic treatise on the organizational structure of the 'mass parties' of the early part of the twentieth century, these organizations tended to become 'self-enclosed'. A highly complex and deeply penetrating bureaucratic apparatus developed, for the purpose of mobilizing a very clearly defined section of the electorate (Duverger 1954).

Another important implication that follows from the cleavage structure of early and mid-twentieth century party politics is that competing 'mass parties' were logically bound to recognize each other's political legitimacy. For, political parties that claim to represent the interests and values of a specific section (i.e. part) of society are bound to recognize that other parties represent the interests and values of other, competing parts. Even though both may also maintain that the interests and values of their specific 'part' better approximate—or indeed actually correspond—to the interests and values of society as a 'whole', when political conflict is framed in these terms, it is difficult to deny that others happen to think differently. This is why Nancy Rosenblum (following Burke) has proposed to understand party democracy (in its ideal-typical form) as a process of 'regulated rivalry' between 'particular interpretations of the common good' that are all '*a priori* equally legitimate' (Rosenblum 2008).[5]

The technopopulist political logic works differently. The first thing to note is that contemporary contenders for electoral office rarely appeal to the interests and values of specific parts of society. They much more frequently portray themselves as representatives of the interests of society as a whole—whether in the form of the populists' unified and monolithic conception of the 'popular will', or the abstract idea of political 'truth' which technocrats claim to have access to in virtue of their competence or expertise. As a result, those competing for political office and power are much less likely to recognize and accept each other's political legitimacy. When the interests of the whole are opposed to those of specific social parts—as in the case of the populist opposition between the 'people' and 'elites' or the technocratic construction of an opposition between 'good public policy' and 'special interests'—the latter appear inherently illegitimate.

This can be conceptualized metaphorically through the idea that the technopopulist logic has the effect of shifting the principal axis of political competition from the *horizontal* dimension of the struggle between left and right ideological poles (which are both construed as representing the interests and values of specific parts of society, and therefore equally a priori legitimate) to the *vertical* dimension

---

[5] In fact, the traditional way of classifying political parties in terms of the ideological categories of 'left' and 'right' captures this feature of the way in which democratic politics was structured in the early and mid- parts of the twentieth century very well. The very idea that some parties can be identified as ideologically 'left-wing' supposes that there must be others on the 'right wing' of the political spectrum. Moreover, the space between 'left' and 'right' is metaphorically situated on a horizontal plane, which suggests that neither part can be considered inherently superior to the other.

of the struggle between the whole and the parts, in which one side of the conflict appears inherently superior. This expresses the way in which we move from an acceptance of the legitimacy of political opponents to a situation where the struggle presumes the superiority of one side over another.

Another important difference between the technopopulist political logic and the way in which electoral competition was structured at the height of the age of ideological political parties concerns the organizational dimension. As we noted, the ideologically driven mass parties of the early and mid-parts of the twentieth century involved deeply penetrating and highly stratified bureaucratic apparatus, whose function was to mobilize specific sectors of the population in the most reliable and totalizing way possible. In contrast, both populism and technocracy are characterized by informal and personalistic modes of political organization, which rely on the cultivation of direct bonds of trust between the leadership and the base, while bypassing intermediary layers of organization. As a consequence, contemporary political actors and organizations end up having a much thinner organizational apparatus, which is meant to appeal as broadly as possible across the electorate by relying on easily identifiable and reproducible personalistic cues.

Both these important differences between the technopopulist and the ideological political logics can be traced back to the different incentive structures faced by political actors in the present day, compared to the early and mid-parts of the twentieth century. Whereas the societies of the early and mid-parts of the twentieth century could be rather unproblematically construed as divided in relatively homogeneous social groups based on the cleavage lines identified by Lipset and Rokkan, contemporary societies appear far more complex and fragmented. Even though the traditional social cleavages based on class, religion, and region have not entirely disappeared, they have been undermined by the emergence of multiple new social divisions as well as the broader social processes of individualization and cognitive mobilization (see chapter 3 for more details). The electoral strategy of appealing to the interests and values of specific groups within society has become less viable since these social formations are more fragmentary, fragile, and fluid. By the same token, it is also becoming more plausible—and strategically profitable—to present oneself as representing the interests of society as a whole. A highly fragmented and individualized electorate is more likely to be receptive to such appeals than a deeply divided and ideologically polarized one.

The means of political mobilization available to contemporary contenders for electoral office are also very different from those which were available in the early and mid-parts of the twentieth century. Even in the not too distant past, the access to political information and other forms of political participation remained relatively limited and costly; the contemporary means of mass communication and information technology make it much easier and almost costless to access a much wider range of political targets. Instead of having to cultivate deep ties of partisan loyalty with a particular section of the electorate through an intensive bureaucratic apparatus, it appears more rational to appeal to as wider section of the electorate as possible, through extensive and easily reproducible personalistic cues that bypass intermediary layers of organization. These complex set of social and political changes imply that contemporary contenders for electoral office face a powerful set of incentives to adopt both populist and technocratic forms of discourse and modes of political organization. This marks its difference with the ideological logic in which rival contenders for electoral office seek to mobilize particular groups within society by advancing ideological packages that are meant to appeal to their specific interests and values.

Two more aspects of the complex relationship between the technopopulist and the ideological political logics ought to be highlighted to complete the comparison between them. First, from what we have stated, it should be evident that the technopopulist political logic cannot simply be understood in terms of the emergence of a new political 'cleavage' between populism and technocracy. As we noted above, the technopopulist logic involves the transformation in the nature of electoral competition, whereby the latter ceases to have the *oppositional* structure of the traditional left/right divide, one which involved a measure of substantive 'goal differentiation', in Kircheimer's terms. Instead, it manifests a form of competition *without* opposition, in which the competing candidates for office all claim to stand for the interests and values of society as a whole. This is what makes it possible for contemporary political actors to combine aspects of both populism and technocracy, in a way that is much harder to do with the traditional 'left' and 'right' ideological poles.

More fundamentally, the technopopulist political logic cannot be understood in terms of the emergence of a new political 'cleavage' because it stems in large part from a process of separation—or *disconnect*—between societal conflicts and divisions, on one hand, and partisan political rivalries, on the other. As we have already sought to make clear above—but will also develop in much more detail in chapter 3—contemporary contenders for electoral office have an incentive to present themselves as representatives of society as a 'whole' precisely because the clear and stable social formations that previous ideologically motivated parties appealed to have ceased to exist, or have at least become much more fragile and fragmentary. The political divisions that exist today, those between the electoral candidates' different *ways* of combining populist claims to represent the people as a whole and technocratic claims to possess the necessary competence for translating it's willing to policy, are removed from the underlying social 'cleavages' that used to structure partisan competition during the year of ideologically motivated political parties. For this reason, the rise of technopopulism is better understood as a manifestation of the *decline in the pertinence of cleavage politics itself*, rather than as the emergence of a new political cleavage between populism and technocracy.

The second important implication of our definition of technopopulism is that even though the technopopulist political logic is clearly different from the ideological one which preceded it and which it in part replaced, the two are not in principle mutually exclusive. To the extent that we currently inhabit a situation in which the previously dominant social cleavages have been blurred, but not completely abolished, while the costs of partisan political mobilization have been greatly reduced, but not an annulled, it is possible for them to be both operative at the same time. In terms of the definitions we have provided, contemporary politicians face two parallel—although in some respects divergent—sets of incentives and constraints: on one hand, to appeal to the interests and values of particular 'groups' within society, according to the traditional logic of ideological political competition, and on the other hand to claim to represent the interests and values of society as a 'whole', according to the distinctive features of the technopopulist political logic. The fact that the former concerns primarily the substantive goals of organized political action, whereas the latter primarily affects the way in which electoral contenders for public office present themselves to voters, makes it possible for political actors for to effectively do both simultaneously—as demonstrated by the several 'hybrid' cases of 'left-leaning' and 'right-leaning' manifestations of technopopulism we consider in chapter 2. It is also possible for a political actor to be quite mistaken about what they think 'the struggle is about', to return to Schattschneider's phrase. They may, for instance, believe that the struggle is still primarily ideological when in fact it is the technopopulist logic that prevails. This was arguably a mistake made by the Labour Party in the 2019 election: it campaigned using heavily ideological language and assumed that its traditional *chasse gardée* would remain loyal. The 'struggle' was encapsulated by a deeply technopopulist slogan ('Get Brexit Done') and traditional Labour voters abandoned the Party in droves. The costs of misunderstanding the nature of the political logic are high.

This is the reason why the key thesis of this book is not that the technopopulist political logic has entirely replaced the previously dominant ideological one, but rather the technopopulism has *in part replaced and in part of superimposed itself upon* the previously dominant ideological political logic. Whether this is a process that will continue in the future, leading to a complete loss of pertinence of the traditional ideological categories of 'left' and 'right'—or may perhaps be reversed, leading to their resurgence—is something we will address in chapter 5, and also especially in the conclusion of this book. For the time being, however, it should be noted that the categories we have proposed in this chapter are meant to offer an adequate interpretive framework for understanding the *present* political situation, not to predict the future. Our argument is that it is plausible to describe contemporary electoral politics in terms of the emergence of a new set of incentives and constraints which encourages all political actors to adopt both populist and technocratic forms of discourse and modes of political organization, while more substantive ideological commitments have lost their centrality and structuring effect on our politics.

Conclusion

In this chapter, we have presented our conceptual definition of technopopulism as a distinctive type of political logic. We have shown that the growing interest in technopopulism has generated a considerable amount of conceptual confusion, especially in the meaning of the prefix 'techno-' and in the relationship between 'techno-' and 'populism'. Our definition of technopopulism as a political logic helps us grasp the way in which appeals to the people and to expertise are not concentrated in specific actors that are different from—and clash with—traditional or 'mainstream' political actors or parties. Rather, there exist a range of incentives and constraints—a political logic—that encourages all actors to make such appeals. Some do more than others, and there are many sorts of technopopulist synthesis, as we shall explore in detail in chapter 2. In defining technopopulism, we have also made clear that it is not just another type of populism but rather that it represents a series of discursive and organizational patterns that are a product of the combination of technocracy and populism. More specifically, technopopulism represents a distinctive development that requires rethinking some of the traditional ways in which we tended to understand the interaction between electoral politics and expertise.

2
Varieties of Technopopulism

Introduction

This chapter approaches the concept of technopopulism from an empirical perspective. It has two parallel goals. First, to demonstrate the heuristic utility of the concept developed in the previous chapter, by pointing to come concrete cases of how the technopopulist political logic has shaped the current or recent European political landscape. Second, to develop the concept of technopopulism itself further, by drawing some distinctions and classifications between different types—or varieties—of technopopulism, which emerge from the empirical analysis.

The method employed is in many ways the inverse of the one pursued in the previous chapter. Whereas there we started from abstract definitions and attempted to build a comprehensive concept of technopopulism by theoretical means, in this chapter we start from an analysis of concrete empirical cases, amongst which we seek to establish some distinctions and classifications through a more inductive process. The hope is that the combination of these two methodologies will lead to an overall concept that is at once theoretically sound and empirically cogent.

The discussion proceeds in two parts. In the first, we focus on what we will be calling 'pure' cases of technopopulism, by which we mean political parties or movements that very clearly offer a synthesis of the appeals to 'the people' and to expertise as a result of the incentives and constraints of the technopopulist logic. Amongst these pure cases of technopopulism, we distinguish three paradigmatic types on the basis of the specific way in which the synthesis between populism and technocracy operates. These are: *technopopulism through the party*, which we discuss with reference to New Labour in the UK; *technopopulism through the electoral base*, which we discuss with reference to the Five Star Movement (M5S) in Italy; and *technopopulism through the figure of the leader*, which we discuss with reference to Emmanuel Macron and his political movement, *La République En Marche!*, in France.

In the second part of the chapter we focus on what we will be calling 'hybrid' cases of technopopulism. These are political parties or movements whose *raison d'être* is much more firmly rooted in the more traditional left/right struggles of the twentieth century. However, they have been forced in various ways to adapt to the technopopulist logic, and we explore the ways in which they do so. The two hybrid cases we discuss are Spain's *Podemos* and Italy's *Lega*—two parties that have long-standing and manifest ideological commitments but whose discourse and organization belies some elements of technopopulism.

Before delving into the analysis, one final preliminary remark is in order concerning the scope of our study and the selection of cases we focus on. The intuitions underpinning the key ideas advanced in this book have emerged out of previous work carried out by its two authors on a set of countries that—for purely biographical and contingent reasons—they know best. This set of countries broadly correspond to 'Western Europe', with a particular focus on France, Italy, Spain, and the UK. This geographic area should therefore be understood as the primary field of applicability of our argument. The advantage of proceeding in this way is that it helps us develop a typology of different varieties of technopopulism which can serve as a baseline for analysing other countries. The goal of the book is not to chart in an exhaustive fashion the technopopulist phenomenon, nor is it to test a series of hypotheses regarding technopopulism. This would require us to test our explanations for the rise of the technopopulist logic against cases where we see no such development taking place. This book aims to introduce and develop in as systematic fashion as possible the concept of technopopulism and to illustrate its applicability as a conceptual framework for making sense of politics in contemporary democracies. For the sheer range of empirical cases to which the idea of technopopulism has been applied, as we outlined in chapter 1, we suspect that many of the core ideas we develop here are applicable to other countries in Western Europe that we did not discuss, as well as further afield. However, this remains a matter of conjecture, to be explored in further research on technopopulism.

Pure Cases

Pure cases of technopopulism are political parties or movements whose political identity is predominantly rooted in its synthesis of technocratic and populist appeals. This means they are difficult, if not impossible, to categorize within the terms of the traditional left/right ideological divide, either because they make it a point explicitly to evade this sort of politics (as in the case of parties who claim to be 'neither left nor right wing'), or because—from an observer's perspective—they simply don't fit within this traditional conceptual framework.

There is not only one possible way of operating such a synthesis, but rather a whole range of possible options made available by the multiple ways in which political actors can creatively reappropriate populist and technocratic tropes, inflecting them and combining them with one another. This is precisely how a political logic works: it establishes a set of incentives and constraints for actors that make certain discursive and organizational patterns more likely, but there remains a vast range of concrete ways in which the technopopulist synthesis can take place. In what follows, we distinguish three different ways in which populist and technocratic modes of political action can be combined with one another. Starting from a concrete case in each instance, we extrapolate three 'pure types' of technopopulism, whose purpose is to serve as referents for the analysis of other, more complex cases.

New Labour: Technopopulism through the Party

The first pure case of technopopulism we shall be considering is constituted by the 'New Labour' experiment carried out by the British Labour Party during the period that broadly corresponded with Tony Blair's and then, more briefly, Gordon Brown's leadership; that is, essentially, from Tony Blair's election as party leader in 1994 to Gordon Brown's resignation as Prime Minister in 2010. This is also the period that included the British Labour Party's longest ever stretch of continued government incumbency, between 1997 and 2010—during which it won three successive elections, by wide and historically unprecedented margins, in 1997, 2001, and 2005, respectively.

Although that period in the British Labour Party's history is now over, the ideas and modes of political organization associated with it remain extremely significant for the present political epoch. The reason is that—for good or ill—Tony Blair and his associates succeeded in establishing many of the basic political coordinates within which many mainstream Western European political parties continue to operate. This is testified by the fact that several contemporary Continental European political leaders and movements can still be identified as 'epigones' of Tony Blair's Third Way Politics: from Italy's Matteo Renzi during his time as leader of the *Partito Democratico* (PD), to Spain's Pedro Sanchez as of the *Partido Socialista Obrero Espanol* (PSOE), up to and including the current French President, Emmanuel Macron.

Indeed, a great many of the so-called 'anti-establishment' parties that populate the contemporary West European political landscape also seem to define themselves with reference to the Blairite brand of Third Way politics—if only *negatively*, by condemning the supposed convergence of all mainstream political parties around a common set of ideological premises. At the time when Nigel Farage was leading UKIP and Jeremy Corbyn was leader of the Labour Party, both were described as 'anti-theses to Tony Blair' (see for instance: Hackett 2017). As Andrew Rawnsley put it at the start of his two-volume history of New Labour, 'New Labour's story is all our stories' (Rawnsley 2010: ix).

Given the amount of academic literature that already exists on this political phenomenon, in what follows we do not offer anything approaching a comprehensive account of New Labour. Rather, what we intend to show is that this political experiment anticipated many of the technopopulist tendencies we focus on in this book, both from an ideational and organizational perspective. As such, it constitutes a paradigmatic case of technopopulism, out of which we will seek to extrapolate an abstract model of what we shall refer to as 'technopopulism through the party'. This will hopefully prove useful to shed more light on the nature of the several contemporary epigones of New Labour that still populate the present political scene, as well as other, more complex cases of technopopulism, which incorporate features of this model while combining them with other traits.

New Labour's populist characteristics have already been pointed out by numerous commentators. In his article, 'Populist or Progressive? The Blair Paradox', the former Labour MP and prominent left-wing intellectual David Marquand wrote that: 'Like Thatcher, Blair is a populist, determined to communicate with an imaginary people over the heads of his colleagues' (Marquand 1999: 216). Similarly, in his analysis of the New Labour phenomenon, Peter Mair wrote that: 'Elements of populism certainly exist within the New Labour approach, and in some cases—as with Blair's 1999 Labour Party conference address—these have been blazoned without inhibition' (Mair 2000: 33). Cas Mudde described New Labour as an instance of 'mainstream populism', even going as far as suggesting that Tony Blair is 'one of the most pure examples of contemporary populism' (Mudde 2004: 551).

Several empirically observable features of the Labour Party under Blair's leadership corroborate these evaluations. First and foremost is the recurrent, almost obsessive invocation of the category of 'the people' as both subject and object of New Labour policies. In his first book on New Labour, Andrew Rawnsley comments on the difference between the Labour government elected in 1945 and the one elected in 1997. Hartley Shawcross, a Labour MP and Attorney General in Clement Attlee's post-war government, is said to have declared in 1946—in a debate in the House of Commons—that 'we are the masters now'. Tony Blair, addressing the newly elected parliamentary Labour Party after his landslide victory in 1997, pointedly avoided making a similar claim. Instead, he qualified his victory. 'We are not the masters now', he told his MPs. 'The people are the masters. We are the servants of the people' (Rawnsley 2000: xiii).

Similar language was present in almost all of Blair's interventions at this time and subsequently. Speaking at the Royal Festival Hall a day after the 1997 election, Blair marvelled that:

> We have won support from all walks of life, all classes of people, every corner of the country. We are now the people's party, the party of all the people, the many not the few, the party that belongs to every part of Britain (cited in Rawnsley 2000: 12).

Far from being an ephemeral reflection of post-electoral hubris, New Labour appropriated the expression 'the people' in the manner of a new political label. Famously, Blair described Princess Diana—at the time of her death in August 1997—as 'the people's princess'. Her funeral was referred to as 'a people's funeral'. Specific projects, such as the Millennium Dome, were known as 'the people's dome'. Blair sought to promote the cause of European integration in the UK by speaking of 'the people's Europe' (Watts and Pilkington 2005).

As Peter Mair points out: 'This is government for, and indeed of, the people' but, crucially, *not* of 'any particular section of that people' (2000: 28). New Labour claimed instead to stand for an 'inclusive' and 'undifferentiated' people, not traversed by any class, interest, or ideological divisions. This is one of the primary hallmarks of the populist conception of the people we identified in the previous chapter, inasmuch as populists claim to stand for the people *as a whole*. There is not supposed to be any specific tie with a particular section of society, but rather a straightforward implementation of the ideal of popular sovereignty, conceived of as a direct translation of the popular will into policy. Consider for example the statement given by the cabinet member in charge of New Labour's constitutional reform agenda, Lord Irvine, in a lecture delivered to the Law Faculty of University of Leiden on the 22nd of October 1999: 'We have' he stated 'set out to be an inclusive Government—a Government truly of the people, for the people, by the people—which returns power to the people, from whom power ultimately derives' (cited by Mair 2000: 27).

Another clearly populist aspect of New Labour's discourse is its way of relating to political opponents. As several commentators have pointed out, the purpose of adding the qualifier 'New' before the Labour Party's traditional label (while at the same time dropping the explicit reference to the idea of a party) was to relegate all political opponents—both on the right, but especially on the left, of the political spectrum—in the camp of the 'Old' (on this point, see for instance: Gamble 2010: 643). In this way, New Labour sought to replace the traditional left/right ideological division with a different conflict rooted in the opposition between the 'New' and the 'Old'. Within the terms of this opposition, opponents of New Labour were automatically disqualified as relics of a past political era, standing in the way of the inexorable march of history: a point frequently alluded to by Tony Blair himself in his recurrent descriptions of his political opponents as 'naysayers', 'obstructionists', and 'enemies of progress' (e.g. Blair 1998).

The same underlying logic also emerges out of the notion of the 'Third Way', which functioned as the overarching label for New Labour's political programme. To the extent that the latter was presented as a 'synthesis'—and therefore an 'overcoming'—of previous ideological orientations (Blair 1998), it left no space for alternative ideological outlooks. Whoever happened to stand against the Third Way must have at best been missing the point, or at worse mischievously trying to further their own interests, thus acting against the people's will as a whole. This point was highlighted already at the time by David Marquand, when he noted that: 'Moral and ideological arguments for the Third Way are unnecessary; it does not have to be defended against alternative visions of the future, based on different moral and ideological premises... There is only one future, and resistance to it is spitting in the wind' (Marquand 1999: 236).

As Peter Mair further points out, New Labour sought to present itself as 'the only possible programme for contemporary government, both necessary and unchallengeable' (Mair 2000: 26). This is consistent with another key feature of populism as we have defined it in the previous chapter; namely, the claim to 'exclusive representation' of the people's interests, which Jan-Werner Müller aptly resumes by suggesting that populists claim 'they, *and they alone*', adequately represent 'the people' (Müller 2016: 20). From this, in turn, it follows that political opponents are not seen as 'adversaries' with an equal a priori claim to political legitimacy. They are disqualified from the start as 'enemies' standing in the way of the people's true interests.

A final distinctively populist aspect of New Labour is in its internal mode of political organization. As Peter Mair noted, 'the process by which New Labour sought to eliminate internal party dissent—marginalizing representative procedures inside the party, introducing plebiscitarian techniques, going over the heads of the party conference and the activist layer in favour of widespread membership ballots—is well known' (Mair 2000: 22). Patrick Seyd describes these changes as amounting to 'the first stages in the development of a new, plebiscitarian type of party in which vertical, internal communication from the leadership and headquarters to the members at home replaces horizontal communications within areas, regions and constituencies' (1999: 401). Andrew Rawnsley writes of a combination of 'big tent inclusiveness' with an 'intensive centralisation of power', which had the effect of transforming the Labour Party in an 'all-embracing self-styled People's Party' directed by a very small leadership team, obsessed with controlling any message emanating from the party: 'less a mass movement, more a junta who had executed a *coup*' (Rawnsley 2000: xiv).

These are precisely the hallmarks of what we have described as the populist mode of political organization in the previous chapter; that is, in Kurt Weyland's words: 'a political strategy through which a personalistic leader seeks or exercises government based on direct and unmediated support from a large number of unorganized followers' (Weyland 2001: 14); or, to put it more precisely, a way of connecting the party leadership with its electoral base, relying on what Robert Barr calls 'plebiscitarian linkages', which bypass the party's internal intermediary bodies by periodically asking the membership as a whole to approve or reject the leaderships' actions, thereby effectively centralizing all power in the figure of the leader him- or herself (see Barr 2009: 34–6).

Alongside these characteristically populist traits, we can also identify a number of more distinctively technocratic features in New Labour's discourse and mode of political organization. This technocratic strain is already implicit in the rhetoric of the Third Way itself, to the extent that the latter was not only presented as a 'synthesis' but also an 'overcoming' of previous ideological traditions and divisions. This is a point on which the exponents of the Third Way insisted at length: rather than being merely a way of staking out an *alternative* position within the traditional ideological spectrum, the Third Way was conceived as a way of *moving beyond* the left/right distinction itself. Anthony Giddens' 1998 programmatic treatise on this concept began by noting that: '[p]olitical ideologies have lost their resonance... In virtually all Western countries, voting no longer fits class lines and has shifted from a left/right polarization to a more complex picture... Social surveys carried out in particular countries confirm the reality of attitude change and the inadequacy of the left/right division as a means of capturing it' (Giddens 1998: 1–22). Similarly, in their co-authored pamphlet entitled *The Third Way/Die Neue Mitte*, Tony Blair and Gerhard Schröder (1998: 3) wrote that:

> Ideas of what is 'left-wing' should never become an ideological straitjacket. The politics of the Third Way is about addressing the concerns of people who live and cope with societies undergoing rapid change... In this newly emerging world people want politicians who approach issues without ideological preconceptions and who, applying their values and principles, search for practical solutions to their problems through honest, well-constructed and pragmatic policies.

This emphasis on 'honest, well-constructed and pragmatic policies' is complemented by a parallel concern for efficiency, delivery and 'getting the job done'. In the same pamphlet, Blair and Schröder write that: 'The public sector must actually serve the citizen: we do not hesitate to promote concepts of efficiency, competition and high performance' (1998: 4). Even more to the point, in a speech delivered to a City of London audience during the 1997 election campaign, Blair declared that: 'What matters is work works.' The concept of 'what works' was later institutionalized in the Home Office's *What Works Programme* for the reduction of penal reoffending. Perhaps the most famous amongst Blair's statements of policy pragmatism, however, was the claim that the choice between 'left or right-wing economic policy' had given way to a choice between 'good or bad policy'.[1]

As Peter Mair notes: 'In a sense far removed from that once mooted by Marx, politics is [here] seen as... a matter of administration—or, in more contemporary parlance, *good governance*' (Mair 2000: 32–3). This is only comprehensible in terms of the assumption that 'objective solutions to social, economic or cultural

---

[1] For more details, see Rentoul 2013.

problems are available' and 'most likely to be found after you have established a judicious mix of institutional correctness and expert, non-partisan judgements' (2000: 33). The consequence is that 'partisanship becomes redundant, democracy depoliticized'. Mair summarizes the overall political project of New Labour as the excising from electoral politics its partisan and ideological dimensions (Mair 2000: 29–30).

These are all features of the technocratic dimension of technopopulism. The assumption that there exist objectively 'right' policy solutions, independent of particular interests or values, from which it follows that ideological conflict and disagreement are at best obsolete, and at worse cover-ups for the illegitimate pursuit of special interests, encapsulates a technocratic outlook on politics. Indeed, as we noted, from the point of view of the internal logic of technocratic discourse, partisanship as such emerges as the main enemy simply because partisan conflict introduces interests and values in a domain that should be a matter of competence and expertise only. To the extent that Mair is correct in describing New Labour as aspiring to realize a form of 'partyless democracy' (Mair 2000), it therefore clearly fits the bill of what we have defined as a technocratic mode of political action.

The same technocratic strain is also visible in New Labour's extensive reliance on 'independent experts' and 'autonomous regulatory bodies' in both the formulation and implementation of public policy (Castellani 2016). As is well known, one of the first measures taken by Gordon Brown as the new Chancellor of the Exchequer upon assuming power in 1997 was to grant full autonomy to the Bank of England in setting interest rates over bonds denominated in British pounds. More broadly, Peter Burnham has identified a general logic of 'depoliticization' as one of the key government strategies employed by New Labour during its period of political incumbency:

> Depoliticisation has taken three main forms in Britain since the mid-1990s. First, there has been a reassignment of tasks away from the party in office to a number of ostensibly 'non-political' bodies as a way of underwriting the government's commitment to achieving objectives... The second form in which depoliticisation has been manifest as a governing strategy under New Labour is in the adoption of measures ostensibly to increase the accountability, transparency and external validation of policy by independent experts... Finally, depoliticisation strategies have been pursued in an overall context favouring the adoption of binding credible 'rules', which limit government room for manoeuvre (Burnham 2001: 136–42).

This concerted drive towards 'depoliticization' was justified at the time by one of Blair's cabinet members, the Secretary of State for Constitutional Affairs and Lord Chancellor, Charlie Falconer, in stating that: 'The depoliticizing of key decision-making is a vital element in bringing power closer to the people' (cited by Mair 2006: 26). Here, we can already begin to see one of the ways in which the two key features of New Labour we have been highlighting—its populist *and* technocratic traits—were brought together at the level of discourse. The key idea is that since politics ultimately boils down to partisanship, and the latter is irreducibly at odds with good governance, the depoliticization of policymaking is instrumental in the pursuit of the people's interests as a whole. Thus, rather than being in tension with one another, the populist call for transferring power from self-interested elites to the people as a whole, and the technocratic pursuit of the ideal of good governance, are here presented as two sides of the same coin. What is distinctive about the New Labour project, however, is that it was not simply an effort to close down political competition and replace it with direct forms of expert rule. It was not classically technocratic in that sense, to return to the different understandings of technocracy that we raise in chapter 1. Rather, it was an explicitly political project, one that was successfully built as a vote-winning strategy. The goal of the New Labour Third Way was to excise ideology and partisanship from politics but not to eliminate political competition as such. Rather, such competition would be reordered around the technopopulist logic, with an appeal to 'the people' as a whole and an emphasis on New Labour's competence, transparency, and expert judgement.

In order to fully grasp how the populist and technocratic elements in New Labour's political strategy were synthesized with one another, it is necessary to move beyond the level of abstract discourse and look more closely at its concrete mode of political organization, namely the political party. Here, Colin Crouch's analysis of the pattern of recent transformation in the organizational structure of mainstream political parties provides us with a useful set of categories. In his 2003 book on *Post-Democracy*, Crouch contrasts the internal structure of what he calls 'traditional mass parties' with a new organizational tendency manifested by what he calls the 'post-democratic party'. The former's core feature is said to be a way of connecting the party leadership with its electoral base through a system of superimposed layers of authority, which Crouch describes as a series of 'concentric circles' (Crouch 2003: 70). In this model, 'leaders are drawn from the activists, who are drawn from the party membership, which is part of and therefore reflects the concerns and interests of those parts of the electorate which the party most seeks to represent' (2003: 70).

By contrast, the 'post-democratic party' links the party leadership *directly* with its electoral base. To achieve this—both in terms of image promotion and policy content—it relies on the recommendations of a number of 'external' professionals, such as 'public opinion pollsters', 'policy experts', and 'media strategy consultants'. For Crouch, this establishes 'the possibility of a curious bond linking the innermost and outermost of the concentric circles, at the expense of the intermediate relationships' (2003: 72). Thus, the system of 'concentric circles' that characterized the mass party's organizational structure is progressively replaced by an 'ellipse' that sees the central leadership's circle reach directly outwards towards the broader public, relying more closely on the services of hired 'campaign experts' than on the internal party network itself (2003: 73–4).

Crouch himself points out that the ideas he puts forward are 'particularly relevant to the contemporary Labour Party' (2000: 15). An earlier version of the text that eventually became the *Post-Democracy* book was in fact first published as a pamphlet by the Fabian Society, one of the Labour Party's original founding organizations and a prominent centre-left contemporary think tank. The idea of a party that progressively replaces grassroots members and intermediate party organizations with 'campaign experts', 'public opinion pollsters', and 'media strategy consultants' is particularly apt for describing the changes undergone by the British Labour Party during the period of New Labour. Peter Mair wrote at the time of a tendency to assimilate the 'people's will' with the outcome of 'focus groups', noting that many of New Labour's policy decisions were 'framed and effectively sanctioned through focus groups', and that the significance of these groups went 'far beyond testing of new ideas'. They were used 'to establish a more or less direct linkage between citizens and government' (Mair 2000: 27). Similarly, in a book recounting his experiences and political role as one of Tony Blair's most trusted 'spin doctors', Philip Gould (2011) observed that:

> From being a party driven by a platform with an election manifesto hammered out at a faction-ridden conference, the British Labour Party has been transformed into a party driven by PR men, opinion polls and advertising agencies.

In this sense, New Labour seems to lie at the origin of a broader political tendency, which has since become very widespread and has already been amply commented upon in academic literature: that of 'public opinion-driven' and especially 'poll-driven' politics (see Holtz-Bacha and Stromback 2012). Even though today it might seem commonplace that politicians use opinion polls and PR experts to define their substantive policy platform, that was not always the case: in the traditional 'mass party' model Crouch refers to, the policy platform was elaborated *within* the party organization and ultimately rooted in its pre-established ideological commitments. The 'public opinion-driven' and especially 'poll-driven' politics of the New Labour era operates a synthesis between what we have taken populism and technocracy to consist in.

On one hand, in common with populism, it has the idea that the popular will is an objective entity existing 'out there' as a function of the mass of individual opinions, as well as the assumption that the purpose of politics is to translate this public opinion directly into policy outcomes, to be 'servants of the people'. On the other hand, the policies deemed to 'work', 'good' policies rather than 'bad' policies, originate in the ideas of individuals selected for their expert knowledge and brought into the highest echelons of the party as special advisors. The development of policy ideas is divorced from the partisan political machine and their principal testing ground are the 'mini-publics' of the focus group.

The figures of the 'policy consultant' and the 'public opinion pollster' are the *embodiments* of this specific type of technopopulism. They make the substance of political competition the two dimensions of the technopopulist political logic: the direct appeal to the people, and the emphasis on expertise combined with a presentation of policies are justified on objective, scientific grounds, 'evidence-based' policies as opposed to partisan—and hence more biased—policies. To the extent that New Labour relied extensively on such figures in the curation of its public image as well as the formulation of its substantive policy platform, in a way that broke very clearly from the traditional workings of the Labour Party as a mass party, we can consider it a distinctively technopopulist political movement.

In this sense, we can describe the New Labour case as a form of 'technopopulism through the party'. Discursively, this type of technopopulism is often associated with a claim about renewal or renovation of an *existing* party structure, particularly one that brings the party closer to the people. An effect of this dismantling of barriers between the party and society is that the party's particular interests and claims to represent specific sections or groups within society are replaced by a more general claim about representing the people as a whole. The definition given of the people is the responsibility of the party, which it does via a number of different tools and procedures, such as through opinion polls and focus groups. These tools take on a central strategic importance in this variant of technopopulism and thus greatly empower experts in the measurement of public opinion and the analysis of polling data. They also include the procedures developed to open up the political party itself, such as open primaries, which have become popular in a number of countries such as France and Italy. In all such cases, the purpose of these changes is to replace the exclusive association of a party with the social identity of its members, and to put in its place a more general and more 'popular' identity for the party. The justification is that in becoming less ideological, the party is able to become more effective in responding to people's needs. In short, the party opens itself up in order to perform better. The party's *raison d'etre* is to realize a set of identifiable goals that benefit 'the people' as a whole rather favouring one segment of society over another. Identifying these goals is the preserve of experts, often employed directly by party leaders and ministers in the form of special advisers, whose expertise lies in individual fields of public policy. As the party opens up, it concentrates power within the hands of a small number of experts tasked with identifying its goals and key policy platforms.

The consequence of this variant of technopopulism is that experts become the new mediators between the party leadership and the public. They replace the traditional links to society provided by party activists and local government representatives. In contrast to the other varieties of technopopulism outlined below, the manifestations of the technopopulist logic occur *within the political party itself*. Whilst party leaders cultivate more direct links to 'the people' by effacing the boundaries between party members and the general public, the elevation of expertise comes with the enormous authority invested in the polling and communications experts as bridge between society and the party leadership. In this type of technopopulism, the destruction of historic state–society relations—a crucial condition for the emergence of the technopopulist logic which we describe in chapter 3—operates in a concentrated form, inside of actually existing parties.

The Five Star Movement: Technopopulism through the Electoral Base

The Italian Five Star Movement (M5S) is our second pure case of technopopulism. Founded in October 2009 by Beppe Grillo, a popular comedian and independent blogger, and Gianroberto Casaleggio, a little-known and reclusive web strategist, this political operation has over the years grown into one of the mainstays of Italian politics. It first fielded candidates in a number of regional elections in 2010, obtaining marginal but encouraging results. By mid-2013 it had already obtained the largest share of the vote for any single party (excluding the votes from Italians abroad) in the national legislative elections. Three years later, two of its candidates—Virginia Raggi and Chiara Appendino—were elected mayors in two of Italy's main cities: Rome and Turin. Finally, at the 2018 national legislative election the M5S again emerged as the largest single party on a national scale, with over 35 per cent of the votes, ultimately going on to form a coalition government with Matteo Salvini's *Lega* in the first Guiseppe Conte government, and then with the PD in the second Conte government. The M5S is still in office at the time of writing.

Despite this impressive electoral record, commentators have had a hard time classifying the M5S. In many ways, it confounds traditional analytical tools and categories. Ideologically, the M5S has made a point of being 'neither left- nor right-wing'. For instance, writing on his personal blog—which for the first few years served as the M5S's principal organ of communication—its founder and charismatic leader asserted that: 'The days of ideology are over...The M5S is neither left- nor right-wing. It is above and beyond' (cited by Tronconi 2015: 196). In light of its eclectic mix of policy proposals—which range from environmental 'degrowth' to universal basic income, the renationalization of basic public services and proposals for more direct democracy, up to a critical stance on immigration and an ambivalent though largely sceptical attitude with respect to the European Union and especially the euro—commentators have various described the M5S as 'post-ideological' (Biorcio and Nartale 2013), 'multi-ideological' (Bordignon and

Ceccarini 2018), 'catch-all' (Diamanti 2014), or simply 'anti-establishment' (Mosca 2014).

At the same time, the M5S is characterized by an 'elusive organizational model', suggesting a variety of terms to describe it—'movement party', 'personal party', and 'business firm party'—but ultimately concluding that 'none of the labels... can fully capture it' (Tronconi 2015: 175, 177). According to Ceccarini and Bordignon, the M5S—along with *Podemos*, UKIP, the *Rassemblement National*[2] and the AFD in Germany—'belongs to an indistinct category difficult to define using the traditional concepts of political science' (2016: 131). What all these parties and movements have in common, for them, is that they are 'all expressions of populism'. However, these same authors also accept that the M5S can plausibly be seen as an 'organizational hybrid', one that is

> in part the party of a charismatic leader, typical of populist formations in particular, in part a participatory party, like those of the environmental movement and the new left.... It is a party in public office, born as a web-based party, but particularly attentive to the rank-and-file through the network of MeetUp groups.... [I]n certain respects it has the characteristics of a catch-all (anti-party) party, based on non-traditional divisions, and/or on (anti-political) sentiments which, far from dividing, unite groups of citizens whose ideological orientations are otherwise very different (2016: 132).

A further difficulty in identifying and classifying the distinctive nature of the M5S has been that both its discourse and mode of political organization have changed, often markedly and unpredictably, over time. What used to be a radical and in many ways also 'anti-system' political force, run in a highly personalistic way by its founder and charismatic leader (e.g. Pasquino 2014), has now become a much more moderate political entity, which has assumed many of the trappings of a traditional political party, and has participated in two different coalition governments (Bordignon and Ceccarini 2018). A crucial *caesura* in this respect was Beppe Grillo's departure as leader 2014 and the handover of power to a 'directorate' of younger militants, out of which Luigi Di Maio has emerged as the leader until his own departure in January 2020.[3]

We aim to solve at least some of these interpretive puzzles by suggesting that the M5S is best understood as manifesting a particular type of technopopulism, which we refer to as 'technopopulism through the electoral base'. This political movement is an exemplary expression of the same technopopulist political logic

---

[2] The *Front national* (FN) changed its name to the *Rassemblement national* (RN) in 2018. We refer throughout to the RN rather than the old FN unless we are clearly speaking of a political moment—e.g. the 2002 election surprise in France—where we then refer to the *Front national*.
[3] Di Maio stepped down as leader of the M5S but at the time of writing had retained his position in the government.

that was so central to understanding New Labour but the manner in which it synthesizes its appeals to the people and the appeals to competence and expertise is different. Given the changes in the M5S, this analysis applies most cogently to a particular phase in the rapid evolution of the M5S's history, which is that corresponding to Beppe Grillo's leadership between the M5S's foundation in 2009 his resignation in 2014. Restricting our focus to this period is justified by the fact that our goal in the present section is not to provide a comprehensive analysis of the nature and historical evolution of the M5S as such, but merely to identify the latter as a paradigmatic case of the broader political logic we are describing in this book.[4] We begin by identifying the populist and technocratic features manifested by the M5S during the time of Grillo's leadership, then focus on the ways in which these have been synthetized with one another, and finally extrapolate from this a more general 'pure type'.

The populist elements in the M5S's political discourse are obvious for all to see and are the reason for which many commentators have described this political force as a 'populist' movement (Diamanti and Lazar 2018; Ivaldi et al. 2017; Müller 2016). Although Grillo's rhetoric hasn't made a particularly extensive use of the category of 'the people', he effectively translated the notion of *la casta*—developed by two Italian journalists in 2007—into a political weapon deployed as a way of denouncing not just government graft and corruption but also the whole Italian political establishment. In Grillo's political vocabulary, 'the caste' refers to a wide variety of different elites, united with one another in the reciprocal protection of their established privileges, at the expense of honest and hard-working common people. In one blog post from 2013, Grillo wrote that:

> The caste is not just one: there are many. They are united together and form an immense body, a super social group, which feeds on the blood of those who produce... The political caste, the caste of the newspapers, the bureaucracy caste, the caste of the central government, the caste of unnecessary bodies... These castes do not derive their power from controlling the means of production, but from controlling the means of information... The Italian caste is like a parasite that kills the body that hosts it (cited by Ivaldi et al. 2017: 359–60).

Here, we find the characteristic opposition between a virtuous and hard-working people and a self-interested and exploitative elite, which we identified as one of the core features of populist discourse in chapter 1. The same opposition is also suffused with a moral dimension which, as Cas Mudde has emphasized, aims to present the people as 'pure' and the elite as 'corrupt' (Mudde 2004: 543). Grillo

---

[4] Nevertheless, when we look back at Di Maio's time at the head of the M5S, the technopopulist lens helps us make sense of a number of things, not least the willingness of this anti-establishment movement to enter into coalitions with its supposed political foes.

was even more blunt about this when he wrote, in another blog post from 2011, that: 'Political parties are evil', adding that they are 'a cancer that is eating up our country and making the lives of honest people impossible' (cited by Bickerton and Invernizzi-Accetti 2018: 136).

Another clearly populist aspect of the M5S's rhetoric are its virulent attacks against political opponents. Even before the M5S was officially founded, Grillo organized two large public rallies, which took place respectively in September 2007 and April 2008, entitled the '*Vaffanculo Days*' (literally: 'Fuck You Days'). They were a blanket rejection of the country's political class and its established elites. Over time, Grillo coined derogatory nicknames for the leaders of all competing political parties, which quickly became part of the M5S's standard political discourse. Mario Monti was 'Rigor Montis', a biting insult for the stiff and technocratic figure that Italians called '*il professore*'. Silvio Berlusconi was dubbed the 'psycho-dwarf' and Matteo Renzi was the 'little idiot from Florence' (Tronconi 2015: 3).

This use of coarse and derogatory language was a way of establishing the M5S's popular credentials. It confirmed its exteriority from the established circles of political power in Italy through a refusal to comply with established codes of political correctness. It also served to undermine the credibility of the political establishment as such, challenging the legitimacy of its principal exponents. Grillo insisted that all the exponents of Italy's political class (apart, of course, from those associated with his political movement) were 'scoundrels', 'thieves', and 'rascals'. Even more telling about the M5S's attitude towards its political rivals, however, was the claim made by Beppe Grillo in an interview with *Time* magazine in 2013. 'We want 100% of Parliament, not 20, 25 or 30%', Grillo declared, implying that in the M5S's world view there is no space for alternative political forces that manifest competing political interests or views (Faris and Bibbona 2013).

Beyond the level of discourse, another clearly populist aspect of the M5S under Grillo's leadership was its mode of internal organization. Throughout this period, the party revolved almost entirely around the figure of Grillo himself, who cultivated a direct—and in some cases even cultish—relationship with the growing mass of online followers of his blog. As Grillo himself explained: 'Folks, it works like this: You let me know and I play the amplifier' (cited by Vignati 2015: 43). The personalism of the M5S during the period of Grillo's leadership was also clear in the hierarchical structure of the M5S. Ownership of the party's brand belonged to Grillo himself, together with Gianroberto Casaleggio through the Casaleggio Associati marketing company. This proprietorship over the party's brand was used as a disciplining tool by its leadership, threatening transgressors of the M5S message with expulsion from the movement and sanction through legal pursuit for copyright violation. Several 'purges' of prominent members of the party, elected to the Italian Parliament after the 2013 national elections, were undertaken in this way (Tronconi 2015).

The concentration of power under Grillo's leadership was never complete, not least because of the vociferous party base, which found expression through the party blog and modified the movement's line on a number of issues. As Diamanti observed in 2014, 'the M5S is certainly personified by its spokesman, Grillo; but its identity is not reducible to personal characteristics' (2014: 10). Organizationally, the M5S under Grillo united in a curious fashion the elements of a 'personalist party' and an online 'grassroots movement'. In Diamanti's (2014: 13) words:

> The M5S is surely a personalized political entity... Nevertheless, the groups and the activists do not belong to the Movement mainly on the basis of personal identification. They are not just 'followers' of Grillo—or rather, they follow him because he offers them a network, a common environment in which to make themselves and their claims visible.

The most important point here is that between the leadership and this largely online base, there were never any intermediate levels of authority or organization. In conformity with Grillo's broader political rhetoric of 'disintermediation' (see Grillo and Casaleggio 2011), the political movement he created involved an essentially *unmediated* relationship between the leadership and the base. The former proposed and disposed on all matters of political relevance (including the sanctioning of dissenters when necessary), whilst the latter were called upon to approve these measures, either by acclamation in the comments section of Grillo's blog, or—over time—through a more structured process of online internal elections.

In this sense, throughout the first phase of its development, the M5S can be described as a 'plebiscitarian' party—which as we noted in chapter 1 is one of the core features of the populist mode of political organization. This point was highlighted by Davide Vittori at the end of his comparative analysis of the M5S and Spain's *Podemos* when he wrote that: 'What the analysis shows is that the main organizational differences between the two parties concern the role of the intermediate bodies, which are almost absent in M5S, and the role of leadership, which is much more plebiscitarian and unconstrained in the Italian case' (Vittori 2017: 324).

Alongside these evident—and widely commented upon—populist traits, the M5S under Grillo's leadership displayed a number of technocratic features that have drawn less attention from scholars. Its origins are telling in this respect. The movement first came together around the comedy routines performed by Grillo in theatres and other public venues around the country. A notable aspect of these shows was Grillo's emphatic refusal to talk about 'politics': a term that in his vocabulary is systematically associated with ideas of 'corruption' and vain 'ideological disputes' (Grillo and Casaleggio 2011: 19). Instead, Grillo made a point of reconstructing cases of public interest, by presenting facts and illustrating scientific theories. As Bordignon and Ceccarini (2013: 134) put it: 'In [Grillo's] widely popular shows, entertainment was mixed with campaigns of mobilisation and denunciation around issues of public interest and the "common good".' Grillo would occasionally bring 'experts' onto the stage in order to corroborate his claims, and on more than one occasion Grillo himself was called upon by public prosecutors to testify in cases brought against private companies and public figures.

This focus on expertise also pervaded Grillo's understanding of politics as an activity that requires a specific type of competence. On numerous occasions, Grillo suggested that elected representatives should not be understood as 'leaders', but rather as employees hired to achieve specific tasks, akin to one's hiring of a plumber to fix broken pipes in a house. For instance, in one of his public speeches, he stated:

> If your plumber were to spend his time on television enunciating important (and unrequested) 'political' thoughts, writing articles and presenting books, you'd begin to doubt that he was working for you. You'd suspect that he was using his position to gain the visibility in plumbing circles that he would otherwise never have had... It's surreal. And all this happens because you pay him to fix water pipes in your house. You pay a plumber, but if you turn your back for a moment, you find a leader under the kitchen sink (cited in Vignati 2015: 10).

In this analogy between politics and plumbing, we find an underlying conception of politics as a purely technical activity, which requires a specific type of competence. Whilst there may be more than one route to fixing a pipe, the options are reasonably limited and the purpose of the intervention is as clear as it could be: to fix the leak. A good plumber knows what needs to be done; all that is necessary is to get the right person to do the job. Grillo's suggestion is that, by analogy, politics is an exercise in problem-solving best undertaken by those with practical skills calibrated to complete the task at hand.

Even more telling in this regard was Grillo's claim that, if the M5S were to win the national elections, they would put 'a housewife with three kids', not an 'economics professor', at the Ministry of Finance (Buzzi 2013). Whilst this was generally interpreted as a swipe at Mario Monti's technocratic government in office in Italy at the time, Grillo's point was actually one about *competence*. He was arguing that a housewife had a much better grasp of financial issues because of her day-to-day management of her family's finances. Grillo's intervention was not about the democratic credentials of Monti, it was an argument over who is the best technocrat. Grillo never called into question the idea that the Minister of Finance should be chosen on the basis of his or her competence, rather than in relation to the political values (or social interests) he or she stands for. We find here a key issue about the 'techne' in technpopulism. As we highlighted in chapter 1, the technopopulist logic heralds a disaggregation in the notion of expertise, pitting as part of political competition one sort of expertise against the other. Grillo's celebration of the housewife as budgetary expert is consistent also with a number of policy positions that the M5S has adopted over the years, including the embrace of anti-vaccination campaign. Such positions and campaigns reflect the M5S's embrace of alternative sorts of knowledge, and their scepticism about the expertise emerging from the state or the ruling establishment. This sort of expertise is tainted with the special interests and privileges that are defended at the same time.

This competence-based and matter-of-fact approach was carried over into the M5S itself. In the run-up to the 2013 parliamentary elections, candidates were not required to provide a statement of their political views. Only their CVs were uploaded on the party's website, the assumption being that their personal competences mattered more than their politics or their values. The same kind of technocratic approach is evident in the M5S's very name. The 'five stars' refer to five issues remarkable for their apolitical and technical nature: 'water', 'environment', 'transport', 'connectivity' and 'development'. These are all policy areas understood pragmatically, as 'problems to be solved' (Grillo and Casaleggio 2011). The M5S takes the view that there are right and wrong solutions to these problems and finding the right solution is a matter of competence, not ideology.

This approach has been evident in the behaviour of those M5S representatives who entered Parliament after the 2013 elections. In the words of one: 'We go project by project. We don't have an ideological line or party line—we have projects' (cited in Passarelli et al. 2013). With much the same message, Manucci and Amsler cite the Grillo blog as saying: 'If a law is good, we vote for it, if it is bad we do not vote for it' (2018: 109). An analogous approach is also visible in the M5S's record at the municipal level. Commenting on the actions of Rome's current M5S mayor, Bordignon notes that Virginia Raggi has brought several non-partisan 'technicians' into her cabinet. 'From the whole controversy over Raggi's cabinet', he writes 'there emerges another recurrent element of the M5S's history: its flirt with technocracy.' According to Bordignon, this is 'the other side of the Five Star's populism': '[t]he idea that technicians, experts and professionals can replace professional politicians' (Bordignon 2016).

Others have highlighted the way in which the M5S's political offer combines some distinctively technocratic elements with a broadly populist appeal. In another article written shortly after the M5S's electoral breakthrough in Rome's municipal elections, Lorenzo Castellani observes that:

> [T]he victory of the 5-Star Movement in Rome is an interesting politico-institutional case because it clearly manifests the two main pillars around which political power is in the process of being re-organized: populism and technocracy. On one hand, the 5-Star Movement won by presenting a candidature drawn straight out of the Casaleggio & Associates marketing firm's strategy,

which succeeded in capturing the protest votes against the corrupt elites that have been governing the capital...On the other hand, once arrived on the Capitol, the *grillini* realized they did not have a political class capable of confronting the intrinsic complexity of the activity of government. The only solution was therefore to constitute a predominantly technocratic cabinet (Castellani 2018).

In Castellani's reading, the combination of populist and technocratic elements is a fall-back option, as if the M5S's exponents were forced into a reliance on technocrats after having assumed power because of their own inexperience in government. We suggest here that the technocratic strain cuts much deeper into the M5S's political discourse and mode of political organization.

How exactly has the M5S synthesized the populist and technocratic elements into a single political offer? As in the case of the New Labour movement we considered above, this is an operation that happens first of all at the level of discourse. During her victory speech in Rome on the 19th June 2016, newly elected M5S mayor, Virginia Raggi, made the following statement:

> We of the M5S are just normal people, like you. This normality scares [the politicians, the establishment] because they know that our team is not just our candidates here. Our team is you, the whole square, the whole city... [The politicians and parties] have ruined our city, left in the hands of criminals. We want efficient trains and public transport; we want efficient accident and emergency units in our hospitals. We believe in the common good and want to strengthen it (cited in Bock 2017).

Here is a common discursive trope already present in our analysis of New Labour: the idea that since party politicians are inherently corrupt and in the service of 'special interests', taking key areas of decision-making out of the political domain, by entrusting them to supposedly 'independent experts', is a way of ensuring that policy outcomes are closer to the true interests of the people as a whole. This assumption enables Raggi to connect the (characteristically populist) claim that the M5S's political exponents are 'just normal people, like you', with the (inherently technocratic) promise that this will enable them to deliver on 'efficient trains and public transport', 'efficient accident and emergency units', and 'the common good'.

To grasp what is *distinctive* about the M5S's way of combining populist and technocratic traits, however, we must look more closely at the specific role this political organization has always assigned to technology, manifest in its online platform, 'Rousseau'. Inspired by its late Internet guru, Gianroberto Casaleggio, the M5S has advanced a form of web utopianism where the technological power of the World Wide Web is assumed to dramatically improve the problem-solving capacities of human societies. As a space of 'unmediated communication', the Internet can harness the 'specific competences' and 'best practices' of dispersed individuals and communities (Grillo and Casaleggio 2011: 26). This is expected to lead to a dramatic increase in 'collective intelligence', making it possible to solve political problems in a more efficient and effective way (Natale and Ballatore 2014: 113). As Casaleggio himself put it, the Internet is 'a brain that sees, understands, communicates, acts' (cited in Mosca 2018). For this reason, he also supposed that the development of online technologies would ultimately 'make politics itself redundant'. Instead, humanity's interests would be served by probing the web's 'collective intelligence' for efficient solutions to common problems (Grillo and Casaleggio 2011). Here, the emancipatory potential of the Internet is not justified with respect to any recognizably 'political' (i.e. contestable) principles as it is with, say, the Pirate Party movement (whose emphasis is on civil liberties). The only claim is both a populist and technocratic one: that this technology will allow for better representation of the people's interests through the formulation of more effective solutions to common problems.

We see this even more clearly in a discussion by Casaleggio of how the Internet can help revive the ideal of Athenian democracy. As Mosca notes, Athens is a common reference point for Grillo and Casaleggio's attempts at reviving the ideal of direct democracy. However, they do this in their own way. In 2013, speaking at an international conference in Cernobbio, on the edge of Lake Como, Casaleggio argued that

> We are far from the Athenian democracy; the story took a different turn... [However], maybe the Internet can help to regain that inspiration, in that it *makes us equal in being smart* (cited in Mosca 2018; italics added).

The formulation of 'equal in being smart' is the core of the technopopulist synthesis operated by the M5S. The language of citizenship and popular sovereignty is deployed using a conception of politics that is primarily epistemic in character—that is, about finding the 'right' answers to common problems. Technology can help us arrive at better policy outcomes through the mobilization of 'collective intelligence'. In contrast with standard variants of technocracy, where expertise is concentrated in certified bodies and professional institutions, here we find competence diffused amongst the population at large. The M5S' message is that *everyone is an expert*, from which it follows that the people as a whole must make the best political decisions. This is the populist element that the M5S grafts onto its technocratic conception of politics, thereby operating a synthesis of the two.

From this, we can extrapolate the core features of a second 'pure type' of technopopulism, which we shall refer to as 'technopopulism through the electoral base'. As a political discourse, individual citizens are mobilized using the language of 'the people', popular sovereignty, and direct democracy. However, citizens are addressed using the language of competence and expertise, not the more traditional language of rights. Each citizen matters not only or simply because s/he is a bearer of rights that need to be realized via representation in the state. The value of each citizen comes from what they *know* as members of civil society. Citizens bring their professional competences—as doctors and nurses, as engineers, as teachers—into the political field and are valued as such. Twenty-first-century technology harnesses this collective expertise by elaborating the most effective solutions for common political problems.

What occurred in New Labour by the transfer of power from intermediate party cadres to public opinion pollsters and PR strategists is accomplished in the M5S by entrusting collective decisions to the wisdom of online platforms and the World Wide Web. This satisfies the populist demand for inclusion *and* the technocratic goal of effective and efficient policy delivery. However, the logic of these 'pure' cases is different. In the case of New Labour, discovering and implementing the people's desire is delegated to a new professional cadre of policy and public opinion experts. For the M5S, the people's will itself, as manifested by the outcome of online aggregating procedures, has an epistemic value. Producing the best policy outcomes is thus a matter of empowering the people as a whole.[5]

Emmanuel Macron's La République En Marche!: Technopopulism through the Leader

Our third pure case of technopopulism is constituted by Emmanuel Macron's *La République En Marche!* First created as *En Marche!* in March 2016, this political movement (which has consistently refused to be identified as a political party) initially served as a vehicle for the presidential bid of its founder and current leader, Emmanuel Macron. Obtaining 24 per cent of the vote at the first round of

---

[5] There is here a certain degree of overlap—or at least affinity—between the M5S's form of 'technopopulism through the electoral base' and the particular strand of contemporary democratic theory usually referred to as 'epistemic' theories of democracy. In the work of authors such as David Estlund (2008) and Hélène Landemore (2013), for instance, democracy is defended against what these authors call 'epistocracy' (i.e. rule by the competent few) on the basis of the argument that the 'collective intelligence' of the many in most cases surpasses the problem-solving skills of even the most competent few. This is essentially the same idea that also underpins the M5S's faith in 'crowd-sourcing' as a political problem-solving tool. An important difference, however, lies in the fact that both Estlund and Landemore still assign an important role to the traditional mechanisms of political mediation—such as collective deliberation, political representation, and institutional checks and balances—in disclosing the collective intelligence of the whole. The M5S, instead, appears to subscribe to a far more simplistic version of the epistemic conception of democracy, according to which the procedure of online voting can ultimately replace—or at least bypass—the more traditional mechanisms of political mediation. It is this emphasis on disintermediation through technology that makes theirs a truly technopopulist conception of democracy, as opposed to the one we find in authors such as Estlund and Landemore, which merely operates on the terrain of technocracy itself.

the 2017 presidential elections, it succeeded in propelling him into the second round. Macron defeated Marine Le Pen with over 66 per cent of the votes and took up the highest political office in the country at the age of thirty-nine. In the subsequent legislative elections, the renamed *La République En Marche!* (LREM) obtained 308 of the 577 seats, granting the newly elected President a comfortable majority in the National Assembly, with which he has governed France up to the time of writing.

As in the case of the Italian M5S, commentators have had a hard time classifying Macron's political movement. Although Macron himself was for a brief time a member of the French Socialist Party, and also served as a cabinet member in François Hollande's government between 2014 and 2016, from the very beginning LREM has presented itself as a 'post-' and indeed 'anti-ideological' political force. When he launched his presidential campaign in December 2016, Macron declared that LREM was 'neither left- nor right-wing' (*ni de droite ni de gauche*). This formula gradually morphed into 'both left- and right-wing' (*en même temps de droite et de gauche*) as it became clear that Macron's principal contender, Marine Le Pen, had adopted the same slogan for her own campaign. In his campaign manifesto-cum-memoir, Macron elaborated on the point further:

> I cannot resign myself to being confined within the divisions of another time... Our current political life is organized around a longstanding division which no longer allows us to meet global or national challenges... My desire to go beyond the conflict between Left and Right has been represented by the Left as neoliberal treason, while the Right has depicted me as a hypocrite of the Left (Macron 2016: 19–21).

While some commentators have interpreted this as amounting to a form of ideological 'centrism' (Elgie 2018)—and indeed Macron's electoral victories as a sign of the possible 'renewal of centrist politics' across Europe (e.g. Collins 2019)—others see Macron as a 'classical liberal', recovering a long-standing but historically marginal tradition of specifically French liberalism going back to Alexis Tocqueville, François Guizot, and, more recently, Raymond Aron (Manent 2017). Still others have focused on his representation of 'business interests', in a political agenda that favours 'capitalist globalization' and 'free market deregulation' (Pinçon and Pinçon-Charlot 2019).

Equally confounding has been LREM's mode of political organization. On one hand, this political movement displays some of the characteristic features of the 'personal party', having served as a vehicle for its founder's presidential ambitions. On the other hand, a recurrent element in LREM's own discourse has been the need to transform the traditional modes of political organization, replacing the 'top-down' and 'bureaucratic' methods of established political parties with a more 'participatory' and 'bottom-up' approach. Indeed, the idea of a grassroots popular movement transforming French politics 'from below' has been a central aspect of LREM's self-presentation from the start. In his book, Macron argued that: 'Change will not be dictated from above. It will be driven at the grassroots level' (Macron 2016: 115).

Many of these interpretive puzzles can be resolved by construing LREM as a technopopulist political force. The specific way in which this movement operates the synthesis between populist and technocratic elements is different from the two other pure cases of technopopulism. It is almost entirely focused on the personal characteristics of Emmanuel Macron himself. For this reason, we suggest that LREM should be seen as manifesting a variant of technopopulism which we refer to as 'technopopulism through the leader'. We proceed in a manner similar to the previous sections: first highlighting the populist and technocratic elements in LREM's discourse and mode of political organization, then focusing on how these are synthetized with one another, and finally extrapolating an abstract model of technopopulism from this analysis.

Several commentators have already pointed out that there exists a populist strand in Macron's mode of political action. In a cautious assessment, Marc Lazar writes that Macron 'flirted somewhat with a populist political style' (2018: 303). Along the same lines, Pierre Rosanvallon has observed that Macron stands for an 'elegant version of populism' (cited by Mauduit 2018: 135). Marcel Gauchet called his a 'velvety form of populism' (*un populisme de velours*) (2018: 10). *Le Monde's* chief political editor, Solenn de Royer, has been more trenchant. 'By standing against "the system" and by-passing intermediary bodies', she argued, 'Macron has clearly adhered to a form of populism.' 'The paradox', she notes, 'is that he draws from the populist playbook in order to fight back against the populist tide.' A similar point was alluded to by Fabio Bordignon when he described Macronism as a form of 'anti-populist populism' (Bordignon 2017), a point to which we return later in the book.

At a discursive level, these populist elements are manifest first of all in the manner in which Macron deployed anti-elitist and anti-establishment rhetoric in his election campaign. Macron spoke regularly in the name of 'the people', whom he opposed to the country's social and political elite. At a speech given in Angers in February 2017, Macron declared that: 'It shall be the people, not those at the top, who will take up the challenge that faces France' (cited in Lazar 2018: 303). Macron also sought to mobilize a growing feeling of *dégagisme* across France: a seething sense of dissatisfaction with the political class that amounts to something similar to the Italian M5S's '*vaffanculo*' slogan. This sentiment was present already in the *Nuits Debout* movement, which ran at the same time that *En Marche!* was launched. As Adam Plowright puts it, '*En Marche!* aimed to offer a different vision for the future that was anti-establishment, but would also appeal to middle class voters, small business owners and professionals' (2018: 205).

Even though his own career trajectory had been entirely through elite institutions—from education at the Lycée Henri IV, to Sciences Po, the *Ecole Nationale d'Administration*, and a partnership at Rothschilds bank—Macron's youth played in his favour by creating some distance between himself and the familiar worn faces of French politics. In a manner resembling Tony Blair's New Labour, Macron emphasized his youth and dynamism, portraying his political rivals as belonging to a bygone political era and himself as the harbinger of change, novelty, and progress. As Marc Lazar and Ilvo Diamanti have pointed out, this discursive opposition between the 'new' and the 'old' functions as a structural equivalent of the more traditional populist opposition between 'us' and 'them' (Lazar and Diamanti 2018: 128–9). Macron pushed this a step further claiming in his 2017 book that what he is standing for is nothing short of a 'Revolution!' (Macron 2016: 1).

On occasion, Macron deployed quintessentially populist terms, such as language of *la casta*. Attacking the vested interests of professional politicians and political parties, he argued that: 'What is unacceptable is when a caste builds itself up, closes ranks and imposes its own rules' (2017: 229). 'The parties' he added 'have given up on fighting for the common good. They focus on their own interests—to survive, come what may' (2017: 225). To this anti-party rhetoric, Macron adds a broader criticism of what the French call the *corps intermédiaires*. In a 2016 interview with the prominent French journalist Eric Fottorino, he asserted that: 'The principal blockages in our society come from these corporatisms, these intermediary bodies, and from the political system itself.' Warming to his theme, he added that: '[t]he political, administrative and economic elite have developed their own corporatism' and 'in a majority of cases, unions and political parties defend the interests of those who are part of the system' (Fottorino 2017: 44).

Carrying the same themes into his campaign speeches, Macron often started by describing a country that was blocked, at an impasse, struggling to free itself of its own negativity. He then presented *En Marche!* and his programme as a chance to liberate people from the burden of the old ways. His appeal stemmed not just from the fact that he was new and different; he was also a *redemptive* solution to the country's long-standing political problems, to use a term belonging to the study of populism (Canovan 1999). Once in power, Macron has described himself as 'populist' on a number of occasions. During a meeting held with the country's Mayors at the Elysée palace in November 2018, he asserted that '[w]e are the real populists, because we are with the people, every day', later adding that

> '[w]hen we are divided amongst ourselves we offer avenues of opportunity, not to the populists—I prefer not to use this term to describe them...but to the demagogues: those who want to simplify things, who revel in the day-to-day bickering of politics, and who like to say: "I am for less taxes, more public

expenditures, more tolerance but also more concern for the environment, and no transition constraints"' (quoted in Jublin 2018).

From an organizational perspective, Macron's populism is visible in the personalization of his political movement and in his attempts to establish a direct link with the broader electorate. Even though LREM has cultivated an image of itself as a grassroots movement, in practice it functions as an extension of Macron's political will and ambitions. As Lazar puts it, Macron 'created a movement the acronym of which corresponds to his own initials. [It is] a personal movement that served him as a tool for his conquest of power' (2018: 303–4). Similarly, Plowright has written that:

> Despite his love of horizontal organizations and start-up culture, Macron's movement was a highly centralized organization built around him. He inspired complete devotion and often took the big decisions alone, after consulting [his wife] Brigitte. Despite the 'kids' [Macron's term for his closest inner team] often being around the same age as him, there was no doubt who the boss was (2017: 209).

Running parallel to this personalization of political power was an attempt at establishing a relationship of 'embodiment' with the broader electorate. Isabelle Mathieu has commented on the 'evident relish with which the President seeks to make contact with the French people' (Mathieu 2019). 'Uncontestably', for her, 'Emmanuel Macron enjoys meeting the French, touching them, kissing them, talking to them without barriers—and especially without intermediaries.' During his victory speech after the May 2017 presidential election, Macron stood before a large crowd in the courtyard of the Louvre palace. With his arms spread wide, in a Christ-like pose, he declared that: 'France has won!...Everybody was telling us that it was impossible, but they don't know France!...What we represent, what you represent, tonight, here...is France's fervour, its enthusiasm, the energy of the French people!' (Macron 2016).

In a later attempt at reconnecting with this initial fervour, and in response to the *gilets jaunes* protest movement, Macron launched an initiative dubbed *Le Grand Débat National*. This involved Macron touring the country, meeting with representatives from different regions and professional sectors, in a highly mediatized show of his personal willingness to listen and engage with ordinary French people's concerns. As Luc Rouban has commented, this offered a 'perfect snapshot of [Macron's] conception of political representation: the French people on one side, neatly arranged by professional categories...and the President on the other side, intently listening to the concerns being raised and ultimately answering all the questions' (Rouban 2019). Far from being in tension with the extraordinary degree of centralization of Macron's political movement, these staged performances of collective participation and dialogue between the President and French citizens reinforced its principal organizational logic, namely that of establishing a direct link of communication between Macron and his followers.

Alongside these distinctively populist features, 'Macronism' has many technocratic traits. Francois Bayrou, who entered into an alliance with Macron and was briefly Minister of Justice in his government, deplored this in late August 2017. In his words, a type of 'techno-managerialism' (*téchno-gestionnaire*) was taking hold of French politics. 'If we continue techno-France, techno-Europe, we're dead', he warned. Responding to Bayrou's accusation, Macron dismissed the idea that there was any real distinction to be made between politics and technocracy. 'We must finish with this dilemma between politicians and civil servants', he argued, pointing out that the Fifth Republic had worked perfectly well at a time when many civil servants were appointed as ministers. 'I am myself a civil servant', he added, referring to his brief stint as a tax inspection officer after graduating from the prestigious ENA school. When Macron speaks of eliminating the distinction between politics and technocracy, he does not mean an end to political competition or the political domain. After all, he himself made the leap from civil servant to politician. Rather, he means that within the political domain we should accept that expertise and competence has its place; and that politics is above all a space where 'things are done'. In his own words, 'I am not interested in politics', meaning the squabbles between parties and associated backroom deals, 'I am interested in doing' (Pedder 2018: 226).

Macron's political movement has been built with collaborators chosen primarily for their competence and achievements, as well as their personal devotion to Macron himself. Political views or previous partisan affiliations have been less important. The group of the so-called 'Macron Boys' around which the project of *En Marche!* first came together in the summer of 2016 was constituted entirely by 'graduates from the *grandes écoles* such as ENA and HEC, communications specialists and some former political advisors,... all—with one exception—in their mid-to-late thirties'. What brought them together was not their alignment or loyalty to a particular party or ideology, but rather their belief in the need and opportunity to try 'something new' (Plowright 2018: 179).

The government personnel chosen by Macron after his rise to power was remarkable for its technical and largely apolitical profile. While Macron's first government was led by Edouard Philippe, a former member of the centre-right Republicans, he also nominated Gérard Collomb, a long-standing Socialist Party politician as his Interior Minister, in an evident attempt to form a government that drew on figures from both the left and the right. The greatest part of Macron's appointments were non-political figures, that is to say people drawn from different parts of civil society, who were chosen for their specific achievements or recognized competence. A former Olympic fencer was appointed Minister of Sport, whilst one of France's leading haematologists was chosen to run the

Ministry of Health (Bucur 2017; Drochon 2017). The taste for non-political appointments was manifested again in LREM's list of candidates for the National Assembly in the 2017 legislative elections: out of 521 candidates, 298 were drawn from civil society and had had no political role prior to standing for election. Paul André Taguieff remarks that whilst such individuals were not professional politicians, they were not very representative of civil society either. Ninety percentage of the new arrivals at the Palais Bourbon were drawn from professional and managerial classes that amount to only 13 per cent of France's population as a whole (Taguieff 2017: 257). The criterion was therefore clear: competence, rather than ideology or political affiliation, is the necessary prerequisite for serving on Macron's political team.

We see Macron's distinctively technocratic approach to governing in the importance he places on competence and service delivery. A former Socialist deputy from Gironde, Gilles Savary, noted in an interview with *Le Monde*: 'It's Bercy [that is, the headquarters of the national civil service] who's taken over power and is now running the country' (de Royer 2019). For Savary, this has led to a 'hyper-centralized, very technocratic form of government...with elected officials kept on an extremely short leash' (de Royer 2019). Similarly, an 'influential and high-ranking civil servant' who preferred to remain anonymous in the same article joked that: 'It's a technocrat's dream:... as if we could finally put in practice the plans for reform that have been sleeping in Bercy's drawers for the past forty years!' (de Royer 2019). Commenting on these developments, Laurent Mauduit has argued that, in an ironic reversal of Macron's rhetoric of overthrowing France's established elites, his electoral victory in fact represents the 'ultimate victory of the technocratic class' (Mauduit 2017). In the same analysis, Mauduit identifies in some detail the wide network of contacts which Macron built up over a number of years and which he has been able to draw on both as Minister, as presidential candidate, and then as President. Comparing these career paths with that followed by Macron himself, Mauduit concludes that the President's move from ENA, to a high-ranking position within the national civil service, through a brief stint in the private sector, before occupying political office is 'only the most successful instance of a more general trend' (Mauduit 2017: 151). This is what Bayrou refers to as France's 'technostructure' and serves as the deep foundation of Macron's power system. What we need to remember, however, is that—in the words of an article in *Le Monde*—it is 'technocracy in power' that we observe here, not the transfer of power *away* from political institutions into the bureaucracy or into independent institutions. The victory of the technocratic class under Macron stems from the fact that in making the political case for his programme of reforms, Macron's justification is a technocratic one: this is the best policy to pursue and the one most likely to resolve the problem at hand. Macron left the 'technostructure' in order to enter into the political domain, bringing his technocratic appeals with him.

As in the case of the Italian M5S, the combination of populist and technocratic elements in Macron's political movement has already been highlighted by several commentators. Writing at the time of his election victory, Mark Leonard argued that Macron's great promise was his ability to combine these two trends, which would otherwise appear to be at odds with one another. 'To bring true change', Leonard argued, 'Macron will have to transcend the two contradictory but mutually reinforcing political models that have defined the last decade of EU governance: technocracy and populism' (2017). Leonard presents the 'Macron method' as a way of overcoming the conflict between them. Castellani writes that: 'The current President of the French Republic, who is directly elected by the people and has already shown a centralizing tendency in the elaboration of his policies, is surrounded by technocratic ministers.' He adds that '[h]aving primarily undergone technical training before entering into politics, these ministers are more oriented towards putting into practice the Elysée's decisions than to contributing to their formation.' '[T]he new French government', he concludes, is 'a curious form of techno-caesarism' (Castellani 2018).

Closer analysis suggests that there is not just a coincidence of populist and technocratic elements in Macron's mode of political action, but a *synthesis* between the two. To a certain extent, this synthesis is operated in ways that appear analogous to the two 'pure types' of technopopulism we have already extrapolated from our analysis of New Labour and the M5S, respectively. Like New Labour, Macron's political movement has from the start relied systematically on public opinion polls and PR marketing strategies to tailor its political offer, albeit of a particular kind. Immediately after launching his presidential bid in the spring of 2016, for instance, Macron embarked on what he described at the time as *La Grande Marche*. This was essentially an itinerant series of 'focus groups', targeting specific segments of the population across the country, whose declared aim was to 'make an assessment of the state of our country as it is seen by those who are primarily concerned: the French people themselves' (LREM 2016). The information, gathered from over 100,000 respondents, was fed back up to the top of the organization and then used as the basis for moulding Macron's electoral campaign. In the words of one who ran this exercise:

> What were the main conclusions? When we asked people what was wrong with France, their first response was: the politicians... So we knew the campaign was going to be structured around that. And that was the whole reason behind [*En Marche!*] (cited by Plowright 2018: 207).

Here, we find a particularly candid expression of a logic we already encountered in our analysis of New Labour. This is the idea that a value-neutral 'science' of public opinion, as practised by a category of professional experts with specific competences, can help elected (or aspiring) politicians discover and implement what 'the people' really want. The added twist in the case of Macron is that what the 'experts' discovered was that 'the people' were unhappy with the way in which they were being represented by the political class as a whole. The experts therefore recommended adopting a populist, or at least an anti-establishment, stance. A difference with New Labour is that rather than absorbing established professional expertise into the upper echelons of the party, *En Marche!* was built by a small group working together at a distance from established political machines and cohering entirely around the person of Macron. We also find in Macron's discourse some of the elements of the way in which the synthesis between populism and technocracy is operated by Italy's M5S, which we described as a form of 'technopopulism through the electoral base'. In the last chapter of his 2017 campaign manifesto, entitled 'Returning Power to Those Who Get Things Done', Macron calls for a form of 'de-convergence' which involves:

> [T]ransferring power and responsibilities from the central administration to authorities on the ground and in direct contact with the general public. Those on the ground are aware of the solutions, and are often able to reach practical agreements with other stakeholders (2017: 235).

This is a version of the idea that there exists a diffuse competence in 'the people' at large, which implies that the best way of making effective political decisions is to allow this collective intelligence to manifest itself. Indeed, it is interesting to note that the members of the 'general public' are understood here primarily as 'stakeholders' with pragmatic 'solutions' to collective problems, rather than citizens with distinctive interests, values, and rights. There is, however, also an important difference with the way in which this specific form of technopopulism is manifested in contrast to the Italian M5S. Macron and LREM do not seem to place as much emphasis on the idea that technology—and especially online platforms—can help to harness the collective intelligence of the people. Instead, this intelligence can develop spontaneously, as long as the artificial blockages introduced by an over-extended public administration and political class are removed. The function performed by 'technology' in devising efficient solutions to collective problems—crucial in the M5S's discourse—is devolved in Macron's case to 'the market' as a mechanism of aggregation and articulation of individual preferences.[6]

There is, however, also a more distinctive way of operating the synthesis between populism and technocracy transpiring from Macron's politics, which revolves around the figure of Macron himself. As well as seeking to present

---

[6] In this sense, there also appears to be a deeply technopopulist strain in the more general neoliberal faith in 'the market' as an efficient problem-solver. This is a point that is alluded to by David Harvey in his *Brief History of Neoliberalism*, when he points out that, especially in its early phases, 'free-market fundamentalism' was often combined with an 'anti-establishment' and indeed even 'revolutionary' rhetoric, focused on the 'efficient solution of collective action problems' (see Harvey 2005: 39–63).

himself as an embodiment of the French people in a characteristically populist fashion, Macron has from the start also cultivated an image of himself as an effective and successful 'doer'. A significant portion of his election manifesto-cum-memoir is in the form of a list of his multiple life achievements. This extends from his early successes at school and as a piano player, to his performance in the final exams of the *Ecole Nationale d'Administration*, up to his lucrative stint as a partner at Rothschild's bank, before entering politics directly as the Minister of Economics in François Hollande's cabinet. As he puts it himself towards the end of the volume: 'I am a product of the French meritocracy—I achieved success there, but I never went along with the traditional political system' (Macron 2016: 212). For this reason, he maintains: 'I believe I can succeed in making changes.' The precise content of this 'success', or the domains in which it was achieved, matters less. Macron implies that the capacity of 'doing' is a transferable skill which qualifies the person possessing it regardless of the domain in which it is applied. Macron emerges from his own self-portrait as a sort of 'polyvalent hero' with a vocation for saving France from its current stagnation. Upon assuming political office, Macron has on several occasions spoken explicitly of the need to recover a sense of 'political heroism'. In an interview conducted with the German political magazine *Der Spiegel* in October 2017, he asserted that: 'I am a strong believer that modern political life must rediscover a sense of political heroism... We need to be amenable once again to creating grand narratives' (Brinkbäumer et al. 2017). Later in the same interview, he also added that: 'Personally... I think it is only possible to do great things in a specific moment once you have understood the *zeitgeist*, and it is only possible to move things forward if you have a sense of responsibility... That is exactly the goal I have set for myself.'

The kind of hero Macron seems to have in mind is a sort of 'collective problem-solver on a grand scale'—which is precisely the image that emerges from his book when he writes that: 'Some believe that our country is in decline, that the worst is yet to come, that our civilisation is withering away... I am convinced that they are all wrong. It is their models, their recipes, that have simply failed' (2016: 1–2). Later he reassures his readers that: 'Anything I do, I will do with you by my side' (2016: 212). The synthesis between populism and technocracy takes place here through the figure of the personal hero, the providential man with whom one has a personal relationship, but who is also able to act and deliver in ways that established politicians cannot. The relationship that matters is between Macron and the French people, though Macron is not representing 'the people' in its diversity so as much as appealing to their desire to see someone act effectively. Macron makes this point explicitly in his election manifesto when he writes that: 'The French people are less concerned with representation than action. They want politicians to be efficient, and that's all there is to it' (2016: 222).

From this, we can extrapolate a third paradigmatic type of technopopulism, which we shall refer to as 'technopopulism through the leader'. Put very simply, it is a form of technopopulism from above, in contrast to the first variant which was technopopulism through the party organization, or the second variant which was technopopulism from below. In this third kind of technopopulism, we find the leader combining a conventional claim about embodying the popular will, with a less conventional emphasis on his own competence and expertise. The leader becomes the people's problem-solver, a doer, a fixer; the process of incarnating 'the people' combines with claims about effective and efficient government.

In this variant of technopopulism, the citizens are not the holders of knowledge; they are bearers of problems to which the leader has solutions (Garrigues 2012). Organizationally, this places the emphasis neither on activists nor on the political party but rather on the leader who builds a direct and personalized relationship with 'the people'. Political organizations, such as they may exist, tend to be personalized campaign vehicles deployed during elections. Whilst they often endure beyond individual campaigns, they generally function as 'vehicles for dominant personalities' (Roberts 2006: 82), with a marginal and secondary role for activists.

Hybrid Cases

Having considered three pure cases of technopopulism, we move on to consider some 'hybrid' cases, defined as political parties or movements responding to the incentives and constraints of the technopopulist logic whilst also remaining products of a more traditional ideological logic. Such cases of technopopulism are interesting because they highlight that the technopopulist political logic has not simply *replaced* the more traditional ideological logic, but is rather *superimposed* upon it, as an additional (though potentially also alternative) structuring logic of contemporary democratic politics. As such, hybrid cases of technopopulism give us a glimpse into the complex ways in which the technopopulist and the ideological political logics coexist and interact with one another. Our purpose in this section is not to downplay the ideological dimension of the cases which we discuss. Indeed, we find in these cases evidence that the ideological logic remains crucial in explaining the behaviour of political actors and also the substance of their political offer. However, we also find that even if their relationship to the ideological logic is strong, such actors cannot ignore the force of the technopopulist political logic. The extent to which they display populist and technocratic traits is thus evidence of the power of this logic and its ability to shape the actions of even the most ideologically driven political movements.

To illustrate, we will be focusing on two rather different cases. We view Spain's *Podemos* as an instance of a technopopulist political party that is situated ideologically on the left. In terms of the three pure types of technopopulism we identified above, *Podemos* manifests a combination of 'technopopulism through the leader' and 'technopopulism through the electoral base'. We observe that *Podemos* operates on the ideological field as a traditional left-libertarian political party and that indeed, this has been its *raison d'être* for many of its founders and supporters. Nonetheless, the party has embraced some aspects of technopopulism in its quest for political power.

The second hybrid case of technopopulism we will be focusing on is Matteo Salvini's *Lega*, which we interpret as manifesting a form of far-right technopopulism. In terms of the three pure types of technopopulism we have identified, this political force displays a combination of 'technopopulism through the party' and 'technopopulism through the leader'. Salvini's *Lega* is clearly situated ideologically on the far right and amounts to a markedly different overall combination of technopopulist and ideological elements from Spain's *Podemos*. However, the same interesting effect is at work with the *Lega*, namely its adoption of some technopopulist features in spite of its strongly ideological character. We think these hybrid cases are crucial in highlighting the strength of the technopopulist logic. Whilst the 'pure' cases illustrated the variety at work in the syntheses of populism and technocracy, these hybrid cases show how even for the most ideologically driven of political movements, technopopulism can still structure political competition and shape discourse and political organization.

Spain's Podemos: A Case of Left-Wing Technopopulism

Founded in January 2014 by a small group of academics and political activists emerging out of the 15M protest movement, over the course of its brief existence *Podemos* has profoundly transformed Spanish politics. Obtaining a surprising 8 per cent of the vote at the 2014 European parliamentary elections, it went on to win around 20 per cent in the 2015 national legislative elections and 21 per cent in the following year's electoral consultation. Some of its candidates were elected in several important local and municipal races, such as for instance in Madrid and Barcelona in 2016. Along with the parallel formation of another distinctively technopopulist political force—the more right-leaning *Ciudadanos*—this has effectively broken the long-standing duopoly of the centre-right *Partido Popular* (PP) and the centre-left *Partido Socialista Obrero Espanol* (PSOE) that has dominated Spanish politics since the post-Francoist transition to democracy in 1978. *Podemos* failed to achieve the '*sorpasso*' it originally aimed for, i.e. overcoming and replacing the PSOE as the primary political expression of the Spanish left. It suffered a significant setback at the 2019 national and European elections, where it only obtained 14.3 per cent and 10.1 per cent of the votes respectively. However, it entered into a coalition government with the PSOE, and *Podemos'* leader, Pablo Iglesias, became the 'second' deputy Prime Minister and Minister for Social Rights.

Just like the three pure cases of technopopulism we considered in the previous section of this chapter, *Podemos* has confounded political observers and commentators. It has consistently refused to be identified as a traditional political force of the left, claiming instead to operate within the terms of a different political axis. However, all of the key figures in its leadership emerge from an avowedly left-wing political background, and most of its policy proposals appear consistent with such an ideological orientation. Some commentators doubt the extent to which *Podemos* represents a 'new' kind of political actor (e.g. Zarzalejos 2016).[7] We argue that the best way to make sense of *Podemos* is to think of it as a left-libertarian political force, committed to an unquestionably ideological form of politics. Nevertheless, *Podemos* has been obliged by the force of the technopopulist political logic to find a synthesis of its own between appeals to the people and appeals to expertise. The movement consciously embraced populist forms of discourse and organization but its synthesis with expertise was thrust upon it by the power of the technopopulist political logic. *Podemos* is thus a case of a political movement whose original essence is not technopopulist but rather one that has had to accommodate itself to this logic.

---

[7] The specific political issues that *Podemos* has chosen to focus on in its public discourse and policy platform are clearly ideologically connoted as left wing, even if its exponents have sought to present them as a matter of 'common sense'. To this effect, for instance, Gilles Ivaldi et al. have noted that: 'Podemos in Spain presents a clear left-libertarian universalistic profile, advocating minority rights, gender equality and civic liberties, while also pledging to fight discriminations' (Ivaldi et al. 2017: 364). Moreover, the same authors also note that: 'Podemos' economic populism embraces socialism, opposing austerity measures and advocating redistributive social policies, public spending and state intervention in the economy, including for instance a state-led banking sector, introducing a universal basic income for those under the poverty line, as well as energy price caps for low-income households' (Ivaldi et al. 2017). *Podemos*' leaders have frequently reminded voters of their left-wing political credentials. For instance, in his 2015 book Pablo Iglesias offers an extensive account of how the 'Podemos hypothesis' emerged organically out of the experience of the 15M protest movement and an ongoing confrontation with both the limits and the possibilities of 'standard left-wing political discourse' (Iglesias 2015: 115–16). Inigo Errejon writes that 'it is of course undeniable that we come, biographically, familially and personally, from the tradition and commitment of the left. I come, for instance, from a family persecuted by Francoism'. *Podemos*' continued—albeit implicit—reliance on the traditional ideological categories of left and right has also been evident in the complex game of political alliances and coalitions it has had to engage in upon entering the halls of power. Upon entering the European Parliament in May 2014, its MEPs joined the ranks of the '*Gauche Unitaire Européenne*' ('United European Left') group: the most left-leaning group in the European Parliament, with which *Podemos*' exponents have also renewed their affiliation in the aftermath of the 2019 European elections. At the domestic level, the main strategic questions for *Podemos* have been around forming an electoral alliance with *Izquierda Unida* (United Left) and entering into coalition government with the PSOE—both of which ended up happening at different stages. No parallel forms of collaboration with the centre-right PP (or let alone the far-right Vox) have ever been envisaged. *Podemos*' roots in the political left are consistent with much of its voter base. As Sola and Rendueles have pointed out: 'According to data from the 2015 barometers of the CIS...voters locate Podemos around 2.3 in the left-right scale (ranging from 1 to 10), further left than the PSOE (4.5) and even more so than *Izquierda Unida* (2.5)' (Sola and Rendueles 2017: 109). 'The bulk of Podemos' voters (around 70%)', Sola and Rendueles observe, 'self-identify as being left-wing, whereas around 18% self-identify as being center...An insignificant 1.5% self-identify as being right-wing and 10% do not respond' (2017: 109). It is difficult to deny that *Podemos* is clearly identifiable within the terms of the left/right ideological logic in spite of its leadership's claim that these political categories are historically surpassed.

Podemos displays some characteristically populist features. This has been mentioned by academic observers but also positively asserted by prominent members of its own leadership. Many of *Podemos'* founding members have an academic background, which has led them to adopt an extraordinarily 'reflexive' attitude with respect to their own political activities (Kioupkiolis 2016; Kioupkiolis and Seoane Pérez 2019). Some have drawn quite openly on Ernesto Laclau's and Chantal Mouffe's work on populism as a possible avenue for the revitalization of left-wing political projects. As a result, they have explicitly reclaimed that label as a positive description for *Podemos'* political identity and this movement has been the bedrock of what observed have called 'left populism' (Mouffe 2019; Jäger and Borriello 2019; Jäger 2019). In a book he co-wrote with Chantal Mouffe, the party's historic second-in-command, Inigo Errejon, maintained that 'provided we strip the term of the pejorative and anti-democratic connotations that are characteristic of the loose way in which it is used in the dominant discourse', *Podemos* can indeed be described as 'populist' (Errejon and Mouffe 2016: 125–6). The same point has also been reiterated by numerous academic observers. Alexandros Kioupkiolis argued that: 'At the core of Podemos' discourse lies the antagonistic divide which characterizes populism from a formal-structural perspective: the antagonism between the social majority and the privileged minority' (Kioupkiolis 2016: 1903). Similarly, Jorge Sola and Cesar Rendueles have written that: 'The keystone of Podemos' strategy has been "transversality"... It addresses its message to "the people" in order to articulate a broad social bloc not shaped by the pre-existing divisive identities' (Sola and Rendueles 2018: 107–8).

Another characteristically populist feature of *Podemos* has been its mode of internal organization, which revolves around a tight-knit and highly centralized leadership focused on the charismatic figure of Pablo Iglesias. The social base is diffuse and periodically mobilized by largely plebiscitarian means, with very few intermediate layers of organization in between. As Kioupkiolis put it, this has resulted in 'a strong "vertical" dimension' in *Podemos'* organizational model, which appears 'at odds with the "horizontal" layer of egalitarian participation and the 15M spirit' but reflects 'a particular reading of populist theory which is prevalent among the party's intellectual leadership and assigns a decisive emphasis to the leader' (Kioupkiolis 2016: 100–6). Pablo Iglesias himself has been candid about the role played by 'a leadership figure with a high recognition factor', describing himself as 'an indispensable ingredient in the Podemos hypothesis'. He used this to explain why, in the 2014 European parliamentary elections, the party ran with an image of his face as its symbol on the ballot papers (Iglesias 2015: 189–90).

Alongside these well-known and highly commented-upon populist features, *Podemos* has displayed a number of less evident but equally significant technocratic traits. As we shall see, some of these originate in the conscious attempt by *Podemos* to distinguish itself from traditional left-wing movements, such as the dominant social democratic parties in Europe and the Communist parties of old. Other components of the technocratic appeal stem from their awareness of the need to play the current political game, which is increasingly structured around a technopopulist political logic. One of the founding claims of *Podemos* is that the traditional ideological categories of left and right are historically exhausted, and that political innovation is required for all those who want to pursue radical and progressive forms of politics in Spain and beyond. In his 2015 book, *Politics in a Time of Crisis: Podemos and the Future of Democratic Europe*, Iglesias wrote that: 'The configuration of the political field into a left/right division created a setting in which change, in a progressive direction, was no longer possible in Spain' (2015: 185). He added that: '[o]ur most important political-discursive task was to contest this symbolic structure of positions.' Similarly, in response to probing over this issue by Chantal Mouffe, Inigo Errejon wrote in their co-authored book that:

> Left and right are not the main frontier for producing political change in Spain... Anybody who believes that that division is the key for understanding what's happening in our country wouldn't understand why it is that, all of a sudden, within the space of a year, the electoral map has changed so much... A change in the frontiers that order the political arena has brought about a potential change in the balance of forces, the possibility of a new vote, defined in patriotic, civic and democratic terms (Errejon and Mouffe 2016: 118).

Errejon admitted in the same text that such statements suggest that the party stands for a form of 'extreme pragmatism' according to which 'there's no longer any frontiers; there's only management and technical differences' (2015: 122). In other words, if it is not around ideological goals that a party stakes its reputation, then it will be around its competence and ability in achieving a given set of goals. Errejon insisted this was not the case, and there is much evidence to suggest that *Podemos* as a movement and as a party has indeed been driven by its commitment to a set of policies that are ideologically on the left. We find some of this ambivalence in the electoral literature produced by *Podemos*, which balances familiar ideological tropes with an appeal to a more epistemic conception of democracy. The manifesto it produced for the 2015 Spanish general election is a case in point. The title—*Queremos, Sabemos, Podemos* ('We Want, We Know, We Can')—suggests that politics is a matter of knowledge and will, and that *Podemos* is the appropriate agent to tease them out and transform them into practicable policies.

When we look closer at the 2015 document, we find more evidence of *Podemos'* technocratic traits, though in this case they were adopted in a conscious way as part of a general awareness by the party that it needed to emphasize its credentials as a competent political force whose ideas are rooted in evidence and expert opinion.[8] The document's Prologue asserts that its purpose is to function as 'guide', offering 'simple and effective solutions' for 'leaving behind the Spain of the five million unemployed, insecurity, exploitation, competitiveness, shrinking wages and energetic dependence' (Podemos 2015: 11). The document states that 'the frameworks, approaches and policy proposals that shape this programme are the result of the articulations of voices by experts and thousands of other people committed to their present and the future of this country' (2015: 10). The role assigned to 'knowledge' and 'expertise' throughout the document is so prominent that, in addition to the explicit reference to knowledge in the title, the manifesto ends with a list of all the 'experts' that contributed in drafting it, alongside the party members and organs of civil society also involved (2015: 311–22). This list was provided precisely in order to ensure that *Podemos* was able to situate itself within a political domain organized around the technopopulist political logic: its populist appeal was self-consciously—and not always very willingly—supplemented by an appeal to competence and expertise. Even for the most ideologically charged of Europe's new political movements, some technopopulist synthesis was required.

This conscious appeal to competence was not a complete rupture for *Podemos*, as it chimed with some aspects of its own self-understanding and self-presentation. Emphasis had been given from the start to its principal political exponents' academic backgrounds as evidence of their possessing a specific kind of political expertise. As Felix de Azua has pointed out, *Podemos* purposively appropriated its image as a *partido de profesores*, transforming it into a trademark feature of its communication style (De Azua 2014). The punctual use of figures and poll data, the consistently calm and pedagogical tone, and the recurrent use of academic jargon—these are all central features of *Podemos'* rhetoric that fit with the identity of their leaders as professional pedagogues. This approach was defended by Inigo Errejon in the aftermath of *Podemos'* failed electoral strategy in 2016 saying that: 'The street not only demands epic narratives and demonstrations, the street asks for guarantees, public policies' (cited by Zarzalejos 2016: 191).

These parallel populist and technocratic features are synthetized with one another through a combination of what we have called, respectively, 'technopopulism through the leader' and 'technopopulism through the electoral base'. The first thing to note in this respect is that *Podemos'* leadership has not only cultivated an image of itself as a team of competent, academically-trained experts. In addition, it has also insisted on its 'ordinariness' through a strategy Alexandros Kioupkiolis refers to as a 'communing of representative politics' (Kioupkiolis 2016: 108). *Podemos'* elected representatives have, by and large, refused to comply with the established standards of political fashion by not wearing 'jacket and tie' in

---

[8] Our thanks to Pablo Bustinduy Amador for his insights into this particular aspect of *Podemos'* political offer.

television appearances or parliamentary sessions. They have frequently used colloquial and sometimes even coarse language, alongside and in conjunction with more elevated academic jargon. Even Pablo Iglesias' iconic and much-discussed ponytail is part of the same goal: to signal that *Podemos*' leadership belongs to the category of what they call 'normal people'; that is, emphatically *not* professional politicians. This is a well-known populist rhetorical strategy, of which we have also found some traces in the (early) M5S's mode of self-presentation. In the case of *Podemos*, however, the representation of its leadership as constituted primarily by 'normal people, like you and me' (to use language from a statement by Virginia Raggi cited above), is fused with their parallel portrayal as calm, competent, and policy-savvy experts. This is a form of 'technopopulism through the figure of the leader', though there are important differences between the way in which technopopulism through the leader is manifested by LREM and *Podemos*. Whereas Macron has sought to present himself as a sort of 'heroic problem-solver', breaking through the blockages in the French political and economic system on behalf of a people he claims to embody directly, in the case of *Podemos* the direct relationship with the citizenry has been sought for primarily through the leadership's claim to ordinariness. However, in both cases the political actors in question are presented as both embodying the people directly and possessing a particular kind of competence that enables them to solve problems *because of their personal characteristics*.

A second key channel through which *Podemos* has sought to operate a synthesis between its populist and technocratic features is closer to what we have called 'technopopulism through the electoral base'. Like the Italian M5S, *Podemos* has placed a significant degree of discursive and organizational emphasis on the role of 'collective intelligence' in solving political problems. Kioupkiolis calls this the '"technopolitical" dimension' (which he later develops in the idea of 'reflexive technopopulism'). He notes that social media and new digital technologies were very popular in Spain and used extensively by 15M activists. In his words,

> *Podemos*' organizers did not simply endorse this technopolitics of ordinary citizens, but they made a qualitative leap. They amplified digital participation with new tools and they placed it at the heart of *Podemos*' development as a network-movement to an extent that remains without precedent in any traditional or new party in Spain...An open multitude of citizens can thus get involved in political action on different scales and in various ways which do not require their constant physical presence and dedication (Kioupkiolis 2016: 105).

This notion of 'collective intelligence' that underpins the justification for this extensive reliance on online platforms as decision-making tools operates a synthesis between populist and technocratic elements. As we saw with the M5S as well, it implies that 'the people' as a whole can make better (i.e. more competent) decisions than even the most highly trained individual experts. The populist demand for social inclusion and direct political participation is reconciled with the technocratic concern for good governance, through the idea of mobilizing collective intelligence as a way of making collectively binding decisions.

An additional channel through which *Podemos* operates a synthesis between its populist and technocratic features is the emphasis on the concept of 'common sense' (*sentido común*) as both an underlying intellectual justification and overarching descriptive label for *Podemos*' policy platform and political project as a whole. As Jorge Sola and Cesar Rendueles observed, 'Podemos has intentionally avoided reference to traditional symbols and stances of the left.' Instead, they note, 'it has given great prominence to other demands able to appeal to a wide social bloc...framing these as a matter of *common sense*' (2018: 104, emphasis added). Kioupkiolis notes that: 'The discourse of Podemos as elaborated by its leadership draws on the "common sense" of Spanish political culture' adding that 'the terms of the common sense are inflected in the direction of social rights, inclusion and egalitarian democracy' (Kioupkiolis 2016: 108–9). Pablo Iglesias himself has commented on this aspect of *Podemos*' discourse, affirming in an interview that: 'The key is to succeed in making "common sense" go in the direction of change' (Iglesias 2014).

Several aspects of this politicization of the notion of 'common sense' illustrate how *Podemos* fuses together populist and technocratic appeals in its political offer. This rhetoric assumes there is such a thing as common sense in the first place; that is, a set of shared principles and practical precepts that cut across existing social distinctions and disagreements. As we pointed out in chapter 1, this is a background condition for the possibility of both populism and technocracy, inasmuch as both rely on the notion of a social 'whole'—whether in the form of a unified and monolithic popular will or an objective and value-neutral political truth—which is opposed to the idea of a society irreducibly divided into conflicting 'parts'. The application of the notion of common sense to the political domain is at odds with more partisan and ideological outlooks that are more divisive and more confrontational. Secondly, the notion of 'common sense' also carries an implicitly anti-intellectual connotation. This makes it particularly well-suited for the populist politicization of the opposition between ordinary people and elites, which may be why we find it at work both in this case and—as we shall see below—in the case of Matteo Salvini's *Lega*. This point is mentioned by Antonio Gramsci in his *Prison Notebooks* when he writes that: 'Common sense is the "philosophy of non-philosophers", the conception of the world a-critically absorbed from the various social and cultural contexts in which the "common man" forms his moral individuality' (Gramsci 1922–33: Q8:173). As such, Gramsci adds, common sense is rhetorically opposed to 'the abstruseness, intricacy and obscurity of scientific and philosophical exposition' (Gramsci 1922–33: Q11:13). Here, we already find *in nuce* the characteristically populist opposition between the solid and grounded values of the 'common man' on one hand and the abstract and self-referential theories of out-of-touch elites on the other. The notion of 'common sense' also carries a connotation of immediate validity and objective reasonability, which makes it apt to function as the vehicle for a distinctively technocratic mode of justification, consisting in the claim that the proposition being justified corresponds to 'right reason' or 'objective truth'. As Clifford Geertz once put it, '[i]t is an inherent characteristic of common sense ... to deny itself as a system of thought and to affirm that its tenets are immediate deliverances of experience, not deliberate reflections upon it' (Geertz 1975: 772). By implication, the inverse of common sense is 'foolishness', 'idiosyncrasy', or simply 'sheer stupidity' (Geertz 1975: 773–5).

This emphasis on common sense is thus another form of 'technopopulism through the electoral base'. It is, in short, a form of popular expertise. To portray one's political project or platform as validated by 'common sense' effectively amounts to saying that it is: a) objectively true, or at least eminently reasonable; and b) already agreed upon by all ordinary people. As such, the political use of the notion of 'common sense' operates a synthesis between the core elements of both populist and technocratic discourses. However, what is at work here is a slightly different logic from that of 'collective intelligence' we discussed above. For *Podemos*, the key claim is not that ordinary people possess a diffuse competence which can be harnessed by technological means. Rather, it is the idea that what ordinary people already believe is true—or at least reasonable—precisely because it is not mediated by the abstract intellectual constructions of the elites. The politicization of the notion of common sense can therefore be understood as amounting to a different variant of 'technopopulism through the electoral based' compared to the idea of 'collective intelligence' which the M5S rely on.

This understanding of *Podemos* as a strongly ideological political force that nevertheless has had to accommodate itself to the technopopulist political logic, and has indeed found that such an accommodation chimes with some of its own understanding of itself as a political project, helps us better make sense of its own political trajectory. On one hand, the fact that *Podemos* presents itself as a 'new' kind of political party, standing for the interests of the social whole beyond traditional ideological divisions, is what distinguishes it from the more established parties of the centre-left and the far-left. This has allowed it to capitalize on the widespread sense of dissatisfaction with existing left-wing formations, scoring some encouraging electoral results. On the other hand, the fact that *Podemos*' never really entirely relinquished its left-wing ideological commitments is one of the reasons why it hasn't succeeded in replacing the more traditional left-leaning political forces with a different political logic, as it initially claimed to want to do. In practice, it has joined the left camp of Spanish electoral politics, contributing to its further division and fragmentation.

One way of reading the overall effect of *Podemos*' irruption on the Spanish political scene is to suggest that instead of replacing the traditional left/right ideological divide *Podemos* has paradoxically ended up reinforcing it. This is because the distinction between 'new' (i.e. technopopulist) vs. 'old' (i.e. ideological) parties is manifests itself *within* the traditional left and right ideological camps in the form of the internal competition between the PP and *Ciudadanos* on one side and the PSOE, *Izquierda Unida*, and *Podemos* on the other side. Though the terms upon which the two sides compete has evolved significantly to include a transversal opposition in which technopopulism is key, left and right persist as the main structuring poles of contemporary Spanish politics. For this reason, *Podemos* is best thought of as a hybrid case of technopopulism, combining both populist and technocratic features with a more traditional ideological profile.

Matteo Salvini's (Northern) League: Far-Right Technopopulism

The second hybrid case of technopopulism we shall be considering is the Italian (Northern) League under the leadership of Matteo Salvini. This is an even more complex case than *Podemos* because, in addition to combining both populist and technocratic features with a more traditional ideological profile, Salvini's *Lega* is the result of a rather long developmental process, in which successive discursive and organizational layers have built up, one on top of the other. Indeed, this party is today effectively the oldest on the Italian political landscape, even if what it has become, both ideologically and organizationally, would have been difficult to foresee on the basis of what it originally set out to be (Jori 2009).

Founded in 1991 on the eve of the implosion of the three mass parties that had dominated the Italian political scene since the end of the Second World War—the Christian democrats, the Communists, and the Socialists—the *Lega Nord* was a 'regionalist' party that claimed to represent the interests of the more affluent North against what were portrayed as the extractive and unfairly redistributive policies of the Italian central government (Cento Bull and Gilbert 2001). As such, it did not have a very strong ideological connotation but rather aimed to represent the interests of Northerners of all persuasions against 'thieving Rome' (*Roma ladrona*). Commentators at the time described it primarily as a 'protest' or 'anti-system' party, noting however also that:

> Throughout most of the 1990s, the League's voters were situated close to the median position within the electorate; a fact that could be interpreted as a direct consequence of the substitution of Christian Democratic votes with Leghist votes, in a sort of 'extremism of the center' (Ignazi 2003; Passerelli and Tuorto 2018: 92).

Over time, this ideological profile changed profoundly. Already by the early 2000s, the party had begun to move markedly towards the political right—first by espousing a more radical secessionist project, based on an ethnically tinged anti-Southern sentiment, and then by entering into an explicitly centre-right government coalition with Silvio Berlusconi's *Forza Italia* and the post-Fascist *Alleanza Nazionale*.

The clearest *caesura* in the party's history came with the leadership change that occurred between 2012 and 2013, after the party's original founder and charismatic leader, Umberto Bossi, was sidelined for a mixture of personal health reasons and a financial malpractice scandal. Initially, Bossi's first successor—Roberto Maroni—sought to bring the party in a more moderate and institutional direction, in the hope of stemming the backlash from the succession crisis by cultivating an image of the League's exponents as competent and efficient administrators, especially in its historic heartlands of the North and North-East. Through the so-called *'movimento delle scope'* (movement of the brooms) Maroni sought to clean up the party's internal organization from a 'rot' that he claimed had set in because of its implication in national politics. At the same time, Maroni hoped to reconnect with the party's roots in the 'Northern' values of efficiency and hard work (Passarelli and Tuorto 2018). This strategy proved short-lived. After Matteo Salvini became leader in December 2013, the party embarked upon a radically different strategy of renewal, without however relinquishing entirely the more 'technocratic' allure that the League had sought to cultivate for itself during Maroni's transitional leadership. As we will seek to demonstrate in what follows, Salvini incorporated this into a much broader ideological and organizational makeover. The key changes introduced by Salvini to this effect developed along two main axes, which we shall consider in turn.

First, Salvini steered the party much further than Bossi had ever dared to do in a rightward direction. This clear ideological orientation was manifested in a number of substantive value statements and policy commitments. To begin with, Salvini almost completely dropped—or at least sidelined—the League's originally regionalist political identity, adopting a nationalist political profile instead. The political entity that the League had initially claimed to defend against the Italian central government was enlarged to include the Italian nation as a whole, while simultaneously recasting the principal villain from *Roma ladrona* to the out-of-touch Brussels of European technocrats. This was achieved by dropping the qualifier 'Northern' from the party's name and by revising its principal slogan from *'Prima il Nord'* (Northerners First) to *'Prima gli Italiani'* (Italians First). Salvini also undertook a major act of political refoundation. As Albertazzi et al. observe,

> Despite delivering his maiden speech as leader at the League's conference of December 2013 under a banner that read 'The future is independence', only a few

days later Salvini went on to apologize for the insults he had directed at southerners throughout his political career and claimed to have become persuaded that, either Italy saved itself *as a nation*, or else all of its regions, without exception, would face ruin. The main argument here was that, even if it could go it alone, the North would still be the victim of regulations imposed by a 'totalitarian' EU... In this way, the EU (rather than 'Rome') came to be portrayed as the locus of real power (Albertazzi et al. 2018: 649).

Closely connected with this shift from regionalism to nationalism in the League's political profile was the much greater emphasis given to the theme of immigration in the party's discourse. Just as Brussels replaced Rome as the principal focus for the party's narrative of institutional oppression, so the figure of the 'immigrant'—and especially the 'clandestine'—replaced that of the Southerner as a target of ethnically and economically motivated resentment. Gianluca Passarelli and Dario Tuorto have written that: 'The growing importance assigned to the issue of immigration in the League's recent political rhetoric is perhaps the dimension that most evidently captures the gist of its recent transformation.' In their view, 'Salvini has systematically operated to stoke up anti-immigrant sentiment, sometimes laying more emphasis on the economic dimension ("they steal our jobs") and others on more symbolically-laden issues (portraying immigrants as a "cultural danger" or a threat for "social cohesion")' (Passarelli and Tuorto 2018: 24–5).

A third notable aspect of Salvini's turn to the right has been the adoption of markedly conservative and 'traditionalist' positions over a variety of civic and moral issues, including abortion, euthanasia, homosexual marriage and, more broadly, the role of religion in public life and the limits to individual freedom and self-expression. This represents an important change with respect to Bossi's leadership, which had instead taken a much more liberal—and indeed 'libertarian'—position on many of the same issues. This was in part because the attacks on moralism and the oversized influence of the Catholic Church over Italian politics went hand in hand with the broader condemnation of Rome's interference in Northern Italians' private and political matters. In contrast, Salvini has made a point of reviving an identitarian and socially conservative form of Christianity, in part in an anti-Muslin (and therefore implicitly anti-immigrant) vein, but also as a way of marking a distinction with what he portrays as the elitism of the liberal left. This is consistent with a broader authoritarian strain in Salvini's political discourse. Salvini has presented himself as a champion of 'law and order', in a country where levels of petty criminality have recently been at historical lows but where there is a widespread perception of insecurity. After its strong showing in the 2018 general elections (at which the League obtained its best ever result, with around 17 per cent of the votes), Salvini insisted on being granted the position of Minister of the Interior, in order to address 'crime and immigration' which he claimed were spiralling 'out of control' (Diamanti and

Pregliasco 2019). Once in post, he spearheaded a series of hard-nosed 'law and order' campaigns such as the extension of the right to use arms in cases of self-defence and the closure of maritime ports to boats carrying illegal immigrants into the country.

Salvini's stances in socio-economic policy matters have veered markedly to the right of his predecessors' ideological positions. Under Salvini's leadership, the League has endorsed proposals for a 'flat tax' which would radically decrease both the marginal tax rates and the progressivity of the fiscal system as a whole. It has redoubled calls for a radical overhaul of the Italian system of public administration, aimed at cutting what Salvini refers to as 'red tape' and 'bureaucratic waste' (Diamanti and Pregliasco 2019). These proposals are complemented by parallel projects for the expansion in the provision of certain public services (in particular those that take the form of cash transfers to the population, such as most notably the pension system) and increases in some areas of the state budget (most notably policing). However, the overarching formula remains 'that liberal-authoritarian model embodied for instance by Hungary's so-called Orbanomics, which combines a deep faith in the "animal spirits" of the capitalist economy, with a strong and highly centralized state'. The role of the state, in this model, 'is to guarantee the efficient functioning of the market, while at the same taking care of those who get left behind, by either providing for them or ejecting them from the country' (Passarelli and Tuorto 2018: 108). Concluding their assessment of the *Lega* today, Passarelli and Tuorto (2018: 23) argue that:

> If one wanted to identify a single characteristic feature of the contemporary League, the attention would most likely have to fall on its politico-ideological orientation, where the party has assumed the characteristic traits of a far-right formation, combining xenophobic racism, authoritarian state policies, with anti-Europeanism and a form of economic neo-liberalism.

The second key pillar of Matteo Salvini's restyling of the party has been an escalation of the populist elements that were present in the League's political offer from the start. As Ivaldi et al. have argued:

> Anti-elite attacks were a mainstay in Umberto Bossi's speeches and writings, in which he established a typical populist framing of pitting a corrupt and distant elite against a virtuous people... The current League shows no significant departure from—but has instead radicalized—this anti-elite populism, displaying a continuous pattern of explicit delegitimation of the political establishment and parties (Ivaldi et al. 2017: 359).

Upon joining the coalition government formed by his *Lega* and the M5S in the aftermath of the March 2018 legislative elections, Salvini declared that: 'We are at a total overthrow of all political perspectives. The issue today is not the right against the left, but the people against elites' (cited by Urbinati and Saffon 2019: 3). Salvini's populism also includes the moralization of his political discourse. The League may be the oldest political party on the Italian political landscape, with its own share of corruption scandals and financial malfeasance accusations. Salvini himself has been a professional politician for over two decades. And yet, Salvini has consistently presented himself and his party as a 'new' kind of political actor, far removed from the corrupt and self-regarding practices of traditional political parties. The coalition government with the M5S, inaugurated in May 2018, has dubbed itself the 'government of change' (*governo del cambiamento*). One of the slogans it has adopted for itself is 'honesty in power' (*l'onestà al potere*).

A distinctively populist feature of the changes Salvini has introduced in the League's political profile concerns the party's internal organizational structure. Under the leadership of Bossi—and even more so Maroni—the League had sought to root itself primarily in its heartlands of the North and North-East by building a strong and rather capillary political organization. This was, in many ways, reminiscent of traditional mass parties. Maroni once joked that "We are the last remaining Leninist party in Italy". Salvini's move to give the party a national political dimension has corresponded to a thinning of the intermediate party organization, and a parallel concentration of power in the leadership. Passarelli and Tuorto (2018: 38) observe that:

> Under Salvini's leadership, we can observe a profound reshaping of the party's internal structure, both from the point of view of its organizational model and the specific personnel occupying the intermediate layers of authority between the party leader and the base. This has all contributed to a strong verticalization in the party's internal governance structure in favor of the leadership: it is not a coincidence that all the most important party posts are now nominated by Salvini himself, leaving little room for the development of internal factions, as was the case with the leadership under Umberto Bossi... Salvini's position within the party is now unquestioned and unquestionable, also in light of the strong personal appeal he holds both with the party's base and with the electorate at large.

A clear indication of this increasing personalization of the party structure around the figure of Salvini himself is given by the fact that, in addition to dropping the qualifier 'Northern', the party's logo has recently been amended to include an explicit reference to Salvini's name. The party is therefore now officially called '*La Lega—Salvini Premier*' (The League—Salvini for President) in a move that mimics something Silvio Berlusconi had done with his own party. Other versions of this personalization trend include Emmanuel Macron's LREM (the original initials of which corresponded to Macron's own) and Pablo Iglesias' *Podemos* (which used his image as a party icon on the ballots for the 2014 European elections).

This combination of an ideologically far right orientation and a populist message national in scope suggests that Salvini's League can be understood as a standard 'far-right populist party' akin to several other European instances of this party family, identified and amply studied by academics since the early 2000s (e.g. Mudde 2007). To this effect, Albertazzi et al. have written that: '[i]f the essence of the populist radical right resides in a combination of nativism, authoritarianism and populism... there does not seem to be any reason not to include Salvini's new *Lega* into this party family today' (Albertazzi et al. 2018: 660). Similarly, in their overview of 'Varieties of populism across the left/right spectrum', Ivaldi et al. class Salvini's League as a 'clear case of far-right populism' (Ivaldi et al. 2017: 362).

What is still missing from this picture, however, is adequate recognition of the markedly technocratic strain that runs alongside both its populist features and its far-right ideological orientation. This is another key ingredient of the contemporary *Lega*'s political profile, which has so far received less attention, but remains essential in explaining its political rebirth after the crisis of 2012–13, as well as its current electoral success. As with *Podemos*, we are describing the *Lega* as a hybrid case. That is to say that the technopopulist synthesis it achieves may not be as central to its existence as it is for the purer cases. However, in these hybrid cases we find the strength of the technopopulist logic evident in the manner in which some combination of populist and technocratic appeals is undertaken by the party or movement out of a recognition of the rules of the current political game.

As in the case of the other technopopulist parties we have considered in this chapter, the *Lega's* technocratic strain is manifested first of all in the 'non-' or at least 'post-ideological' allure that Salvini has sought to give his party by claiming that the left/right ideological distinction has lost political relevance. In a book he published in 2016 to explain his overarching political vision, Salvini asserted that:

> Only the indefeasible laziness of some contemporary journalists and political commentators allows them to continue to classify us as a 'far-right' or 'xenophobic' party... When, in the few seconds that I am allowed on television, I highlight the contradiction that exists between those who do not have the money to buy medicines and the thirty-five Euros per day spent by the state for every asylum seeker *I am simply doing my job: indicating a problem and proposing a solution* (Salvini 2016: 61, italics added).

This statement was intended to defuse lingering anxieties about the return to political prominence of the far-right in a country with a history of Fascist dictatorship. Nevertheless, Salvini chooses to do this by portraying his 'job' in the depoliticized terms of 'identifying problems and proposing solutions'. This conveys an underlying conception of politics as a purely technical activity, independent of particular interests or value commitments. The same point is then also conveyed in another statement by Salvini:

> I want to be given the responsibility to govern this country not to transform it into some kind of earthly paradise, but rather into *a normal place*...A place where the laws protect everyone and are respected by everyone, where rights exist alongside duties, and where our shared idea of the future is not measured as a percentage of GDP, but in the number of children we make, in the quality of the air we breathe, and the food we have on our table (2016: 12, emphasis added).

All the issues Salvini's highlights are striking for their apolitical and consensual nature. The image Salvini is going for is that of a competent and responsible *pater familias* who can solve ordinary people's day-to-day problems.

Another clearly technocratic feature in Salvini's discourse is his recurrent appeal to the authority of expertise to validate his policy positions and proposals. In discussing the euro in his book, he writes that: 'The common currency has proved a net gain for the Germans, but a terrible swindle for us Italians...A currency without a people is without future and must be overcome, *as has already been certified by no less than seven Nobel prize winners in economics*' (2016: 205, emphasis added). In presenting the coalition government put together by the League and the M5S in the aftermath of the 2018 legislative elections (which is led by the non-partisan figure of Giuseppe Conte and also includes a number of 'technicians' in key positions), Salvini declared: 'In putting together this team we have not been guided by partisan affiliations or power play, but rather by the *criterion of recognized competence* in the specific tasks to be performed' (cited by Cottone 2018). In both these cases, the authority of a presumptively 'objective' external authority is used to validate what are essentially political decisions. Over time, Salvini has claimed for himself and his party associates the specific competence that he initially attributed to the non-partisan members of his government. Already in his 2016 book, Salvini had asserted that: 'The League has all the necessary credentials for governing the country effectively', with reference to the party's 'over twenty years of experience' in local and regional administrations in its historic heartlands of the North and North-East (Salvini 2016: 22). Upon assuming national political office as Minister of the Interior in June 2018, Salvini has consistently sought to draw a contrast between the 'amateurishness' and 'inexperience' of his coalition partner, the M5S, and his party's competence and expertise in government. This was evident in the case of the ongoing disagreement over the completion of a project for building a tunnel for high-speed trains connecting Turin and Lyon, which has become a national political issue in Italy. Whereas the M5S has ridden the anti-establishment sentiment associated with popular resistance to the project, Salvini has taken a clear stance in its favour in a move interpreted as a way of reassuring both the private sector and international partners that he is a reliable administrator with whom it is possible to 'do business' (e.g. Fittipaldi 2019).

It would be difficult to understand the roots of Salvini's current electoral and political strength without taking into account the sustained effort he has put into presenting himself and his own party as competent and reliable administrators. This is not to suggest that the ideological overhaul of the *Lega* is any the less important, nor is it clear whether Salvini's own conception of politics is shaped by this technocratic outlook or whether it is just adopted because it is what he thinks is important in contemporary Italian politics. The issue is not intentionality so much as the way that the technopopulist political logic shapes both political discourse and political organization. It is insufficient to describe the current incarnation of the Italian *Lega* purely as an expression of 'far-right populism'. Passarelli and Tuorto are closer to the mark when they describe it as a 'far-right party with a vocation for government' (*una estrema destra di governo*). This captures at least an aspect of the technocratic strain that Salvini and his team have injected into the League's political profile in order to make it into a credible governing force. A more accurate way of capturing all the distinctive aspects of Salvini's League is to construe it as a hybrid case of technopopulism, marrying both populist and technocratic features with a more traditional far-right ideological profile.

How has Salvini's League managed to reconcile these apparently incongruous traits in a single political offer? In terms of the three pure types of technopopulism we have identified in the first part of this chapter, Salvini's League is a combination of 'technopopulism through the figure of the leader' and 'technopopulism through the party'. The former is most clearly visible in a feature Salvini's League has in common—somewhat counter-intuitively—with Spain's *Podemos*. Although neither Pablo Iglesias nor Salvini himself have ever claimed to embody their respective peoples in the way Emmanuel Macron has done in France, they do claim to possess something else that establishes a direct relationship with their electorate, namely 'common sense'. In the case of Salvini's League, the discursive emphasis on this notion has been even more systematic and pervasive than in the case of *Podemos*. The party manifesto that the League launched in preparation for the 2018 legislative elections was known as 'The Revolution of Common Sense' (*La Rivoluzione del Buonsenso*). All of its specific policy proposals were related, in one way or another, with the notion of 'common sense'. The League's economic programme was referred to as the 'common sense programme' (*manovra del buonsenso*), whereas its proposal for extending private gun possession and use rights was described as a 'common-sense provision' (*una proposta di buonsenso*). During the campaign for the 2018 European parliamentary elections, Salvini described his party's team of candidates as 'extremists of common sense' (*estremisti del buonsenso*), later going on to form a pre-electoral agreement with a number of other far-right parties from different European countries, which ran under the banner of 'Europe of common sense' (*l'Europa del buonsenso*) (Bickerton 2019).

As we already pointed out in our discussion of *Podemos*, the political mobilization of this notion of 'common sense' operates a synthesis between populist and technocratic tropes. It unites the populist dimension of anti-elitism (and in particular anti-intellectualism) with the technocratic appeal to objectivity in what is effectively a form of people's expertise. Whereas in the case of *Podemos* this expertise (*sentido común*) is represented as lying diffusely within the people themselves, thereby yielding a conception of the party's role as aggregator and amplifier of a collective intelligence, in the case of Salvini's League, 'common sense' (*buonsenso*) is represented as residing primarily in the accumulated experience of the party's leadership, and in particular in the figure of Salvini himself. In the case of Salvini's League, the rhetoric of 'common sense' functions primarily as a vector of 'technopopulism through the leader' rather than 'technopopulism through the electoral base'.

A form of 'technopopulism through the party' is visible if we look more closely at the way in which Salvini has operated to transform the League's internal organizational structure. As well as favouring the 'verticalization' of this structure (Passarelli and Tuorto 2018), Salvini has relied extensively on a team of hired political consultants and public opinion experts who have carefully curated his public image and the party's outward political message for the past six years. The key role played by these expert consultants in the League's ideological and organizational makeover has been captured in detail by Pucciarelli (2019). In his words (2019: 17),

> What transformed a strategy that might have stalled under another leader... was the appearance of Luca Morisi, a 45-year-old informatics expert from Mantua and a past councillor for the League with a penchant for philosophy. Morisi ran a company called Sistema Intranet with his business partner Andrea Paganella; they had no employees, but plenty of institutional clients. Taking Salvini in hand when he was already inseparable from his tablet, they set up a social media staff for him, which quickly became far more important than any party body... The result was a media operation functioning like a daily newspaper, thanks to a publishing system created in-house and known as 'the beast'. Content was published at fixed times on affiliated pages and reactions monitored instantly. Soon Morisi and his colleagues were publishing eighty to ninety posts a week on Facebook alone, where Renzi managed no more than ten (Pucciarelli 2019: 17).

As we already noted in the context of our discussion of New Labour, this kind of transfer of strategic and organizational power from grassroots activists and intermediate party cadres to external experts hired to tailor the party's image to public opinion at large operates a synthesis of populist and technocratic features. The presumptively value-neutral 'science' of public opinion on which such experts rely supposes the existence of a unified and homogenous 'popular will' constructed out of the individual preferences of disaggregated citizens. It also empowers these experts themselves to speak in the name of the popular will. Salvini's League has employed such external political consultants, instead of relying on the more traditional mechanisms of intra-party communication, which is consistent with what we have called in this chapter 'technopopulism through the party'.

Conclusion

This chapter has deployed the concept of technopopulism as a distinctive political logic to understand a number of empirical cases. We use these cases to develop a typology of technopopulism, which is based on distinctive ways in which appeals to the people and appeals to expertise and competence are synthesized into a single political offer. We identify some cases that are 'pure' instances of technopopulism, by which we mean that their political rhetoric and organizational mobilization is heavily and exclusively ordered around the technopopulist political logic. Other cases we describe as hybrid, which means that their roots and origins may well lie in the ideological left or right or within the ideology of nationalism. However strong this ideological orientation, we find that in various ways these parties and movements adapt to and are shaped by the technopopulist logic, sometimes very consciously and at other times more spontaneously as an accommodation to the dominant rules of the contemporary political game. These hybrid cases pose once again the question of how the ideological and technopopulist logics relate to one another. The following chapter will deal with this question in a historical manner, by tracing the emergence of the technopopulist logic out of the crisis and decomposition of the ideological logic.

3
The Origins of Technopopulism

Introduction

This chapter examines the origins of the technopopulist political logic. The goal is to provide an explanation for the rise of technopopulism as the main structuring logic of contemporary democratic politics. Our explanation highlights the historical distinctiveness of this political logic and provides an account of the reasons for its emergence, in part replacing and in part superimposing itself upon the more traditional left/right ideological logic. The approach is historical, in the sense that we do not seek to isolate a number of independent causal factors and then justify them empirically by statistical means. Instead, we weave a variety of historical threads together into an overarching historical narrative of how we got from a situation in which political parties and candidates for office competed primarily in terms of rival ideological platforms rooted in conflicting interests and values within society, to one in which parallel claims to embody 'the people' as a whole and to possess the necessary expertise to translate its will into policy have become the mainstays of electoral competition.

Our main thesis is that technopopulism stems from a broad process of separation—or disconnection—between society and politics, and more precisely between societal dynamics and divisions, on one hand, and the logic of electoral competition on the other. Traditionally, political parties and ideologies had the role of mediating the relationship between society and politics. They did this by articulating particular interests and values present within society into an overarching—though still partisan—vision of how the latter ought to be governed and to what ends. Over the course of the second half of the twentieth century, their capacity to do so was undermined because of a number of deep sociological transformations whose translation into political life was partial at best. The effect of the growing disconnect was to undermine the legitimacy of existing party systems, leading to a demand for closer connection between society and politics. In absence of any effective mechanisms of mediation between them, the relationship between the social and the political took the form of a mass of disaggregated social interests and values, on the one hand, and unitary conceptions of the 'popular will' or the 'common good', on the other. The political logic that emerged from this unmediated relationship between society and politics was technopopulism.

This outcome was the result of a number of underlying factors and did not operate in a purely linear or uniform way across the different historical and political contexts that constitute the object of our analysis. One of this chapter's challenges has been to weave together both structural and conjunctural factors—while also considering the role of sequencing between them—in order to account for the variable trajectories of our specific case studies. At the same time, we have built up an overarching narrative that explains the parallel emergence of technopopulism across these cases. To these ends, we have divided up our narrative in three broad historical periods, highlighting both the common trends that unite our case studies and the historical specificities that account for contextual variation.[1]

We begin with a description of what we call the era of the emergence and eventual supremacy of the ideological political logic, which we claim lasted roughly from the end of the nineteenth century to the middle part of the twentieth. This is intended to offer a foil for our account of the emergence of the technopopulist logic, by illustrating how political action and competition were structured *before* the emergence of populism and technocracy as mainstays of electoral competition. The key claim is that during the era of the ideological political logic, society and politics were closely connected to one another by the mediating action of political parties and ideologies. Partisan divisions were largely a reflection of underlying conflicts of interest and value within society, whilst also shaping the very fabric of social life. There were, we recognize, important differences in the way partisan ideologies structured political action and competition in this period. During the first few decades of the twentieth century, social and ideological conflicts were so severe that they often threatened to undermine the democratic order itself. In the aftermath of the Second World War there was a more sustained effort to contain political conflict within the framework of democratic orders. We distinguish between an early phase of ideological conflict that corresponds to the class war of 1918–45 and a later phase of regulated ideological conflict, which lasted more or less until the mid-1960s. What straddles both

---

[1] There is always much debate around periodization, of course. Our choice is informed by the manner in which cognate but independent literatures—in political science, political theory, and political sociology—all adopt roughly these same three periods, though the labels they give to them are different. In the literature on party politics, we have the era of the mass party, the catch-all party, and then the cartel party (Katz and Mair 1995, 2018). In the literature on democratic representation, we have the eras of parliamentarism, party democracy, and audience democracy (Manin 1997). In political sociology, we have the era of organized modernity, which corresponds to ideological political competition. Then we have the crisis of organized modernity—which is our era of transition—followed by the era of disorganized modernity, our era of technopopulism (Wagner 1994; Crouch 1999). Even in nationally specific historical debates, we have something of the same. Stuart Hall and Bill Schwarz argued that 1880–1930 was the period that formed British social democracy, on the back of the crisis of the nineteenth-century liberal state. They situate the ideological crisis of social democracy in the 1970s, and argue that Thatcherism has come to replace it as the new ideologically hegemonic project (Gamble 1988).

periods is a sense in which modern society was organized by and structured around group identities which shaped everyday life and political competition.[2]

The second historical period we identify is what we call the era of transition, which lasted roughly from the mid-1960s to the end of the 1980s. This period is defined in relation to the main historical phenomenon we seek to explain, that is, the rise of technopopulism. It is characterized by a progressive breakdown of the main logic of political competition during the previous period, but not yet by the emergence of the technopopulist political logic itself. Our key claim is that during this period the social bases for the partisan political conflicts that dominated the era of ideological competition were progressively undermined. However, the political parties themselves, and the logic of competition between them, remained largely in place. This led to a growing disconnect between society and politics, initially manifested by growing social tensions and—paradoxically—an exacerbation of ideologically charged conflicts. These occurred as their underlying social bases were being progressively hollowed out, and indeed this hollowing out was partly driving the ideological polarization. By the end of the transitional period, an empty form of ideological political conflict remained whilst its concrete social content, and in particular the organized interests and social actors that provided this content, had disappeared.

Our third historical period is that of the rise of the technopopulist political logic, from the beginning of the 1990s to the present day. This period was ushered in by the end of the Cold War—a key historical development which shattered the empty carapace of ideological politics and cleared the way for the rise of populism and technocracy as the main structuring poles of contemporary democratic politics. A second critical juncture was the worldwide economic crisis that followed the financial meltdown of 2008–11. In absence of any organized political forces and ideological projects to deal with this crisis, political responses were shaped by

---

[2] Sociologists and political scientists describe this 'ordered modernity' using terms such as 'pillarization' and 'segmented pluralism' (Lorwin 1971). Colin Crouch refers to this as 'structured sociological liberalism' (1999: 34). This way of organizing society did not emerge from a vacuum. Crouch describes in detail its roots in the institutional forms taken by religious tolerance in the aftermath of the Protestant Reformation. By the middle of the eighteenth century, Dutch society in particular was structured around three 'pillars': a reformed Calvinist Church, a more fundamentalist branch of Calvinism, and a Catholic minority (which was the strongest pillar, reflecting its status as a minority). These pillars stood for a combination of separation and cooperation that would form the basis for relations between organized interests in the twentieth century. Moving beyond these confessional divides, Western European societies at the time were developed in a way that favoured this form of 'structured tolerance' between distinctive social groupings and communities. Writing about the importance of the growth of towns and cities, Crouch argues that they 'signalled a model of political development different from that of the aristocratically ruled countryside' and most crucially they 'also expressed the concept of long-term co-existence of rival and antagonistic organized forces' (1999: 17). The urban social order built around guilds, corporations, and local government, which together made up the emerging identity and interest known as bourgeois, was constantly forced to negotiate and manage its relationship with powerful landed interests and with the religious organizations. It is this form of coexistence of distinct and rival interests that Crouch claims 'became the hallmark of a distinctive, Western European form of social organization' (1999: 17).

the technopopulist logic, whilst also reaffirming its centrality to democratic political discourse and organization. Populism and technocracy emerged as the dominant modes of political action in a situation in which a fragmented and disorganized society, under conditions of ideological disorientation and economic duress, gazed at its self-referential political rulers across what Peter Mair called 'the void' (Mair 2013). After discussing the impact of these historical developments at the beginning of this section of the chapter, we follow closely the development of technopopulism in each of our cases.

Approach and Method

The chapter provides a 'thick description' of political life within the different historical periods we have identified. That is to say, we provide some sense of how political action and competition were structured in each of these periods.[3] We do not provide any systematic account of the actions of particular individuals but are interested in uncovering the main determinants of political action in each period. In so doing, the chapter provides some analytical clarity regarding why ideological competition has given way to the new political logic we call technopopulism. Our aim is to understand both what a change in the structuring logic of democratic politics means for political action and competition and to inquire into the principal reasons for that change.

Regarding our method, we avoid the language of dependent and independent variables and prefer to follow Hannah Arendt in thinking in terms of the *origins* of technopopulism.[4] One reason for this is that the language of dependent and independent variables introduces a misleading degree of formalism to political explanation. In tracing the origins of a political object—such as a new political logic—we will inevitably find that there are elements in the object itself that have social, economic and cultural properties. For instance, we stress in chapter 1 that the technopopulist political logic is associated with a relationship between individuals and politics that is increasingly less mediated. We can therefore include within our understanding of what technopopulism *is* the growing absence of organized interests in society. At the same time, by way of an *explanation* of the emergence of technopopulism, the decline of these organized interests is a crucial part of the story.

In social science, there is always a degree of overlap between the dependent and independent variables. This is the result of a social world built around the relative

---

[3] The term 'thick description' has generally been associated with the work of Clifford Geertz (1973). The term itself was originally developed by the Oxford metaphysician, Gilbert Ryle, in his lecture on 'the thinking of thoughts'. For a discussion of this, see White (2020): 117.
[4] Arendt's book, *The Origins of Totalitarianism*, has been the basis for an extensive debate around the meaning of causal explanation in the social sciences.

interdependence and interpenetration of political, cultural, and economic spheres. Pretending that we can firmly separate these spheres and categorize them as dependent and independent variables is to mislead the reader. In our narrative in this chapter, we try to maintain as much separation between cause and effect as possible, in order to avoid circularity. However, we also try to avoid introducing distinctions and categories that pretend that political phenomena can really be either 'outside' or 'separate' from society, culture, or the economic sphere.

A second reason for preferring the narrative approach, and for focusing on origins, has to do with our objects of study. We find that, in existing accounts of the causes of populism and of technocracy, there is a marked tendency to promise more than can be delivered. The language of dependent and independent variables suggests a degree of precision in causal explanation which has thus far been quite absent from the scholarly debate on both populism and technocracy. What we find instead is a curious amalgam of precise scientific language around causal hypotheses and rather vague historical claims about the emergence of both populism and technocracy.

In one of the seminal texts in the study of populism, Mudde's 2004 article on the 'populist zeitgeist', we find a section on 'the causes of the *current* populist zeitgeist' (2004: 552–6, italics added). The structure of the explanation is a simple list of causes. Mudde dismisses some of them whilst others he believes are more convincing. This list is so broad, however, that the 'populist zeitgeist' could have occurred at any time from the 1960s through to the 2000s. Cognitive mobilization, which Mudde cites favourably as an explanation, began in the 1950s and 1960s (with the baby boomer generation reaching adulthood). Depillarization in the Low Countries dates also from the 1960s (Andeweg 2019). The depoliticization of democracies, which Mudde discusses, is already a prominent concern of Kirchheimer's, writing in the 1950s and 1960s, and is a core part of his concept of the catch-all party (1969: 346–71). Mudde himself notes that '[f]or decades, authors have noted a development towards apolitical or non-ideological politics in western democracies' (2004: 555) but without recognizing that this poses a problem in terms of temporal accounts of the rise of the current wave of populist mobilization. The media is an important cause but, once again, Mudde observes that this factor began in the late 1960s as newspapers in particular uncoupled themselves from political parties.

Mudde is not alone in providing such a 'laundry list' of causes without specifying why populism should emerge with greatest force in the 1990s and 2000s rather than in the 1960s or 1970s.[5] There are some scholars for whom

---

[5] For more details, see Abromeit 2017. Referring to Mudde and Kaltwasser's 2017 book, *Populism: A Very Short Introduction*, he writes that 'they do not seem to believe that there is any single explanation for populism' and instead they 'provide a laundry list of conditions, whose existence facilitates populism, such as a perception of threat or crisis, economic downturn, systematic corruption, a weak state unable to collect taxes or redistribute wealth, and an increasingly diversified and

populism is a product of a very specific set of factors that are clearly rooted in time, such as Judis (2016) for whom populism is an historically specific revolt against neoliberal policies in Europe and North America. By adopting the framework of causal hypotheses and then selecting the most relevant variables, we observe that a populist 'window of possibility' opens up stretching from the 1960s to the 2000s. Sometimes the window is even wider. Hawkins, Read, and Pauwel use Durkheim's ideas on anomie, a notion first proposed at the end of the nineteenth century, to explain contemporary populism (Hawkins et al. 2017). It is a peculiar feature of academic studies of populism that whilst they stress the contemporary relevance of it, their explanations take us back almost half a century or more. The distinction between demand-side and supply-side explanations tends to exacerbate this problem. Demand-side explanations are notoriously bad at explaining why events happen when they do, which is why scholars have turned increasingly to supply-side factors. Some of these—such as electoral rules—change so infrequently that they are equally indeterminate in terms of timing.

We observe the same problem in the explanatory literature on technocracy, though scholars in this field tend to be less attached to the language of dependent and independent variables. Explanatory accounts of technocracy are marked in particular by a gap between broad brushstroke accounts of the macro-historical causes of technocracy and the actual development of technocratic institutions or the actions of technocrats in political life. Technocracy is principally understood in terms of the birth of industrial society and subsequent iterations of the industrial revolution—from the development of steam power to the birth of computer technology (see Esmark 2020; Akin 1977; Meynaud 1969; Putnam 1977; Porter 1995). Some recent writings on technocracy in Latin America and Europe have associated technocracy with the effects of economic crises and the demand for technocrats to run finance ministries (see Alexiandou and Gunaydin 2019; McDonnel and Valbruzzi 2014). Work on the rise of the 'regulatory state' relies on very broad macro-historical accounts, related in particular to arguments about the functional requirements of capitalist societies (see Majone 1994).

We believe that in its search for 'causal adequacy', political science has become too ahistorical. We need more history in political science, in order to explain why things happen when they do. More specifically, we need more history in the study of populism and technocracy.[6] For this reason, we adopt a chronological 'thick

---

competitive media market that focuses more on the sensational issues favoured by populists' (2017: 182).

[6] In a critical review of recent contributions to the debate on populism, John Abromeit remarks that 'in contrast to the older debates about populism, historians have been...notably absent' (2017: 177). A problem with existing attempts at bringing history into these fields is that there is a tendency simply to add to the existing literature a new strand of 'populist' literature that focuses on earlier historical periods (e.g. Abromeit et al. 2015). We see this in the expanding literature around populism and interwar fascism (e.g. Finchelstein 2017). What is still missing is the application of historical methods

descriptive' and narrative approach to this chapter. Our overarching narrative aims to explain the shift from an ideological logic to a technopopulist logic. Within this shift, we identify a series of different moments, with a complex interplay between the social and the political and changes within each respective domain. The most important causes we highlight include the decline of organized interests, the process of cognitive mobilization, and the cartelization of national party systems. By developing our account chronologically, we try to account for the uneven development of these factors.

The Era of the Ideological Political Logic (1890-1965)

The Birth of Ideological Politics

The era of the ideological political logic was characterized by the existence of strong mechanisms of mediation between society and politics. Political parties, but also trade unions and other forms of interest organization and representation, such as religious institutions and civic associations, articulated the particular interests and worldviews of individuals within society. They transformed them into more encompassing ideological orientations which competed with one another for the exercise of formal political power through the state. Partisan political divisions were largely expressions of underlying social conflicts of interests and values, but at the same time contributed in shaping the very fabric of social life itself. As a character in Hugo Claus's classic novel, *The Sorrow of Belgium*, puts it, 'we are infested with politics!'. Claus's novel, set in the late 1930s, captured the complex relations between lower and upper classes in Belgium, between religious and secular forces, and the transformative effect exercised by Flemish nationalism on politics and society. What Claus describes in the case of the Low Countries also characterized the structured and stratified societies of Western Europe, including our own cases of the UK, France, and Italy.[7]

This close connection between societal divisions and dynamics, on one hand, and the political process, on the other, is captured in the concept of sociopolitical 'cleavage' (Lipset and Rokkan 1967). The central thesis advanced in Lipset and Rokkan's 1967 essay is that the partisan political conflicts that structured electoral competition in most advanced Western democracies throughout the first few decades of the twentieth century were the reflection of underlying social divisions. These divisions were the result of the two revolutions that ushered in the modern

---

and argument to contemporary populism and technocracy. Important exceptions include the work of Anton Jäger and the recent contribution by Rosanvallon (2020).

[7] Hugo Claus's novel was originally published in Dutch in 1983.

period: the political revolutions that abolished the *anciens régimes* and established modern democratic states; and the industrial revolution that marked the transition from feudal to capitalist modes of production and economic organization. The former sparked a conflict between the centre and the periphery of the newly established nation states, as well as a conflict between religious and secular citizens and institutions. Meanwhile, the latter lay at the origin of the class conflict between the proletariat and the bourgeoisie (Lipset and Rokkan 1967: 33–5).

These conflicts were manifested politically through different partisan organizations, which embodied 'constellations' of specific interests and values. The British Labour Party was founded in 1900 out of the confluence between specific class and religious interests that opposed both the Tory Party (which had previously been an expression of traditional landed interests and aristocratic values) and the Whig Party, which had instead been a primarily urban party, championing the interests of the industrial and commercial bourgeoisie.[8] The Christian Democratic parties that emerged in several countries of Continental Europe between the end of the nineteenth century and the first few decades of the twentieth initially coalesced around the goal of protecting the privileges of organized religion and in particular the Catholic Church. However, they also sought to mobilize the rural peasantry and the conservative elites around a defence of the traditional order and especially the principle of private property (Kalyvas 1996; Invernizzi-Accetti 2019).

The 'mass parties' of the early part of the twentieth century were not merely an expression of underlying social conflicts and divisions. As agents of social organization and political change, they also contributed in shaping the lives of their members and of society at large. Consider for instance the following description of the daily life of a member of the French Communist Party offered by Maurice Duverger (1954: 117) in his classic treatise on the nature and organizational form of mass parties:

> Every day in his factory or in his workshop he must serve as an officer on his party's cell; that is, communicate the directives coming from the central party offices, interpret the essential portions of *L'Humanité* or the local communist newspaper, and make sure that the revolutionary ardor of the other members remains kindled. He is also a member of the CGT [the Communist Trade Union], which is in effect a branch of the party and in which his activities as a member of the cell are extended and completed. The same happens with his free

---

[8] Tony Judt observed that 'the British Labour Party was born in 1906 from a coalition of organizations and movements which drew heavily on non-conformist congregations' (2010: 158). 1906 is the date of the general election when Labour candidates did well enough (twenty-nine were elected) for them to change their organizational basis from the Labour Representation Committee to the term that we know today, the Labour Party. Candidates for an earlier incarnation of what we know today to be the Labour Party first stood for election in 1900, however. For more details on the origins of the Labour Party, see McKenzie (1963: ch. 8).

time: a significant portion of which is absorbed by the meetings of the party itself or contiguous institutions, such as the Association for Peace, or the Friends of the USSR etc.... What remains is also organized by the party: sports clubs, civic associations, celebrations and picnics, even cinema sessions and literary clubs sponsored and organized by the party punctuate its members' diversions. Finally, the party even penetrates private life, since his wife is probably registered in the Union of French Women, as well as various housewife committees, whereas the children are part of the Republican Youth Union and its subsidiaries.

As Duverger himself comments, 'there is no distinction between public and private life [here]' (1954: 117). Ideology and partisan organizational requirements permeate all aspects of individual and social life. Duverger recognizes that this is an extreme example and that not all political parties were as rigorously regimented as the French Communist Party (PCF), even at the height of ideological political conflict. However, the overarching thesis of his book is that, in order to resist the political challenge posed by these kinds of organized mass parties, rival political forces increasingly had to adopt similar organizational forms, according to a logic he describes as a form of 'contagion from the left' (1954: 215). As a result, the lives of large sections of society were permeated by ideological principles and partisan organizational requirements throughout the first few decades of the twentieth century.

The overall political dynamics this gave rise to are described in detail by Pierre Rosanvallon in *Le Peuple Introuvable* (1998).[9] Rosanvallon's broad claim is that modern democracy should be viewed as a process of 'filling in' the powerful but abstract concept of 'the people', something which only occurs when a society of individuals is replaced by a society of groups or of organized interests. Modern democracy requires the 'sociologization' of politics; that is, the giving of social content to the empty rallying cry of popular sovereignty (Rosanvallon 1998: 12). Focusing in particular on the case of France during the first few decades of the twentieth century, Rosanvallon maintains that this led to the emergence of a 'structured democracy', which refers to three pillars: the political parties, which had traditionally been divided along the left/right ideological continuum since the French Revolution; industrial relations, which were based on social representation via trade unions and employer associations; and the 'consultative state', which for him encompassed the variety of economic and social councils created in the late nineteenth and early twentieth century, such as the *Conseil National Économique* (National Economic Council), which aimed to structure the relationship between civil society and the state around a set of professional and expert concerns (1998: 27–9).

---

[9] The translations of Rosanvallon (1998) are our own.

A key argument advanced by Rosanvallon is that during this period class divisions progressively asserted themselves as the main sociological basis for the traditional ideological distinction between left- and right-wing parties, supplanting or in any case encompassing the previously more salient divisions between centre and periphery or between religious and secular citizens. 'At the turn of the century', he writes, 'after the storms unleashed by the Dreyfus Affair, the emergence of an urban proletariat and the so-called "social question" completed the fragmentation of the original monism [of the French Revolutionary era] entrenching the recognition of a legitimate and quasi-structural opposition between right and left' (1998: 235). The consolidation of the ideological political competition in France therefore coincided with the structuring of French society around class lines. As Henri Mendras and Alastair Cole observed, by the outbreak of the Great War, French society was clearly and firmly divided into 'four great social groups, each of which had its own characteristics' (cited in Crouch 1999: 3; see also Mendras 1988: 29). These groups were the bourgeoisie, the proletariat, the peasantry, and the 'middle class'.

The main political parties that dominated the politics of the French Third Republic broadly corresponded to these social groups. The *Parti Républicain* (founded in 1901) was a classical liberal party that championed the interests and values of the urban and commercial bourgeoisie. The *Section Française de l'Internationale Ouvrière* (founded in 1905) was an expression of the country's workers' movement that emerged out of the fusion of a variety of other previous socialist groups. The *Fédération Républicaine* (founded in 1903) was a conservative political organization that sought to federate the interests and values of the former landed aristocracy (that had rallied in favour of the republic and against the monarchy) with those of the rural peasantry and the agricultural sector more generally. The *Action Française* (founded in 1899) was an explicitly monarchist political organization. It militated against republicanism and had its social base mostly amongst the urban middle classes and the more reactionary sections of the peasantry and former landed aristocracy.

The Italian experience was similar to the French in many ways, though industrialization took place more slowly and in a more stunted and patchy way. The 1911 census recorded that almost 59 per cent of the workforce depended on agriculture, making it clear that Italy remained an 'overwhelmingly rural society' at that time (Duggan 2014: 177). There was mass movement away from the countryside but it took the form of emigration (to the US especially) rather than the creation of an urban proletariat. As a result, the main ideological division between the parliamentary coalitions of the historical Right (*la Destra*) and Left (*la Sinistra*) still corresponded primarily to conflicts over the role and legitimacy of the centralized state and its relations with other forms of more localized power, as well as the Roman Catholic Church and the so-called 'Roman question'. Nevertheless, during the first few decades of the twentieth century, industrialization began to reshape the class structure of Italian society. FIAT was founded in 1899, in Turin, and Lancia and Alfa Romeo both in 1906. The textile sector boomed in the early 1900s, expanding employment in this sector. This led to the formation of a workers' movement. The *Partito Socialista Italiano* had already been formed in 1896. The *Partito Comunista Italiano* followed in 1921 (Duggan 2014: 189–200).

In other countries, the evolution of the class structure differed in many ways, though the overall direction of change was the same. In the British case, early industrialization had created a large working class and a class of capitalists at a time when other societies were still primarily agrarian. However, British political life was oriented around the relations between three estates—the Church, the landed aristocracy, and the Commons—until after the First World War (Moran 1999: 185). In the early 1900s, religion and territory dominated political debates more than class. It was in the course of the 1920s that British politics was irremediably ordered along class lines, with the Conservatives the party of the established order and Labour the working-class party of opposition.

The gradual reorganization of partisan political competition along the lines of class conflict had the effect of escalating the divisions and tensions within the existing systems of political representation. Indeed, during the first few decades of the twentieth century, the severity of the class and ideological conflict between the labour movements and the liberal bourgeoisie (who were aligned with the representatives of the old order) was such that it often called into question the viability of the existing democratic frameworks. In Italy, the class tensions and economic hardships that exploded in the aftermath of the First World War led first to a wave of strikes and organized revolutionary activity which became known as the '*biennio rosso*' of 1919–20. This, in turn, sparked a reactionary movement supported primarily by the urban middle classes and rural elites known as the '*biennio nero*' of 1920–21 (Mack Smith 1997). The latter culminated with Benito Mussolini's 'March on Rome' and subsequent rise to power at the helm of the Italian Fascist party. Upon assuming power, Mussolini sought to restore order by imposing his own organicist and corporatist conception of society through dictatorial means and progressively banning all forms of political opposition. The Italian electoral system remained formally in place throughout the 1920s and 1930s, but after the murder in 1924 of the head of the Italian Socialist party, Giacomo Matteotti, the very idea of legitimate political competition had been effectively eviscerated. Italy was on its way towards the consolidation of what Mussolini himself would later describe as a 'totalitarian' system of government (Gentile 2002).

Although the French Third Republic remained formally in place until the German invasion and the subsequent establishment of the Vichy regime in 1940, Henri Mendras notes that throughout the first decades of the twentieth century 'an underlying violence underpinned all the relations between classes' (Mendras 1988: 53). In 1936–38, he adds, 'the bourgeoisie lived the era of the

Popular Front with the fear of the revolution that would uproot the social order entirely'. The Resistance and the Liberation (1939–45) were, for him, 'the last patriotic and revolutionary events where French citizens were physically afraid of other French citizens' (1988: 53). The prospect of violent social revolution, as well as of an extra-institutional reassertion of order by reactionary forces, were real possibilities during the last few years of the French Third Republic, crystalizing in the form of a non-democratic authoritarian regime sponsored by the German Nazis during the Second World War.

Even in the United Kingdom—which is the only one of our case studies to have remained formally democratic throughout the period under consideration—the class tensions of the first few decades of the twentieth century reached unprecedented proportions. The first Labour government of 1923, under the leadership of Ramsay MacDonald, was portrayed by the Tory opposition as 'the negative of everything Britain has ever stood for' (Pugh 2011). The publication of a forged letter by Grigory Zinoviev, the Soviet head of the Communist International, speaking openly of the possibility of Communist revolution in Great Britain, led to a veritable 'Red Scare' in 1924 contributing to the Conservative Party's landslide electoral victory of that year (Kadish 1987). The British Union of Fascists under the leadership of Oswald Moseley was formed in 1932 and after only a year had acquired a membership of over 50,000. It was banned by the British government after the country's entrance into the Second World War against the axis powers in 1940 (Benewick 1972).

The Regulated Conflict of the Post-War Period

In the aftermath of the Second World War there was a much more sustained effort to contain ideological conflict within the framework of established democratic procedures. This led to what has been described as the 'golden age' of party democracy (Mair 2013: 77–8). Political parties remained the expression of particular constellations of interests and values within society but nonetheless agreed to compete with one another according to a set of commonly recognized democratic procedures. Elections became a mechanism for evaluating the respective balance of power between competing social groups, whilst parliaments functioned as a sort of bargaining chamber, in which compromises and agreements were struck between these groups, on the basis of their performance in elections. Colin Crouch (1999: 33) describes this as a form of 'structured tolerance' that settled into place after 1945:

> People would be organized around one of the great divisions, and from that vantage point would at best pursue an active cooperation with old enemies, at worst accept an armistice across enemy lines. Workers and employers, having

organized themselves for industrial conflict, used their organizations to make deals with each other. Different religious denominations, while remaining proud of the distinctive beliefs and practices defended by their particular organizations, ... set up various types of cooperation with theoretically rival denominations. Political parties cooperated in government, or at least in sustaining democracy; nation-states which had defined themselves against each other and set up state machines for making war against each other, now used those same machines to launch an ambitious movement for a European economic community.

Seymour Martin Lipset observed something similar, describing it as a shift from conflict between social groups to a form of bargaining-based politics where 'each group accepts the others' right to legitimate representation within the structure of representation and discussion' (Lipset 1964: 271). He argued that 'domestic politics in most of these [Western European] societies became reduced to the "politics of collective bargaining", that is, to the issue of which groups should secure a little more or less of the pie' (1964: 274). It was taken for granted that these societies were socially stratified along the lines of class and religion and that these cleavages led to organizationally specific forms of political mobilization.

This stabilization of party democracy around the principle of regulated ideological conflict gradually inscribed itself into Western European party systems. Otto Kirchheimer has argued that the 1950s signalled the birth of a new type of political party, the 'catch-all party', which came to replace the mass parties of the interwar period. When we look closely at the notion of the catch-all party, we find that it is still built around the ideological political logic and that it corresponds to societies still divided by traditional cleavages. Kirchheimer is developing an argument about a change in the relationship between the party and its social base rather than any break in that relationship. The new function of parties is to be 'brokers' between different social groups. Mass parties had tended to have very firm ties to specific groups and sought only to mobilize their own voters at election time.

The political parties of the post Second World War period were no longer the 'political arm of social groups', as they were in the early twentieth century and the interwar era, but their role as brokers testifies to the segmented nature of post-1945 societies (Katz and Mair 2018: 14). There were limits to this brokering role of parties, given the power of the ideological logic. Italy's *Democrazia Cristiana* could play down its religious roots, but it could not openly court the country's anti-clerical elements (Kircheimer 1969: 355). The same would apply to the German SPD or to the British Labour Party. Neither party could realistically aim to win over landed or propertied interests or the big farming fortunes. Rather, they sought to forge coalitions between blue- and white-collar voters or between private and public sector workers. The notion of the 'catch-all party' designates a political party seeking to expand its share of the vote but without being able to escape its social roots or ignore the ideological logic that structured political competition in Western democracies at the time.

Writing about British political life at the time of the 1951 general election, the British diplomat and politician, Harold Nicholson described it as 'two Nations facing each other like two blocks of cement' (cited in McKibbin 2014). These 'two Nations' were the Conservatives and the Labour Party. The historian Ross McKibbin suggests that Britain at that time was 'a two-party state, Labour and anti-Labour, which meant Conservative'. The two parties, he continues, 'appealed to brute social loyalties and antagonisms solidified in the 1940s'. And yet, at the same time as these two 'blocks of cement' coldly observed one another from their respective positions of strength, Britain was a country governed by consensus.

'By the mid-1950s', writes Tony Judt, 'English politics had reached such a level of implied consensus around public policy issues that mainstream political argument was dubbed "Butskellism": blending the ideas of R.A. Butler, a moderate Conservative minister and Hugh Gaitskell, the centrist leader of the Labour opposition in those years' (Judt 2010: 49). In Italy, post-war political and social organization corresponded closely to what political scientists have called 'segmented pluralism' or pillarization. Such terms are usually applied to Western Europe's smaller 'consociational democracies': the Low Countries and often Austria, all practising what Lijphart called 'the politics of accommodation' (Lijphart 1968). However, as Judt (2005: 260) also observes, there are clear parallels to be made between Italy and these more typical consociational democracies.

Throughout the 1950s and 1960s, the Christian Democrats governed Italy, in coalition with small centrist parties and then from 1963 onwards in coalition with the non-Communist left. During this time, the political parties slowly took over various parts of the state apparatus, allocating funds and jobs along political lines. This was a form of state capture and patronage—what critics called the *partitocrazia*—but much of the same occurred in those other 'segmented pluralist' societies. It was a clear illustration of the interpenetration of the political and the social, both at the individual and at the group level.

The French Fourth Republic has been similarly described as a 'republic of parties' (Rioux 2005). The new constitution established after the end of the Second World War enshrined the principle of proportional representation, leading to a proliferation of political parties representing competing interests and value orientations within society. These parties were broadly located within three camps: the left, which included the Communists and the Socialists; the centre, which was composed of the secular Radical Party and the Christian Democratic *Mouvement Républicain Populaire*; and the right, which included the Gaullists, the remnants of the traditional right and pro-Vichy social forces united in the *Centre National des Indépendants et Paysans*, and the Poujadist far right. Although for a time several components of this highly fragmented political landscape managed to cooperate with one another—such as during the so-called Tripartite government headed by General de Gaulle between 1944 and 1946—very soon the deeply entrenched political and ideological divisions between them proved difficult to surmount. This led to a protracted period of political instability, which ultimately brought the Forth Republic down over the Algerian crisis of 1958.

Transitions (1965–89)

Our second historical period is the era of transition. This was a period during which change and continuity were interwoven in complex ways. We saw the return of ideological radicalism and political violence. It was also a time of industrial strife and attempts at reviving corporatist institutions. Whilst these developments pointed to the return of the instability and conflicts of the interwar years, deep social transformations ensured that no such return was possible. The ideological *form* of politics remained throughout the period, but the social *content* changed profoundly. This era of transition is therefore marked by a growing disjuncture between social (and cultural) change and political continuity.

One interpretation of the disjuncture is that it reflects the difficulty political systems experience when required to adapt to rapid social change. Another view is that the disjuncture had some purpose or function. In an era of social flux, might citizens not find some comfort in the familiarity of an unchanging political landscape?[10] This explanation would suggest that once the need for the disjuncture had disappeared—perhaps due to the end of the period of rapid social change—then the tension between the political and the social would manifest itself much more powerfully. This is indeed what we find, though the disjuncture itself outlived the social transformations that we describe below.

This section on the era of transition is important in explaining the origins of the technopopulist logic because it helps grasp why there was so much delay in some social factors having their effects on the political landscape. Many social changes corresponding to the emergence of technopopulism—growing individualization, decline in class identities and the fragmentation of organized interests, as well as cognitive mobilization—first occur in the course of the 1960s and 1970s. However, the continued rigidity of ideological political competition meant that these changes were not translated into new forms of politics until the 1990s.

---

[10] Judt suggests as much when he discusses pillarization in the Low Countries. He writes that 'the pillars thus survived into the 1960s—anachronistic echoes of a pre-political age that lasted long enough to serve as cultural and institutional stabilizers during a period of hectic economic transformation' (2005: 265). Mair also makes a similar argument. In his words, 'despite the massive social change and enormous structural mobility, which has seen large sections of the population move from rural areas to urban areas, and from agriculture to services and industry, large numbers of voters have nevertheless *maintained* their traditional voting preferences' (2014: 276, italics in original).

Social Change and Political Stasis

The sustained period of peace and economic growth of the post-war years, coupled with the consolidation of welfare states and the incipient tertiarization of the economy, led to enormous social transformations by the beginning of the 1960s, which profoundly altered the conditions for political competition. The first and most important transformation concerned the *class structure* of Western European societies. Whereas during the first few decades of the twentieth century Western European politics had been dominated by class warfare and then by the regulated conflict between the proletariat and the bourgeoisie, by mid-century these class divisions had become more fuzzy.

One way of thinking about this is in terms of an expansion of the 'middle class', which progressively incorporated large swathes of the former proletariat and bourgeoisie, tempering and to a large extent defusing the conflict between them. Henri Mendras suggests that French society gradually shifted from a class structure represented in the shape of a 'pyramid'—with the bourgeoisie at the top but numerically very small, a larger middle class, and then a much larger working class and peasantry at the bottom—towards a 'tear drop' shape signalling a vastly expanded middle class. At the very top we still find the social and political elite, but the large 'central constellation' dominates the middle and is also relatively internally heterogenous. Below it lies the 'popular constellation' and below that lies the numerically much smaller precariat that some call an 'underclass' (Mendras 1988).

What Mendras calls the 'central constellation' corresponds to the birth a 'new middle class', one associated with the shift towards services in advanced capitalist economies. Within this constellation, a new managerial class—*les cadres*—make up the core. They earn a wage but are not working class; they manage teams but are not the CEOs of companies. They are an intermediary layer whose importance grew rapidly as large-scale businesses—the corporation—began to dominate economic life from the 1960s onwards. These managers earn well, but they are not the functional equivalent of the bourgeois rentier of the early twentieth century. Their professional expertise defines them, and they are products of the expansion of national educational systems. At the same time, this new category of the cadres has an air of monotony and conformity to it. It is associated with the expansion in suburban life and has all of the pathologies associated with this development, captured by the British author J.G. Ballard and mocked ruthlessly in films such as *Les Bronzés* (1978) in France.

The consequence of the expansion of this 'central constellation', as Mendras highlights, was the progressive dissolution—or at least the decline in pertinence—of other class formations and loyalties. By the mid-1980s, he argued that: '[t]he peasantry has disappeared, the bourgeoisie's own attributes have been diffused across the rest of society, proletarian culture is dead and the middle class is no longer made up principally of shop owners, artisans and employees, but of managers' (1998: 30). 'If there is no longer a proletariat', he added 'then there can be no bourgeoisie... By disappearing, the bourgeoisie, peasantry and proletariat are also making disappear a class system in the strong sense of the term.' In his definition of this class system, Mendras captures the way in which class shaped individual experience whilst also being a powerful force of collective action. In his words, the class system amounted to 'civilised universes that encompassed all of life and all one's personality and all the ambitions of its members, and ... organized groups fighting for power and for the domination of society as a whole' (1998: 30). Both of these dimensions were lost as societies were increasingly less structured around class identities.

Another way of thinking about the transformation of the class structure of Western European societies in the middle part of the twentieth century is in terms of a growing 'differentiation' and 'stratification' *within* existing class formations (e.g. Pakulski and Waters 1996). While the proletariat and bourgeoisie originally constituted relatively homogenous social formations (think of Nicholson's 'blocks of cement'), the changes in the mode of economic production and the growing levels of socio-economic security of the post-war period led to a growing pluralization of individual life experiences and expectations. In this respect, Jan Pakulski writes that: 'In class society, property/market-generated inequalities are most salient', whereas 'complex social inequality and hybrid stratification refer to configurations in which no single system of inequality predominates' (Pakulski 2005: 172). Pakulski concludes that 'increasing hybridization heralds the decomposition of the industrial classes and the concomitant departure from class society' (2005: 165–73).[11]

The combined effect of the expansion of the 'central constellation' and the internal 'hybridization' of existing social classes was manifested in the growing difficulty experienced by political parties to retain the vote of the specific classes they had traditionally relied on as their basis for electoral support. This process—which has been widely documented and commented upon by political scientists—is known as 'class dealignment'. John Goldthorpe (1980), for instance, reports that while in 1964 the British Labour Party could count on 64 per cent of the vote share of the manual working class, by 1987 that share had declined to 43 per cent. Similarly, in France, David Boy and Nonna Mayer found a clear decline in class voting between manual and non-manual employee groups regarding support for the socialist parties from 1978 to 1997 (Boy and Mayer 1997). More broadly,

---

[11] By way of illustration of this shift towards more pluralization, Mendras notes that if the formal dinner was the archetypal ritual of bourgeois life—with its demands in terms of cooking, the elaborate dinner service, the attention to detail in the dining room, the formality of the dress code—then the new ritual of the central constellation is 'the barbecue'. It is an occasion that lacks any formality, has no recognized or systematic hierarchy, and much of the stuffiness and tension of eating in the dining room is lost in the open setting of the back garden (Mendras 1988: 84).

Russel Dalton, Scott Flanagan, and Paul Allen Beck have found that since the mid-1960s it has become increasingly difficult to specify the 'class identity' of mainstream political parties in advanced industrial democracies, since the electoral choice appears to be increasingly dominated by individualized value orientations and lifestyle preferences (Dalton et al. 1985).

A second key process of social change that manifested itself from the early 1960s onwards is that of religious *secularization*. The idea that modernization would involve a generalized decline in the social significance of religion had been a central tenet of classical social theory at least since the time of Marx, Durkheim, and Weber. The mid-1960s saw a proliferation of sociological works that purported to demonstrate this empirically, on the basis of evidence drawn from declining rates of church attendance, participation in religious rituals such as baptism, confirmation, and religious marriage, and sharply declining rates of entry into the clerical professions throughout most Western European countries (for an overview of this evidence, see Wilson 1966; Berger 1967).

Several aspects of these early sociological formulations of the theory of secularization were soon criticized. Scholars pointed out that the empirical evidence on which they relied did not support the idea that general levels of religious *belief* were declining. Thomas Luckmann, for instance, suggested that declining rates of church attendance and participation in religious rituals did not necessarily imply that people were becoming 'less religious' but could also be explained on the basis of the supposition that the specific *way* in which people experienced and practised religion was changing. He therefore introduced the concept of religion '*à la carte*' to suggest that individuals were increasingly constructing their own forms of religious practice and belief, independently of established religious traditions and institutions (Luckmann 1967).

In her 1994 study of *Religion in Britain since 1945*, Grace Davie argued that British society had increasingly opted for a form of 'believing without belonging', whereby individual citizens did not necessarily stop believing in God or self-identifying as 'religious' (or, even more so, 'spiritual') but increasingly withdrew from organized—and especially institutionalized—forms of religious practice and belief. For Davie, secularization operated primarily at the level of religious organization and institutions, and far less at the level of individual belief. What has been declining, she contends, is the social role of religion as an 'aggregating force' capable of creating structured 'communities of belief', not religious belief per se (Davie 1994).

These revisions tend to reinforce our argument here, which is not about the issue of personal 'faith' as such but rather about the organizational dimension of religion and its structuring effect on social and political life. The theories of secularization developed in the 1960s and 1970s can be inscribed within a broader theory of 'modernization', conceived of as a generalized process of 'individualization' and 'differentiation' of life experiences (Giddens 1990; Beck and Beck-Gernshein 2001). More recently, authors such as José Casanova and Karel Dobbelaere have folded the notion of secularization into an even broader theory of modernization as a process of 'functional differentiation of spheres' (Casanova 1994; Dobbelaere 2002). Whereas religion previously permeated all spheres of individual and social life, modernity corresponds to a generalized process of 'autonomization' of different spheres of action, such as the political sphere, the economic sphere, the private sphere and—separately from all of the above—the religious sphere. Without necessarily declining per se, or not as much as we may have thought, religion becomes a self-enclosed activity even within the sphere of individual consciousness and it has little bearing on other aspects of individual and social life (see also Taylor 2007). These different theories of secularization bring out the way which, over the course of several decades in the middle part of the twentieth century and especially since the 1960s and 1970s, organized religion lost much of the influence it had previously exercised on other spheres of social life—and in particular the political sphere—across Western Europe.[12]

To the extent that the religious divide had constituted one of the main social and political 'cleavages' of the era of the ideological political logic, this implies that from the early 1960s onwards political parties were in the process of losing another key basis of social mobilization and support. The more fragmented—and especially individualized—nature of religious belief meant that they couldn't count as effectively as they had in the past on the wide range of religious organizations, civic associations, and communities of faith that had previously constituted one of the backbones of partisan political mobilization. Whereas the parties of the ideological left—i.e. the Socialists and Communists in Italy and France, and the Labour Party in the UK—were more vulnerable to the process of 'class dealignment' we discussed above, it was the parties of the historic right and centre right—i.e. the Christian Democrats in Italy and France, and the Conservative Party in the UK—that were hardest hit by this process of religious secularization. The generalized retreat of Western European citizens from religious organizations and other forms of structured religious belief has been cited as one of the main reasons for the progressive decline and ultimate collapse of the French *Mouvement Républicain Populaire* (MRP) beginning in the 1960s and the Italian *Democrazia Cristiana* beginning in the 1990s (Papini 1978; Mayeur 1980; Invernizzi-Accetti 2019).

---

[12] The question of whether the theory of secularization applies across the world, or whether Western Europe constitutes some kind of 'exception' in this regard, has been fiercely debated in the relevant sociological literature (on this point, see for instance: Berger 1999; Berger et al. 2008). However, the one thing most participants in this debate seem to agree on is that Western Europe is the one area of the world in which the empirical predictions of the classical theories of secularization seem to have been borne out most accurately. The debate is in effect over whether these theories also apply as cogently elsewhere.

A third extremely important process of social change that also began to become manifest during the 1960s and 1970s is *cognitive mobilization*. Like secularization, this is a complex concept that captures a variety of related social processes. The term was used for the first time by Ronald Inglehart in the late 1960s to describe the effect of increasing education levels and public exposure to new forms of mass media (such as, most notably, the television) on the post-war 'baby boomer' generation. His claim was that these processes were leading to an 'increasingly wide distribution of the political skills necessary to cope with an extensive political community' (Inglehart 1970: 47). The concept was taken up some years later by Russell Dalton (1984: 265), who wrote that

> The dramatic spread of education in advanced industrial democracies is producing a qualitative change in the political sophistication of Western mass publics... At the same time, these societies have experienced an information explosion through the mass media and the cost of political information has decreased substantially. Because of this cognitive mobilization, more voters now are able to deal with the complexities of politics and make their own political decisions.

In both Inglehart's and Dalton's work, the concept of cognitive mobilization was tied to the acquisition of new political values, new attitudes, and changes in political behaviour. Inglehart suggested that the increasing levels of education, prosperity and access to information characteristic of the post-war period led to the new generations' acquisition of what he called 'post-materialist' values, such as 'self-expression', 'individual autonomy', and 'concern for the quality of life' (Inglehart 1977). Whereas previous generations had been primarily interested in what he called 'materialist' issues, revolving around the 'satisfaction of basic needs' and the 'distribution of key socio-economic resources', by the mid-1960s, cultural emphasis was shifting 'from collective discipline to individual liberty; from group conformity to human diversity; and from state authority to individual autonomy' (Inglehart and Welzel 2005: 7).

Dalton focused more closely on the connection between cognitive mobilization and what he calls 'partisan dealignment'. Already in his 1984 work on the concept of cognitive mobilization, he drew a distinction between 'party mobilization' and 'cognitive mobilization'. The former was measured by the strength of party identification and the latter measured by an index combining formal education and interest in politics (Dalton 1984: 270). Later, he explicitly formulated the hypothesis that more cognitively mobilized citizens would be less likely to participate in traditional forms of partisan activity due to the inherently hierarchical and bureaucratic nature of partisan organization: 'With more political information available to a more educated electorate', he wrote, 'more citizens now possess the political skills necessary to become self-sufficient in politics. These changes mean that contemporary publics are less likely to defer to party elites or to support a party simply out of habit. Instead, people may question elites or resort to non-partisan forms of political expression' (Dalton and Wattenberg 2002: 11).

In describing the profile and preferences of the cognitively mobilized citizen, Dalton also describes a set of attitudes that echo with the outlook of voters shaped by a technopopulist political logic. Cognitive mobilization can therefore help to understand not only the sentiment of rejection vis-à-vis existing party structures but also the positive content of what individuals began looking for as a replacement. When voters are asked about what they expect from their political representatives, 'apartisans' are most likely to stress the policy-oriented and problem-solving aspects of representation. They are least interested in the party-related dimensions of politics and view legislators primarily in policy terms rather than in partisan terms. In short, they judge on the basis of a representative's policy expertise, not their 'partyness' or degree of party loyalty (see also Dalton 2013). Cognitive mobilization thus leads to a situation where a growing number of voters are hostile to traditional political parties *and* are inclined to view elected representatives in terms of their expertise in problem-solving. This combination of features overlaps with our description of the technopopulist logic and the modes of political action that it generates.

Despite these enormous social changes, the political systems—and in particular the systems of partisan competition—of most Western European democracies remained largely unchanged throughout these decades. This is consistent with the 'freezing' hypothesis first advanced by Seymour Martin Lipset and Stein Rokkan in their 1967 essay on cleavage structures and party systems: 'The party systems of the 1960s', they wrote, 'reflect with but few exceptions the cleavage structures of the 1920s' (Lipset and Rokkan 1967: 50). As a result, they added, 'the party systems, and in remarkably many cases the party organizations too, are now older than the majority of their national electorates.'

The most obvious example of this amongst our case studies is Italy, where the same political party—the *Democrazia Cristiana* (DC)—remained in power continuously from the immediate aftermath of the Second World War to the early 1990s, often with many of the same individuals in key government positions. Although by the beginning of the 1960s there was a widespread sense that this party was losing touch with the values and aspirations of the society it had governed for close to twenty years, a variety of factors contributed in keeping it in power for almost three more decades (Scoppola 1996). The most important was the fact that the main opposition party in Italy at the time remained the Communists, which were at least formally committed to overthrowing the system of 'bourgeois democracy' instituted in the aftermath of the Second World War. Since this was perceived as foreclosing the possibility of democratic alternation (not least because of Italy's international position within the context of the Cold War), the DC opted from 1963 onwards for a progressive expansion of its government coalition, including a variable combination of parties of both the centre left and the centre right, all in order to keep the Communists out of power. The result has been described as a form of 'imperfect bipartism' since it involved two main political parties, only one of which remained consistently in power from 1948 to 1992 (Galli 1967, 2004).

The United Kingdom saw some political alternation in this period but without any fundamental change in policies corresponding to the sorts of social transformations we have described above. Labour returned to power in 1964 after a protracted period of Conservative rule. It was replaced by a Conservative government in 1970 but governed again by Labour from 1974 to 1979. Notwithstanding the change of party, the policy platforms converged around 'Butskellism' well into the 1970s, even though the underlying sociological reality had been profoundly transformed by then. During this period of extensive social ferment, the Labour and Conservative parties colluded with one another to entrench their duopoly in political power, refusing to change the country's first-past-the-post electoral system. This is most visible in the vicissitudes surrounding the Liberal Party's attempts to reassert itself as a significant 'third force' in British politics over this period. Even though—under the leadership of Jo Grimond and subsequently Jeremy Thorpe—this party experienced a revival in the mid-1960s, which allowed it to poll even up to 20 per cent nationally by appealing primarily to young middle-class and suburban voters, it never managed to win more than the fourteen seats it obtained in the 1966 general election, compared with the 364 seats won by Labour with 43 per cent of the vote and the 253 seats won by the Conservatives with 38 per cent of the vote in the same electoral contest (Cook 1976).[13]

The case of France is slightly different. As we have already mentioned, the combination of the political instability of the 1950s and the Algerian independence crisis of those years ultimately led to the collapse of the Fourth Republic and the return to power of General de Gaulle in 1958. This provoked a significant realignment of the existing party system, in particular after the introduction of a two-turn majoritarian electoral law in the Fifth Republic's constitution later that year. In line with the more Presidential and personalized nature of the new republic, the party system was axed around the figure of General de Gaulle himself, with a Gaullist front—the *Union Pour la Nouvelle République*—uniting most elements of the right and centre right, on one hand, and the non-Gaullist Socialists and Communists, on the other. Under the leadership of General de

---

[13] When the Liberal Party finally succeeded in coming to power for the first time since the beginning of the century through the minority Lib–Lab coalition that was created after the February 1974 general election, the Labour Prime Minister Harold Wilson refused to accede to its key demand of a shift to a proportional system of representation, preferring to call for renewed elections in October of that year, through which he was able to secure enough seats to form a majority Labour government without the support of the Liberal Party.

Gaulle himself, and subsequently of Georges Pompidou and Valéry Giscard d'Estaing, the Gaullist party remained in power effectively from the foundation of the Fifth Republic in 1958 up to the election of the Socialist François Mitterrand in 1981 (Cole 1993).

The 'freezing' hypothesis originally formulated by Lipset and Rokkan in 1967 therefore continued to remain valid for several decades after they advanced it. One reason for this is that if parties are understood as mechanisms for the solution of 'collective action problems', then once they are established it is easier to work for political change *within* existing partisan structures than to create entirely new partisan organizations. Another reason suggested by Lipset and Rokkan is that political parties are not merely a 'mechanical reflection' of underlying social changes; they are also 'actors' within the existing political system (Lipset and Rokkan 1967: 52–4). They can therefore use their political power to entrench their dominant positions in the electoral system. Labour and the Conservative parties have been doing so in the UK for over a century, the *Democrazia Cristiana* did it in Italy for over five decades, as the Gaullists did in France for almost twenty years. Commenting on this more than two decades after Lipset and Rokkan's freezing hypothesis was originally advanced, Peter Mair (1992: 274; italics added) wrote that:

> [W]hen society changes, we assume that politics also automatically changes and thus, when class or other social boundaries become blurred, we assume that electoral change must inevitably follow... [W]hile this may well be true as far as the issues which divide parties are concerned, in that substantive policy differences do change in line with new social problems and new government concerns, such social changes do not necessarily imply the emergence of new parties. Indeed, *perhaps the most striking feature of the survival of the old parties of Western Europe is that this survival has occurred within a context of massive social change.*

The combined result of the massive social changes that took place in most Western European democracies throughout the 1960s and 1970s, and the unchanging ('frozen') quality of their party systems, was a growing disjuncture and disconnect between societal dynamics and the logic of electoral competition. Whereas the societies that had emerged from the large-scale sociological transformations of the post-1945 period were in many ways similar to our own—secularized, individualistic, fragmented, and highly educated—the parties and party systems that were supposed to represent them politically were the product of a previous, more collectivist, and deeply ideological age. This made it more and more difficult for the political demands and aspirations expressed by society to be adequately addressed by the political systems in place.

The events of 1968 help us illustrate this argument as they captured this disjuncture between politics and society in a dramatic fashion. The coexistence of a radically heightened sense of individual autonomy felt by the new generations alongside political parties forged in an earlier - more collectivist - age generated enormous amounts of frustration at the political system and political leaders, eventually turning many of the members of the 'central constellation' away from traditional party politics altogether.[14] In this reaction against the established party systems, we see some important developments of relevance to the emergence of the technopopulist logic. The changing social context of the 1960s and 1970s already anticipated some of the features a technopopulist political logic, as we noted with regards the increasingly unmediated quality of social life and the focus on expertise and knowledge emerging out of the processes of cognitive mobilization. However, there was no corresponding change at the political level. The same ideological logic continued to prevail even when the social conditions for it had given way to something new.

Politicians responded to the uprising of 1968 as they would to a return of class warfare. French President Charles de Gaulle was ready to leave France if the violence got out of hand. In Italy, serious consideration was given to a military coup as a solution to the student uprisings (Wagner 1994: 141). The country's secret services set up a hidden armed network ('*Gladio*') whose purpose was to contain—and if necessary eliminate—the threat from the radical left (Ginsborg 2001: 172; Ganser 2004). Socially, however, the mobilization was of a quite different order. The student protests were followed by waves of industrial action in France and elsewhere, but there was little by way of coalition-building between workers and students. Global ideological confrontation was at the heart of the lifeworld of the *soixante-huitards*—and this continued with the political violence of the 1970s in Italy and in Germany—but there was little practical interest amongst the student groups in mobilizing the masses.

Recounting his experience in a 1968 protest in Paris, the philosopher Alain Badiou described how surprised he was when the crowd of protestors walked straight past the French National Assembly without giving it a second glance. Seizing power was not the aim of this revolt, he observed. It was driven instead by a desire for authenticity, a striving for being oneself. Whereas the ideological logic of politics in the previous few decades was associated with a closely and richly articulated relationship between social groups and their competing visions of how society as a whole ought to be governed, we see in 1968 the unravelling of this relationship. All that remained were the hypostatized ideological declarations of Maoist students, on the one hand, and an increasingly individuated and atomized social body, on the other. This 'deracination' of politics, its uprooting from the social structure, was what Tony Judt described as the 'unbearable lightness of

---

[14] For a further discussion of this argument about 1968, see the account of '*les évenements*' in Wagner 1994.

politics' of the 1960s and 1970s. Its impact on politics in Western Europe was considerably delayed by the persistence and rigidity of traditional party systems.

Economic Crisis, Cartelization, and State Transformation in Western Europe

Far from moderating the disjuncture between politics and society that first became manifest between the mid-1960s and the mid-1970s, the political developments of the ensuing two decades exacerbated it even further. In this section we focus on three such developments in particular. The first is the economic crisis of the mid-1970s and especially its political fallout in the ensuing decade. The second refers to changes in the party systems which increased their isolation and distance from society at large, what Katz and Mair have called 'cartelization'.[15] The third development refers to the process of regional integration that reshaped state structures in ways that deepened the 'void' between voters and politicians. This began haltingly in the late 1970s and then changed gear dramatically from the mid-1980s onwards. It is also a feature of the 1990s and 2000s which—as with cartelization—serves to reinforce the technopopulist logic.

These more proximate origins of technopopulism need to be understood in conjunction with the more gradual processes we discussed in the previous section, which hollowed out the organizational forms so crucial to the strength and operation of the ideological political logic. Together, these two sets of processes amount to what we refer to as the end of 'organized modernity' (Wagner 1994) or the end of what Rosanvallon described as 'structured democracy'. That is, an end to a certain way in which collective political identities provided a structure and meaning to the individualism of capitalist social relations.

Economic crisis and the end of the alternative to the market

The economic crisis of the 1970s itself had many different strands to it, but its disintegrative effects on the organization of social interests are clear. Signs of a coming crisis were already present in the 1960s (in the UK especially). These included industrial action and a steady breakdown in cooperation between workers, management, and government (Wagner 1994: 124). Other signs included a fall in the rate of productivity growth, increasing inflation, and growing

---

[15] By identifying this factor at this stage in the narrative, we highlight its role in the story about the origins of the technopopulist logic. However, cartelization continued well beyond the 1980s and in some cases only really became a pronounced trend later. Cartelization has both had some role in creating the technopopulist logic and is also an important element that sustains it, a factor which emphasizes for us once again the difficulty of separating independent causes and analysing their 'impact' in temporally discrete ways.

macro-economic imbalances. The United States had put an end to the post-war Bretton Woods system by uncoupling the dollar from gold. This eased the pressure put on the US economy generated by the war in Vietnam but also caused inflationary pressures throughout advanced capitalist economies. The outbreak of the crisis is commonly associated with developments in the Middle East. In 1973, the oil-producing cartel OPEC raised its oil prices in retaliation for the West's support for Israel in the Yom Kippur War. Whether or not this decision can be 'responsible' for the outbreak of the crisis is debatable. One alternative view is that underlying conditions in Western economies—tied specifically to what some have called the 'full employment profit squeeze'—meant that many other such 'sparks' would have had the same effect (Marglin and Schor 1990; Maddison 1991; Wagner 1994).

By way of reaction, Western European governments initially held onto the policy goals of the post-war era—full employment in particular—and used 'neo-corporatist' methods to achieve them (Schmitter 1974, 1985). However, this revival of corporatism was short-lived and a sign already that the organized interests of the pre–Second World War era could not be so easily mobilized decades later.[16] Over the course of the later 1970s and 1980s, relations between capital and labour changed profoundly. This was hardly surprising: unemployment in Europe increased from 5 to 6 million in 1973 to 19 million by 1993, empowering employers over workers (Ginsborg 2003). The growing power of capital over labour was evident in the fall in the share of wages as a proportion of national income, which emerged as a secular trend across all Western European economies (Baccaro and Pontusson 2016). The economic crisis of the 1970s was not just a crisis of capitalist profitability, however. It was also the beginning of the end of the system of interest representation which first emerged in the late nineteenth century and which, as we have described in this chapter, was so central to the formation of the ideological political logic.

As Robert Boyer has written, as well as prompting the 'reconsideration of the contours of most post-war organizational forms', the crisis entailed the 'tearing up of solidarities and of constituted interests' (cited in Wagner 1994). The 'new left' and the social movements of the late 1960s and early 1970s were hostile to corporatism. They were more interested in empowering the shop in the name of workers' democracy—what in France was called *autogestion* (i.e. self-management) and in Italy formed the basis of the *autonomia operaia* movement. The social changes described above, in particular the rise of a new class of service-based workers that blurred the boundaries between blue- and white-collar workers, also made corporatist practices difficult as they were heavily reliant on a clear boundary between workers and employers.

---

[16] On the rise of corporatism in Western Europe after the First World War, see Maier 1975.

Lucio Baccaro and Chris Howell (2011) have argued that for all the variety of industrial relations that existed in Western Europe, since the mid-1970s we have witnessed a steady and unrelenting process of 'convergence'. This has involved the dismantling of a system of bargaining between organized interests and its replacement by individual firms and workers operating and acting within an unmediated field of action. Based on data for fifteen advanced capitalist economies (twelve Western European, plus the United States, Canada, and Australia), they observed that between 1974 and 2005 there was a 'generalized weakening of trade unions', a fall in rates of industrial conflict, and a decentralization of collective bargaining structures (Baccaro and Howell 2011: 529).

Organized interests had been crucial to ideological political competition. They were part of the 'sociologization of the political' that characterized the first half of the twentieth century (Rosanvallon 1998). The legacy of the 1970s economic crisis was a shrunken role for these organized interests, entirely absent in some cases or reduced to pursuing localized deals for individual companies or sectors in other cases. The United Kingdom during the Thatcher era provides a particularly vivid illustration. Building on the developments of the late 1970s, the three successive Thatcher governments of the period between 1979 and 1990 went to great efforts to eliminate the remnants of organized interest representation in the UK. The result was what Jessop et al. have called a 'dual crisis' of the British state: a weak political channel of legitimation and the destruction of the organized interests required for policy coordination and policy implementation (see: Jessop et al. 1984: 1–28).

Although Margaret Thatcher herself paid rhetorical attention to the importance of the family unit as a mediating organism between individuals and the state, her governments did little to fight against the social changes that were making the traditional idea of the family obsolete and difficult to sustain materially. In discussing the actual policies implemented by the Thatcher governments in the social domain, Andrew Gamble notes that: '[d]espite occasional outbursts from Ministers, little was done positively to reinforce the family. Social engineering on the scale required to refashion social relationships to conform to the Conservative ideal was too much to contemplate' (Gamble 1988: 200).

Even though Thatcher's famous statement of 1987 that 'there's no such thing as society' was followed by the assertion that 'there are individual men and woman *and there are families*' (italics added), her legacy was in the realm of a growing individualism and not in the strengthening of family ties. Gamble adds to this a broader point about Thatcherism, noting that it would be wrong to think of it as an ideologically led revolution, as writers for *Marxist Today* did at the time (e.g. Hall 1980).[17] Instead, it was more ad hoc and opportunistic; destructive of existing social organisms but without the capacity to fashion its own.

---

[17] Gamble himself was a contributor to *Marxism Today* in the early 1980s.

Gamble notes that Thatcherism resembled most of all a 'passive revolution from above' (1988: 190). It lacked the sort of mass mobilization of the kind we saw in the interwar era. In the words of Jessop et al. (cited in Gamble 1988: 190), whose own interpretation of Thatcherism emphasized the contrast with the interwar decades of ideological mobilization: 'Where are the Thatcherite new model unions, the Tebbit Labour Front, the Thatcherite Youth, the women's movement, Thatcherite sports leagues, rambling clubs etc.? They do not exist...' The Thatcherite decade of the 1980s ended with a government and state elite increasingly autonomous from society, able to communicate with the mass public principally through the media. The fragmentation of society was due to the longer-term social changes described earlier in this chapter.

The economic policies of the 1980s carried further this hollowing out of state–society relations. The British economy was denationalized and privatized, its labour market made more flexible and specialized (Edgerton 2018: 466). Whilst these policies had an impact across British society as a whole, they were particularly destructive of working-class solidarities that had come to form part of Britain's political and social landscape. Another consequence of the 1980s was the destruction of the left politically, the consequences of which extended to the political right as well. The left and the right need one another for ideological political competition to be sustained and plausible in the eyes of voters. The development of a politics of 'There is No Alternative' (TINA) was therefore a blow to both sides. Stripped of the possibility of articulating alternative political projects, Britain's two main political parties began to converge in the years after Thatcher's departure from power.

Developments in France were very different from Britain, but the underlying effect of a closure of ideological conflicts following the economic crisis of the 1970s was consistent across these cases. An important difference in France was that ideological change at the top was only achieved in 1981, very late in the history of the Fifth Republic. François Mitterrand's 1981 victory was perceived by many as an historic win for the left. The symbolic importance of Mitterrand's victory should not be underestimated, and it leant to the left–right confrontation in France a vitality that was ebbing away from other advanced democracies. Nevertheless, the Mitterrand era was a time of change in France, and as ever with Mitterrand—whose nickname was 'the sphynx'—appearances were deceptive. Mitterrand's electoral success was due in large part to votes coming from the managerial class working within the private sector (Mendras 1988: 64). This change did not last, and many of these voters switched once again in 1986 and in 1993, which gave way to the experiences of cohabitation described above. Mitterrand himself was not a conventional figure for the left and bore little sociological resemblance to the French working class. He peppered his political interventions with references to Greek and Roman myths that left even the most erudite of journalists perplexed. His victory in 1981 was as much a sign that the left had become 'realistic' and was capable of government as it was a testimony to the political capture of the French state by socialism as an ideological project.

When we look more closely at the evolution of Mitterrand's time as President, which ran from 1981 to 1995, we see that he found some resolution to the core constitutive disputes of France's ideological political era, thus ushering in a more consensual age as part of his political legacy. Relevant here is the dispute over the governing of the economy. Mitterrand's ideological 'volte-face' in 1983 signalled—in Mendras's words—a definitive end to French anti-capitalism both on the left and the right (1988: 21). Importantly, it confirmed a long-standing belief on the right that the economy operates according to rules that should not be subject to political manipulation. Mitterrand thus oversaw and reinforced the separation of the economic from the political realm, a striking development given that the unity of the two had been one of the central identifying features of French social democracy. As the journalist Philippe Bauchard put it, the experience for French Socialists in the 1980s was one of a movement 'from dream to reality' (Bauchard 1986). Mitterrand was therefore the socialist President who presided over France's embrace of the market. Whereas in the UK this trajectory was embraced by the government as its main aim, in France it occurred in a more muted and backdoor fashion; the direction of change, however, was the same.

The cartelization of party systems

The second key political development of the period under consideration was a generalized process of 'cartelization' in Western European political regimes over the final few decades of the twentieth century. The latter is a point that has been emphasized in particular by Richard Katz and Peter Mair (1995, 2009, 2018) in their influential work on the evolution of dominant party forms during this period. The key idea is that mainstream political parties responded to the progressive erosion of their traditional bases of social support over the 1960s and 1970s by 'retreating into the state' and beginning to collude with one another to share the benefits of office and power amongst themselves. In Katz and Mair's (1995: 15–17) words,

> A variety of social, cultural and especially political developments may be cited as facilitating or even encouraging a movement towards the anchoring of political parties within the state. These include a general decline in the levels of participation and involvement in party activity... Parties have therefore been obliged to look elsewhere for their resources, and in this case their role as governors and law-makers made it easy for them to turn to the state... In short, the state, which is invaded by the parties, and the rules of which are determined by the parties, becomes a fount of resources through which these parties not only help to ensure their own survival, but through which they can also enhance their capacity to resist challenges from newly mobilized alternatives... Hence we see

the emergence of a new type of party, the cartel party, characterized by the interpenetration of party and state, and also by a pattern of inter-party collusion.

The emergence of the cartel party was consistent with a decline in the substantive competition between political parties. As Katz and Mair explained, '[while] the parties still compete, they do so in the knowledge that they share with their competitors a mutual interest in collective organizational survival and, in some cases, even the limited incentive to compete has actually been replaced by a positive incentive not to compete' (1995: 19–20). Amongst the several important consequences of this, Katz and Mair focus in particular on what they describe as a 'constriction of the policy space'. 'If the "product" offered by parties is policy', they write, 'cartelization would be indicated by limiting competition over policy offered by cartel members, reflected both by narrowing the range of options proposed with regard to any particular policy question and by removing potentially disruptive, cartel-threatening questions from active competition altogether' (Katz and Mair 2018: 136).

Cartelization goes hand in hand with a narrowing of what Otto Kircheimer has called the degree of 'goal differentiation' between mainstream political parties: to the extent that they form a cartel, the latter are encouraged to de-emphasize ideological differences amongst each other, focusing instead on substantive goals they can all agree to. Cartelization adds to the already significant gap between society and the state. As party programmes increasingly resemble one another, there is a 'shrinkage in the degree to which electoral outcomes can determine government actions'. The distinction between parties 'in' office and those 'out' of office becomes blurred, meaning that elections 'cease to be effective channels of communication from civil society to the state' and 'democracy becomes a means of achieving social stability rather than social change' (Katz and Mair 1995: 22–3). We see here how a feedback loop is established within the cartelization process: parties respond to their loss of social bases of support by 'retreating into the state', but this makes them less responsive to societal demands and aspirations and therefore contributes to their further alienation from society.

This dynamic was manifested most clearly by the case of Italy in the late 1970s and early 1980s. In absence of the (perceived) possibility of democratic alternation in power, the *Democrazia Cristiana* continued to expand the government coalition throughout this period. They even managed to include the Communists after the 'historic compromise' struck in 1976. This granted a minority DC government external support from the Italian Communist Party (PCI) in exchange for a variety of offices and benefits at the regional and local levels (Barbagallo 2004). As Luca Falciola has noted, '[a]longside the sempiternal DC, ... the PCI increasingly morphed into a "party of administrators", adept at manipulating the resources of the state and distributing them at the grassroots level using entrepreneurial techniques' (2015: 42). Two years before the 'historic compromise' of 1976, all the mainstream parties of Italy's First Republic cooperated with one another to approve a law instituting public funding for political parties, the so-called 'Piccoli Law' of 1974. By the 1980s, Italy was effectively governed by the '*pentapartito*', a coalition structure composed of all the mainstream political parties within the 'constitutional arch' (i.e. with the exception of the Communists, who returned to opposition at the national level after 1979), which shared out public offices and resources amongst each other according to the logic of '*lottizzazione*'. In Pietro Scoppola's telling, this implied that elections ceased to function as a mechanism for establishing 'who governs' and became instead a way of 'allocating the proportions of public offices and other spoils of government each party was entitled to' (Scoppola 1996).

The other two countries we have been focusing on in this chapter also manifested the logic of cartelization, albeit in slightly less vivid ways. In France, after a brief period of ideological revival surrounding the presidential election of François Mitterrand in 1981, there was an unmistakable convergence in the substantive political agenda of the two main electoral formations (the centre left and the centre right). We observed above how this occurred with regards French political economy and an acceptance—from 1983 onwards—of a separation between the economic and political realm (Bernard 2015). Despite Mitterrand's own ideological grandstanding, particularly in the international sphere, most of his period in office was marked by a rather consensual form of policymaking, made necessary by the two periods of *cohabitation*—between 1986 and 1988 and between 1993 and 1995.[18] While Mitterrand himself focused primarily on foreign policy, two Prime Ministers from the opposite political formation—Jacques Chirac and Edouard Balladur—pursued a programme of market-oriented reforms.

Mitterrand himself was also responsible for some of the ideological closure that occurred during his time as President. One of his promises in his electoral campaign of 1981 was to absorb the French private education sector—made up in large part of Catholic schools—into a single national and secular educational system. Resistance by the country's religious establishments, by the political right,

---

[18] The notion of '*cohabitation*' is used in French political jargon to indicate a situation in which the Presidential and Prime Ministerial positions are occupied by exponents of different political formations. This was made possible by the fact that the constitution of the French Fifth Republic originally set the Presidential term to seven years, whereas the legislative body was to be elected every five years. Thus, after the first five years in office, a President could lose majority support in the National Assembly, which is responsible for nominating the Prime Minister. Although this was always a theoretical possibility since the Fifth Republic's constitution came into effect in 1958, it only materialized in practice for the first time in 1986, when Mitterrand's Socialists experienced a sore defeat in the legislative elections, and then again in 1993 for the same reason. The French constitution was amended in 2000, shortening the Presidential term to five years and therefore effectively foreclosing the possibility of *cohabitation* (even though this still remains in principle possible, since the legislative and executive bodies continue to be elected through separate procedures, which are now separated only by a short interval).

and by a large part of the public, eventually forced Mitterrand to abandon this promise in 1984. This provoked the resignation of his Prime Minister, Pierre Mauroy, who was replaced by a typical representative of the Parisian bourgeoisie, Laurent Fabius. Mendras (1988: 21) summarizes thus:

> The two major conflicts which have divided the French—public sector versus private sector, Church versus the Republican state—promptly disappeared in 1983 and 1984 along with the great myths which had animated them. Unexpected, these events put a symbolic end to a whole century of republican ideology.

Consistent with the logic of cartelization, the Mitterrand era signalled an historic end to some of the country's principal ideological conflicts. Unsurprisingly, their connection to specific social bases weakened, political parties looked beyond dwindling membership fees for new avenues of party financing. Chirac's Gaullist movement (known as the RPR at the time) turned increasingly to the state, but in the form of illicit funds obtained by virtue of Chirac's position as the Mayor of Paris. This scandal involved individuals working directly for the RPR but whose jobs were falsely given as being based at Paris City Hall (*la Mairie de Paris*). Former Prime Minister Alain Juppé was found guilty in 2004 for involvement in this scandal, as was former President Chirac in 2011. Neither served any time in prison.

State transformation in Europe

The third political development of the last few decades of the twentieth century, which contributed in further exacerbating the process of separation between society and politics manifest already by the 1970s, was the process of regional European integration and international cooperation which gathered pace from the mid-1980s onwards (Bickerton, Hodson, and Puetter 2015; Bickerton 2012). After various moves in the late 1970s (from the creation of the European Council to the establishment of a monetary 'snake' arrangement for national currencies) came the Single European Act of 1986, followed by the Maastricht Treaty of 1992, the establishment of the World Trade Organization in 1995 and a succession of revised European treaties over the next two decades.

The key idea here is that from the early 1980s onwards, national executives responded to their growing incapacity to satisfy political demands and aspirations coming 'from below' (i.e. from society) by first forging and then appealing to a new type of political legitimacy 'from above' (i.e. from the international arena). This legitimacy consisted in membership in a series of international treaties and supranational organizations—such as the European Union and the World Trade Organization—which were presented as if they were *ipso facto* markers of political credibility and economic success.

In order to qualify for membership in these supranational organizations, national executives often had to impose rather severe sacrifices on their domestic societies, as was notably the case of Italy, and to some extent also France, during the push in the 1990s to comply with the so-called Maastricht 'convergence criteria' (De Grauwe 2009; Dyson and Featherstone 1999). However, these efforts were justified on the grounds that membership in the relevant regional organizations and international treaties constituted a strategic goal for the country as a whole. These objectives constituted a mechanism for insulating national executives from their domestic societies, through the appeal to intergovernmental agreements that the national executives themselves had made with one another.

Framed as a process of state transformation, we can understand this development in Europe as a transition 'from nation states to member states' (Bickerton 2020a, 2012). Western European nation states had traditionally drawn their political legitimacy from the connection they established between society and politics through the democratic process. The process of European integration in the last couple of decades of the twentieth century has involved a transformation in the nature of statehood itself, whereby member states increasingly draw their political legitimacy from their reciprocal agreements with each other, rather than from their capacity to respond to their domestic societies' political demands and aspirations. This is the distinctive nature of 'member statehood' and it has involved an exacerbation of the disjuncture between domestic societies and their national political systems.

'Member statehood', Bickerton argues, 'is based upon the presumed antagonism between state and society, such that the national government understands its vocation as that of limiting the power and discretion of national populations' (Bickerton 2012: 188). This dramatic acceleration in the process of top-down European integration began in earnest in the mid-1980s onwards, but efforts along these lines marked out the later part of the 1970s already. This process empowered governments, and indeed it was the aim, but in ways that cemented the divorce between political classes and their voters. This process of state transformation in Europe was part of a 'revolt of the elites' whereby the political systems of most advanced Western European democracies responded to the breakdown of their social bases of legitimacy by gradually cutting themselves off from the established mechanisms of domestic political accountability.

The revolt of the elites

The notion of a 'revolt of the elites' was first used by Christopher Lasch (1996) to describe a rather different set of processes taking place at around the same time in the United States. The book emphasizes the secession of the 'upper classes' from their obligations of solidarity with respect to their fellow citizens. We find it apt as a general label to describe the various ways in which the Western European political elites' reacted to their growing loss of legitimacy in the 1960s and 1970s by distancing themselves further from their respective national publics.

Lasch's phrase brings together the three main political developments we have discussed in this section. Whereas the social content of the ideological logic was transformed over the course of the 1950s and 1960s, it was in the 1970s and 1980s that Western political systems adapted to this change. They did so by consolidating their separation from society through changes in economic policy, cartelization, and the turn to transnational policymaking. Instead of seeking to create new mediating links between the society and politics, they capitalized on the collapse of mediating bodies to develop horizontal ties amongst themselves in ways that distanced them even further from voters. This new—and highly attenuated—relationship between politics and society was the basis for the emergence of the new political logic, what we call technopopulism.

The Rise of the Technopopulist Political Logic (1990–2020)

By the beginning of the 1990s, all the structural factors for the emergence of the technopopulist political logic were in place. As we have seen in the previous sections of this chapter, society and politics had for decades been undergoing a process of gradual separation from one another. Peter Mair powerfully summed up this situation at the start of his book entitled *Ruling the Void*, when he stated that, by the end of the twentieth century, the era of party democracy had effectively 'passed': 'Although the parties themselves remain', he wrote, 'they have become so disconnected from the wider society and pursue a form of competition that is so lacking in meaning, that they no longer seem capable of sustaining democracy in its present form' (Mair 2013: 1).

In addition to this separation, and partly as a result of it, Western European societies had experienced an unravelling of its organized interests and various forms of collective solidarity that were the mainstay of the era of the ideological logic.[19] As we stressed in the first section of this chapter, ideologies not only provided frameworks for collective political. They also played a role in structuring the everyday life of individuals—from the sorts of holidays people would take and with whom, to the newspaper they read at home, which football club they supported and which café they would socialize in. The result of this great unravelling was an unmediated relationship between society and politics. Societies were no longer organized around a small number of social cleavages, each with their own extensive organizational accoutrements. They were relatively disorganized and marked by a multiple set of overlapping divisions. A pronounced sense of

---

[19] For an account of this in the case of the United States, see Packer (2013).

individuation, disaggregation, and atomization shaped individual outlooks and sentiments.

This situation was not a stable one but, as we have seen, there is no direct or neat correspondence between social and political change. A number of the processes we describe in our era of transition—such as cartelization and state transformation through regional integration—continue throughout the period we describe here. These processes are as important in sustaining technopopulism as they are in explaining its origins. Before we proceed to look at the development of the technopopulist logic over the last three decade in each our three cases, it is necessary to discuss two more exogenous developments. We situate these outside of the ongoing narrative and discuss them more analytically. This is in part because of their generality but also because one of the two—the Great Recession—has an intermediary role in this narrative, occurring both once the technopopulist logic had emerged and playing some role in its further development. After discussing these two conjunctural factors, we return to our three cases and our ongoing narrative regarding the development of the technopopulist political logic.

The End of the Cold War

The dramatic moment of historical change which precipitated—or at least rendered far more probable—the break-up of the empty carapace of ideological party politics was the end of the Cold War. As several commentators have noted, the Soviet regimes had also been largely 'hollowed out' of their political substance by the end of the 1970s. Nevertheless, their survival as institutional forms into the late 1980s was crucial in maintaining the faith on the left—and the fear on the right— that another type of socio-economic and political regime from the liberal-capitalist one remained possible. When the whole Soviet bloc suddenly collapsed between the end of the 1980s and the beginning of the 1990s, it dealt a fatal blow to much of what remained of the Communist faith in the West (Furet 1995; Hobsbawm 1994).

The most immediate consequence of the collapse of the Soviet bloc in the West was the implosion of virtually all explicitly revolutionary Communist parties, such as the Italian PCI and the French PCF (although the latter happened somewhat more slowly)—two instances that we discuss in more detail below. Above and beyond the fact that the Soviet Union had been materially supporting both these parties throughout the post-1945 period, its collapse had an effect also on the 'radical political imaginary' of Western societies (Furet 1995: 24). The implosion of most Western European Communist parties in the first few years of the 1990s had important repercussions on the organizational and ideological unity and coherence of right and centre-right parties as well. As most Western European conservative—and especially Christian Democratic—parties had effectively morphed into 'anti-Communist coalitions', the latter's disappearance deprived them of their *raison d'être*.

In many cases, the party system and the individual parties within it remained in place. More often than not, there was no change in name. Germany's CDU remained the CDU, as did the SPD. However, the end of the Cold War meant that parties more readily sought out new frameworks through which to preserve the competitive dynamics between themselves. The dynamics of cartelization created internal incentives within the political system itself for a shift away from ideologically charged electoral contests. The end of the Cold War provided a new external environment for parties that complemented these internal incentives, one that obliged parties to rely on new political logics.

This new environment was captured in Fukuyama's well-known 1989 article on 'The End of History', followed up by his 1992 book, *The End of History and the Last Man*. At the end of his 1989 article, Fukuyama had written that 'the end of history will be a very sad time'. 'The struggle for recognition', he continued, 'the willingness to risk one's life for a purely abstract goal, the worldwide ideological struggle that called forth daring, courage, imagination, and idealism, will be replaced by economic calculation, the endless solving of technical problems, environmental concerns, and the satisfaction of sophisticated consumer demands' (Fukuyama 1989: 17–18). Fukuyama hypothesized that this more consensual form of technocratic politics would be likely to generate a political backlash, given its retreat from the more elevated struggles of the ideological era. 'I can feel in myself and see in others around me', he wrote,

> a powerful nostalgia for the time when history existed. Such nostalgia, in fact, will continue to fuel competition and conflict even in the post historical world for some time to come... Perhaps this very prospect of centuries of boredom at the end of history will serve to get history started once again (1989: 18).

A similar reasoning was also applied to the Western European context by Katz and Mair in their reflections on the consequences of the process of cartelization in the 1980s and 1990s. They noted that in 1995 that 'the self-protective mechanisms that the cartel parties have created... have their own internal contradictions' since 'attempts at exclusion offer excluded neophytes a weapon with which to mobilize the support of the disaffected' (Katz and Mair 1995: 23). In their 2018 book on *Democracy and the Cartelization of Political Parties*, Katz and Mair (2018: 180) go further, arguing that:

> What we have been seeing over the recent decades is a growing alliance between the mainstream parties and technocracy (under such labels as the 'regulatory state')... So long as things went well, the parties could maintain this privileged

social position while the technocrats managed societal governance and the populists had little basis for support beyond blatant racism or xenophobia. When things ceased to go well, however, the parties found themselves as the most visible targets for dissatisfaction. From the populist side, they had failed to attend to the interests of the people, instead protecting 'the establishment'. From the technocratic side, they were too quick to bend to political pressure. The result has seen increasingly prominent calls to bypass the politicians, either by granting them ever more independent authority to the technocrats or by replacing them with 'amateurs' at the polls.

The end of the Cold War thus served as a catalyst for the various changes we have described in this chapter. As we show below, the effect was not automatic. It was felt through the specific national experiences of each party system. In some instances, the movement beyond the old ideological order was dramatic and quick, in other cases it was slow, gradual, and worked out from within the existing political order. Nevertheless, both the domestic social content of the ideological logic had gone, along with the international confrontation that had long supported it even after the domestic social struggles had waned.

Technopopulism and the Great Recession

Katz and Mair's comment above about 'when things ceased to go well' refers to a final conjunctural factor which we discuss here - the Great Recession sparked by the global financial meltdown of 2008–11. As Katz and Mair highlight, 'so long as things went well' mainstream political parties managed to hang on to their positions of power in at least some Western European countries (such as most notably France and the UK), despite having lost virtually all connection with their social bases by the beginning of the 1990s. However, the sharp economic downturn experienced by the whole region in the wake of the financial crisis of 2008–11 crystalized the seething social resentment against the established economic and political elites. The strong demand for political renewal made possible the emergence of some of the new and distinctively technopopulist actors we have discussed so far, such as the Five Star Movement. At the same time, the political responses to the economic crisis were themselves shaped by the technopopulist logic, a sign that the logic was already in place and generating its own modes of political action and reaction.

Political establishments across the world, and in advanced democracies in particular, responded to the events of 2008 and the aftermath by reaffirming the economic and political logics that had led to the crisis in the first place. We witnessed a technocratic *fuite en avant*, which involved first of all a massive bailout package for the financial institutions considered 'too big to fail' and subsequently the imposition of tough austerity measures on the populations that were held to be most responsible for the massive expansion in public debt that resulted from this. As Adam Tooze has pointed out in his detailed account of the unfolding of the Great Recession and the political responses to it, this effectively involved a massive upward redistribution of resources, according to the logic of 'socializing risk and privatizing profits' (Tooze 2018).

This particular reading of the financial crisis—namely, the technocratic management of the crisis and the populist backlash to it—has been explored in the existing academic literature on the political consequences of the Great Recession. Various scholars have highlighted the technocratic nature of the way in which the political establishment responded to the economic crisis. Despina Alexiadou and Hakan Gunaydin have shown that the economic crisis led to a significant escalation in the number of explicitly 'technical' or 'technocratic' ministers and governments in office in Continental Europe (of which Italy's Mario Monti and Greece's Lucas Papademos are merely the most prominent examples). The latter were seen, they argue, as a response to 'commitment problems' faced by ordinary politicians (Alexiadou and Gunaydin 2019).

Jonathan White has suggested that the general way in which the crisis was managed manifested a technocratic 'emergency logic' that involved a growing transfer of power from, democratically accountable politicians to informal transnational governance bodies, such as the so-called Troika composed of the European Central Bank, the European Commission, and the International Monetary Fund (White 2020). A former Deputy Governor of the Bank of England, Paul Tucker, argued that one of the principal legacies of the financial crisis was the elevation of central bankers to the 'third great pillar of unelected power, alongside the judiciary and the military'. Tucker warned that this vast expansion in technocratic authority needed to be properly legitimized if citizens were not to feel disenfranchised (Tucker 2018).

Numerous studies have also sought to establish a direct connection between the way in which the Great Recession was handled politically and the proliferation of a wide variety of different forms of anti-establishment populism in its wake. In their book, *European Populism in the Shadow of the Great Recession*, Hanspeter Kriesi and Takis Pappas argue that '[a]s austerity became the new policy norm, economic and social inequalities grew larger, and as European integration appeared to many constituencies as a hopeless project, newly emergent populist leaders rose in several countries to defend the powerless people against sinister elites (Kriesi and Pappas 2015: 1–2). In *The Populist Explosion. How the Great Recession Changed the World*, John Judis (2016) maintains that the Eurocrisis is '*the* triggering factor' that has led to the recent proliferation of both left-wing and right-wing political forces in Continental Europe.

These accounts connect populism and technocracy with the fallout from the financial crisis but they frame them as opposite responses, destined to clash with one another. Kriesi and Pappas recall that when the former Italian Prime Minister Mario Monti stood for re-election in 2013, he appealed to voters to avoid a 'return of populism'. At the same time, the former President of the European Council, Herman Van Rompuy, was sending alarming messages about the 'winds of populism' threatening Europe (Kriesi and Pappas 2015: 1). Conversely, a key component of both Tooze's and Judis's accounts of the political consequences of the Great Recession is the idea that the rise of populism constituted a 'backlash' against the establishment's technocratic way of dealing with it.

We argue instead that populist and technocratic appeals can and are combined in many different ways. At the same time, we need to situate the technocratic and populist dimensions of the financial crisis within the broader narrative about the emergence of the technopopulist political logic. Whilst the events of 2008–11 had the effect of further catalysing this existing development, political responses to the crisis are themselves evidence of the way in which the long-term social and political developments we have been describing in this chapter served as incubators for these types of responses. In the remainder of this chapter, we return to our three cases studies, Italy, France, and the UK. We complete the narrative about the transition from an ideological to a technopopulist political logic, identifying the key events and developments in the national politics of these countries. Doing so helps us see the enduring effects of the end of the Cold War and to understand better the sorts of responses we saw to the 2008 financial crisis that reinforced the existing technopopulist logic.

Italy's Second Republic

Unique amongst the Western democracies considered here, the collapse of Italy's ideological political logic was swift and full of drama. Within the space of just two years, all the main parties that had come to define Italian politics in the course of the twentieth century had disappeared and new political forces had emerged that began to rely upon the synthesis of technocracy and populism for the mobilization of voters. Writing about the 1994 election, Mair observed that 'on the face of it, there is no other established Western party system that has undergone such a profound change' and 'in terms of format, the [Italian party] system has also been totally transformed, with the emergence of new parties and the reconstitution of established parties' (2014: 294).[20] The political crisis of 1992–94 has internal and

---

[20] Mair continues: 'At the electoral level, ... following decades of relative stability, the 1994 contest resulted in a level of volatility of some 37.2%, which is not only the highest figure recorded in Italian history but, even more strikingly, is substantially higher than that recorded in almost any election held in Western Europe between 1885 and 1989 ... [V]irtually none of the parties currently represented in the new 1994 Parliament was represented under the same name or in the same form as recently as 1987' (2014: 294).

external roots, but it is important to recognize it as a crisis of the political logic rather than a crisis of political regime. At the time, there was some comparison made between the collapse of Soviet regimes in Eastern European and the dramatic collapse of Italy's political class. Ginsborg rightfully cautions against this view. As he puts it, 'Italy's crisis was one *within democracy*, in a country which for nearly fifty years had enjoyed free elections and universal suffrage' (2001: 205, italics added).

The first episode in the uprooting of the ideological logic was the disappearance of the Italian Communist Party, the PCI. After the fall of the Berlin Wall towards the end of 1989, the PCI leadership realized that history was moving fast and announced that it would change its name. A few months later, the party decided to call itself the *Partito Democratico della Sinistra* (PDS). A small breakaway faction, *Rifondazione Communista* (RC), retained the original association with the Communist movement. Though many remained loyal to the Communist cause, the double-blow of the swift collapse of the Soviet Union and the symbolic death of the PCI, one of Italy's great mass political parties, was hard to stomach. The disappearance of the PCI—and its evolution into an ideologically much more ambivalent electoral vehicle, the PDS—was a key moment in the waning of ideological political competition in Italy.

Whilst the PCI was hit the hardest by the end of the Cold War, the other governing parties were swept away in part by events but also by a popular reaction against the 'blocked' decade of the 1980s and the cartelized form that Italian politics had assumed during this time.[21] This dissatisfaction was given a clear focus in the crisis of political corruption—*tangentopoli*—which broke out very soon after the April 1992 elections.[22] Led by a team of Milan-based magistrates, this scandal spread over the course of the next six months. It reached the very top of the Italian state in December when Socialist Party (PSI) leader Bettino Craxi was served his first Notice of Guarantee, which was a signal that he was under investigation by the magistrates. Unable to contain the corruption crisis, the government tried to put an end to it altogether. A proposal to decriminalize the illegal financing of political parties was denounced by the public, by leading journalists, and by the President of the Republic himself. By the end of April 1993, the government had collapsed and in its place we saw the formation of a 'presidential government', meaning one put together by the President of the Republic and composed of unelected technocrats.

Carlo Azeglio Ciampi, a respected figure who had been governor of the Bank of Italy since 1979, led the first technocratic government. As Ginsborg observes, 'with his arrival at Palazzo Chigi, the tendency for the Italian "core executive" to

---

[21] The phrase 'blocked decade' refers to the title of one of Ginsborg's chapters in his 2003 book. He describes Italy in the 1980s as having 'a blocked political system'.

[22] *Tagenti* meaning bribes, *tangentopoli* meaning 'bribesville'.

be dominated by non-political experts... reached its apogee'. Ciampi's 'technical administration' ruled for almost a year, until the national elections of March 1994.[23] During Ciampi's time in power, both the DC and the PSI disappeared. The events of 1992–93 signal no less than the complete dismantling of the ideological awning that had been spread over Italian politics for so long. The relative electoral stability of the 1980s and the hegemony of the 'CAF'— the triumvirate of Craxi, Andreotti, and Forlani—had survived in spite of being quite out of sync with a much-changed Italian society. When this awning was blown away by the winds of *tagentopoli*, the first element to replace it was a technocratic government. The elections of March 1994 brought the second element, the new politics of Silvio Berlusconi. If we consider the 1994 election closely, we see that Berlusconi's electoral victory was straight out of a new technopopulist playbook.

Berlusconi had no political organization to speak of when he decided—in late 1993—to enter Italian politics. Though the international media have often presented Berlusconi as something of a buffoon, his movement *Forza Italia* was put together with as much precision as New Labour and its army of spin doctors. As Ginsborg notes, 'never in Italy had the creation of a political force been studied so minutely and scientifically' (2003: 290). In his televised address of the 26th January, announcing his decision to run in the March 1994 elections, Berlusconi denounced the actions of the governing 'left-wing cartel'. In his words, '[n]ever as in this moment does Italy... need people of a certain experience, with their heads firmly on their shoulders, able to give the country a helping hand and to make the state function....'[24] This emphasis on 'good government' and competence were central to Berlusconi's political appeal. His southern coalition with Gianfranco Fini was called *Il Polo del Buon Governo* (the Pole of Good Government). Berlusconi repeatedly presented himself as a force for moderation and balance. Whilst pursuing a deeply personalized campaign that emphasized his role as outsider to the existing political *casta*, Berlusconi chose the mantra of 'I have the necessary competence' as a key message. Ginsborg notes that Berlusconi's 'appeal to many Italians lay in the fact that he was an immensely successful businessman, the incarnation of many of the individual and family dreams that had their origins in the economic "miracle", the antithesis of the career politician who was his opponent' (2003: 292).

At the time, it was common to argue that this victory represented the opening of something new in modern democratic politics. Sartori called it the rise of 'videocracy'; Seisselberg described Forza Italy as a 'media-mediated personality-

---

[23] In his discussion of Ciampi's government of experts, Ginsborg notes that it 'was relatively free from the interminable intra-party feuds of the past, and of the so-called "party delegations" which had ensconced themselves so improperly in the Council of Ministers of previous governments... Ciampi managed to forge his ministers into a team... quite new for Italian politics' (2003: 277).

[24] Cited in Ginsborg 2003: 290.

party' (1996). Guy Hermet tried to capture the paradoxical quality of Berlusconi by arguing that he stood for a form of 'post-ideological anti-politics' (cited in Tarchi 2008). In fact, Berlusconi's originality lay in his ability to draw on both the anti-system sentiments prevalent across Italian society, fuelled in large part by disgust at the discoveries of private gain by vast numbers of elected representatives, and the desire for better and less partisan forms of politics that were rooted in competence and experience. When the ideological scaffolding of Italian politics was brought down by the complex crisis of 1992–93, these two pillars—populism and technocracy—were swiftly erected in the place of the void left by the collapse of the governing parties.

As yet, however, technopopulism had not stabilized itself as a political logic. In the 1994 campaign, Berlusconi had not really fused technocracy and populism into a single and coherent political offer. Technocracy was still bound up with a notion of governing 'outside of politics', at a distance from electoral competition, in the style of the Ciampi government of 1993–94. Most importantly, the crisis of 1992–93 was not yet over. In November 1994, at a G7 meeting in Naples, Berlusconi was given his own Notice of Guarantee. This was enough to lead to the collapse of the centre-right coalition and the formation of a second 'presidential government' of technocrats, led this time by Lamberto Dini, an economist who had served in Berlusconi's short-lived government but was not a politician in any classical sense.[25] Though Berlusconi was not to return until 2001, the centre-left government which ruled between 1996 and 2001 was as far a cry from a return to ideological politics as one could imagine. This period reinforced the move away from an ideological logic and the narrowing of political possibilities that came with an increasingly technocratic form of public debate. This shrinking of the policy space was principally due to the centre-left government's determination that Italy should join the euro in the 'first wave', thus imposing upon it a series of restrictive macro-economic conditions. During this time, elements of the old political party cartel returned to Italian politics, generating another round of political disenchantment.

The beginnings of a technopopulist synthesis occurred when Berlusconi returned to power five years later. This time he won a majority in both the Parliament and the Senate. The Forza Italia vote reached almost 30 per cent whilst the DS won 16.6 per cent.[26] Forza Italia's electoral campaign was both intensely personal and focused on the same theme of competence. Berlusconi continued to emphasize his identity as an entrepreneur rather than a career politician. The importance of the notion of entrepreneur to Berlusconi's political campaigns was illustrative of its technopopulism. The term itself is non-ideological and socially

---

[25] Ginsborg 2003: 299–300.
[26] The PDS had renamed itself the DS, the Democratic Left. It would soon become just the Democratic Party (PD), dropping the ideological identifier altogether.

empty, that is to say that it can potentially mobilize all the electorate rather than a particular segment and it does not play on the typical ideological tropes of either left or right. Berlusconi's celebration of the entrepreneur was a celebration of action, of doing, in opposition to just talk or mere thinking. It associated Berlusconi with this 'man of action' and suggested his voters could aspire to the same. As an actor, the entrepreneur is outside of party politics, and Berlusconi was thus able to cement his own appeal as someone quite different from the career politicians. By focusing on the entrepreneur, Berlusconi was able to combine his attack on the political *casta* with a promise of governing through action and through results.

If we think of his politics within the context of the technopopulist political logic, we can see that there is a thread of continuity that connects Berlusconi to the rest of the Italian political system, on the left in particular. In the 1990s, the centre left had governed in a way that advanced above all the 'technocratization' of Italian politics, particularly around securing Italy's place within the new European single currency. We have observed since then a certain 'Berlusconization' of the left, which in essence means its own embrace of many aspects of technopopulism.[27] If we consider some of the features of Matteo Renzi, who took over the leadership of the Democratic Party in 2013, we can see how the structuring logic of technopopulism spread from the Italian right to the left.

Renzi quite explicitly adopted some of the populist tropes of Berlusconi, above all in his savvy use of the media and in his cultivation of a populist style that was both anti-intellectual and self-consciously light-hearted. This was done in order to differentiate Renzi from the austere and highbrow figures usually found on the Italian left. Renzi appeared on a popular TV show, *Amici*, aired on one of Berlusconi's channels, wearing a black bomber jacket and giving high-fives to audience members. He even joked about his resemblance to Fonzi from *Happy Days*. When he was asked once by Guiliano Amato, a serious and cerebral political figure, the title of the last book that he had read, Renzi was only able to give an awkward and vague response. However, far from this being a weakness, Renzi made this combination of celebrity status and anti-intellectualism into a badge of honour and used it as a basis for interacting in a more 'authentic' way with those he calls *la gente* (ordinary folk).

Renzi also emulated Berlusconi in his relationship to the *Partito Democratico*, the PD. Like Tony Blair's transformation of the Labour Party, Renzi took up the reins of the party but in a manner that firmly established himself as an outsider. He first made a national name for himself when he declared in 2010 that the PD should 'junk' its political leadership, a statement which resulted in Renzi having the moniker of '*il rottomatore*', the scrapper. In his own bid to take over the

---

[27] This section draws on Bickerton and Invernizzi Accetti (2014), especially the part 'The Legacy of "Berlusconism" for the Italian left', 24–7.

leadership of the PD in 2013, Renzi successfully argued that the primaries should be open, to include the electorate at large and not only restricted to party members. Well aware of the strength of the PD political apparatus, which harks back to its origins as the mass party of the radical left, Renzi wanted to efface the boundary between the party and wider society in order to recast the PD as a 'People's Party', as Blair did with the Labour Party. Successful in his bid for leadership, Renzi used the support he enjoyed from outside of the party to weaken the internal opposition. Renzi's own campaign for the leadership created as much distance as possible from the PD. He relied on images of himself and eschewed entirely the use of the PD's traditional symbols. Renzi argued that his goal was to appeal to as many people as possible and associate them with an inclusive and common project, not to divide Italy across partisan or ideological lines. As with New Labour, this plebiscitarian approach to party management sought to create a more direct and personal relationship between the party leader and the electorate, whilst at the same time empowering a select group of experts and officials deployed by the leader to study and monitor public opinion.

Another way in which Renzi built upon Berlusconi's technopopulism was in his adherence to what Ivo Diamanti (2010) described as *l'ideologia del fare* (the ideology of doing). On the populist side, there is the insistence that one's record be judged in line with a set of personal engagements made directly with the people themselves. Just before the 2001 elections, Berlusconi signed live on television a 'contract with the Italian people'. Renzi built his leadership of the PD around a similarly limpid and synthetic approach. He won the PD leadership on the back of four simple proposals: to abolish the senate, streamline the administrative state, reform the electoral law, and reform the justice system. Renzi contrasted these clear set of personal commitments with the tortuously long (150 pages) government programme drafted by Romano Prodi's coalition in the run-up to the 2006 election. The technocratic bent of this 'ideology of doing' comes from the definition of goals in advance, evacuating any need for ongoing debate or deliberation. Judgement takes the form of an assessment of whether the promises were met, of whether the 'job was done' or not. This oriented politics entirely around the notion of results, which is the obvious corollary of the focus on 'doing'. As Diamanti (2010) observed, if the defining feature of one's political identity is that one is capable of 'Doing', then it doesn't matter so much *what* one does, just that one *can* do it. In taking over the leadership of the PD, Renzi said nothing about the economic crisis or austerity; he simply promised to honour Italy's commitments to the EU. In the orientation towards outputs and results, we find the thread that connects Berlusconi with Renzi. Berlusconi's emphasis on the entrepreneur was aimed at highlighting his ability 'to deliver results'. Renzi has similarly sought to build his political offer around ideologically neutral terms, such as 'change' or 'progressive reform'. He associated his political programme with the notion of 'youth', which Renzi defined as a state of mind rather than any particular age. In the same way that, according to Berlusconi, anyone could be an entrepreneur, Renzi claimed that anyone could be 'young'.

Given this account of the emergence of the technopopulist logic in Italy, we can see that the *Movimiento Cinque Stelle* (discussed in detail in chapter two) did not develop in a vacuum. The 1992–94 crisis in Italian politics brought down in spectacular fashion the ideological politics that had existed for many decades in Italy. The technopopulist logic, more consistent with the social changes that Italy had known in the preceding decades, swiftly took its place. This was principally the work of Silvio Berlusconi, but as a structuring logic of politics it was taken up by Matteo Renzi on the left. Whilst the M5S has always portrayed itself as viscerally opposed to both Berlusconi and the PD, its own technopopulist political synthesis draws extensively on their legacy.

The Hollowing Out of the French Party System

French politics in the post-Mitterrand era was characterized above all by a social and political malaise that grew in intensity throughout the two terms of the Jacques Chirac presidency (1995–2002 and 2002–7). Traditional parties and political rhetoric continued to dominate the political scene but without being able to convincingly translate the wishes and aspirations of voters into political outcomes. Suzanne Berger writes about this period that 'the traditional contours of the left and the right have evolved and have become vaguer, without any new conception of how society should be organized...or the role of France in the world being developed in its place' (2006: 426). She calls this the crisis of the French representative system. The 1990s and early 2000s saw the emergence of a strong sentiment of '*dégagisme*', that is, the desire to punish and kick out incumbents. Some of this was a response to the political scandals that tainted the end of Mitterrand's rule and remained a constant of Jacques Chirac's time in office, particularly regarding illegal methods of party financing.[28] In the legislative elections of 1997, after which a socialist government had to 'cohabit' with a right-wing presidency, around half of those on the electoral lists abstained or voted for an 'anti-system' party (Berger 2006: 424). Those candidates present in

---

[28] One such scandal, known as *l'affaire Elf*, involved the use of embezzled funds for financing political parties, self-enrichment, and the payment of bribes. Some leading Socialist politicians were implicated in the affair, such as Mitterrand's former Foreign Minister, Roland Dumas, who held the office between 1986 and 1993. German Chancellor, Helmut Kohl, was also implicated, as some of the money from Elf had been used to finance the Christian Democratic Union (CDU). The other scandal which dogged Chirac for many years, and which we described above, was the creation of fictitious jobs at the Mayor's office in Paris in order to raise money for his political campaigns. On the Elf affair, see Heilbrunn 2005.

the second round of presidential elections had won 54 per cent of the votes in 1981 and 1988; in 2002, they won no more than 36.6 per cent of the votes (Balme 2006: 383).

It is in this context that we must situate the electoral 'earthquake' of the first round of the presidential election on 21st April 2002. The main contenders were the incumbent President Jacques Chirac and his socialist Prime Minister, Lionel Jospin. Both had been widely expected to make it to the second round run-off. In the end, with a low turnout of 71.6 per cent (cf. 81.4 per cent in 1988), Jospin won only 16.18 per cent of the vote, approximately 200,000 votes behind the leader of the *Front national*, Jean-Marie Le Pen. The election was marked by remarkable fragmentation, particularly on the left where around six different candidates stood with scores varying from 5.72 per cent for the Trotskyite Arlette Laguiller to 0.47 per cent for another Trotskyite, Daniel Gluckstein. The most significant development was the downwards trajectory in the vote share of the French Socialist Party (PS). From a height of 34.1 per cent of the vote in the first round of the presidential election in 1988, its vote had more than halved by 2002. The vote itself came as an enormous surprise and generated much soul-searching within the French elite, in the media, and amongst the public at large. In its aftermath, journalists travelled far into the provinces, writing profiles of the *Front national* voter, a 'species' hitherto unknown to the urban middle classes. Writing about the 2002 result, Richard Balme (2006: 379) argues that

> [T]he crisis revealed in 2002 is, in essence, the result of a growing distance between citizens and politics, which takes two forms. One is that citizens have lost their identification with the main political cleavages that structure the partisan system. The other is that the public perceptions around mediocre government performance and corruption have generated scepticism and suspicion vis-à-vis political organizations and their leaders.

We can see in Balme's description of public sentiment the beginnings of the new political logic of technopopulism. The growing obsolescence of class-based cleavages for understanding political behaviour point towards a generalization of political outlooks and the multiplication of appeals to the people as a whole rather than to distinctive groups within society. Widely felt anger at the poor performance of the political class creates demand for effective government, for improved performance, for more competent leaders.

We also find in the crisis of 2002 a confirmation of France's retreat from the 'structured democracy' described by Rosanvallon earlier in this chapter. Mediating bodies capable of connecting individuals with the exercise of power and its symbolic expression in the form of the republican state tradition have atrophied. One of France's leading journalists, Serge July, captured this in his editorial for *Libération* a couple of days after the first round of 2002, when he wrote that:

All the intermediary bodies are in an advanced state of decomposition, and have been over the last twenty years. We can see that this process of disaggregation is picking up pace and the discontent is continuous. Political parties, trade unions, social forces, administrations, and schools are all weakened, none is able to support society, to organize its words, to provide accountability, to create links between political powers and social actors, salaried workers or those excluded from society and politics (cited in Berger 2006).

Chirac's victory in the second round of the 2002 presidential election, with over 82 per cent of the vote, did nothing to address these problems. At the time, the second round was described as a choice 'between a crook and a fascist'—the height of political disenchantment.[29] In the regional elections of 2004, the political spectrum swung wildly in the other direction, with the Socialists wining power in almost all of the country's regions. Then in 2005, again much to the surprise of all the country's political elite and its media, a majority voted to reject the Constitutional Treaty of the European Union. These votes had no common ideological thread running through them. Instead, each was connected by the wish to sanction the parties in power—the left in 2002, the right in 2004, and both the left and the right in 2005 (Berger 2006: 425).

Partly due to his own origins within the French ideological political framework—born in 1932 and the leading figure on the French Gaullist centre right for four decades—Chirac was unable to bring together the two strands of populism and technocracy which had begun to structure political life in France around the turn of the twenty-first century. The beginnings of the technopopulist synthesis came instead with Nicolas Sarkozy, President of France for one term (2007–12). The 2007 election was itself an indication of changes within French politics. The Socialist Party candidate, Ségolène Royale, chose to run at a distance from her own party, creating from scratch an election vehicle known as *Desirs d'Avenir*. This mobilized large numbers of young activists but failed to connect with the French population at large. In organizational terms, Sarkozy was able to take control of the centre-right party, known then as the *Union pour un Mouvement Populaire* (UMP), and avoid the divisions and infighting that plagued Royale's bid for the presidency. Sarkozy's treatment of the UMP was, however, largely instrumental. For instance, he hired the Boston Consultancy Group, a management consultancy firm, to help him write his election manifesto (Musso 2008: 108). By way of a justification for this, Sarkozy's *chef de cabinet* explained that BCG's role was principally to 'give coherence' to the UMP leadership. BCG recorded interviews with members of the public who held contradictory views on

---

[29] 'Votez escroc, pas facho', *Liberation*, 23 April 2002: https://www.liberation.fr/evenement/2002/04/23/votez-escroc-pas-facho_401301.

a subject and asked leading UMP politicians to respond. Initially, the politicians would simply agree with the person asking the question in order to avoid conflict. BCG's role was to train the UMP politicians to be more consistent and less deferential to public opinion, so that voters would come to associate UMP with a set of principles, to believe, in other words, that politicians stood for something beyond their own self-interest. We find here a remarkable reversal in the functions of the political party and the content of its partisan offer. The UMP under Sarkozy became an electoral vehicle, quite empty in terms of substantive principles. In order to find these principles, the party sought the help of outside experts. Management consultants had become, in the French political system, the means by which politicians could be 'trained' in how to be principled and consistent in their messaging to voters.

Unsurprisingly, given the leading role played by Boston Consultancy Group in the creation of his programme, Sarkozy as a politician embraced the technopopulist contours beginning to emerge in the post-ideological French political landscape. The greatest emphasis in his campaign was on 'results', on delivering changes that the French people were asking for. From the outset, Sarkozy was defined—and ridiculed—for his incessant energy, for the speed with which he wanted to achieve changes. His 2007 campaign was full of policy promises and political rhetoric that cut across ideological lines. He denounced 'hooligan CEOs' in his bid to win over those worried about corporate excess and rising inequality. He also put great emphasis on environmental policies. There was no single ideological thread that held his campaign together. It was defined by his commitment to 'deliver' on his promises and his undeniable personal energy and desire to 'get things done'.

Once in power, Sarkozy carried these promises over into his role as President, taking a largely pragmatic approach to most issues. Upon taking up the rotating presidency of the European Union in July 2008, Sarkozy declared that he was committed above all to a 'Europe of results'. When it was announced that France would rejoin NATO's integrated military command structure, he argued that this was not an ideological betrayal of the Gaullist legacy but simply a common-sense approach to ensuring the security of French citizens. The choices Sarkozy made regarding the composition of his government are revealing. He made much during the campaign of opening up to the left, and in his first government he appointed key figures from outside the Gaullist right. Bernard Kouchner, a famous humanitarian activist and founder of *Médecins Sans Frontières* (MSF) was appointed Foreign Minister; Eric Besson and Jean-Pierre Jouyet, the former a high-ranking Socialist official who left the PS to join Sarkozy and the latter a senior civil servant who had been in the cabinets of two prominent French socialist politicians, Jacques Delors and Lionel Jospin, both entered Sarkozy's government. Jouyet is particularly interesting since he has been both a mentor and prominent supporter of Emanuel Macron (Jouyet 2020).³⁰

Though much of the writing about Sarkozy has been through an exclusively ideological lens (e.g. Badiou 2009), some observers did grasp the novelty of the 2007–12 presidency. Pierre Musso coined the term '*Sarkoberlusconisme*' to describe the style of political rule common to both Nicolas Sarkozy in France and Silvio Berlusconi in Italy (Musso 2008). In Musso's definition of *sarkoberlusconisme*, he emphasizes the manner in which both Sarkozy and Berlusconi tried to model politics on the world of business. His neologism refers to 'a Latin neo-liberalism deploying references to business and to a managerial dogma, presented theatrically by marketing and audio-visual tools' (2008: 14). As Musso notes, Sarkozy transformed this fondness for jogging (principally in the Bois de Boulogne, which was adjacent to Neuilly-sur-Seine where he was Mayor for almost twenty years) into a political mantra. On his website under the heading 'what I believe', the answer was 'I believe in movement. In a world that is constantly changing, France cannot stay still' (2008: 115). Much as with Matteo Renzi's own ideology of 'doing', Sarkozy's commitment to constant movement makes it difficult to reflect at length on where one wants to go. In fact, this is relegated as secondary to the importance of movement itself.

Positioned in between the presidencies of Sarkozy and Emanuel Macron was the presidency of François Hollande (2012–17) This did not constitute any real caesura in the development of the technopopulist logic. Hollande's attempts at reviving ideological conflict were noteworthy for their weak and almost accidental quality. During the campaign of 2012, where he ran against Nicolas Sarkozy, Hollande promised that anyone earning over a million euros would be taxed at 75 per cent. This proposal made sense as part of a programme defended by a Socialist candidate committed to social justice and reducing income inequality. However, in 2012, it bore the hallmarks of the sort of soundbite politics we associate with Blair and Berlusconi. Hollande's announcement took his campaign team entirely by surprise and had to be retrospectively put together in the hours and days following his declaration. Once in power, it was steadily abandoned. The same artificial quality to Hollande's pronouncements can be found in his speech in January 2012, where he declared that 'my real enemy is finance.' As two journalists have recounted in their published interviews with Hollande, as this speech was

---

³⁰ There is an interesting parallel between Bernard Kouchner and Nicolas Hulot, who Macron appointed as his Environment Minister in his first government. Both Hulot and Kouchner were known as principled activists, willing to break with political protocol in order to achieve what they considered morally justified ends. Their appointment signalled both a non-partisan approach to politics and a favouring of interventionist and active figures rather than more cautious diplomats. Hulot was only minister for just over a year (May 2017–September 2018). Kouchner was foreign minister between 2007 and 2010 and had a longer career of various government appointments.

delivered, a person in the audience threw a shoe at the presidential candidate. It failed to hit its target, landing a few feet in front of him and sliding up to the bottom of the lectern. Hollande himself remarked that had the shoe hit the spot, his campaign would probably have been over.[31] As it happens, this was the speech that 'turned' the campaign in his favour. Politics often rests upon a certain degree of chance and good fortune, but Hollande's own presidency seems to have been almost accidental. He was successful principally because he capitalized on enormous anti-Sarkozy sentiment, itself an extension of the anti-incumbency feeling described above that shaped the 2002 presidential elections, the 2004 regional polls, and the 2005 EU Treaty referendum. This sentiment carried him to the Elysée palace but faded quickly, leaving Hollande as an unpopular and much-mocked figure for the duration of his time in power. Far from reaffirming the vitality of the ideological politics in France, Hollande's presidency was a testimony to its obsolescence.

The UK after Blairism

We discussed in detail in chapter 2 the phenomenon of New Labour, which covers an important part of the time period that we associate with the establishment of the technopopulist logic. As a result, in this section we focus on British politics *after* Tony Blair's departure from power in 2007, where we see different ways in which the Blairite technopopulist synthesis was taken up and modified by his successors. Our starting point for our narrative is the policy consensus that reigned in the UK over the course of the 2000s, what British historian David Edgerton has called 'Blatcherism' and which he suggested was far more powerful as a form of consensus than the Butskellism of earlier decades. According to Edgerton, '[t]he period from the mid-1990s was the period of the greatest identity of views between the major parties since 1950, or indeed since 1900 . . . The lack of contestation over the key issues and practices of government was by twentieth-century historical standards extraordinary' (Edgerton 2018: 507). This lack of contestation had created a systematic division between the British political class and 'the rest', in the words of the British journalist Peter Oborne, who wrote a book in 2007 entitled *The Triumph of the Political Class*. Oborne found that British politics had been to all extents and purposes fully cartelized.

Following Tony Blair's resignation as Prime Minister in 2007, the British Labour Party remained in power under the leadership of Blair's long-time political ally (and former rival), Gordon Brown. Lacking his predecessor's charisma and popular appeal, Brown was never able to offer as effective a synthesis of populist

---

[31] Davet and Lhomme 2016: 18. See also Bickerton 2017.

and technocratic traits, though this was not from want of trying. During his decade as Chancellor of the Exchequer, Brown had gained the reputation as a competent administrator, one committed deeply to policy issues (whilst also prone to micro-managing and to fits of anger with his staff). This reputation continued upon his assuming the prime ministership. Brown's first major policy decision as Chancellor in 1997 had been to grant independence to the Bank of England in the setting of monetary policy and exchange rates (King 2005), a move which aimed to take controversial macro-economic decisions out of the hands of elected politicians. Ironically, most of his time as Prime Minister was consumed by the fallout of the global financial meltdown that was triggered by the collapse of the US investment bank Lehman Brothers in September 2008, just over a year after he took office. This involved major policy decisions about the state's role in the economy and how to support and then regulate an outsized financial sector. As we noted above, political responses to the financial crises were highly technocratic in the manner in which they were taken and also presented to the public. Brown acted promptly and decisively but also in a top-down and opaque way. By October of 2008, Brown's government had passed a £500 billion bank rescue package, modelled on the one also put in place by George Bush in the United States. This succeeded in stymieing the immediate threat of a run on the banks but it could not prevent an economic recession, which lasted into the second quarter of 2009 (Tooze 2018).

With a lagging recovery and growing social resentment against the way the crisis had been managed, Brown was voted out of office at the 2010 national elections. Most other Western European incumbents that faced re-election at the height of the economic crisis enjoyed the same fate, with the notable exception of Angela Merkel. However, Brown's tenure as Prime Minister was also cut short in part due to the difficulty he found in complementing his obvious expertise and grasp of policy detail with the more direct and personal connection with an electorate that is critical when political competition is shaped by the technocratic political logic. Brown flirted with the odd populist slogan, such as his call for 'British jobs for British workers', made at his first Labour Party conference speech as leader in September 2007. This was reiterated once again during wildcat strikes of 2009 that broke out across oil refineries and power plants in the UK, in opposition to reliance by employers on workers from other EU member states. But what defeated Brown was his inability to 'connect' with voters. One episode of the 2008 general election was telling in this regard. Visiting the former textile-manufacturing town of Rochdale in the North of England, Gordon Brown's stage-managed walkabout included a discussion with Mrs Duffy, a pensioner. Duffy challenged Brown about the number of EU migrants coming into the UK. After amicably ending the conversation, Brown was overheard in his car complaining bitterly about this 'ridiculous' meeting, dismissing Duffy as some 'bigoted woman'.[32] Brown's contempt was unmistakeable, and the incident cemented his reputation as competent but lacking in any 'personal touch'.

The return to power of the Conservatives under the premiership of David Cameron (initially relying on a coalition government with Nick Clegg's Liberal Democrats and then governing alone with a majority of twelve after the 2015 election) demonstrated the influence of technopopulism on the British political system. During the 2010 election campaign both Cameron and Clegg expressed admiration for Blair's achievements. Cameron went as far as to present himself as an 'heir' to Blair's legacy, in a backhanded attempt to draw a wedge between himself and Brown's more stolid, old-school approach. The most striking element of the 2010 campaign, however, was the emergence of Nick Clegg, leader of the Liberal Democrats and a figure relatively unknown to the public before the start of the campaign. Though the origins of his party go back to the early period of the British party system, Clegg stood out for his technopopuist appeal. Clegg cast himself as the outsider, the leader of the 'third' party that would finally break the monopoly on power held by Labour and the Conservatives. He presented himself as the answer to what he called 'this huge disillusion at the ding-dong two-party stuff' (Ferguson 2010). Though his opponents were not old (Brown was fifty-nine, Cameron was forty-three), Clegg made much of his 'youth' (forty-three, the same age as Cameron). This disruptive image was relayed incessantly and proved very successful in light of the parliamentary expenses scandal of the previous year, an unprecedented political crisis which had galvanized public disgust with mainstream politicians. At the same time, Clegg's political offer emphasized his competence and his dislike for ideological grandstanding. Clegg's own relationship to liberalism as an ideology was far from dogmatic: during his time in Brussels working at the Commission, his boss was the Tory grandee Leon Brittan. Trying to understand Clegg's success in the 2010 campaign, one observer found the answer in Clegg's commitment to policy detail. Asked a difficult question about pay in the Royal Air Force, 'Clegg's answer was so detailed, in terms of specifics about the money and what he would really do to service accommodation, that it won spontaneous applause' (Ferguson 2010). In his own retrospective account of his time a Deputy Prime Minister, entitled *Politics Between the Extremes* (Clegg 2016), Clegg's arguments draw heavily on his many technocratic traits. He defends the Liberal Democrats' decision to enter into government as a junior coalition partner with the Conservatives in the name of responsible and sensible government, particularly given the scale of the economic crisis at the time. He

---

[32] Brown had left switched on the lapel microphone installed for the walkabout. Sky News captured the discussion and it was replayed to Mrs Duffy, who was visibly appalled at the way the Prime Minister spoke about her.

describes his time as Deputy Prime Minister—where he was heavily criticized for giving up on certain policy commitments, such as the promise not to raise tuition fees for university students—as trying to 'deliver sensible policies' and to 'moderate Tory extremism' (Runciman 2016). In his review of Clegg's book, David Runciman notes that 'Clegg keeps telling us that he took decisions on their merits, having done his homework, unlike his Tory partners in government who were more often looking for party political advantage.' Clegg's principal defence of his time in office is that he was driven by his commitment to 'doing the right thing' rather than just what was in the interests of his political party.

Assuming office at the head of a coalition in 2010, Cameron declared that he intended to 'put aside party differences and work hard for the common good and for the national interest' (Hough 2010). In a famous joint press conference with Cameron and Clegg in the Downing Street rose garden in May 2010, Cameron justified the compromises of being in a coalition as necessary for 'good government'. In practice, this took the form of a rather tough set of austerity measures, which were intended to balance the budget by extending many of the market-oriented reforms that had been pursued by the New Labour government. Under Cameron's premiership, the Royal Mail was privatized, and severe spending cuts were imposed on various areas of public service, including transport, research, and defence. Although the National Health Service's budget was in principle 'ring-fenced' from the austerity measures, it was nonetheless put through a significant structural overhaul, which was widely perceived as 'gutting' the much-cherished national programme (Borges et al. 2013). Much of these measures were justified as part of the economic emergency which had broken out in 2008, as well being attempts at resolving problems brought about by Labour's immediate response to the crisis. In terms of its own distinctive and substantive contribution, Cameron's time as Prime Minister is emblematic of the desubstantialization of the techno-populist era. Some of the larger ideas that he aired in the early years of his leadership—such as 'the big society'—had little by way of policy substance. When Cameron launched his 'big society' idea in 2010, he described it as 'the biggest, most dramatic redistribution of power from elites in Whitehall to the man and woman on the street', and one that would lay the basis for better policies in areas such as transport or the development of broadband internet (Watt 2010). However, this 'redistribution' coincided with a significant reduction in state support for a variety of social initiatives, making it easy to paint Cameron's idea as a return to some notion of Victorian philanthropy.

It is unsurprising that Cameron's principal political legacy was neither in the realm of policy or shifts in Conservative Party ideology; it was the pledge he made in the run-up to the 2015 national elections to hold a referendum on British membership in the European Union. Re-elected with a small majority, Cameron proceeded with the vote, which was held in June 2016. The Brexit vote itself has shown the extent of the British political class's detachment from society and the degree to which the technopopulist political logic has penetrated into its partisan politics and institutional culture. Both the mainstream political parties—as well as the vast majority of the country's political, economic, and cultural establishment—supported the Remain option. However, the electorate proved to be much more divided on the issue. The way in which the Remain campaign attempted to persuade it was through what was described as 'project fear'; that is, by maintaining that Brexit would have disastrous consequences, both socially, politically, and especially economically (Clarke et al. 2017). This had the effect of configuring the options as a choice between economic rationality on one hand and a fusion of patriotic nationalism and anti-establishment sentiment on the other; that is, in a sense, technocracy vs. populism. This opposition was emblematically captured by one of the most prominent exponents of the Leave campaign, Michael Gove, in the rum-up to the 2016 vote when he stated that: 'the people in this country have had enough of experts' (Mance 2016).

The results of the referendum revealed a deep fissure not just within British society as a whole, but also within the electorates of the two main political parties. Although Leave won a narrow majority of 52 per cent, the division cut across the traditional partisan divide. This made it difficult for the incumbent political class to deliver on the results of the referendum. The Leave camp was marked by internal divisions and disarray in the immediate aftermath of the vote, since by most accounts they had not expected to win. The person who rose to fill the power vacuum left by Cameron's immediate resignation was the Home Secretary, Theresa May, a supporter of the UK remaining in the EU but who had taken a back seat during the referendum campaign. May's reputation as a politician was built around her hard work and determination, more 'tenacity' than 'flair' (Runciman 2017). Whereas Cameron's rise to the Tory leadership had an air of ease and inevitability about it, May's rise to the top was a product of effort and came with a list of policies that she had been responsible for as minister, particularly at the Home Office.

It was a paradox of the post-Brexit political landscape that a politician with very little popular appeal, whose success had stemmed from the seriousness with which she treated every task she undertook, was made Prime Minister in order to implement the result of a popular referendum, which its supporters had described as a populist backlash against the establishment. May's time as Prime Minister, from mid-2016 through to the summer of 2019, was shaped by this paradox, and there are many different manifestations of the technopopulist logic bound up with the attempts by May to honour her pledge that 'Brexit means Brexit'. The British institutional framework still required any deal to be approved by Parliament, which remained deeply divided on the issue. While there was always a negative majority able to strike down any concrete proposal, there was never a positive one in favour of anything specific. As well as there being an obvious division between

Leave and Remain supporters both within Parliament and in the country as a whole, the divisions around Brexit also pointed to an overall *fragmentation* of political values and interests, which made it difficult for any positive political programme to succeed (Hagemann 2018). May's difficulties also stemmed from the dissolution of political party discipline within the parliamentary parties: for a good deal of the time that she was Prime Minister, the traditional whipping operations that ensure that the government's will can be transformed into law disappeared altogether, leaving May exposed to repeated and uncontrolled outbreaks of rebel behaviour from within her own party. A similar difficulty faced the Labour leader, Jeremy Corbyn, whose own MPs regularly flouted his policy on Brexit. Fragmentation took on a very concrete form when some individuals MPs abandoned their parties altogether, forming an independent group within Parliament.

May's own actions were also constrained by outside pressures which followed a technopopulist logic. May's ambitions for her premiership were centred not only on delivering Brexit but on responding to the anger she felt existed across the country, articulated by those who thought of themselves as 'just about managing' (the 'jams'). As she delivered her first speech to the British public as Prime Minister, on the 13th July 2016 on the steps of Downing Street, she addressed this despair head on: 'I know you are working around the clock', she said, 'I know you are doing your best and I know that life can sometimes be a struggle'. 'The government that I lead', she promised in a swipe at her Etonian-educated predecessor, 'will not be driven by the interests of the privileged few but by yours'. And yet, at the same time, helicopters circling overhead were policing a demonstration outside the gates of Downing Street, where protestors demanded that the new Prime Minister 'trigger Article 50 now'. These demands did not come with any answers to the question of what future relationship exactly the UK would have with the EU—in or out of a Customs Union, what sort of free trade deal, or the implications of Brexit for the Northern Irish border. Rather, they amounted to a simple populist demand that May honour the 'wishes of the people'. As one campaigner put it, 'The entire elite wants to delay Article 50. We must fight them' (Whelan 2016). Ironically, the effect of triggering Article 50 was to tie the UK into a time-limited negotiation that removed the substantive discussion of the shape of future UK–EU relations from the public sphere, and relocated it entirely behind closed doors, where negotiations would take place between nominated groups of experts. Triggering Article 50 ushered in a period of Brexit negotiations overseen by Michel Barnier's team in the European Commission and the UK government team led by first by Ollie Robbins and then later by David Frost. May's Brexit policy was built up out of this fusion of populist and technocratic elements, which itself mirrored the ways in which appeals to the people and appeals to expertise had shaped the British debate on EU membership throughout the referendum campaign. Byond her capacity for hard work and diligence, May had built her political career around the firm conviction that if a promise is made, then it should be honoured.[33] The fact that her premiership was so marked by these populist and technocratic pressures, at the exclusion of any progress on those issues she felt most strongly about, demonstrates once again the force of the technopopulist logic. In the unravelling of May's prime ministership, we see the capacity of this logic to subsume politics in fractious debates about the means deployed, at the expense of any real consideration about the proper ends of government and political office.

Conclusion

This chapter has provided a narrative of the origins of the technopopulist political logic. Whilst focusing in most detail on the three cases of the UK, France, and Italy, it has also provided a more general argument about the origins of an ideological logic of politics over the course of the twentieth century and the transition to a technopopulist logic. The main claim has been that ideological politics was rooted in a relationship between society and politics that was mediated by a wide variety of organization forms, including but going far beyond the mass political party. At the same time, societies themselves were structured and segmented in ways that connected individual experience with collective action. We trace the origins of the technopopulist logic in the demise of this form of 'organized modernity', paying particular attention to the collapse of many organized interests and the corresponding gap that has opened up between voters and their politicians. Given the complexity of historical developments, and the often messy and overlapping quality of different social and political processes, this chapter has aimed to provide some understanding of the ideological and technopopulist political logics from the inside, so to speak. Our started point has been the level of lived experience as well the more abstract analyses of macro-social historical change that make up this analytical narrative. We have also stressed the overlapping and complexity of factors involved in undermining the ideological political logic and encouraging the emergence of technopopulism.

---

[33] As Runciman (2017) puts it, May 'takes a position and then she sticks to it, seeing it as a matter of principle that she delivers on what she has committed to'. This contrasts with what some call 'transactional politicians', i.e. those who treat policy commitments as mere 'lines in the sand', offered up as the basis for intra- and inter-party negotiations.

4
The Consequences of Technopopulism

This chapter explores some of the consequences of the rise of technopopulism as the new structuring logic of contemporary democratic politics. Following an approach similar to the one pursued in the previous chapter, we inscribe the rise of technopopulism within a broader narrative, by pointing to some of the attendant political phenomena it is historically and conceptually related to. The hypotheses we put forward are therefore probabilistic and contextual in nature, rather than deterministic and linear (Marini and Singer 1988; Sayer 2010).

The analysis is divided in two parts. In the first we focus on what we call the 'internal' consequences of technopopulism, by which we mean the effects that it tends to have on the primary domain of which it is a structuring logic; that is, the domain of electoral competition itself. In the second part, we focus on what we call the 'external' consequences of technopopulism, by which we mean its broader effects on other domains of contemporary politics and society.

Internal Consequences

Increasing Conflictuality

"Come the fuck in or fuck the fuck off"[1]

The first and most immediately apparent consequence of the rise of technopopulism as the new structuring logic of contemporary democratic politics concerns the latter's outer texture or form. It is by now almost a commonplace to point out that partisan competition has become increasingly hostile and confrontational over the past few decades, a development reflected in the increasingly coarse language used by politicians and attributed to them in fictional accounts such as *The Thick of It*. As Andy Beckett has noted in a recent article entitled 'The Death of Consensus: How Conflict Came Back to Politics', the adjective most commonly employed by commentators to describe the tenor of contemporary political competition is 'toxic'. 'From the US, to Italy and Australia', he writes, 'politics

---

[1] This was the famous line delivered by the main character in the British comedy, *The Thick of It*, modelled on the era of New Labour. The main character, Malcolm Tucker, gave this answer when someone knocked on his office door.

Technopopulism: The New Logic of Democratic Politics. Christopher J. Bickerton and Carlo Invernizzi Accetti,
Oxford University Press (2021). © Christopher J. Bickerton and Carlo Invernizzi Accetti.
DOI: 10.1093/oso/9780198807766.003.0005

has become tribal, contentious and increasingly combative... Opposing factions no longer seem able to talk to each other, or even to agree on what they should talk about' (Beckett 2018; see also Chua 2018).

One way in which political scientists have attempted to measure this phenomenon is in terms of the notion of 'polarization', defined either as 'the distance between the policy positions of different political parties' or 'the extent to which partisan preferences and preferences on substantive issues are correlated within individual voters' (Stanig 2011). However, the results yielded by these measures have been less clear-cut than what the tenor of contemporary political language might have led us to expect. Writing about the United States, Alan Abramowitz and Kyle Saunders observe that 'there is widespread agreement among scholars concerning the growing importance of ideological divisions at the elite level... However, there is much less agreement concerning the importance of these divisions at the mass level' (Abramowitz and Saunders 2008: 543). Other scholars, such as Morris Fiorina and his collaborators, argued that 'when it comes to the political beliefs of the mass public, very little has changed since the 1950s' (cited in Abramowitz and Saunders 2008: 543; see also: Fiorina et al. 2006).

Similarly inconclusive results were obtained by recent attempts at measuring rising levels of ideological polarization in Europe. For instance, in their collective volume on *Political Conflict in Western Europe*, Hanspeter Kriesi and his collaborators report that 'Switzerland is the only country that constitutes a strong case for our hypotheses. The Swiss party system is strongly polarized, having started at a low level, and by the 1990s and early 2000s had become as polarized as the German or French systems' (Kriesi et al. 2012: 115). In most other Western European countries, ideological polarization seems to have remained 'surprisingly low' throughout the past few decades. For instance, Kriesi et al. write that:

> The declining polarization in the three high-conflict countries (France, Germany and the Netherlands) is difficult to reconcile with the hypothesis of a new cleavage... Mobilization linked to the new integration/demarcation issue apparently has not been able to outweigh the decline of mobilization linked to the old cleavages or to the new social movements of the 1970s (2012: 115–16).

We argue that the failure of the available measures of political polarization to register the increasingly conflictual nature of contemporary democratic politics is due to the fact that their focus on substantive *ideological* differences misses the mark. The rise of technopopulism as the new structuring logic of contemporary democratic politics corresponds to a decline in the salience of previous ideological divisions. It is therefore not at the level of substantive policy differences that the effects on electoral competition are likely to be most visible. Rather, it is at the level of its outer texture or form that we should expect the consequences of technopopulism to be most visible.

We see this in the language and reciprocal perceptions of members of different partisan groups, where large and important trends are clearly apparent. For instance, in an article entitled 'Fear and Loathing Across Party Lines: New Evidence on Group Polarization', Shanto Iyengar and Sean Westwood report on the increasing amount of hostility across party lines in the United States. In their words, 'negative views of the out-party and its supporters have risen sharply since the 1980s, and the specific content of outgroup stereotypes has followed suit. While Republicans view fellow partisans as patriotic, well-informed and altruistic, Democrats are judged to exhibit precisely the opposite traits' (Iyengar and Westwood 2015: 591). Commenting on this and similar evidence, David Brady and Bruce Cain have suggested that 'political polarization is no longer just—or even mainly—about policy differences, but now shapes how partisans understand each other as human beings' (Brady and Cain 2018: 100).

Similar empirical results have been replicated in Europe. In an article on the impact of the 2016 Brexit referendum on British public opinion, Sarah Hobolt et al. have found a particularly marked effect on what they call 'affective polarization', defined as 'the emotional attachment to ingroup partisans and hostility to outgroup partisans' (Hobolt et al. 2018: 4). 'Remainers and Leavers' they write 'are much more likely to attribute positive characteristics to their own side and negative characteristics to the other side... Only around half would be happy to talk politics with the other side, whether that side is defined by Brexit or party identity.' 'Even more strikingly', they add, 'only a third on average of those with a Brexit identity would be happy about a prospective son or daughter in law from the other side' (Hobolt et al. 2018: 18–19).

This sort of disparaging opinion of political opponents has become an endemic feature of contemporary democratic politics precisely where the technopopulist political logic is most evident. From the start of his political career, the founder of the Italian Five Star Movement, Beppe Grillo, employed dismissive and insulting epithets to describe the leaders of rival political parties—such as *'rigor Monti'* for Mario Monti, *'psiconano'* (psychotic dwarf) for Silvio Berlsuconi, and *'ebetino di Firenze'* (little idiot from Florence) for Matteo Renzi (Mazza 2012). Although the tone has been slightly moderated under the leadership of Luigi di Maio (2016–20), and especially since its accession to political power in 2018, government exponents continue to describe the opposition as 'obstructionist', 'malicious', and recently even accused it of practising a form of 'mediatic terrorism' (Vecchio 2018).

The current French President Emmanuel Macron has displayed a similarly dismissive attitude with respect to his political opponents, who are invariably qualified as representatives of 'special interests' or the 'old order' (Macron 2016: 2545). In the run-up to the Presidential election in May 2017, Macron spoke about a 'democratic emergency' in the case of an *Front National* victory, presenting himself as the 'protector of the Republic' and its 'democratic institutions' (Poussielgue 2017). Upon taking office, he then proceeded to declare that his party would not form any electoral alliances or government coalitions with other parties in the upcoming legislative elections and has later at several junctures described political opponents as either 'imbeciles', 'do-nothings', and 'enemies of the Republic' (Develey 2018).

The overall picture is therefore one where decreasing levels of *ideological* polarization go hand in hand with sharply rising levels of *affective* polarization, which involve critical or even derogatory views of one's political opponents and ultimately also challenge their legitimacy as political actors in the first place. As Michael Ignatieff has suggested, this points to an erosion of the distinction between political 'adversaries' and 'enemies', which in turn implies a souring—and potentially even a breakdown—of political confrontation and debate. 'An adversary', he writes, 'is someone you want to defeat', whereas 'an enemy' is 'someone you have to destroy'; what we are observing today is 'what happens when a politics of enemies supplants a politics of adversaries' (Ignatieff 2017).

This new conflictuality is closely tied to the way populism and technocracy function as incentive structures within the new political logic. As we explained in chapter 1, populism and technocracy both constitute ways of claiming to stand for the interest of the social *whole*, as opposed to any specific *parts* within it. In the case of populism, this whole was said to be the 'popular will', whereas in the case of technocracy it is the specific kind of political 'truth' which technocrats claim to have access to in virtue of their 'competence' or 'expertise'. Correspondingly, both populists and technocrats construe their political opponents as representatives of specific groups within society, whether in the form of the corrupt elites that populists stand against, or the special interests and rent-seekers that technocrats portray themselves as antidotes to. Since the whole is by definition superior to its parts, from this it follows that political opposition must begin to appear normatively illegitimate. As populism and technocracy become the dominant modes of contemporary democratic politics, political opponents are therefore increasingly be perceived as 'enemies' rather than 'adversaries', and the outer texture of democratic politics becomes more sour and confrontational.

This kind of attitude with respect to political opponents can be further explained with reference to other distinctive features of populism and technocracy we highlighted in chapter 1. As we noted, populism rests upon a claim to 'exclusive representation' of the popular will, which—as Müller puts it—implies that 'whoever does not support populist parties might not be a proper part of the people' (2016: 10–11). Moreover, as Cas Mudde emphasized, populist discourse also implies a distinctively 'moralizing' component. The problem with the political elite is not just that they pursue their own interests, but it is also that they are viewed as 'morally bankrupt' (Mudde 2017: 29). From this too it follows that populists are ill-disposed to recognize the legitimacy of their political opponents, since morality is predicated on a categorical opposition between good and evil, which excludes the possibility of compromise and even dialogue between them.

There is no point in trying to come to terms with evil; thus, to the extent that opponents are seen as 'malicious', 'dishonest', and 'corrupt', the only reasonable course of action can be one that is oriented towards their destruction.

The same exclusivity is found in populism's organizational dimension, where it is presumed that the leader directly embodies the people as a whole. To doubt this means challenging the personalistic way in which the populist leader relates to voters. Thus, any expression of difference or dissent must appear as a challenge to the leadership's capacity to speak in the name of the people, explaining the populists' virulence with respect to both critics and opponents. From their perspective, any expression of disagreement or dissent constitutes a direct attack against the populist leadership's position as legitimate representatives of the people, which elicits a retort in kind.

Technocracy as we have defined it operates in a similar way, further undermining the very idea of legitimate opposition. From the perspective of someone claiming to have access to some kind of political 'truth' in virtue of their competence or expertise, disagreement or dissent can only result from one of two sources: either ignorance of the objectively rational solution to the given policy problem, or wilful neglect of the latter in the service of a particular interest. Political opponents tend to be perceived as either flat out wrong, or actively malicious. Either way, their political stances are not to be taken very seriously— or indeed deliberately ignored. This is reflected in the fact that arguments about education levels and hidden motivations are assuming such a central role in contemporary democratic politics.

Politicians that don't recognize each other's legitimacy in spite of their substantive disagreements are bound to attack each other more virulently and directly, and to be more sceptical of each other's motivations, leaving less and less space for compromise and reconciliation. The reason they don't recognize their opponents as legitimate is that populism and technocracy are serving as the political coordinates in relationship to which these politicians are developing their political offers and identity. As Jan-Werner Müller pithily put it, 'if you disagree with a populist, you are declared a traitor to the people; if you disagree with a technocrat, you'll be told politely that you are not clever enough' (2020).

Desubstantialization

They convey neither conviction nor authority... Convinced that there is little they can do, they do little. The best that may be said of them, as so often of the baby boom generation, is that they stand for nothing in particular... (Judt 2010: 133–4).

As the outer texture of democratic politics is becoming increasingly hostile and confrontational, its substantive content is being progressively marginalized.

Concrete policy and value differences recede in the background, leaving the foreground of political contestation to other issues, such as the personal characteristics of the politicians involved, their dexterity and resourcefulness in employing modern means of mass communications, as well as their capacity to deliver on policy goals framed as being in everyone's interest. Thus, whilst political life is becoming increasingly ordered around the use of invective and threat, its long-term goals—that is, the representation of specific interests, values, and policy platforms—have lost importance, giving way to a preoccupation with personality, image, and competence.

This *desubstantialization* of democratic politics – what the historian Tony Judt referred to as the problem of standing 'for nothing in particular' – has been the subject of ongoing commentary. In the early 2000s, Colin Crouch lamented the fact that, despite the seemingly planetary expansion of democracy as a system of government, 'the content of party programs and the character of party rivalry are becoming ever more bland and vapid' (Crouch 2003: 7–8). 'Devoid of any comprehensive political vision and increasingly unable to discern what demands are coming to it from the population', he added, 'party politicians are having recourse to the well-known techniques of political marketing, which give all the advantages of discerning the public's views without the latter being able to take control of the process itself' (2003: 8). The British historian, Tony Judt, called this the 'unbearable lightness of politics'. In his words:

> [W]e have now become so accustomed to this that we take it for granted that a party's program is a 'product' and that politicians try to 'market' their message. Yet this is not really at all obvious. Other successful models of how to talk at large numbers of people were potentially available... but political journalism and politics more generally began to model themselves on advertising copy: very short messages, requiring extremely low concentration spans; the use of words to form high-impact images instead of arguments appealing to the intellect (Judt 2010: 131–3).

This preoccupation with the 'emptiness' of political debate takes us back to the 1990s and the rise of what some called 'the politics of spin'. As John Corner put it, this referred to the normalization of phenomena such as 'the soundbite, the pseudo-event, the orchestrated party conference, the emphasis on the telegenic' (1996: 354). Writing in 1999, Giampietro Mazzoleni and Winfried Schulz described this as the 'spectacularization of political communication', meaning that 'the language of politics has been married with that of advertising, public relations, and show business' (Mazzoleni and Schulz 1999: 251–2).

As a result of this change in the nature of political debates, we see other factors assuming a greater relevance in the contemporary political landscape. The most obvious and frequently noted are the personal characteristics of the politicians competing for office. As Musella and Webb put it in 2015: 'The century that has just started will be the age of personalization, just as the previous one was the century of mass collective actors' (2015: 226). Writing almost a decade earlier, McAllister (2007: 571) observed that 'it is now commonplace for governments to be named after the leader, rather than after the party that holds office, particularly if the party and its leader have won successive elections.' This type of 'personalization' involves leaders fashioning parties in their own image rather than in line with a set of abstract principles or values. As Curtice and Holmberg argue, 'a competent leader creates the impression of a competent party' (2005: 236). As a result, '[t]he power of the leader lies in their ability to lead and mold their party rather than their ability to appeal to voters independently of their party.'

We can therefore think of 'personalization' as denoting organizational change within parties as much as a shift of power from parties to individuals. This is what the work of Calise and others capture in the concept of the 'personal party'. Calise defines this as 'a transformation of the political party where a combination of charismatic and patrimonial resources replace the collective and legal-rational original party structure' (2013: 304). What the 'personal party' tells us is simply that the nature of the political struggle has changed: ideological conflict matters less, whereas conflicts between personalities, each of whom embody a different set of claims about their suitability and competence in office, matters more.

The declining salience of substantive policy disagreements in the contemporary political landscape is also manifested by the rise of so-called 'valence issues'. These are defined as 'issues on which there is agreement on the ends of politics' and therefore competition turns on the 'relative competence of different actors in achieving them' (Green 2007: 629). This is in contrast to 'position issues' where 'voters and parties are divided on the ends of politics' (see also Butler and Stokes 1969; Stokes 1985, 1992). In an article explicitly devoted to the question of the increasing salience of 'valence issues' in the era of New Labour, Jane Green writes that: 'British political competition has become competence-based because the major parties and the electorate have converged on the dominant left/right dimension' (Green 2007: 629). Sergi Pardos-Prado similarly observes that the consequence of the rise of 'valence issues' is that 'the politicians' perceived capacity to deliver on largely consensual policy goals' is more important that 'their substantive placement on contentious ideological issues' (2012: 349–50).[2]

---

[2] One of the clearest cases of this transformation in the quality of political competition was found in Central and Eastern Europe in the decade preceding membership of the European Union. Writing in 2003, Anna Grzymala-Busse and Abbey Innes observed that 'Eastern European public policy is overwhelmingly dominated by valence issues, or by issues on which all parties declare the same objectives (e.g. open and competitive markets, balanced budgets, reduced public spending and entry into the European Union)'. The result of this has been that elites have had little option but to 'dispute each other's *competence* in achieving the desired result' (Grzymala-Busse and Innes 2003: 66). Political competence is thus centred on the means—on 'the parties' modus operandi'—rather than on the ends, that is 'over substantive programmatic alternatives or ideological commitments'. The authors sum this

The limit point of these various interlocking tendencies—the personalization of politics, its spectacularization, and the rise of competence-based voting—is what, following Ilvo Dimanati, we propose to call the 'politics of doing'; that is, a politics that ceases to be about *what* is to be done, and instead becomes more and more about *who* does it, *how* it is done, and ultimately *that* anything is being done at all. Commenting on the grounds for the political success of Silvio Berlusconi, Diamanti claimed that 'the mythology of being a "doer" has always been at the heart of his image: as an entrepreneur he was a "self-made man"; as a real-estate tycoon he was a "builder"; as a media mogul, a "creator" and an "innovator"; even as a sports magnate, his whole persona has always been constructed around the capacity for "achieving results"' (Diamanti 2010).

Referring back to our discussion in chapter 2, we find that the idea of 'getting things done' has been at the heart of the technopopulist political field. The Five Star Movement's discourse does not refer to any substantive principles or value orientations, but rather to broad policy areas—water, mobility, development, connectivity, and environment—in which it is assumed that action is required, even though it is never really specified what this action is supposed to consist in. Even though the M5S has committed to some specific policies (notably, a Citizen's Income), its electoral appeal has principally been in its 'style of communication' and anti-establishment message (Tronconi 2015, 2018). As such, more attention has always been devoted to the curation of the movement's image through the staging of elaborate public events—such as the early V-days and, more recently, the movement leadership's TV appearances—than the definition of a substantive policy platform.

The political programme of France's current President, Emmanuel Macron, has also been similarly vague. Although Macron has been keen to present himself as a 'doer' and an '*enfant prodige*' who has been enormously 'successful in all his previous endeavours', his electoral campaign was described as 'singularly light on content' (Di Pasquale 2017). Not unlike the M5S's, his electoral manifesto contained a list of abstract *desiderata* but little detail as to how these would be implemented in practice or the fundamental value orientations that informed them. In contrast, a great deal of space was devoted to the construction of Macron's image as a young and energetic reformer, with appealing images of him greeting supporters and engaging in various kinds of activities looming large on almost every page (LREM 2017).[3] Recently, Macron was described in extensive

---

up as an uneasy coexistence of technocratic political competition and a growing populist challenge; in other words, the emergence of a technopopulist political field. Writing in 2019 on the crisis of democratic liberalism, Krastev and Holmes (2020) make a similar argument about the failure of the politics of 'imitation' in Central and Eastern Europe.

[3] In an article describing the vicissitudes that preceded the publication of Macron's official portrait, we learnt that 'ninety-one separate versions of the image were saved', with work on it spanning three

interview with the *Financial Times* as 'hyperactive'; his predecessor but one, Nicolas Sarkozy, was widely known and derided as 'the hyperactive president' (Khalaf and Mallet 2020; Duhamel 2012).

As in the case of the increasing conflictuality of contemporary democratic politics, our contention is that the rise of technopopulism as the new structuring logic of contemporary democratic politics can at least in part explain these developments. The first thing to recall is that both populism and technocracy were defined as 'modes of political action' and as such were said to be unmoored from any specific policy platforms. Jan-Werner Müller, for instance, noted that 'populism isn't about policy content', but rather about 'making a certain kind of moral claim' the content of which can come from 'any particular ideology' (Müller 2016: 160). Similarly, Frank Fischer pointed out that 'technocrats are to be found across the political spectrum. In both conventional ideological and programmatic terms, they can as a group disagree on almost anything... Like the rest of us, and for many of the same reasons, technocrats are quite divided on the pressing policy issues that confront modern society' (Fischer 1990: 20-1).

This is one of the things that we claimed distinguish populism and technocracy from traditional political ideologies such as liberalism, socialism, and conservatism, which are instead inextricably tied to an at least broadly defined set of specific policy measures. As populism and technocracy become the main structuring poles of contemporary democratic politics, overlaying and to some extent also replacing the more traditional political ideologies of left and right, substantive policy issues are bound to recede in the background and be replaced by the kinds of issues and features that are more central to the populist and technocratic modes of action. In other words, inasmuch as populism and technocracy are just modes of political action—as opposed to substantive policy platforms—the rise of technopopulism is bound to be correlated to a progressive desubstantialization of democratic party politics, which sees politicians increasingly competing with each other over their respective *ways* of doing politics, rather than their substantive policy goals.

Beyond this general logic, it is also possible to discern some more specific connections between the distinctive features of populism and technocracy we highlighted in chapter 1 and the particular forms of political competition that appear to be replacing that based on substantive policy divergences. To begin with, it is worth recalling that both populism and technocracy attribute great importance to the personal characteristics of political representatives. In the case of

---

days. The last tweaks were made just minutes before Macron's release of the image on Twitter. These tweaks touched on details such as the 'specific page of Charles De Gaulle's *Mémoires de Guerre* that is left casually open on Macron's table', and the time on his table clock, set precisely at 8.20, which is 'reasonable but early, by French standards' (Quito and Yanofsky 2017).

populism, this is because the leader's charisma—or some other combination of his or her personal qualities, such as class or ethnic background, life history, or personal achievements—are supposed to validate his claim to speak for the people as a whole. Similarly, in the case of technocracy, the leader's education, training, or accumulated experience are supposed to validate his or her claim to possess the necessary expertise to govern effectively. Thus, in both cases, the leader's biography and his or her personal life—as opposed to their substantive policy platform—become of paramount importance in validating their political standing. This suggests that the rise of technopopulism plays a part in the increasing personalization of contemporary democratic politics.

In addition, it is also worth noting that, since both populism and technocracy place very little emphasis on the role of formal procedures, the kinds of connections they establish between their leadership and the popular base are largely of the order of the symbolic. In the case of populism, the leader is somehow supposed to connect with the people directly; whereas in the case of technocracy he or she is supposed to know what is in the people's best interest, without these connections receiving any procedural validation. This implies that in both cases there is a constant need to reactivate the connection between the leadership and the base in order to make it appear real, even though it is of the order of the symbolic. And this in turn implies that the techniques of theatre and spectacle are bound to assume a particular relevance for technopopulist modes of political action. Spectacular measures such as large public gatherings and ritualized predictions of future economic performance, portraying the leaders precisely in their capacity as legitimate representatives of the people or competent experts about their true interests, have a well-known capacity to render palpable what remains only of the order of the symbolic (Balandier 1980). It is unsurprising that the rise of technopopulism as the structuring logic of contemporary democratic politics should also correspond to an increasing spectacularization of electoral competition.

Finally, the rising salience of 'valance issues' and the attendant tendency to evaluate politicians on their competence and capacity to 'deliver' are also clearly related to the rise of technopopulism as the new structuring logic of contemporary democratic politics. The presumption that there exists a procedure-independent criterion of political truth—whether in the form of a substantive and monolithic 'popular will' or set of 'correct policy solutions'—implies that politicians are not to be evaluated on the basis of their particular policy goals (which are assumed to be consensual), but precisely on the basis of their capacity to deliver on these presumptively consensual policy ends. The image of the politician as a 'doer' who is capable of 'achieving results', irrespective of what these actually happen to be, is therefore one that should be expected to gain much greater prominence in the context of the technopopulist field.

External Consequences

Democratic Discontent

"Que Se Vayan Todos!" (Out With Them All!)[4]

At the same time as politicians present themselves as exclusive representatives of the 'people's will', and claim to possess the necessary competence for delivering on their 'objective' interests, citizens of advanced Western democracies are increasingly dissatisfied with their performance, demanding in many instances that the political class as a whole is cleared out, as the *Indignados* movement wanted. The rising rates of popular discontent with elected politicians, as well as with democratic institutions more generally, have become a prominent feature of contemporary democratic regimes. Disaffection with politics has become generalized in the form of public cynicism towards politics and distrust of political actors. As Judt put it, the feeling is that '[s]ince "they" will do what they want in any case—while feathering their own nests—why should "we" waste time trying to influence the outcome of elections?' (Judt 2010: 131). In a recent book on what he calls 'imperfect democracy', Yves Mény compares the institutional apparatus of contemporary democratic regimes to trees that are suffering from a malady and vulnerable to being swept away in the next powerful gale (2019). The bark is still there, he writes, but the sap has gone.

There is robust empirical evidence underpinning this sense of democratic malaise. In *The People vs. Democracy* (2018), Yascha Mounk notes that recorded levels of 'trust in politicians' have been consistently declining over the past few decades. Even during the 1974 Watergate scandal, which eventually forced Richard Nixon to resign, 'a clear majority of Americans retained confidence in people holding office.' Today, by contrast, 'a clear majority of Americans say they distrust people in public life' (Mounk 2018: 99). This collapse of trust in politicians is mirrored by a soaring mistrust of institutions in general. In June 2014, Mounk notes, 'only 30% of Americans reported having confidence in the Supreme Court...29% expressed confidence in the Presidency.' For the legislative branch, the figures are dramatic: 'In the 1970s, over 40% of Americans had expressed confidence in congress. By 2014, that figure had fallen to 7%' (2018: 100). Far from being restricted to the United States, this political discontent is found across advanced Western democracies. It is evident in declining electoral participation rates and in rising rates of protest-oriented politics. Writing in 2013, Peter Mair observed that average turnout rates across Western Europe fell

---

[4] This was one of the slogans adopted by the *Indignados* protest movement in Spain during the 2014 protests against the country's two mainstream political parties, out of which *Podemos* emerged.

from 81.7 per cent to 77.6 per cent in the last decade of the twentieth century, falling further in the 2000s (Mair 2013: 24). 'Although there is no undisturbed downward trend', Mair observed, 'record lows now come with greater frequency and in a greater number of polities.'

A rise in protest politics has accompanied this decline of trust in democratic politics. The growing frequency of all sorts of protest movements, concerning issues as wide-ranging as financial regulation ('Occupy Wall St'), public health ('No Vax'), and carbon taxes (the *gilets jaunes* in France) is a recurrent feature of contemporary democratic politics. What in the 1960s and '70s appeared extraordinary and potentially even threatening for the stability of democratic regimes, has now become virtually normal (Krastev 2014). To take an example, in recent years Italian politics has become increasingly oriented around the gathering of citizens in squares across the country. This sort of mobilization was a key component of the rise of the Five Star Movement, with its famous '*Vaffanculo*' protests that began in 2007. More recently, it has been the preferred *modus operandi* of those opposed to the growing dominance of the *Lega*'s anti-immigrant agenda. As we note in more detail in the conclusion, the 'sardine' movement, launched in late 2019, has taken the form of anti-*Lega* protests held in the squares of towns and cities across Italy. The name itself derives from the idea of protestors standing together as tightly packed fish, intended as a sign of conscious solidarity (Poggioli 2019).

It is easy to see this democratic discontent as a *cause* of populism and technocracy's contemporary prominence. However, we argue here that it should also be seen as one of the main *consequences* of the rise of technopopulism as the new structuring logic of contemporary democratic politics. The reason is rooted in a key feature of these two modes of political action, which we already highlighted in chapter 1; namely, the fact that both populism and technocracy are based on unmediated conceptions of the public good—popular will and an objective 'truth'. Neither of these conceptions emerge out of a process of articulation and reconciliation between conflicting interests and values within society but are rather assumed to be given in advance of the political process itself. Both populism and technocracy dispense with the dimension of *political mediation* because they claim to have direct access to the ultimate ground of political legitimacy itself. This is reflected in their distinctive modes of political organization. Populism relies on the cultivation of a direct relationship of 'embodiment' between the populist leader and his or her electoral base whilst technocracy is based on an informal relationship of 'trust' between the technocrat and those he is supposed to govern, rooted in the assumption that the former possesses a specific 'competence' or 'expertise', tied to his or her personal qualities and professional qualifications. Both populism and technocracy dispense with 'intermediary bodies' and other forms of mediation between society and politics, seeking to establish a more 'direct' kind of relationship between the two (see Urbinati 2015).

Both these aspects are captured by the notion of 'disintermediation' that was introduced in the Italian political vocabulary by Beppe Grillo. In one of his blog posts from the 11th of January 2013, the founder of the Italian Five Star Movement wrote explicitly that: 'The M5S wants to realize direct democracy, the disintermediation of the relationship between the state and citizens, the elimination of political parties, and binding referendums without a quorum. In a word: the citizen in power'. This ideal of 'direct democracy' as a form of disintermediation was further elaborated upon by the original founder of the Italian M5S, Gianroberto Casaleggio, in a 2004 book entitled *Web Ergo Sum*, in which he stated that:

> The term direct democracy describes a new relationship between citizens and their representatives... Contemporary democracies operate on the principle of delegation, not participation. This means that the relationship between voters and their representatives is exhausted by the vote... The Web has the opportunity of redefining the relationship between citizens and politics by allowing for direct access to information at any time and constant control over the activities of government... Thus, *direct democracy introduces the centrality of the citizen through the means of disintermediation* (Casaleggio 2004; italics added).

A similar emphasis on the need to cut down on all the mechanisms of mediation between individual citizens, on one hand, and the state, on the other, can be found in Emmanuel Macron's political statements, speeches, and interviews. He argued in his 2016 book that 'if we want politics to serve the French People once again we need to get down to the job of making politics more effective' (Macron 2016: 2601). In the ensuing analysis, he blamed France's 'intermediary bodies' (*les corps intermédiairies*) as the main culprits for the inefficiency and ossification of the country's political system. 'We need' he wrote 'to reinvigorate our fossilized political apparatus. This is the blind side of democratic debate. In our times, the parties have given up on fighting for the common good. They focus on their own interests—to survive, come what may' (2016: 2539). Later in the same text, the future French President added that: 'What is unacceptable is when a caste builds itself up, closes ranks, and imposes its own rules. And here the parties and institutions are far more to blame than the representatives themselves' (2016: 2557).

This sort of call for direct democracy is a plausible way of facilitating the transmission of popular demands from society directly into the political domain, and thereby increasing the quality of political representation by simplifying it, but we argue that its effect is the opposite. Far from empowering individual citizens by giving them a greater opportunity to have their voices heard in the political domain, disintermediation dilutes their political agency, increasing their sense of alienation from the political system as a whole. This is because of the enormous difference in scale between individual interests and values, on one hand, and the idea of a 'general will' or an objective political 'truth', on the other. Faced with these unmediated conceptions of the common good, the individual is bound to perceive him or herself as an infinitesimally significant entity, with little chance of affecting the political direction of society as a whole. When the interests of society as a whole are opposed to those of its constituent parts, in the way that both populists and technocrats imply, the individual is bound to feel disempowered and alienated from the political system.

This was Hans Kelsen's point in his 1929 treatise on *The Essence and Value of Democracy*. In his words, '[i]t is a well-known fact that, because he is unable to achieve any appreciable influence on government, the isolated individual lacks any real political existence' (Kelsen 1929: 39). For this reason, Kelsen maintained that '[d]emocracy is only feasible if, in order to influence the will of society, individuals integrate themselves into associations based on their various political goals... Collective bodies, which unite the common interests of their individual members as political parties, must come to mediate between the individual and the state' (1929: 39). Another way of saying this is that the activity of political mediation between society and politics—which is normally carried out by intermediary bodies such as political parties, trade unions, churches, and other civic associations—plays a key role in giving citizens a sense of effective political representation. To the extent that contemporary populism and technocracy construe the activity of political mediation as an obstacle rather than a necessary condition for the realization of the democratic ideal of effective political representation, they actively contribute to an *exacerbation* of the widespread sense of democratic discontent from which they stem in the first place. With the rise of technopopulism as the new structuring logic of contemporary democratic politics, increasingly atomized individuals are bound to get a sense that political representation is being hollowed out, even if—or indeed precisely because—political actors claim to represent the substantive interests of society as a whole in a 'direct' and 'unmediated way'.

There is another way in which democratic discontent and the technopopulist logic are connected. If politics is increasingly ordered around the combination of appeals to the people and to expertise and competence, then political actors and parties have a vested interest in perpetuating democratic discontent as a condition for their own political survival. However, this implies that their political exponents also run the risk of becoming the objects of the same kind of popular dissatisfaction and resentment they have fostered against the political system as a whole, wherever they succeed in coming to power. We can observe this dynamic in all the paradigmatic examples of technopopulism we considered in chapter 2.

Italy's Five Star Movement began by denouncing what Beppe Grillo called as far back as 2008 a 'democratic emergency' caused by the 'confiscation of popular sovereignty' by 'political parties', 'economic interests', and 'international organizations'. That discourse has remained a centre piece of the movement's rhetoric even after its accession to government in 2018. Subsequently, voices both within and outside the movement—including Beppe Grillo himself—have criticized the M5S for having 'lost touch with its roots' and 'sold out to be powers that be' (Musso 2019). After being elected on a platform that promised to 'clean up French politics' from the 'endemic corruption' and 'self-referentiality' of traditional political parties, the current French President Emmanuel Macron has dismissed criticisms directed against him and his government as 'attacks against the state' and 'perversions (*détournements*) of democracy'. This has been widely perceived as a sign of arrogance and lack of empathy with the electorate, and Macron has struggled with approval ratings that at times have been as low as those of his much-reviled predecessor, François Hollande. In effect, what we see with technopopulism is a personalization of politics and a move towards making the process and the means—rather than the ends—the substance of political debate. This may enable a movement or a party to succeed electorally, but it also means they will be subject to the same standards of assessment and critique. Whilst presenting themselves as *solutions* to the current sense of democratic malaise, the technopopulist logic reproduces the crisis, albeit in a different form.

The New Authoritarianism

"In Galera!" (Lock Them Up!)[5]

A second external consequence of the rise of technopopulism is closely connected to the one we discussed in the previous section. If it is true that technopopulism not only feeds on but also fosters a widespread sense of dissatisfaction with the quality of democratic representation, it must also implicitly call into question the very grounds of political authority in democratic societies. If the ultimate foundation of political legitimacy is assumed to be the democratic principle of collective self-government, the fact that the rise of technopopulism tends to weaken the sense of effective representation that citizens feel with respect to the government implies that it must also weaken the grounds for their compliance with it. Demands to 'lock up' political leaders because of their corrupt behaviour express very vividly this crisis of representation.

The way in which contemporary political systems have responded to this increasing deficit in democratic legitimacy is by securing compliance by other, more repressive means; that is, in relying more and more on the threat of punishment rather than the promise of collective self-government. This suggests

---

[5] Slogan chanted by M5S supporters at the first 'Vaffanculo Day' organized by Beppe Grillo and Gianroberto Casaleggio on 14 June 2007.

a connection between the rise of technopopulism as a structuring logic of contemporary democratic politics and what we shall call the 'new authoritarianism' of contemporary democratic societies, manifested by increasing rates of punitiveness, incarceration, surveillance, and police activity in general, even while crime rates appear to be generally declining or at least stagnating. In what follows, we first establish a number of relevant facts and then critically assess some of the criminological explanations that have been provided for the 'repressive turn' of contemporary democratic states (Wacquant 2009).

The empirical data on the degree of punitiveness of contemporary Western democracies is remarkably solid and consistent. Rates of incarceration, surveillance, and police activity have increased more or less across the board over the course of the last few decades, even while rates of reported crime have mostly decreased, or remained constant. According to the US National Research Council's 2014 report on 'The Growth of Incarceration in the United States', 'in 1973, after fifty years of stability, the rate of incarceration in the United States began a sustained period of growth. In 1972, 161 US residents were incarcerated in prisons and jails per 100,000 population; by 2007 that rate had more than quintupled to peak at 767 per 100,000...In absolute numbers, the prison and jail population had grown to 2.23 million people, yielding a rate of incarceration that was by far the highest in the world' (NRC 2014: 33). The European Society of Criminology's 2016 newsletter offers a similar overall picture. 'Data from West European countries', it states, 'indicates astonishing changes in prison population rates. The Netherlands, which had traditionally displayed low levels until the 1980s, experienced a quadrupling of prison population by 2006...In Spain, the proportion of prisoners per 100,000 of the national population increased from 40 in 1984 to 133 in 2016, whereas in England and Wales the same figure almost doubled from 80 to 147 over the same period' (Dunkel 2016).

The same report also notes that some Western European countries appear to display counter-tendencies, or at least more complex overall patterns. For instance, the rate of incarceration has actually declined by about 46 per cent in the Netherlands between 2006 and 2016, whereas in Italy an 'ebb-and-flow pattern' responding to the vagaries of 'electoral politics' has been discerned against 'a background increase in incarceration since 1970, amplified particularly after 1990' (Gallo 2015). The overall trend remains nonetheless unmistakable. 'Since the 1980s', David Garland writes,

> sentences of imprisonment have increased in length, average time served has increased, custodial sentences have been used in a larger proportion of cases and the likelihood of being returned to custody from parole has greatly increased. There has thus been a shift—more pronounced in the USA than in the UK but present in both countries—towards a much greater and more intensive use of custody...This more punitive trend is echoed in America by the increased

frequency of judicial execution, which have recently reached levels not seen since the 1950s (Garland 2001: 168).

Analogous trends can also be discerned in levels of surveillance and police activity in general. For instance, in his 2004 book entitled *CCTV and Policing: Public Area Surveillance and Police Practices in Britain*, Benjamin Goold notes that 'since the late 1980s, over one million closed circuit television cameras have been installed in towns and cities across Britain, with an estimated five hundred or more being added to this figure every week... As a consequence, whether they like it or not, going about their daily business under the watchful eye of CCTV has become a fact of life for many citizens' (Goold 2004: 1). This has led some commentators, such as David Lyon, to talk of a new 'surveillance society' as the principal means of crime prevention in advanced Western democracies (Lyon 2001). More broadly, as Garland notes, 'in the policing sector, there has been a shift of emphasis away from reactive strategies and 911 policing towards more proactive community policing efforts, and, more recently, to more intensive policing of disorder, incivilities and misdemeanors' (Garland 2001: 169). 'Information technology and new management techniques', Garland adds, 'have been combined to produce tighter control of resources and more directed, problem-solving conduct... As a result, policing has become "smarter", more targeted, more attuned to local circumstances, more responsive to public pressure, and more willing to emphasize prevention' (2001: 169).

What is most striking about all this, is that the increases in the rates of incarceration, surveillance, and police activity in general have happened against a backdrop of generally *decreasing*—or, at the very least, stagnant—rates of reported crime itself. The annual FBI reports on crime in the United States, for instance, show that the violent crime rate has declined by about 49 per cent between 1991 and 2017, at the same time as property crime rates have declined by almost 54 per cent and aggravated assault rates have declined by around 39 per cent (FBI 2017). Similarly, the European Union's Eurostat service reports that 'while there was relatively little change between 2006 and 2011, EU-wide police recorded robberies fell by 24% between 2012 and 2016, even though the downward trend flattened out in the last two years of that period' (Eurostat 2016). There has been an 'overall downward trend in homicide rates since 2008' and a 'marginal increase in rates of assault', which is mostly attributed to increasing rates of reporting, particularly in the case of sexual assault, rather than an increase in the incidence of crime itself (Eurostat 2016).

A wide variety of different explanations have been supplied to account for this 'punitive turn' of contemporary democratic societies, ranging from the emergence of a 'culture of control' tied to the insecurities of modern social life (Garland 2001), to the declining levels of welfare provision resulting from the ascendancy of a 'neoliberal ideology' (Wacquant 2009; Harcourt 2010), up to the evolving dynamics of 'racial politics', particularly in the US (Alexander 2010). What interests us here is a particular strand of contemporary criminological literature which focuses on the connection between electoral politics and the degree of punitiveness of the repressive apparatus of the state.

In his 2007 book, *Penal Populism*, John Pratt advanced the argument that recent increases in the rates of incarceration of most advanced Western democracies are at least in part due to the fact that 'governments have developed penal practices in line with the sentiments and aspirations of the general public, rather than their own bureaucratic organizations' (Pratt 2007: 1). As such, the notion of 'penal populism' refers to the idea of 'politicians tapping into and using for their own purposes what they believe to be the public's generally punitive stance' (2007: 2). As Pratt himself further notes, this idea has recently gained significant traction, making its way into the mainstream media and political commentary, as well as academic criminology.[6]

This notion of 'penal populism' establishes a direct connection between one of the two key political forms we are concerned with in this book and the rising rates of incarceration and general punitiveness of contemporary democratic societies. At the same time, as Peter Ramsay has noted, it is problematic to assume that increasing rates of incarceration and police activity in general are 'popular' since the very phenomenon of penal populism has 'occurred at a time of falling participation, both in elections and more generally' (Ramsay 2016: 84). Indeed, Ramsay adds, 'the period in which incarceration rates have risen has also been a period in which the idea of collective self-government has been more or less evacuated from the content of electoral politics' (2016: 98). In his view, 'it is a mistake to understand contemporary criminal justice policy as being popular'; rather, it is 'better understood as one of many symptoms of the unpopularity of politics and the decline in participation in public life' (2016: 84).

Ramsay's suggestion is that the increasing degree of punitiveness of contemporary democratic societies is not the result of an *excess* of democracy (as the notion of 'penal populism' is normally used to imply) but rather the symptom of a *deficit* in democratic representation, which is in line with the way in which we have proposed to understand the notion of populism in this book. The underlying logic here is one of substitution: to the extent that a state's democratic legitimacy is progressively undermined, it compensates by relying on increased punitiveness in order to secure compliance from its citizens. With an eye to understanding the changing nature of the British state, Ramsay argues that contemporary democracies are becoming more 'Hobbesian' precisely to the extent that 'the normative grounds of their political legitimacy are being eroded', which in turn implies that

---

[6] For further discussions, see Bottoms 1995 and Roberts et al. 2003.

greater punitiveness should not be seen as a sign of 'strength' of contemporary political regimes but rather of their 'weakness' (Ramsay 2012: 215–19).[7]

Further evidence to the same effect on the penal implications of austerity politics in Italy was recently provided by Zelia Gallo. Starting from the assumption that austerity politics amounts to a 'technocratic' mode of government, premised on 'executive discretion' and used to push through a particular socio-economic policy agenda in spite of widespread popular discontent, Gallo argues that 'the contemporary restriction of those spaces in which state and citizen can interact on neutral, participative terms' is leading to a 'weakening of state authority and norms', to which the state reacts by 'using the penal law to try and enforce compliance' (Gallo 2018). Her conclusion is that the 'weakening of democratic norms' associated with the rise of austerity politics is likely to lead to an exacerbation of punitive practices; 'punishment is used to impose cohesion on an ever more fragmented polity' (2018).

Our analysis of the consequences of technopopulism chimes with this strand of criminological literature inasmuch and can help our understanding of the underlying causes of the 'weakening of democratic norms'. As we have shown in the previous section, the rise of technopopulism constitutes an important contributory factor to the widespread sense of dissatisfaction with the quality of democratic representation. This is because technopopulism undermines the mechanisms of political mediation that play an essential role in enabling individual citizens to meaningfully influence the political decisions to which they are subject. This implies that the rise of technopopulism can at least in part explain the 'punitive turn' of contemporary democratic societies, since it poses the conditions for the widespread sense of political discontent to which states have been responding with increasing rates of incarceration and police activity in order to secure compliance in the face of waning democratic legitimacy.

This connection between technopopulism and the contemporary 'punitive turn' can be found in some of the paradigmatic instances of technopopulism we considered in chapter 2. Tony Blair made the notion of being 'tough on crime' as

---

[7] A similar argument has also been recently advanced by Vanessa Barker with respect to the United States. In a book chapter entitled 'Prison and the Public Sphere: Toward a Democratic Theory of the Penal Order' she writes that: 'the breakdown of American democracy partially accounts for the unprecedented rise in incarceration over the past thirty years... Americans by and large have retreated into the private sphere and eroded the quality and character of the public sphere. These dual processes have major implications for the rise of state coercion against marginalized social groups' (Barker 2013: 125). To substantiate this thesis, Barker provides a comparative study of various US states, showing that the quality and vitality of state-level democracy is closely correlated with the degree of 'penal populism'. California, which for her is a state with 'surprisingly low rates of civic engagement' and 'a long history of social conflict and social insecurity', is said to display 'some of the highest incarceration rates in the country' (2013: 139). In contrast, Barker writes, 'in Washington state, democratization, particularly as it was part of a deliberative process and communicative action, defused growing social conflict and social insecurities and suppressed reactionary calls for punitive penal sanctioning' (2013: 141).

well as 'tough on the causes of crime', into a trademark element of his broader revision of the British Labour Party's traditional approach in this domain (Matthews and Young 2003). In fact, during his premiership the country experienced the biggest expansion in levels of incarceration and policing in post-war history (McLaughlin, Muncie, and Hughues 2001), along with extensive policy innovation in this area such as the introduction of anti-social behaviour orders (ASBOs) (Ramsay 2008).

The Italian Five Star Movement first rose to national prominence with a message laying great emphasis on the idea of prosecuting and sanctioning both politicians and businessmen for illicit behaviour. This type of *'giustizialismo'* was the main reason offered for Beppe Grillo's consistent refusal to stand for elected office, despite playing a key role in founding the movement and spurring it to political success. The M5S's original statute demanded a prohibition on individuals with a criminal record standing for elected office, and Grillo himself does not satisfy that criterion, having previously been convicted for manslaughter in the context of a car accident. Upon entering a government coalition with the far-right *Lega Nord* in 2018, the M5S supported a controversial 'security decree' proposed by Matteo Salvini which greatly enhanced policing and prosecutorial powers, especially in the domain of petty crimes assumed to be tied to illegal immigration (Trocino 2019).

Most prominent in this regard has been Emmanuel Macron's extensive reliance on the repressive apparatus of the state since assuming office in 2017. This had already been an important aspect of his electoral campaign, with respect to the issue of domestic terrorism, which for Macron showed that 'a continuing police presence in our country is now a necessity', since 'proximity is the only way to collect information, and to identify and monitor dangerous individuals' (Macron 2016: 1957). It was, however, manifested even more explicitly in the reaction to the *gilets jaunes* movement. As many commentators pointed out, this took an extraordinarily—and, for French standards, unprecedently—repressive form. Using emergency measures that had remained in place since the terrorist attacks of November 2015, Macron's administration presided over a massive expansion in police powers and activity. This led to over 2,500 serious injuries (1,843 reported hospitalizations amongst protesters and 1,048 amongst policemen) and a total of ten deaths over several weeks of confrontations between police forces and protesters (Mauger 2019).

If political actors undermine the sense of effective democratic representation by eroding the existing mechanisms of mediation between social demands and political offers, then we understand why they might resort to more repressive means of state control to ensure citizen compliance when they encounter opposition once in power. We refer to this as a *new authoritarianism* to emphasize the difference between our analysis and the claims of 'penal populism', which attribute the same developments to the changing preferences of the electorate at large.

Far from being a sign that democratic representation is working well, we argue that the technopopulist logic leads to a *decrease* in the quality of democratic representation, one of the effects of which is an increase in state punitiveness.

Closure of the Revolutionary Horizon and the Rise of Identity Politics

"There Is No Alternative"[8]

The last external set of consequences of the rise of technopopulism as the new structuring logic of contemporary democratic politics we shall consider concerns the horizon for radical political change. Despite their ostensibly 'anti-establishment' appeal, a striking feature of the types of political actors produced by the technopopulist political logic is their refusal to envisage radical transformations to existing the social and political systems. Their aspirations ultimately boil down to make the existing social and political systems 'work better' according to their own stated principles. As such, there appears to be a distinctively 'conservative' dimension to the technopopulist logic, which restricts the horizon of possible political change to the sphere of reform of the status quo.

This is not just a case of promises left unmet. Technopopulist political actors do not promise to overthrow the status quo while failing to deliver on that promise. They promise no such thing in the first place. None of the instances of technopopulism described in this book are 'revolutionary' political movements which aim to usher in an entirely new form of politics and society. Instead, they are modes of political action that remain firmly *within* the horizon of democratic electoral politics and claim only to make the existing system work better, despite their discursive flirtation with the rhetoric of revolution and radical social and political transformation, which appears to have a primarily cosmetic function.

In a blog post written at the time of the delicate coalition negotiations that preceded the M5S's first accession to government in 2018, Beppe Grillo wrote in a characteristically flamboyant way that 'only a revolution can save us.' However, he quickly went on to explain that he did not mean a 'violent seizure of state power' since those kinds of revolutions 'always end up producing winners and losers, friends and enemies, some who command and others who obey' (Grillo 2018). Instead, he maintained that 'real political change...only happens through slow, very slow, almost imperceptible transitions.' On this basis, Grillo then concluded

---

[8] This was a slogan originally used by Margaret Thatcher, later adopted also by Angela Merkel in the context of the Eurozone crisis and the policies she and her finance minister (Wolfgang Schauble) supported. See Müller 2018.

that what was needed was 'to abide by the fundamental democratic principle that everyone—and that means every vote—is worth one' (Grillo 2018).

In his 2016 book, *Revolution*, Macron explained clearly that what he offered was not *'le grand soir'* of revolutionary lore. On the issue of constitutional reform, he argued for preserving the status quo against the likes of Jean-Luc Mélenchon and Benoît Hamon, who have long called for the creation of a new Sixth Republic. To this effect, he wrote that '[i]t is my conviction that French people are fed up with the promises regularly made to them that their institutions are going to be changed—either to be "remodelled", or to be "adapted to the needs of the times" ...I do not believe that such changes are a priority for the French people' (Macron 2016: loc. 2498). Later in the same text, the future French President also added that '[o]ur country was able to flourish for a long time with that same constitution, and without any storms of anger brewing', in an evident appeal to political moderation and respect for established institutions and political patterns (2016: loc. 2486).

Despite rhetorical appeals to the contrary, the technopopulist political logic does not generate the sort of 'anti-system parties' that were a regular feature of democratic politics during the age of the ideological political logic (Bickerton and Invernizzi Accetti 2018: 134–5). Instead, it participates in a broader contemporary pattern whereby the scope for revolutionary political change appears to have been foreclosed. Writing in 1999, Russell Jacoby already observed that 'we have entered an era of acquiescence in which we build our lives, families and careers and conduct our politics with little to no expectation that the future can transcend the present' (Jacoby 1999: xi). In 2010, Tony Judt articulated a similar sentiment. '[W]e seem unable to conceive of alternatives', he noted, 'which is something quite new from a historical point of view' (Judt 2010: 2).

Various explanations have been provided for this phenomenon, which some call the TINA—There is No Alternative—mentality (Seville 2017a, 2017b). We argue that there is a clear relationship between the dynamics of the technopopulist logic and the foreclosure of the revolutionary horizon. This relationship has its roots in the 'unmediated' nature of populist and technocratic modes of political action and the implications of this for political agency. Principled political organizations are central to the history of modern revolution, a point made forcefully by Michael Walzer in his path-breaking work on the history of revolutionary ideas and practice in Western civilization. His key argument in *The Revolution of the Saints. A Study in the Origins of Radical Politics* is that 'a politics of conflict and competition for power, faction, intrigue and open war is probably universal in human history.' By contrast, the 'politics of party organization and methodical activity, opposition and reform, *radical ideology and revolution*' is historically specific, and as such must have identifiable ideal and material conditions (Walzer 1965: 1; italics added). Walzer (1965: 1–2) points to the historical significance of the Calvinist conception of 'sainthood' in opening the horizon for modern revolutionary politics:

> What Calvinists said of the saint... other men would later say of the citizen: the same sense of civic virtue, of discipline and duty, lies behind the two names... Saint and citizen together suggest a new integration of private men into the political order, an integration based on a novel view of politics as a kind of conscientious and continuous labor, which... formed the basis for the politics of revolution and shaped the character of the revolutionary.

Walzer suggests that disciplined social organizations dedicated to the transformation of the world through conscientious work are a necessary condition for the emergence of revolutionary politics. Without such social groups, utopias will certainly exist, as people have always imagined 'ideal societies' situated temporally in some 'mythical past', 'projected future', or 'supra-temporal domain' (Walzer 1965: 29–30). However, what remains unavailable is the idea of transforming the present world in accordance with a higher plan through dedicated political action.

Looking at the nature of the technopopulist political logic, we see that it is precisely such organizations—and the social groups they are related to—which are most directly undermined by contemporary democratic politics. The processes of political 'disintermediation' we have described have undermined the kind of organized and conscientious political activity that Walzer identifies as a necessary condition for the disclosure of the revolutionary horizon. The key connection between technopopulism and the closure of revolutionary politics therefore lies in the instances of *political mediation* we identified earlier in this chapter as being so important for individuals to conceive of themselves as being able to meaningfully affect political outcomes. Without such modes of articulation and aggregation of particular interests, both partisan and especially radical political change appear impossible. Even modest changes are difficult to imagine if the only perspective to see the world is from an individual one.

Disintermediation has an effect on those forms of political activity that we label 'radical'. Several commentators have recently sought to draw a connection between the foreclosure of the revolutionary horizon and the growing salience of a different form of politics, centred around claims to recognition and inclusion by marginalized social groups, which is commonly referred to as 'identity politics' (Bickford 1997). Already in 1993, for instance, in an essay entitled 'The Rise of Identity Politics', Todd Gitlin maintained that 'two hundred years of revolutionary tradition, whether liberal or radical, were predicated on the ideal of a universal humanity', whereas, in his view, 'seized by the logic of identity politics, and therefore committed to pleasing its disparate constituencies, the contemporary left has lost interest in the commonalities that undergird its obsession with difference' (Gitlin 1993: 174–7). In *The End of Utopia*, Russel Jacoby maintained that: 'To avoid contemplating the defeat and its implications, the left now largely speaks the language of liberalism—the idiom of pluralism and rights... Stripped of a radical vision and robbed of utopian hopes, it has retreated in the name of progress to celebrate diversity... Whereas it once rejected pluralism as superficial, it now worships it as profound' (1999: 10–11). To be sure, Jacoby recognizes, 'the goal of including more people in the established society is certainly laudable'; however, he notes, 'it hardly seems radical' (1999: 33). Thus, he concludes: 'The rise of identity politics correlates with the decline of utopia, an index of the exhaustion of political thinking' (1999: 33). More recently, in *Identity: The Demand for Dignity and the Politics of Resentment* (2018), Fukuyama has pointed out that, as a form of political radicalism, 'identity politics' seems to have moved out of the confines of the ideological left. Increasingly, 'the right is redefining itself as patriots who seek to protect traditional national identity against the corrosive forces of globalization and liberal multiculturalism, an identity that is often connected to race, ethnicity or religion' (Fukuyama 2018: 4). In Fukuyama's view, this stems from the fact that liberal democracy and market economy have entrenched themselves as an 'inescapable horizon', making people look elsewhere in their need for 'heroism and recognition' (2018: v–vi).

To the extent that the rise of technopopulism is connected to the present foreclosure of the revolutionary horizon, these passages suggest that the salience of questions of identity and recognition must also be seen as closely related to the contemporary political logic of technopopulism. To begin with, the fact that both populism and technocracy have the pretension of standing for the interests of the social 'whole' makes them particularly vulnerable to claims of exclusion or marginalization. Whoever can prove that the particular interests of their specific identity group are not being adequately taken into account is able to attack a populist's or a technocrat's conception of the whole for not representing them. Challenges to technopopulist politicians are therefore likely to take—both in theory and in practice—the form of claims to political exclusion or marginalization. We have seen this most vividly in the British Labour Party: the 'pure' case of Blairite technopopulism was swiftly followed by 'Blue Labour' and battles with the 'cosmopolitan' wing of the Labour Party. These internecine battles that shaped the Labour Party in the post-Blair era were each symptoms of the embrace of identity politics by the British left. The Corbyn era which followed was itself an amalgam of traditional socialist politics and a heightened form of left identity politics.

At the same time, in both appeals to the people and to expertise, the language of contestation is distinctively *moral*. Just as populists and technocrats both appeal to a moralized conception of the interests of the 'whole', which undercuts the legitimacy of any form of partisan opposition, contemporary claims to exclusion and recognition by marginalized social groups operate on a level of moral reprobation that leaves little room for political disagreement and debate. How could one possibly disagree with the injustice of political exclusion? As such, both technopopulism and the logic of identity politics seem to belong to a political world in which the very conception of politics as a struggle between competing—but equally legitimate—interests and values has been abandoned in favour of one in which the goal of politics is to implement some presumptively consensual set of moral ends, policing against deviations and disagreements.

More deeply, we can say that identity politics expresses the same collapse of the dimension of political mediation than technopopulism does. As we have insisted on at several junctures in this chapter, both populist and technocratic modes of political action involve appeals to the interests and values of society as a whole that do not attach onto or originate in any particular or determinate social interest. In contrast, identity politics is a form of political mobilization based exclusively on the appeals to the interests of specific 'parts', without any claim that the latter better approximate the interests and values of society as a whole. As such, identity politics can be seen as the flipside of technopopulism: the former trades in abstract (i.e. unmediated) generalities (such as the 'people's will' and the notion of an objective political 'truth'), the latter asserts a form of *pure particularism*, in which the interests and values of specific social 'parts' are construed as inherently valuable, precisely because they are marginalized or excluded.

What is missing in both cases is the dimension of political mediation whereby the interests and values of a 'part' of society are articulated into some conception of how the whole ought to be governed. Revolutionary politics requires political mediation in order to reconcile individual will and collective agency. Both technopopulism and identity politics, as unmediated forms of politics, are instances of a form of political action that has cast off any revolutionary trappings, committing itself instead to marginal improvements of the status quo.

5
Normative Reflections on Technopopulism

This chapter proposes some normative reflections on the set of developments we have analysed so far. Thus far, we have sought to identify and explain the nature, varieties, origins, and consequences of the technopopulist political logic in a way that did not prejudge the question of their normative desirability. We now take a step back in order to evaluate critically whether the general logic we have uncovered is normatively desirable or not, and then (since our answer to that question is in the negative) consider some possible remedies for it.

The discussion proceeds in three parts. We begin by clarifying the standpoint from which we evaluate the normative valence of technopopulism. This is constituted by a conception of democracy which lays emphasis not just on the formal mechanism of electoral competition, but also on the availability of substantive political options for electors to choose from. From this perspective, we contend that technopopulism undermines the *quality* of democratic regimes because political actors competing on the basis of parallel claims to represent the 'people' as a whole and to possess the necessary expertise to deliver on its 'objective' interests leave no room for meaningful political contestation, even if they do not challenge the formal mechanisms of electoral competition itself.

In the second part of the chapter we consider some of the remedies that have been suggested in the existing academic literature on populism and technocracy for dealing with the specific problem we focus on. We observe a recurrent tendency to posit populism and technocracy as possible *remedies for one another*. On one hand, advocates of populism often portray it as a corrective for the depoliticization implicit in the transfer of power away from elected politicians to presumptively neutral experts. On the other hand, arguments for technocracy often turn on the claim that the depoliticization of key areas of decision-making is necessary to prevent populists from taking hold of them. Our contention is that both these lines of thought are problematic because they rely on the implicit assumption that populism and technocracy are merely opposites of one another. What emerges from our analysis is that there is an important degree of complementarity between them, first of all because they often develop as reactions to each other, but also because they can be fruitfully combined in a variety of ways, which we have attempted to identify through our discussion of the varieties of technopopulism in chapter 2. From this it follows that more of one does not necessarily imply less of the other. On the contrary, to the extent that populism

Technopopulism: The New Logic of Democratic Politics. Christopher J. Bickerton and Carlo Invernizzi Accetti,
Oxford University Press (2021). © Christopher J. Bickerton and Carlo Invernizzi Accetti.
DOI: 10.1093/oso/9780198807766.003.0006

and technocracy go hand in hand, they can only be overcome together, by moving beyond the underlying technopopulist logic itself.

In the third part of the chapter we suggest one possible way of doing so, by examining the prospects for a revitalization of the dimension of *partisanship* implicit in a conception of politics as the struggle between competing interests and values within an institutionalized electoral framework. The starting point is a recognition that the rise of technopopulism is the result of a deep crisis of traditional political parties and ideologies, the contours of which we have spelt out in chapter 3. This implies that it is not possible (and would in any case also be normatively undesirable) simply to return to the 'old' way of doing politics. At the same time, we maintain that the dimension of partisanship itself is neither historically obsolete or normatively undesirable, to the extent that it is construed as a way of connecting a set of contestable political values rooted in particular interests within society with a mode of political organization that enables like-minded individuals to cooperate in the pursuit of those values.

The question therefore becomes how to revitalize the element of partisanship associated with the ideological political logic, while at the same time extricating it from the specific historical incrustations that have made it appear both obsolete and normatively undesirable. To answer this question, we focus on the idea of democratizing the internal structure of existing (or potentially entirely new) political parties. This suggestion is based on the intuition that the fundamental reason for the present crisis of political parties and ideologies is not that individuals have become uninterested in politics or unwilling to take part in it, but rather that the available avenues for political participation have become unattractive for them, because they remain tied to historically obsolete ideologies and modes of political organization. Allowing individuals more scope to determine the terms and modes of their political engagement could therefore provide a greater incentive for them to engage in partisan political action.

This proposal is not a political project in its own right, only an attempt to specify the conditions for formulating one that might be successful. We do not take that to be a problem but rather a strength because to specify in advance the substantive content of the political project required to overcome technopopulism, as some who write on the contemporary democratic malaise do, would end up doing the work of democratic citizens for them and fall back into a technocratic logic. The ambition of the third part of this chapter is therefore to navigate our way through the Scylla of *nostalgia* (fantasizing about the return to a 'golden age' of party democracy, which is now obsolete) and the Charybdis of *utopianism* (recommending a solution that appears attractive in theory but has no real connection with the actual interests and desires of individuals on the ground, and therefore has little chance of being realized in practice).

What's Wrong with Technopopulism?

We begin by explaining why we believe that the rise of technopopulism constitutes a normative problem that needs to be remedied. It is common in the existing academic literature on populism and technocracy to maintain that these political forms pose a challenge to the very survival of the democratic regimes in which they develop. Towards the end of his book on *What is Populism?*, for instance, Jan-Werner Müller writes:

> The major differences between democracy and populism should have become clear by now: one assumes fallible, contestable judgments by changing majorities, the other imagines a homogenous entity outside all institutions whose identity and ideas can be fully represented... The one presumes that decisions made after democratic procedures have been followed are not 'moral' in such a way that all opposition must be considered immoral, the other postulates one properly moral decision even in circumstances of deep disagreement about morality and policy... Finally—and most importantly—the one takes it that the people can never appear in a non-institutionalized manner and, in particular, accepts that a majority (even an 'overwhelming majority', a term beloved by Vladimir Putin) in parliament is not the people, the other presumes precisely the opposite (Müller 2016: 77–8).

On this basis, Müller reaches the conclusion that populism is 'an exclusionary form of identity politics' which 'poses a danger to democracy' (2016: 6). Even more explicitly, in *How Democracies Die*, Steven Levitsky and Michael Ziblatt write that '[w]hen populists win elections, they often assault democratic institutions' (Levitsky and Ziblatt 2018: 6). This leads them to warn about what they call an 'electoral route to democratic breakdown' whereby democratic regimes may 'cross the line into dictatorship' without the traditional 'alarm bells' ringing. 'There are no tanks in the streets', they write, 'constitutions and other nominally democratic institutions remain in place, people still vote... [Yet,] this is how democracies now die' (2017: 4–5).

The existing academic literature on technocracy has been less alarmist, but it has also highlighted a deep element of tension between the technocratic project of favouring expert rule and the democratic principle of popular sovereignty. In his 1993 article on 'The New Leviathan. The Dynamics and Limits of Technocracy', Miguel Centeno asks: 'What are the political implications of the empowerment of a technocratic elite and the imposition of their mentality on policy-making?' (Centeno 1993: 326). In response he maintains that 'the very same characteristics that promote technocratic control also make it inimical to democratic rule' (1993: 326). Similarly, in *Technocracy and the Politics of Expertise*,

Frank Fischer states that '[t]echnocracy's growing influence shields the elites from political pressure from below' (Fischer 1990: 29). This, for him, 'violates democratic principles' and therefore constitutes a 'threat' for democracy's very survival (1990: 30). Recent writings on technocracy make a similar argument. Writing about the expansion in 'technocratic governance' after the Eurozone crisis, Scicluna and Auer (2019) warn about the effects that the 'depoliticized rule of rules' can have on European democracy.

From this, it would seem that a political logic based on the combination of populist and technocratic discursive tropes and organizational features should represent an even greater threat for the health and stability of democratic regimes. Something to this effect has in fact been suggested by Yascha Mounk in his book entitled *The People vs. Democracy*. Here, Mounk makes the case that, as a result of the recent 'populist onslaught' and the establishment's 'technocratic response', the two core components of existing liberal democratic regimes are being pulled apart from one another, producing a split between 'illiberal democracy' on one hand and 'undemocratic liberalism' on the other. This, for him, threatens the viability of liberal democracy since 'the current crisis may end in a dramatic swing from undemocratic liberalism to illiberal democracy, followed by a gradual descent into dictatorship' (Mounk 2018: 254–5).

Our contention is that these suggestions overstate the case, and therefore at least partially misidentify the problem we are concerned with. To the extent that populism and technocracy function as ways of claiming political legitimacy *within* the framework of existing democratic regimes, they do not really threaten the survival of those institutional frameworks themselves. This constitutes an important difference with respect to the 'anti-system' political forces that function as the implicit term of comparison in the analyses we have cited (Zulianello 2018). Whereas the fascist and communist parties that emerged during the interwar period in Continental Europe explicitly claimed to want to overthrow the democratic regimes they operated in, the contemporary manifestations of populism and technocracy insist on respecting the democratic 'rules of the game', and at most claim to want to make existing institutional frameworks *more* democratic (Bickerton and Invernizzi Accetti 2018; Rostowski 2016).

This is confirmed by the fact that the rise of populism and technocracy as the main modes of political action in contemporary democratic regimes has not brought about any major institutional transformations. Even in countries where political actors we have identified as paradigmatic cases of technopopulism have succeeded in coming to power—such as New Labour in the United Kingdom, the M5S in Italy, and *La République en Marche* in France—the basic institutional components of a democratic regime are still in place, at least in the minimal sense that a peaceful changeover of power through electoral means remains a real possibility (which is the main criterion used to establish whether a political regime can be considered democratic by most standard empirical classification methods).[1]

The real problem posed by the rise of technopopulism must accordingly be situated at a different level: not that of the very *survival* of the institutional frameworks that enable a political system to be described as democratic, but rather at the level of the *quality* of democratic representation offered by the political regimes in question. To clarify what we mean by this, it is useful to pursue a brief detour, looking more closely at the way in which the democratic principle of popular sovereignty can actually function in practice. For this, we shall be relying on the discussion of this principle offered by Eric Schattschneider in his seminal book entitled *The Semi-Sovereign People*, which provides a particularly compelling account of the basic normative standpoint from which we intend to criticize the technopopulist political logic.

Schattschneider's starting point is what may be described as a deflationary move. Partially agreeing with critics of the idea that democracy can be anything more than a method for enabling the peaceful circulation of elites through competitive elections (e.g. Schumpeter 1942), he concedes that popular sovereignty cannot plausibly be assumed to require that the people actually govern themselves. A mass of empirical evidence, as well as the growing size and complexity modern societies, suggest that ordinary people simply do not have enough time—or information—to get involved in the day-to-day running of public affairs (Schattschneider 1960: 126–32).

Schatttschneider contends that this doesn't necessarily imply that the idea of popular sovereignty must be discarded. That train of thought is the result of a form of 'pre-democratic thinking' according to which 'the "many" in a democracy are supposed to do the same things that the "one" does in a monarchy and the "few" do in an aristocracy', whereas it is obvious that 'the shift from the "one" to the "many" . . . must also involve a change in the way power is exercised' (1960: 137). More specifically, Schattschneider suggests that the citizens of a democratic polity are in a position similar to that of 'a very rich man who is unable to

---

[1] Whether this is also the case in a number of other empirical cases which the literature we have cited refers to—such as for instance Vladimir Putin's Russia, Recep Tayyip Erdogan's Turkey, and arguably also Viktor Orbán's Hungary—is more doubtful. However, as we have sought to make clear from the start, these are not really the kinds of political actors or regimes we are talking about in this book. Since we understand technopopulism as a new structuring logic of democratic politics, our area of focus is restricted to political regimes that can be considered democratic, at least in the minimal sense that they allow for a peaceful transition of power through electoral means. To the extent that this condition does not obtain, it seems more appropriate to use different labels to describe the political actors operating under such conditions—such as authoritarianism or, indeed, dictatorship. The fact that authors such as Müller and Mounk use the same label to describe what is going on in contexts as different as Russia and Turkey on one hand and the United States and Italy on the other therefore seems to us to be more of a weakness than a strength of their analyses.

supervise closely all of his enterprises', in that 'his problem is how to compel his agents to define his options' (1960: 136).

Schattschneider's argument is that the kinds of *choices* that the members of a polity are offered by the representatives competing for office in elections have become 'the essence of democratic politics' (1960: 136). 'Democracy' he writes 'is a political system in which the people have a choice among the alternatives created by competing political organizations and leaders' (1960: 138). A political regime can be considered democratic only *to the extent* that the choices it offers its members through the mechanism of elections constitute meaningful alternatives that touch on their actual needs, interests and aspirations:

> The whole world—Schattschneider maintains—can be run on the basis of a remarkably small number of decisions. The power of the people in a democracy depends on the importance of the decisions made by the electorate, not the number of decisions they make (1960: 136).

It is *this* specific dimension of popular sovereignty that the technopopulist political logic undermines. The reasons can be gleaned from the analysis of the consequences of technopopulism we provided in chapter 4 and also from the historical account of cartelization given in chapter 3. To the extent that both populism and technocracy involve claims to represent society as a whole (whether in the form of a reified conception of the 'popular will', or in terms of the overarching political 'truths' technocrats claim to have access to) they undermine the scope for meaningful political contestation amongst alternative political projects. The very idea that there might exist alternative political visions corresponding to different sets of interests and values is presented as dangerous and self-serving. Thus, political opposition tends to be construed as illegitimate. Moreover, the concrete political projects being pursued are forced to become more consensual and indeterminate, in order to avoid antagonizing any specific sector within society. The alternatives on offer become substantively more and more similar to one another, what Katz and Mair in their discussion of 'cartelization' described as the 'constriction' or shrinking of the policy space (1995, 2008).

Two more specific consequences we identified are particularly worth highlighting here. The first is what we called the 'desubstantialization' of electoral competition. Since we have defined both populism and technocracy as modes of political action uncoupled from any substantive policy goals, to the extent that they become the structuring poles of contemporary democratic politics, electoral competition tends to centre on different *ways* of doing politics, rather than what is actually being done. The personal characteristics of the politicians competing for office, their particular style of communication and leadership, as well as their capacity to deliver on whatever task they set themselves to accomplish therefore increasingly assume centre stage, at the expense of the substantive content of their policy proposals.

The second relevant consequence of technopopulism is what we have described as the 'increasing conflictuality' of contemporary democratic politics. At the same time as electoral competition loses much of its substantive content, it also becomes increasingly hostile and confrontational. From the perspective of someone claiming to represent the interests of society as a whole, political opponents can only appear as either malicious or ignorant of the people's true interests. The dimension of political opposition itself begins to be perceived as illegitimate, as evidenced by the fact that politicians routinely attack each other personally, questioning each other's motives, morality, and grounds of support, while electors become increasingly distrustful of those who vote for different parties or candidates (Iyengar and Westwood 2015; Brady and Cain 2018).

All this implies that the rise of technopopulism alters the terms of political competition. The choice between contenders ceases to be a matter of particular (and therefore contestable) interests and values, becoming instead an existential decision in which only one option is truly legitimate. Under these conditions, there is not really a *choice* to be had amongst alternative options. Whatever is chosen is construed as absolutely necessary, even if at the level of substantive policy outcomes it doesn't make much difference. The rise of technopopulism undermines the dimension of political *contestation* that Schattschneider identifies as the true substance of democratic politics.

This effect is further compounded by the specific modes of political organization associated with populism and technocracy. As we pointed out in chapters 1 and 2, both these modes of political action purport to bypass—and in some cases explicitly attack—the dimension of formal political organization. Populists claim to offer an unmediated form of political representation, based on a direct relationship between the leadership and the people as a whole. As such, they insist on dispensing with intermediate layers of political organization, presenting them as distortions and even grounds for manipulation of the people's true interests and desires. Technocrats favour informal mechanisms of political influence and cooptation, relying on the cultivation of a particular relationship of trust with the electorate.

To the extent that the dimension of formal political organization is essential to the articulation of competing social interests via alternative political platforms competing with one another on the electoral plane, the challenge to this sort of organization from the technopopulist logic limits the very possibility of substantive political confrontation between competing social parts. Politics becomes a competition between parallel claims to represent the social whole that are *de facto* unmoored from specific interests within society, and therefore fail to constitute an adequate basis for meaningful political contestation. As Peter Mair (2013: 1) put it,

> Although the parties themselves remain, they... become so disconnected from the wider society and pursue a form of competition that is so lacking in meaning, that they no longer seem able to sustain democracy in its present form.

Populism and Technocracy as Remedies for Each Other

Having clarified the reasons why we consider the rise of technopopulism to constitute a normative problem, we move on to discuss some possible remedies for it. In the proposals that have been put forward in the existing academic literature we observe a recurrent tendency to suggest that populism and technocracy can function as effective remedies *for one another*. Normative defences of populism frequently portray it as a corrective for the depoliticization implicit in technocratic calls to transfer power from elected representatives to independent experts. Advocates of technocracy often present it as a bulwark against the danger represented by populists being elected at the polls and entrusted with the responsibility for making policy. Whereas populism is seen as a corrective for technocracy, technocracy is presented as a bulwark against populism.

In his seminal book *On Populist Reason*, Ernesto Laclau defines populism as a mode of political action based on a 'logic of equivalence' whereby a set of 'unsatisfied social demands' are fused with one another in a distinct political identity, by being collectively opposed to a 'constitutive other'. This is contrasted to what Laclau calls a 'logic of difference', whereby different social demands are treated as 'individual problems to be solved', preventing the formation of any clear political antagonisms (Laclau 2005a: 72–100). Laclau thus constructs a categorical opposition between what he calls the 'populist logic' of politics itself, and a 'technocratic logic' that tends towards depoliticization. In a comment he wrote on his own theory a few years after *On Populist Reason*, this is made explicit: '[I] have described', Laclau writes, 'political practices as operating at diverse points of a continuum whose two *reductio ad absurdum* extremes would be a technocratic discourse, dominated by a pure logic of difference, and a populist one, in which the logic of equivalence operates unchallenged' (Laclau 2005b: 45).

Within the framework of Laclau's thought, this distinction is not merely meant to have analytical purchase, but it also clearly has a normative valence. Laclau shares with Carl Schmitt the assumption that there is something inherently valuable in structuring the political space in terms of a dichotomous distinction between 'friends' and 'enemies' (Schmitt 1921). When Laclau asserts that the technocratic integration of society in terms of a series of 'individual problems to be solved' amounts to a form of 'depoliticization', this is clearly meant to function as a critique. Conversely, the claim that the logic of populism is structurally engrained in the very grammar of politics is meant to alert us to a very important function that populism is capable of carrying out. The latter is therefore effectively defended on the grounds that it constitutes an antidote to the depoliticization implicit in the technocratic 'logic of difference'.

The same point is also made, in a more historically specific way, by Chantal Mouffe. In her 2018 book, *For a Left Populism*, Mouffe describes the 'Third Way' politics that she claims has prevailed throughout Europe since the end of the Cold war as a 'technocratic form of politics', one that seeks to 'displace the left/right partisan confrontation' with a presumptively 'neutral management of public affairs' (Mouffe 2018: 15). She goes on to argue that the 2008 economic crisis has manifested this 'hegemonic discourse's' incapacity to deal with the inequalities it engenders. On this basis, Mouffe asserts that: 'The central argument of this book is that to intervene in the hegemonic crisis, it is necessary to establish a political frontier, and that left populism, understood as a discursive strategy of construction of the political frontier between the "people" and the "oligarchy" constitutes, in the present conjuncture, the type of politics needed to recover and deepen democracy' (2018: 17–18).

Explicit arguments for technocracy as a bulwark against populism are not quite as prominent in the existing academic literature. They are, however, a common staple in the semi-academic and political press. In a recent book entitled *Technocracy in America*, international relations expert and political consultant Parag Khanna begins by noting that 'the spread of democracy has hit many stumbling blocks since the end of the Cold War', mentioning in particular that 'populism has hijacked governments from Argentina to Hungary, Russia and Venezuela' (Khanna 2018: 29). On this basis, he goes on to argue that: 'Technocracy becomes a form of salvation after societies realize that democracy doesn't guarantee national success. Democracy eventually gets sick of itself and votes for technocracy' (2018: 32).

Similarly, if somewhat more cautiously, in their book entitled *Democracy in Europe*, the former Italian Prime Minister and European Commissioner, Mario Monti, and the former Member of the European Parliament and current Deputy Governor of the Bank of France, Sylvie Goulard, write that:

> Notwithstanding what the populists may say, the task of government is not to blindly follow the people's passions and desires... It is not through a demonization of expertise, but through a correct combination of technocracy and democracy that public policy will be able to find a better temporal pertinence: reacting rapidly in times of crisis and making wise decisions in anticipation of the future' (Monti and Goulard 2012: 41–7).

What we find here is precisely the inverse of the logic we identified in the normative defences of populism we considered above. There, populism was presented as a corrective for technocracy; here, technocracy is defended as a bulwark against populism. Key elements of this argument about the usefulness of technocracy can be found in a number of recent academic contributions to democratic theory. In his discussion of democratic legitimacy in his 2011 book on this topic, Pierre Rosanvallon argues that democratic legitimacy is a 'complex construct' which requires the combination of a variety of 'modes of representation' in order to be fallibly approximated in practice (Rosanvallon 2011: 1–14). Amongst these, Rosanvallon identifies two which clearly qualify as technocratic according to our definition of the term. The first is what he refers to as the 'legitimacy of identification with generality', which corresponds to the idea of a meritocratic public administration as a separate pillar of democratic legitimacy.[2] The second is what he refers to as the 'legitimacy of impartiality', linking it to the recent proliferation of independent and non-elected regulatory bodies such as 'independent central banks', 'expert commissions', and 'non-partisan authorities' (2011: 87–92).

To the extent that Rosanvallon's overarching conception of democratic legitimacy involves a defence of these two subtypes of legitimacy as necessary for realizing the democratic ideal of popular sovereignty, it can be understood as containing a normative case for technocracy, even if the latter is couched in the terms of an argument for 'enriching' the ordinary forms of democratic representation. What is especially relevant for our present purposes, however, is that this overarching conception of democratic legitimacy as a 'complex construct' is explicitly set against what Rosanvallon calls the 'populist mystification', according to which the people's will can be manifested and implemented directly by the right representatives. We find in Rosanvallon's thought a version of the same idea found in the work of Mario Monti and Sylvie Goulard, namely that democracy and technocracy need to be complemented with one another in order to stymie the threat of populism.

Another interesting example of contemporary democratic theory's flirtation with technocracy as a bulwark against populism is offered by Russel Muirhead and Nancy Rosenblum's recent book entitled *A Lot of People Are Saying. The New Conspiracism and the Assault on Democracy*. In this book, the two authors identify a 'new form of conspiracism' based on 'blatant disregard for facts' as one of the core ingredients of the specific type of 'populism' which for them poses a grave threat for the very idea of 'party democracy' as 'regulated rivalry' (Muirhead and

---

[2] In this respect, for instance, Rosanvallon writes that: 'The neologism technocracy was coined [during the period of creation of independent bureaucracies] to denote a system of government in which experts organize and control the nation's resources for the good of all' (Rosanvallon 2011: 48).

Rosenblum 2019: 62–4). In the last chapter of the book, they propose some possible remedies for it, based on the idea of 'speaking truth to conspiracy'. Muirhead and Rosenblum argue that '[s]peaking truth to conspiracy is not just for political representatives... Experts too, both inside and outside government, whose authority derives from expert knowledge, must speak out' (2019: 153). The main argument developed in the chapter is that reasserting what Muirhead and Rosenblum call the 'epistemic authority' of 'knowledge-producing institutions' is an essential condition for contrasting the conspiracist component of contemporary populism (2019: 141). Since the idea of a politics based on 'truth' is a core component of what we have called technocracy, this can be seen as another version of the idea that technocracy can function as an adequate bulwark against (at least some aspects of) contemporary populism. The contemporary relevance of these arguments should not be underestimated: the *New York Times*' 'truth campaign'—with slogans such as 'the truth is hard', 'the truth can change the world', and 'the truth is more important now than ever'—was one of the leading efforts to challenge Donald Trump's presidency.

Our contention is that both the lines of thought we have just considered—i.e. the idea that populism can function as a corrective for technocracy and that technocracy can function as a bulwark for populism—are fundamentally misguided because they rely on the implicit assumption that populism and technocracy are merely *opposites* of one another, in the sense that the relationship between them is always zero-sum. If this were the case, more populism would indeed imply less technocracy and vice versa, so it would make sense to try to find some 'balance' between them, as a way of contrasting one or the other (or both). The analysis we have conducted throughout the rest of this book, however, shows that this is not the kind of relationship that obtains between populism and technocracy. In addition to some outer elements of tension, we have pointed to some deep elements of *complementarity* between them. Far from being merely opposites, they can also go hand in hand.

Two points are particularly worth highlighting here. The first is that populism and technocracy often appear in conjunction with one another, precisely inasmuch as they constitute political reactions to each other. In chapter 3, for instance, we suggested that the recent proliferation of various forms of anti-establishment populism in Western Europe can be (at least in part) explained as a reaction to the technocratic posture adopted by mainstream political parties as ideological divisions have waned and parties began colluding instead of competing with one another to share the spoils of power. To the extent that mainstream parties form an electoral and political cartel, outsiders have an incentive to try to break it by constructing an opposition between 'the people' and the political establishment as a whole (Katz and Mair 2018: 151–87). At the same time, however, this populist challenge has the effect of reinforcing the establishment's incentives to justify itself in technocratic rather than political terms. As Sheri Berman cogently put it: 'Populism and technocracy are mutually reinforcing. They feed off and strengthen one another' (Berman 2017).

The second point—which has been less often commented upon, but is at the centre of this—is that populism and technocracy can also be fruitfully *combined* with one another by political actors seeking to draw on both their legitimating resources at once. This is the core of the definition of technopopulism we offered in chapter 1, whereas chapter 2 was devoted to a discussion of several concrete examples. In each case we demonstrated that—far from being at odds with one another—the parallel populist and technocratic features of the political forces we considered complement and reciprocally strengthen one another. There is in fact no a priori contradiction either in the idea of using populist discourse to advance a technocratic political agenda, or in the use of technocratic means to foster the presumptive interests of 'the people' as a whole. This constitutes a powerful case against the idea that populism and technocracy can serve as remedies for one another. If they are not just opposites, but also in important ways complementary to each other, more of one does not necessarily imply less of the other, but may on the contrary pose the conditions for an exacerbation of the very phenomenon that was to be contained or reduced.

Since populism and technocracy are part of the same overarching political logic, they cannot function as antidotes for one another. What is needed is to step outside of the technopopulist political logic itself. In the next section of this chapter, we advance one concrete suggestion for how to go about this. This is offered in the spirit of an avenue for further reflection, that will hopefully spur more detailed discussion on this topic, without precluding other aspects of the problem being considered too.

Reviving (and Renewing) Party Democracy

The analysis we have provided suggests that to fight back populism and technocracy together it is necessary to revive a conception of politics as competition between conflicting social 'parts', which stand for the pursuit of substantively different political goals. A condition for that is to revive the dimension of formal political organization as a way of articulating particular interests within society in an overarching vision of how society as a whole ought to be governed. The specific political institution that has historically performed these two functions is the political party. This makes it plausible to suppose that reviving a conception of *party democracy* as a form of politics in which conflicting social interests and values, organized in rival political parties, compete with one another for the temporary exercise of political power over society as a whole might go some way towards contrasting the technopopulist political logic.

Whereas both populists and technocrats claim to stand above partisan divisions, advancing a vision of the interests of society as a whole that is unmoored from any particular interests within it, it is precisely by reaffirming the centrality of partisan conflict as a system of 'regulated rivalry' between organized social parts that the quality of existing democratic regimes can be restored (Rosenblum 2008). There is a sense in which the technopopulist political actors we have focused on in the previous chapters of this book can also be considered partisans, since they compete for political office within the established institutional frameworks, without challenging democracy's basic rules of the game. However, our contention is that theirs is an impoverished form of partisanship, which denies itself as the expression of particular interests and values within society, and for this reason ends up undermining the dimension of substantive political choice amongst the options available to electors. What needs to be revived in order to enable political parties to perform the functions that make them an essential component of democratic self-rule are the dimensions of substantive 'goal differentiation' and formal 'interest organization' that are at the core of the idea of party democracy. Otherwise, all that remains is the empty shell of democratic procedures and partisan competition, without the element of substantive choice that enables electorates to actually have a say in how they are governed.

In what follows, we suggest that a possible way of doing this is to focus on the dimension of intra-party organization, and more specifically to democratize the internal structure of exiting (or potentially entirely new) political parties. To substantiate this claim, we begin by explaining what we mean by a democratization of the internal structure of existing or future political parties. We then explain how this can help revive the two key dimensions eroded by technopopulism; that is, the dimension of substantive goal differentiation between political parties and that of social interest organization within them. Finally, we consider three possible objections to our proposal, offering replies that will hopefully serve to underscore its plausibility.

What we mean by a democratization of the internal structure of existing or future political parties can be explained with reference to a more or less standard model for describing the nature of partisan organizations in general. In the work of authors as diverse as Roberto Michels, Maurice Duverger, and Richard Katz and Peter Mair, we find the idea that party members (or affiliates) can be divided in three broad categories. At the top is the party *leadership*, which is composed of its candidates for elected office, executive committee members, and main figures of authority entitled to speak in the name of the party as a whole. Below them is the party's *middle management*, which is composed of local party officials, active branch members, and registered voters (in countries that have primary election systems). Finally, at the bottom, the party's *base*, which is constituted by the individuals who more or less reliably vote for the party in elections, but do not take a much more active role in running its internal affairs.[3]

In terms of these categories, the internal organizational structure of traditional mass parties can be described as 'top-down'. In his seminal work on the German SPD, for instance, Roberto Michels argues that—under a veneer of 'democratic centralism'—this party had a strongly 'oligarchic' organizational structure, whereby the party leadership made all the most important decisions, controlling the electoral base through the mediation of the middle management (see: Michels 1911: 342–56). Similarly, in his classic treatise on *Political Parties*, Duverger argues that the mass party form (which replaced previous cadre parties in the first few decades of the twentieth century) had an internally hierarchical—and in particular 'bureaucratic'—organizational from, in which the middle management's key function was to mobilize the party's electoral base (which Duverger calls its '*classe gardée*') to vote for the leadership in elections (Duverger 1954: 133).

The specific mechanisms through which this 'top-down' organizational form was sustained need not concern us here. The key point is that the traditional mass parties of the middle part of the twentieth century were *not* internally democratic. Power within them was exercised by the leadership over the middle management and by the latter over the base. Democratizing the internal organizational structure of political parties means inverting this system of power relations. Instead of the party leadership controlling the electoral base through the mediation of its middle management, a political party can be considered internally democratic to the extent that its electoral base is able to control the leadership through the mediation of the middle management.

In this respect, it is important to emphasize the key role played by the party's middle management in the democratization of political parties. The reason is tied to something we have already seen in our analysis of the internal organizational structure of paradigmatic manifestations of the technopopulist political logic in chapter 2. Following a broader organizational trend, many of these have claimed to aspire towards some form of intra-organizational democracy. However, the primary way in which this has been attempted in practice is by establishing more direct links between the party's leadership and its electoral base, which bypass the party's middle management—for instance through the establishment of primary

---

[3] This tripartition roughly corresponds to what Richard Katz and Peter Mair call, respectively: the 'party in public office', the 'party in central office', and the 'party on the ground' (see for instance: Katz and Mair 2018). An important distinction, however, is that what we call the party's leadership also includes powerful figures within the party that don't necessarily run for public office. Similarly, what we call the party's middle management also includes active party members that don't necessarily hold formal positions of responsibility within it. Finally, we also include the party's electorate within its base. Overall, therefore, the difference is that Katz and Mair's tripartition is based on formal status within the party, whereas ours (following Michels, Duverger, and especially May on this) is based on internal influence and prestige. For the same reason, the categories we have proposed shouldn't be seen as discrete or watertight, but rather as defining a spectrum of influence within the party structure, from top to bottom.

elections or other kinds of membership ballots that periodically enable the base to approve or reject the leadership's actions and choices.

As numerous commentators have noted (Seyd 1999; Hopkin 2001; Carty 2013; Katz and Mair 2018), this has had the paradoxical effect of *reinforcing* the degree of control exercised by party leaders over the lower strata of their party's internal organizations, for a reason analogous to the one that explains why the rise of technopopulism undermines the quality of democracy at the system level. Without the availability of substantively different political options, the mere possibility of voting doesn't afford voters any meaningful degree of collective self-government, but rather serves as a mechanism to offer a plebiscitarian type of legitimation to the leadership. The party's middle management is essential for intra-party democracy for the same reason that parties themselves are essential to democracy at the system level. What is needed in both cases is an intermediate stratum of organization that articulates competing interests and value commitments within the electoral base into alternative political options amongst which the latter can choose.

This ultimately translates into a vision of intra-party democracy as a way of empowering the party's middle management against the leadership, by making it function as the organizational stratum through which the party's base can formulate alternative visions for the party's future and choose amongst them. This doesn't mean dispensing with primary elections or membership ballots entirely. However, it does mean that intra-party voting mechanisms need to be complemented with other forms of intermediate partisan organization in order to achieve their purpose. The existence of organized intra-party factions (or currents), as well as institutionalized mechanisms to permit collective deliberation between them and prevent anyone from prevaricating against the others therefore seem essential for realizing the ideal of intra-party democracy, just as inclusive deliberation and institutionalized checks and balances are essential for realizing democracy at the system level (Teorell 1999; Wolkenstein 2016, 2019; Invernizzi Accetti and Wolkenstein 2017).

Intra-party democratization can lead to a revival of the dimension of formal 'interest organization'. Since we have insisted that intra-party democratization requires strengthening the party's intermediate layers of organization to make sure that the base has meaningfully different options to choose from, it could be said that intra-party democratization is *in itself* already a way of reviving intra-party organization. The party's intermediate layers of organization become the mechanism through which particular interests and values that exist within the party's base are articulated with one another into competing visions of how the party as a whole ought to be run, amongst which they can meaningfully choose. This contrasts both with the mass party organizational model—in which, as we saw, the main role of the party's middle management is to mobilize its own base to vote for the leadership in elections in a top-down fashion—and from the technopopulist mode of intra-party organization, which bypasses the party's intermediary bodies entirely, by establishing a direct relationship of embodiment between the leadership and the base. In this sense, intra-party democratization revives the intermediate layers of organization within the party, while at the same time ascribing them a different political role to the one they had in the context of traditional mass parties.

The more complex and interesting point concerns the reasons for which it is plausible to expect that intra-party democratization should also lead to a revitalization of the other key dimension of partisanship undermined by technopopulism, which is that of substantive 'goal differentiation' between political parties. To make this case, we will rely on a relatively common set of assumptions in the existing political science literature on political parties, which is sometimes referred to as 'May's law', following a seminal article on this topic by John May, in which he introduced what he called the 'general law of curvilinear disparity' (May 1973; on this point, see also Kitschelt 1989; Norris 1995).

The core idea is that it is possible to correlate the three different levels of intra-party organization we identified above with what May calls different 'opinion structures', on the basis of the different incentives and potential rewards they face because of their particular position within the party organization. More specifically, May contends that the party leadership's primary incentive is the prospect of winning public office. For this reason, he supposes that they are likely to display a more 'moderate' ideological profile than the party's middle management or its electoral base, since (at least in a two-party system, which is May's primary term of reference), this gives them more chances of capturing the 'median voter' and therefore winning the election as a whole. In contrast, May points out that since the party's middle management doesn't have a vocation for occupying public office, its primary motivating incentive must lie in a commitment to the basic ideological principles for which the party is supposed to stand. For this reason, May supposes that this intermediate stratum is likely to be more ideologically 'extreme' than both the party's leadership and its electoral base. Finally, May assumes that the party's electoral base is constituted primarily by passive voters, whose primary interest is to obtain policy outcomes that reflect their interests and values. For this reason, he supposes they must be ideologically situated somewhere in between the more 'moderate' party leadership and the more 'extreme' party activists.

This set of assumptions yields an overall picture of the likely distribution of ideological preferences amongst party affiliates that is represented graphically by the diagram on the next page (see Fig. 1). The interesting thing to point out in this respect is that May himself thought that his 'general law of curvilinear disparity' would function primarily as an argument *against* intra-party democracy. The reason is that May supposed (just as we have suggested) that intra-party democratization would lead to an empowerment of the party's middle

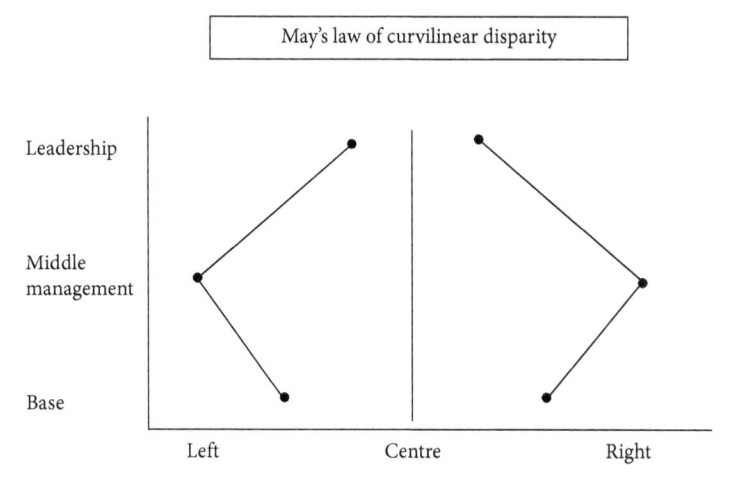

Figure 1. May's Law of Curvilinear Disparity

management and electoral base at the expense of its leadership, thereby resulting in the party's overall ideological profile becoming more 'extreme'. This, for him, was a problem because it implied that the party's overall position would shift away from that of the 'median voter', and therefore make it more difficult for the party to succeed in general elections.

Our contention, however, is that—precisely for the same reason—intra-party democratization can also function as a way to revive the dimension of substantive 'goal differentiation' between political parties. For, if intra-party democratization involves empowering the party's middle management and electoral base at the expense of the party leadership, and if the former two are likely to be more ideologically 'extreme' than the latter, then it is plausible to suppose that intra-party democratization should result in political parties shifting further away from each other on the left–right ideological spectrum. This is represented schematically in the diagram below, where the solid vertical lines represent the overall party positions of 'top-down' political parties (which are assumed to be congruent with those of the party leadership), whereas the dotted vertical lines represent the overall party positions of internally democratic parties (on the assumption that intra-party democratization would result in the party assuming an overall position that is somewhere in between that of the party base and its middle management) (see Fig. 2).

From this analysis it follows that whether intra-party democratization is normatively desirable or not depends on the trade-off between voter maximization and substantive 'goal differentiation' that is implicitly posited by May's 'law of curvilinear disparity'. In a situation in which the parties' ideological positions are already so far removed from one another that there is a risk of gridlock in the political system as a whole (which is not unlike the context in which May was

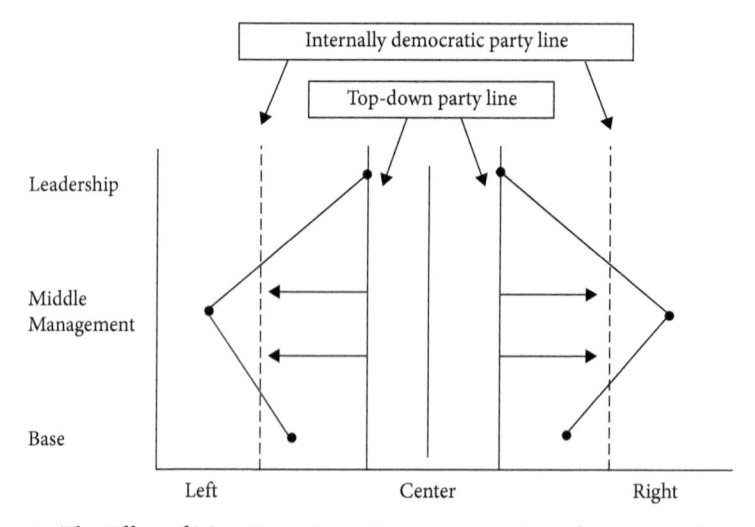

Figure 2. The Effect of More Intra-Party Democracy on Its Substantive Policy Position

writing in the early 1970s), more intra-party democracy may lead to an exacerbation of the ideological divisions that already threaten the viability of the political system as a whole. However, in a situation in which the problem is that there is so little ideological differentiation that electors do not have any meaningful choice between alternative political projects (which is what we have claimed is the problem posed by the rise of technopopulism as the new structuring logic of contemporary democratic politics) intra-party democratization appears more normatively desirable, since it would restore a key dimension of democratic political competition by pushing parties further apart from each other on the ideological political plane.

The central argument we are advancing is therefore that intra-party democratization can help address the problems posed by technopopulism because it would both revive the dimension of formal political organization (virtually by definition) and exacerbate the substantive ideological divisions between political parties (because of May's law of curvilinear disparity), thereby offering electors a more meaningful choice between alternative political projects than are currently available. Of course, in order to exercise their key political function, parties need to remain oriented towards the goal of winning elections. To the extent that, according to May's framework, the party leadership is the internal organizational stratum that is most strongly motivated by this objective, this implies that intra-party democratization need not go so far as to abolish the dimension of party leadership entirely. Parties need to both lead and represent their electorates.

Our suggestion is therefore that *in the present historical context*, the rise of technopopulism has led to an exaggeration of the power of party leaders over their electoral bases, which undermines the quality of democracy at the system level. For this reason, we think that intra-party democratization can contribute in addressing the problems posed by technopopulism, even though it is of course not the only component of what a broader political strategy to definitively overcome this political logic would require.[4]

We now move on to address a number of a number of possible objections to this suggestion. The first objection we shall consider is from *nostalgia*. Its key contention is that the specific conception of party democracy we are proposing to revive is the product of a past historical era—which is sometimes referred to as the 'glorious' thirty years in the aftermath of the Second World War, as in the French expression *les trentes glorieuses*—and it is impossible to reproduce something that is now in the past.

After all, what we have traced in the first few chapters of this book is precisely a historical transition between a form of politics structured primarily by the conflict between different interests and values organized in rival political parties (which we called the ideological political logic) to a form of politics in which rival claims to embody 'the people' as a whole and possess the necessary 'expertise' to translate its will into policy become the main structuring axis of political competition (which is what we have called the technopopulist political logic). As we sought to explain in chapter 3, there are deep historical and sociological reasons for this transition. Thus, even if it were possible, returning to the presumptive 'golden age' of party democracy might still be normatively undesirable, since it would be likely to reproduce the same dynamics that have led us to the present political problems in the first place.

---

[4] One interesting case to consider in this respect is the British Labour Party under the leadership of Jeremy Corbyn. As several commentators have pointed out, the measure of democratization of the party's internal organization that took place during the years that preceded it played a key role in enabling Corbyn to rise to the position of party leader in 2015 (Seymour 2017). This contributed in shifting the party's overall ideological profile markedly towards the left, thereby leading to much starker alternatives being presented to the electorate in both the 2017 and 2019 national elections. This much more polarizing ideological profile has also been widely indicated as one of the main reasons for the Labour Party's resounding defeat, especially in the second of these electoral contestations Proctor 2019). This is based on the supposition that Corbyn moved the party 'too far' to the left by relying on an intra-party basis of support that had lost touch with the interests and demands of the broader electorate (Cruddas 2019; Bickerton 2020b). Other reasons, however, contributed to the party's defeat, including its position on Brexit, which was itself the reflection of deep conflicts of interest and value within the party's electorate, and the charges of anti-Semitism which were a theme throughout the election campaign (Loucaides 2019). At issue, however, is not whether democratization of parties will lead to the victory of one side or the other but whether it will be good for democracy as a whole. The fact that the Labour Party lost the 2019 election is not necessarily evidence that this posed a problem *for democracy*. The fact that electors were presented a clear choice between alternative visions for the future of the country and made an unequivocal decision between them may be seen as evidence of the British electoral system working well. What does appear clear from the experience of the Labour Party under Corbyn is that even if intra-party democratization leads to greater ideological radicalization, there is no guarantee that elections will be fought around—or won on—ideological issues. The 2019 British election was a case in point, where the ideological radicalism was contained to the Labour side, whilst the Conservative Party mobilized—far more successfully—around the technopopulist logic with its slogan of 'Get Brexit Done', a promise to efficiently deliver the popular will.

Our response to this objection is that a distinction can and must be drawn between the aspects of the way in which party democracy was practised during its presumptive 'golden age' that are indeed obsolete (or normatively undesirable) and those that aren't. It may in fact be the case that *specific* political ideologies that parties were competing over several decades ago—or at least the concrete policy positions with which these ideologies were associated—fail to capture the live political issues of our time.[5] Similarly, it is perfectly possible—and indeed likely— that the *particular* modes of organization adopted by political parties in the past are now out of sync with present-day individuals' aspirations and ways of living. However, this does not imply that the dimension of partisanship *itself* is historically obsolete, to the extent that the latter is construed as connecting a particular set of interests and values with a specific mode of political organization in the pursuit of political power within an electoral framework (Rosenblum 2008; Muirhead 2014; White and Ypi 2016; Bonotti 2017).

As long as there are conflicts of interest within society, there are likely to be conflicting systems of values, embodied in different opinions over how society as a whole ought to be governed. As long as individuals will want to try to make sure that their preferred outcomes are translated into policy, they will have to find a way of cooperating with like-minded individuals in some form of organized political action to achieve their goals. What we are recommending is not a return

---

[5] Our position in this regard is that what is more likely to have become obsolete are the particular *policy platforms* that have historically been associated with the traditional left/right ideological divide, rather than the *value systems* that underpin them. In an interesting essay on the history of these labels, Marcel Gauchet reminds us that the notions of political 'left' and 'right' have their origin in the aftermath of the French Revolution, since the supporters of the revolutionary project initially sat to the left of the king in the newly established *Assemblée Nationale*, whereas its opponents sat to the king's right (Gauchet 1996). From the start, therefore, the political left was associated with the values of 'freedom, equality and fraternity', whereas the right stood for 'order, tradition and authority'. Over time, these basic value commitments have been associated with rather different policy platforms. For instance, in the immediate aftermath of the French Revolution, the left stood for the establishment of a republic (or at least a constitutional monarchy), whereas the right aimed for a return to the *Ancien Régime*. Over the course of the nineteenth century, the left became increasingly associated with the idea that the full realization of the values of 'freedom, equality and fraternity' required addressing also the so-called 'social question', whereas the right progressively came to accept the republican political form, while standing for a protection of the rights of private property and restricted franchise. Finally, throughout the first few decades of the twentieth century, the left/right divide revolved primarily around the question of the degree of state involvement in the running of the economy, as the left came to advocate for a form of welfarist redistribution and the right for free market capitalism. Today, few seem to challenge the idea that *some* degree of state involvement in the economy is necessary to compensate for the inequalities and other imbalances produced by the capitalist economy. However, it also seems hard to deny that an overarching vision of society founded on the values of freedom, equality, and fraternity remains very different from one based on authority, tradition, and order. Thus, while it may be necessary to redefine the specific policy implications of what it means to be 'left-' or 'right-wing' in the present historical context, those ideological labels do not appear to us to be obsolete. There may perhaps come a time when the values of freedom, equality, and fraternity are so fully realized that they stop being at odds with tradition, order, and authority. However, that is clearly not the world we live in at present. So, for the time being, we maintain that the traditional ideological poles of 'left' and 'right' are still politically relevant, irrespective of the specific policy platforms with which they have been historically associated.

to a presumptive 'golden age' of party democracy but rather the elaboration of *new* forms of partisanship and political organization, as antidotes to a mode of political action that denies its partisan nature and claims to dispense with the dimension of political organization altogether, thereby undermining the very substance of the democratic ideal of popular sovereignty.

As should already be clear from the discussion we have provided, the specific way in which we are recommending to do this cannot be considered nostalgic because it involves very significant differences with respect to the way in which party democracy was practised during the so-called *trentes glorieuses*. Whereas the mass parties that existed at the time had a 'top-down' organization structure, which committed them to a set of very rigid ideological principles, what we are suggesting is that the condition for a revitalization of party democracy in the present day is a democratization of the internal structure of political parties, which would allow their electoral base and middle management more scope for determining their overall ideological profile and internal form of organization.

Moreover, in this respect, it is also worth noting that the specific reforms we are recommending are in tune with the analysis of the underlying causes of the crisis of the mass party form we provided in chapter 3, and, for this reason, are far from envisaging something obsolete. In particular, a key point that emerges from the narrative we provided in chapter 3 is the centrality of what Ronald Inglehart and Christian Welzel have called 'cognitive mobilization' for understanding contemporary politics. As collective identities and organized interests have become more fragmented, and aggregate levels of education and access to political information have simultaneously grown over the past few decades, individuals have become more politically self-reliant, intellectually sophisticated, and correspondingly less willing to submit to external authorities and hierarchical forms of political organization (Inglehart and Welzel 2005; Inglehart 1990).

This, we suggested, is one of the main reasons why electors have become more receptive to both populist and technocratic registers of appeal. On one hand, they have become more willing to criticize their political representatives, in some cases imagining that the latter could be replaced altogether by more direct forms of political representation. On the other hand, they have become more interested in and capable of evaluating the technical qualities of policymaking, in a way that disposes them more favourably to technocratic forms of politics. The same set of underlying explanatory factors, however, also offers a plausible explanation for the crisis of traditional partisan organizations.

The reason is that—as we noted—traditional 'mass parties' involved both an extremely rigid set of ideological commitments, rooted in a set of predetermined ideological 'packages' that were not really subject to renegotiation, and a markedly hierarchical internal organizational structure, which under the guise of the notion of 'democratic centralism' effectively concentrated power in a bureaucratically selected leadership, leaving little room for individual self-expression and political deliberation within the party's base. This kind of political organization is clearly at odds with the political aspirations and demands for political participation that are likely to be entertained by more cognitively mobilized—i.e. intellectually sophisticated and politically self-reliant—individuals. Thus, it doesn't seem surprising that the societal process of cognitive mobilization has corresponded to a generalized crisis of traditional mass parties (Dalton and Wattenberg 2002; Invernizzi-Accetti and Wolkenstein 2017).

It is important to point out, however, that this line of explanation does not imply that the dimension of partisanship has entered into a crisis because individuals have become less interested in participating in democratic political activity as such. On the contrary, the idea is that more cognitively mobilized individuals are likely to want to take a *more* active role in defining the ideological and organizational terms of their political participation, but this demand for increased political participation is not met by the traditional forms of partisan political organization. As a consequence, individuals have been more inclined to get involved through other, non-partisan modes of political participation—such as civil society organizations and social movements, whose number, size, and importance have grown as those of traditional political parties have waned (Norris 2002).

If the internal organizational structure of existing (or potentially entirely new) political parties were democratized in such a way as to give party members a more active role in defining their ideological and organizational profile, this form of political participation would prove more attractive for contemporary citizens. Democratizing the internal organizational structure of existing or future political parties can address the underlying causes of the crisis of traditional mass parties, by discarding what is indeed obsolete in this specific party form—i.e. pre-fixed ideological packages and strongly hierarchical bureaucratic structures—but at the same time posing the conditions for a revival of what is still actual and normatively desirable in the idea of partisanship itself; that is, connecting a particular set of interests and values with a specific mode of political organization that is suited to present-day individuals' aspirations and ways of living.

The second objection we shall consider is from the *status quo*. Here, the concern is that what we are experiencing at present is not a deficit in ideological conflict and partisan political organization, but rather an excess which is posing serious problems for the stability and viability of existing democratic regimes. A version of this argument has been rather common currency recently in the United States, where a number of empirical studies have purported to show that mainstream political parties have displayed markedly increasing levels of ideological 'polarization' over the past few decades, even while the preferences of public opinion at large have remained rather stable over key issues. This, in turn, has been adduced as an explanation for the rise of ideologically more 'extreme' political figures, such as Donald Trump and Bernie Sanders, and the attendant gridlock of the American political system as a whole (Kelley 2018).

Analogous arguments have also been advanced with respect to contemporary Western Europe. In a series of influential studies, for instance, Hanspeter Kriesi and several collaborators have argued that—contrary to a widespread impression—levels of ideological confrontation have not in fact declined in Western Europe over the past few decades but have been 'displaced' to a different axis of political opposition. Whereas Kriesi et al. suggest, for most of the twentieth century, the principal axis of political confrontation in Western Europe was the 'left/right spectrum' revolving around the 'degree of state involvement in the economy', over the course of the past few decades, the main focus of political competition has shifted to the more 'cultural' and 'symbolic' issues of 'openness vs. closure' with respect to globalization and the modernization of societal mores (see for instance: Kriesi et al. 2012).

From this, Kriesi et al. deduce that the parallel rise of various forms of anti-establishment populism in Western Europe (and technocratic forms of governance as a response) can be seen as a direct result of a 'cleavage realignment' that pits what they call the 'losers of globalization' against its 'winners' (Kriesi et al. 2012). A counter-intuitive implication that follows from Kriesi et al.'s suggestions is that the emergence of populism and technocracy as the main structuring poles of contemporary democratic politics is a result of democratic representation working *well*, not poorly. It follows that heightened degrees of partisanship and ideological confrontation cannot function as an effective antidote to either populism or technocracy, since from this perspective these political phenomena appear as expressions of new—and in some cases even more intense—forms of partisanship and political organization in the first place.

This objection mistakes the outward appearance of contemporary democratic politics for its concrete substance. As we have already highlighted both earlier in this chapter and in chapter 4, we agree that one of the consequences of technopopulism is an 'increasing conflictuality' in the way contemporary democratic politics is conducted, since politicians claiming to stand for the interests of society as a whole tend to deny the legitimacy of their political opponents and attack them personally, questioning their motives, morality, and grounds of support. However, at the level of concrete policy platforms, the substantive differences that exist amongst today's major political forces in Western Europe appear rather slim.

This is not just a consequence of the strictures on socio-economic policy imposed by European regulations and the broader convergence of virtually all major political parties on a form of regulated capitalism in the aftermath of the collapse of the Soviet bloc. Even at the level of what Kriesi et al. call 'cultural' and 'symbolic' issues, the substantive differences between contemporary Western European political parties appear much slimmer than what the 'tone' of political confrontation would lead one to suppose. As several studies have shown, on the key issue of immigration, there is effectively a 'policy consensus' amongst all the major Western European political parties at the moment, inasmuch as no one seems to disagree that the levels of both legal and illegal immigrants need to be severely restricted (e.g. Geddes and Scholten 2016). Even presumptive champions of openness, such as France's Emmanuel Macron and previously Matteo Renzi in Italy, have adopted extremely restrictive measures on immigration during their time in office. If there is any disagreement in this respect, it therefore boils down to the purely technical issue of the *degree* to which immigration ought to be restricted, rather than any fundamental conflict about whether restrictions should be in place or not.

Similarly, on the issues of 'law and order', Western European polities have uniformly displayed what we have described in chapter 4 a as a 'punitive turn' both in rates of incarceration and general surveillance and policing, irrespective of what specific political forces have been in power. As in the case of immigration, the positions adopted by supposedly more liberal candidates such as Tony Blair or Emmanuel Macron over matters of crime, security, terrorism, and civil liberties have not been substantively different from those advocated by the more 'hard-nosed' political forces such as Matteo Salvini's *Lega*, Marine Le Pen's *Rassemblement national*, or the UK Independence Party. What remains the basis for substantive public disagreements are the so-called 'morality issues', such as conflicts over the permissibility of abortion, euthanasia, homosexual marriage, and family rights more broadly. It is precisely the absence of ideological worldviews—which integrates moral questions such as these into political projects founded upon contestable values—that transforms these questions into purely moral ones, which leave little room for a recognition of the legitimacy of alternative views.

What we are observing in the contemporary political landscape is neither a hypertrophy nor a displacement of political partisanship and ideology, but rather a considerable *decrease* in the set of issues over which partisan political opposition still appears possible, which is nonetheless overlain by a marked increase in the degree of conflictuality with which this relatively substance-less kind of political competition is carried out. We do not think that the status quo gives the lie to the idea that what is needed to contrast the parallel rise of populism and technocracy as structuring poles of contemporary democratic politics are greater levels of substantive ideological confrontation and partisan political organization. Rather, we maintain that a proper understanding of what is going on at the moment confirms our key thesis.

A similar point can also be raised with respect to the specific way in which we maintain that the levels of substantive ideological conflict and partisan political organization can be increased—i.e. the democratization of the internal structure of political parties. While it is true that many contemporary political parties (including, most notably, the ones we identified as paradigmatic examples of technopopulism in chapter 2) have made the idea of intra-party democracy a central plank of their political identity and mode of internal organization, the way in which these parties have actually gone about realizing this principle has only resulted in an *apparent* democratization of their internal structure. These parties have relied on an impoverished—and indeed ultimately plebiscitarian—conception of intra-party democracy, based on the introduction of voting mechanisms which allow the base to periodically approve or disapprove of the political actions and choices of the leadership. This has paradoxically ended up reinforcing the power of the party leadership over the base, because it bypasses the dimension of intermediate party organization, which we have claimed is essential to enable the party base to exercise any meaningful degree of control over the leadership.[6]

In contrast, what we have suggested is that a true democratization of the parties' internal structure must pass through an empowerment of its intermediate organizational strata, such that they can function as the mechanisms through which the party base is offered meaningful alternatives between different options for the party's future as a whole, deliberate amongst them, and then choose by means of voting. To the extent that this mode of intra-party organization remains a far cry from the way in which present-day political parties are organized, it shows that what we are recommending is by no means a reiteration of the status quo, but rather a very different form of politics and mode of intra-party organization.

The third and final objection we shall consider is from *utopianism*. This is a complex charge that is usually raised against proposals that are deemed too abstract or difficult to realize in practice. Upon reflection, it can be decomposed in at least two separate charges. The first is that specifying a normatively desirable end-goal is not sufficient to prove that it can be realized in practice. What also needs to be provided is a plausible account of how the goal can be realized, or at least who could do so and why. In absence of such an account, any normative proposal appears incomplete and therefore suspect of unfeasibility. The second problem tied to the notion of utopianism is that specifying a desirable end-goal may short-circuit the democratic process by doing the work of democratic citizens for them, and therefore ultimately fall back into a technocratic logic.

A couple of cautionary examples will serve to illustrate both points. In his book on *The People vs. Democracy*, Yascha Mounk begins the final section on 'Remedies' by suggesting that the only truly democratic way of contrasting the 'deconsolidation' of liberal democracy is to defeat both 'illiberal democrats' and 'undemocratic liberals' at the polls. 'The only democratic protection against

---

[6] For instance, in chapter 2 we suggested that—under a veneer of internal democracy—the reforms introduced by Tony Blair within the British Labour Party's organizational structure, as well as the online membership ballots employed by the Italian M5S, and the participative surveying methods used by France's *La République En Marche* during its early phases of development, have all resulted in highly centralized and 'top-down' political organizations, in which the control of the leadership over the base is virtually unassailable, precisely in virtue of its plebiscitarian legitimation.

authoritarian strongmen', he writes, 'is to persuade people to vote against them' (Mounk 2018: 189). This is consistent with our idea that the present crisis of party democracy is best addressed through *more*, not less, partisanship. However, when Mounk goes on to spell out a concrete proposal for doing so, he advances a series of suggestions that appear to be at odds with the spirit of democratic realism that animates his first point.

Mounk suggests that what is needed is a partisan political project championing a form of 'liberal nationalism' that allies 'raising levels of labor productivity' with a significant degree of 'income redistribution', while at the same time combining the values of 'inclusion and diversity' with a recognition of the fact that 'national borders remain an important symbolic horizon for many people' (2018: 195–252). A similar political project is also hinted at by Jan-Werner Müller towards the end of his book on populism, when he suggests that what is needed to contrast the threat that the latter poses for democratic regimes is 'some sort of new social contract' that seeks to 'bring in those currently excluded... while also keeping the very wealthy and powerful from opting out of the system' (Müller 2016: 99).

While both these proposals may appear normatively appealing (at least to people with left-leaning ideological dispositions), they also display two important limitations that illustrate the problems with what we have called utopianism. The first is that neither Müller nor Mounk provide any account of how their political projects can be linked to the actual interests and political aspirations of specific actors on the ground. Müller concedes that his proposal for a 'new social contract' would require 'broad social support', but he gives no indication as to how the 'very wealthy and powerful' could be kept from 'opting out of the system'. Similarly, Mounk doesn't seem to take into account that many of the specific aspects of the overall political projects he spells out are in tension with one another. It isn't clear what specific social interests or groups Mounk aims to appeal to with his proposals.

The second problem is that, in spelling out the content of what they take to be a 'necessary' political project, even before indicating who is supposed to carry it out and how, both Müller and Mounk do the work of mobilized citizens for them. In this way, they short-circuit the democratic process, by indicating the concrete policy outcomes it should produce even before this has been given a chance to operate. This is tied to a slippage that takes place in both their texts between the 'observer' and 'participant' perspectives. Whereas in the first part of their respective books both Müller and Mounk claim to inhabit the former, the normative proposals they advance at the end are clearly enunciated from the point of view of the latter. What they put forward are *partisan* political projects, which can be broadly described as ideologically left of centre. However, these are presented as the precipitate of a scientific analysis of the conditions required to revive—or indeed save—democracy as a whole, rather than as the expression of a particular set of interests and values. There is therefore a strongly technocratic approach implicit in both Müller and Mounk's proposed ways of overcoming the problems they identify.[7]

Our normative proposal aims to avoid both these pitfalls. To begin with, it is worth noting that the idea of democratizing the internal structure of political parties corresponds to the concrete interests of identifiable actors and groups within society. As we noted above, the societal process of 'cognitive mobilization' translates into an increased demand for political participation, as long as the appropriate channels are offered to satisfy it. A more cognitively mobilized electorate has a clear interest in the internal democratization of political parties, since this will offer them a vehicle for political participation that is more adequate to their demands. What is perhaps even more important, however, is that also the parties' leadership strata have an objective interest in the democratization of existing or future party structures, to the extent that this is indeed a condition for revitalizing participation within them.

The reason is that—even if, from their perspective, intra-party democratization necessarily involves a certain measure of loss of control over the ideological content and organizational form of the party itself—party leaders *need* middle managers and especially solid party bases in order to run successful political operations. Without committed party cadres, activist members, and reliable pools of grassroots political support, they too would find themselves without adequate vehicles for achieving their political goals. No one can win an election alone. To the extent that intra-party democratization is likely to motivate the middle management and attract greater shares of grassroots political support, it is also in the interest of the party leadership itself.

This suggests that the proposal we are advancing is not impossible to realize; it is objectively in the interest of all the actors concerned. All that is required is for them to become conscious of this, through a process that can be easily set in motion by those who stand most to gain from it (i.e. the parties' middle management). The kinds of reforms that are necessary at the intra-party level can then be easily gleaned from the extensive academic literature that already exists on the idea of intra-party democracy (Cross and Katz 2013; Wolkenstein 2016, 2019; Invernizzi-Accetti and Wolkenstein 2017).

---

[7] The problem we are highlighting here has been insightfully discussed by Christopher Meckstroth in a recent book entitled *The Struggle for Democracy* (2015). As he points out, the problem occurs at the point of intersection between normative political theory and democratic praxis. In what Meckstroth calls the 'paradox of authorization', normative political theorists would seem to have to be authorized by democratic means for their specific proposals to be considered democratically legitimate. However, this is a problem if what is at stake is precisely the nature of democratic procedures themselves, or the quality of democratic representation, since that begs the question that is being addressed in the first place. Meckstroth's conclusion is that the only way out of this 'paradox of authorization' is through a recursive dialectical process whereby democratic procedures and normative political propositions reciprocally validate each other. We argue here that neither Müller nor Mounk take adequate account of this problem, and therefore ultimately fall back into what may be described as a purely 'technocratic' form of normative political theory as a direct consequence of their utopianism.

Avoiding the second problem tied to the charge of utopianism is more difficult. On one hand, our proposal does not immediately fall back into the technocratic logic we have found at the heart of Müller and Mounk's proposed remedies for the problems they identify in their respective books, because it does not amount to a partisan political project advocating for any specific policy outcomes. It merely indicates the conditions for a revival of partisanship itself, through an extension of basic democratic principles to the parties' internal organizational structure. On the other hand, one could argue that this proposal does not emerge out of a democratic process and could therefore be said to recommend the democratization of the internal structure of political parties in a technocratic way.

There is, however, a form of recursivity that is implicit in the idea of democratizing political parties and that is absent when one makes recommendations for partisan political projects. To say that the internal organizational structure of political parties needs to be democratized implies that over time this very structure should be reshaped by the dynamics of intra-party democracy itself. The only truly technocratic element of our proposal lies in the way in which this process is set in motion; over time, this is a flaw that can be corrected for by the intra-party democratic process itself. In contrast, Müller's and Mounk's respective proposals specify concrete policy outcomes which do not set up any recursive process of this sort. They therefore remain technocratic in the sense in which we have described, even if they may appear normatively desirable from a partisan point of view.

Conclusion

What may initially appear as a weakness of our normative proposal—that is, its indeterminacy at the level of concrete political outcomes—ultimately turns out to be its strength. This is what prevents it from falling back into the technocratic logic that plagues much normative political theory. This also leaves open the possibility that intra-party democratization might not produce the specific political outcomes we hope for. It might, for instance, lead to an excessive degree of ideological polarization, which makes parties ill-suited for representing the interests of society as a whole. Or, if party members are unable to reach inclusive compromises or agreements over specific issues, it might lead to gridlock or even break-up of the party itself, thereby contributing to further ideological fragmentation. Another danger is that if the political party itself fails to reach out sufficiently into society, then its own internal developments may operate rather like those of a bubble, divorced from wider society and with limited purchase at election time. In other words, there is a question about the precise relationship between transforming the political party and transforming the political logic; greater ideological polarization may exist but have little purchase on political competition firmly rooted in the technopopulist logic. We argue that it is reasonable to suppose that there might be a relationship between the change in the party and the change in the logic, though in practice this relationship is likely to be a complex one.

In short, intra-party democratization is nothing like a 'golden bullet' that will single-handedly solve all contemporary political problems. As we sought to make clear from the start, it can only at most be a *component* of a broader set of social and political transformations that could be reasonably expected to take us beyond the technopopulist political logic. Whether any of this will indeed happen in the foreseeable future is something we take up and discuss in the conclusion. Nevertheless, even in trying to realistically examine plausible avenues for future development, it is useful to have some normative reference points clarified. This can, at the very least, help spot potential dangers and windows of opportunity, if and when they emerge.

Conclusion

Beyond Technopopulism?

Pressures for change constantly operate from within even the most established political systems. Ideological logics were embedded within a rich and overlapping collection of organizational forms—from the local parishes of established churches to the mass political parties of yore. The technopopulist logic has emerged from an organizational vacuum in a way that may leave it more vulnerable to change. In this conclusion, we reflect on current and future changes in the technopopulist logic. We outline ways in which technopopulist actors have evolved over time: some of our most exemplary cases of technopopulism—such as Italy's Five Star Movement—appear to be in decline, at the same time as new syntheses of appeals to the 'people' and appeals to 'competence' emerge. Describing technopopulism as a moveable feast, we chart some of the new developments that highlight the changeable but enduring quality of technopopulism.

In his *Philosophy of Right*, Hegel observed that the owl of Minerva flies at dusk. In the second part of this conclusion, we reflect on the forces and pressures that may take us beyond technopopulism. We understand these to be internal tensions within the technopopulist logic itself. Most obviously, populist and technocratic appeals are not natural bedfellows. It was no coincidence that Michael Gove was able to make such an impact with his claim that 'the people have had enough of experts' during the Brexit referendum campaign of 2016. This surface level tension may over time start to permeate the roots of the technopopulist logic. We also observe that the attempt to use as a political resource a form of legitimacy— expertise—usually legitimized by precisely its *non*-political character certainly has limits. Moreover, appeals to the 'people' also struggle to legitimize authority over time. This is not because anti-establishment movements are unable or unwilling to transform themselves into 'responsible' politicians but because the distributive and zero-sum nature of politics—i.e. the making of decisions that involve favouring some rather than others—cannot be legitimized by appeals to generality of the kind that we find in populist discourses. In order to sketch out some possible scenarios for the future, we look at how the unfolding coronavirus crisis has affected the technopopulist logic. We wrote this conclusion during the first lockdowns of 2020 and this crisis has prompted an extensive public and political debate. We ask whether the crisis will challenge or reinforce technopopulism as the new logic of democratic politics.

The Moveable Feast of Technopopulism

Technopopulism is an idea whose time has come. As one technopopulist synthesis hits electoral hard times, another takes its place. With democratic politics now organized around the technopopulist political logic, we find multiple instances of how appeals to the people and appeals to expertise come together into a single political offer. As we have stressed throughout this book, technopopulism is not a property of a particular actor or political party. As a political logic, it shapes the discursive and organizational dimensions of our politics and the struggle for power that we observe in advanced democratic states. For the most successful and skilled political operators today, this fusion of appeals to the people and appeals to expertise is almost instinctive. It has become the way in which they experience and think about politics, without necessarily being aware that they are doing it.

We described the Five Star Movement in chapter 2 as one of our 'pure' cases of technopopulism. The M5S has reached difficult electoral waters, often outflanked by the powerful *Lega* of Matteo Salvini even in its southern heartlands of Calabria and Sicily. In the regional elections of January 2020, the M5S performed spectacularly badly in places considered part of its core electoral base. In Calabria, the M5S won little over 6 per cent of the vote. These results confirmed an established pattern of decline in support for the M5S, which has been compounded by the resignation of its leader, Luigi Di Maio. As one commentator put it, the movement has lost its sense of purpose since it entered government (Colonelli 2020). Its introduction of flagship policies—such as the Citizen's Basic Income—has also been marred by complexities in the way the policy was designed.

As the M5S wanes, other actors reflect the endurance of the technopopulist political logic. We described the *Lega* in chapter 2 as a 'hybrid' case where far-right ideology combines with technopopulist tropes. The *Lega*'s popularity stems from its promise of action. In Emilia Romagna, the *Lega* presented itself as an efficient alternative to the sclerotic local *Partito Democratico* (PD) machine. In the closely fought regional election in January 2020, the Democratic Party won but only after extensive popular mobilization against the insurgent threat from the *Lega* in a region so long dominated by the political left.[1] Writing about the *Lega*'s role in this election, one account argued that the party's success came from its ability to marshal together an 'anti-politics' sentiment directed at the PD establishment

---

[1] The regional election was held on the 26th January 2020. The campaign was dominated by the mobilization of citizens against Salvini in the form of the 'Sardine' movement. Opinion polls had suggested the *Lega* might win in Emilia Romagna, but in the end, the Democratic Party candidate, Stefano Bonaccini, won 51.4 per cent of the vote; the *Lega* candidate, Lucia Borgonzoni, won 43.7 per cent. Both the DP and the *Lega* obtained over a million votes each and the *Lega* increased its seats in the Regional Council by seven, the PD had three fewer seats than before. On the Sardine movement, see Brody 2020. On its wider lessons for the left, see Donadio 2020.

and a pragmatic willingness to vote for whoever promises to get the job done (Johnson 2020).

In the Emilia Romagna elections, the 'Sardine' movement appropriated the M5S's iconoclastic appeal, managing to create the sort of excitement around bottom-up politics that the M5S once generated.[2] The founders of this movement have emulated some of the technopopulist tropes of the M5S: they aimed to fill the gap left by the crisis of mainstream traditional parties by organizing through social media but also by rejecting any notion of partisanship. Their rule for the mass gatherings was 'no flag, no political party, no insults' (Zampano 2019; Wells 2020). Their message was explicitly non-ideological, which created many tensions within the movement and with more committed left-wing groups. Their core mobilizing message was anti-fascism, but in the further elaboration of their wishes, the 'Sardines' argued for a more respectful and moderate political debate. They called for all participants to be more faithful to the 'facts' and supportive of 'the institutions' (referring to the independent bodies and checks and balances on executive power within the Italian political system). Here we have a good example of a grassroots movement mobilizing within a political domain structured by the technopopulist logic.

Important changes have also occurred in the United Kingdom's political landscape. In chapter 2, New Labour was our paradigmatic case of technopopulism 'through the party'. The transition on the British left towards a post-Corbyn era suggests already that the power of the technopopulist logic is reasserting itself after the ideological caesura of the last five years. The party's new leader, Keir Starmer, is a former barrister whose political project is built around a solid left-wing ideological legacy but one that is presented in a way that emphasizes his legalistic rigour. As one profile put it, Starmer is a 'sensible radical' (McGuire 2020). As opposition spokesperson for Labour on Brexit, Starmer devised an approach to the May government's Withdrawal Agreement that was explicitly technocratic: he established six 'tests' that an Agreement needed to pass, and recommended voting against the agreement because it 'failed' the tests. This recalled Gordon Brown's approach to British membership of the Eurozone, which in that case was subject to five tests (Glover 2000). Rather than frame the decision as one of political judgement, Brown—and later Starmer on Brexit— would frame it as the passing or not of a test, that is conformity or not to an objective standard of truth, in the manner that one can succeed or fail in an exam if one gets the answer 'right' or 'wrong'.

Significantly in British politics, the technopopulist logic has been felt most keenly with the arrival of a new Conservative Party leader, Boris Johnson, who won a large majority in a December 2019 election. Johnson himself, and those

---

[2] Many M5S supporters participated in the Sardines protests, and figures from the M5S gave the 'Sardine' their support.

around him, are demonstrative of yet another kind of synthesis between populism and technocracy. Johnson has styled himself as the leader of a 'people's government'. His election was won by presenting himself as the only defender of the popular will, as expressed in the 2016 referendum on EU membership. After filling the parliament with his MPs, Johnson called the legislature the 'people's parliament'. This multiplication of identifications with 'the people' goes hand in hand with a strong technocratic message. Johnson's winning slogan was 'Get Brexit Done'—a combination of a promise to enact the 'people's will' and an ability to 'do the job', that is to perform, to execute, to deliver. Here we have echoes of Macron's promise to be the 'people's problem-solver' and of Trump's presentation of himself as a 'fixer' after years of dithering.

Perhaps most strikingly in the British case is that the synthesis of populism and technocracy is incarnated in a pure fashion by a single individual—the Prime Minister's chief advisor, Dominic Cummings. Cummings is both iconoclast and provocateur. But his political identity and action is characterized in very simply terms: as the fusion of populist and technocratic forms of reasoning. Cummings has been the author of some of the most popular populist slogans of recent years. In an early 2004 campaign against New Labour's plans to devolve power to a regional assembly in the North-East of England, Cummings led the campaign with slogans such as 'say no more to politicians' and 'they talk; we pay'. He was successful in convincing voters to reject the North-East assembly proposal in what has been called 'Britain's first populist campaign' (McDevitt 2019). Just over a decade later, he was the brains behind 'Take Back Control', the winning slogan of the 2016 EU referendum. At the very same time, Cummings is the author of a curious but widely read blog that celebrates the ability of technology and policy expertise to overcome bottlenecks within the traditional civil service and within the party-political system. Already, Cummings' technopopulist traits have been noticed. James Meek, writing a profile of Cummings for the *London Review of Books*, observed that

> There's a stark mismatch between this utopia of technology-enabled government and the ideology of Brexit, the political-religious project that has given Cummings his power base and reputation. Brexit is an ideal of democracy as a simple expression of majoritarian national will, based on the privileging of faith, hope and anger over expertise. But Cummings' actual governing ideal is antipolitical, ultra-technocratic, excluding all but a tiny fraction of extravagantly trained (in the sciences) high IQ individuals from the levers of control. [Cummings] rejects the EU not because it's undemocratic... but because it's inefficient... He stops short of admiring the Chinese system but describes China as one of the few 'high-performance governments'. His heroes aren't elected: they are visionaries... like the Cold War deterrence expert Michael Quinlan and Leslie Groves, who ran the project to build the first atom bomb (Meek 2019).

As an empirical phenomenon, technopopulism is therefore a *moveable feast*. We have illustrated the power and workings of this political logic through our discussion of the varieties of technopopulism. We expect new combinations in the years to come to add to our list of ideal-types. We also believe that there will be movement in our 'pure' and 'hybrid' cases, as we suggested above, with regards to the British Labour Party and Matteo Salvini's *Lega*.

Internal Tensions within Technopopulism

Technopopulism is a political logic that shapes the discursive and organizational patterns of our politics. As such, it is not a property of any single political actor or party but rather structures the incentives and constraints that such actors face in the present historical and political context. Whilst there are many different syntheses of appeals to the people and to expertise, a change in the logic itself is likely to come from some of its own internal tensions. We observe these tensions in three ways: in the technopopulist syntheses themselves, and in the appeals to competence, on the one hand, and appeals to the people, on the other. We discuss each of these in turn.

Tensions in the Technopopulist Synthesis

We stress in this book the degree to which appeal to the 'people' and appeals to 'expertise' need to be considered as complements rather than opposites. This helps make sense of the various syntheses of these different appeals that we observe and avoids the sort of confusion that paints Macron as a 'non-populist populist' or the surprise that animates observers when figures once dubbed populist embrace expert opinion. Nevertheless, it remains obvious that at a number of different levels, these populist and technocratic appeals are also different and in tension with one another.

Most obviously, an attack on the establishment, the *casta*, the ruling class, is at the core of what we call populism. Appeals to competence and expertise would seem to signal an acceptance and support for those institutions often associated with 'the establishment'. That phrase describes not only the political class but also many other key institutions across society that are characterized by an emphasis on expertise and professionalism. In Anthony Sampson's account of the British establishment, in his famous book of 1962, *Anatomy of Britain*, he included the political, financial, and bureaucratic elites in his account of the establishment. One of Sampson's main claims was that Britain was run by 'a cluster of interlocking circles, each one largely preoccupied with its own professionalism and expertise and touching the others only at one edge', rather than by any cohesive and unified 'ruling class' (Marquand 1962). We should expect anti-establishment movements to direct their fire at institutions and individuals central to the production of knowledge in our society—from universities through to the media all the way to the administrative arm of the state. Conversely, we often find conflict between those who hold dear matters of competence and expertise in politics and those who prefer to speak in the name of the people.

This sort of oppositional tension between technocracy and populism was an ongoing feature of the British debates around Brexit, particularly after the 2016 referendum. Analysts have made much of the fact that education levels were strong predictors of how one voted in the referendum, with supporters of EU membership clustering towards the more educated end of the spectrum. The leading Labour politician Rachel Reeves put it even more baldly: '"Brexiters" voted with their hearts whilst "Remainers" voted with their heads', she argued (Reeves 2018: 18). On this reading of the debate, there is no technopopulist synthesis. Rather, populist emphases on identity clash with technocratic arguments about integrated supply chains, the economic impact of Brexit, and the nature of twenty-first-century 'shared sovereignty'.

There are evident tensions between populism and technocracy but it would be wrong to reduce them to matters of class, taste, or education. Rather, we are dealing with a more fundamental problem, namely that what populism and technocracy have in common is also what divides them. As argued in chapter 1, both appeals to the people and to competence have in common their generality: they are appeals to a certain kind of 'truth', that of the popular will or that of an objective answer of some kind discoverable through formal methods of investigation (Bickerton and Invernizzi Accetti 2015a). This similarity is crucial for the technopopulist synthesis, but such appeals are at the same time appeals to *different sorts of generality*.

Daniele Caramani (2017) has developed this point most systematically, noting that populism and technocracy represent different sorts of ideas about representation (in the form of 'mandate' versus 'trusteeship' respectively), value responsiveness in one case (populism) and responsibility in the other (technocracy). Over time, technopopulist syntheses have to adapt to the consequences of these different sorts of generalities. In some cases, such differences may make it hard to maintain the unity of the technopopulist political identity, and they can lead to an actor concentrating on one element of the logic more than the other. Tensions between these two appeals to generality can also limit the political appeal of a technopopulist strategy, pushing actors to seek an alternative.

The British campaign group, the People's Vote, is a useful case in point. It was established in order to campaign for a second referendum on EU membership. It deployed the language of 'the people' openly and explicitly. This rested on the claim that the first vote lacked legitimacy because voters had not been properly informed and that in so far as there was information, it was misleading (Bellamy

2018). The popular majority in favour of leaving the UK was thus giving way to an active majority in favour of voting again, more aware of the consequences this time. More strategically, the campaign was seeking to claim the populist mantle from the Brexiteers, deploying its own version of popular sovereignty described as 'the right to change one's mind'. However, the core of the campaign was premised on the notion that how one votes will be shaped by understanding an issue better, and in essence getting closer to 'the truth of the matter', in this case the 'truth' being the nature of the UK's membership of the EU. The popular and the epistemic dimensions to the campaign were simply too different to be reconciled. Internal reasons related to clashing personalities played its role, but the fundamental differences between an appeal to 'the people' and a strictly epistemic understanding of democracy was an important reason for the campaign's failure.[3]

Technopopulist Legitimation and Political Competition

Tensions within the technopopulist logic can also occur in each of the two dimensions of that logic—the 'techno' and the 'populist' respectively. In chapter 1, we developed our definition of technopopulism as a political logic, differentiating it from earlier attempts to frame it as an ideology or as the property of a particular type of political actor. This conception of technopopulism implies a distinction between the dynamics of electoral competition and the operations of the modern administrative state. It implies the maintenance of the autonomy of the political realm *vis-à-vis* bureaucratic power. What we describe in this book is not the collapse of the political struggle altogether but rather the *transformation* from an ideological to a technopopulist political logic.[4] The appeals to the people

---

[3] Little has been written so far on the People's Vote campaign. For the most thoughtful treatment of the question of the legitimacy of the first referendum, and the quality of arguments in favour of a second, see Bellamy 2018.

[4] The idea that contemporary politics has been eviscerated, leaving just populism and technocracy in its wake, was captured by Slavoj Žižek in his 2008 book, *In Defence of Lost Causes*. He suggested that populism had become 'the "spontaneous" ideological supplement to post-political administration' (2008: 268). We find something similar in Pierre Musso's idea of the 'enterprise-state' (Musso 2019a, 2019b). He argues that what unites otherwise contrasting figures such as Silvio Berlusconi, Emmanuel Macron, and Donald Trump is the way they have brought the language of business and management into politics. They have cited the practices of the corporate world as a model for running a government (2019b); as in Macron's famous wish that France should become a 'start-up nation' or Berlusconi's promise that under his rule all Italians could become 'entrepreneurs'. According to Musso, the 'company-state' is run by a 'president-entrepreneur'. Berlusconi was the pioneer of this form of politics, but it has now become normalized. A similar sort of idea is made by those writing about depoliticization and anti-politics. These accounts often give the impression that political competition as such has been radically stripped back, leaving us with little more than a fight between charismatic leaders, conducted within a vast landscape of expert rule, what Weber called 'plebiscitarian democracy' (Lassman and Speirs 1994: 339). The concept of the 'entreprise-state' expresses this same collapse of politics into administration, with charismatic leaders transformed into twenty-first-century CEOs.

and to competence combine in ways that sustain political competition, albeit one that is very different from a politics of left versus right.

Considered in this way, we can see a problem with legitimizing political authority through populist and technocratic appeals. Both the appeal to expertise and the appeal to the people are legitimized by their *externality* to the principal dynamic within politics, which is the struggle for power and the seeking of office. As we have argued in this book, technopopulism as a form of politics is disconnected from any particular group within society or any organized interest as such. It is a politics of the 'whole', not of the 'parts'. Nevertheless, by becoming the basis for political competition, these general appeals are subject to the particularizing effects of political office.

An ideological logic is well suited to this because it contains within itself an attempt at mediating between the particular and the general; ideological appeals fuse the interests of particular groups into broader visions for society as a whole. Neither appeals to the 'people' nor to 'competence' do this. Therefore, it becomes much more difficult for them to maintain their legitimacy when politicized as part of the shift towards a technopopulist political logic. In a sense, therefore, technopopulism suffers from a legitimation deficit generated by the very politicization of the appeals to knowledge and to 'the people' that define it. We discuss each dimension of this tension below, starting with the technocratic appeal.

As Weber argued in his account of the development of modern mass politics, the distinction between politics and administration is a fundamental one. It refers to two quite different 'life worlds':

> [T]he true official... should not engage in politics but should 'administer', and above all he should do so *impartially*... The official should carry out the duties of his office *sine era et studio*, 'without anger and prejudice'. Thus, he should not do the very thing which politicians, both the leaders and their following, always and necessarily must do, which is to *fight*. Partisanship, fighting, passion—*ira et stadium*—all this is the very element in which the politician, and above all the political *leader*, thrives (Lassman and Speirs 1994: 330).

Technopopulism subverts this distinction by politicizing expert knowledge. This provides political actors with a new source of legitimacy and creates the space for novel political offers, but it introduces into the political domain that which is usually legitimate precisely because it is not political. Castellani (2020) describes the corrosive effects this can have on the technocratic appeals made in line with the technopopulist political logic. 'Subject to the demands of *kratos*, of power', he writes, '[technocratic governances structures] come up against the invariable cycle of politics. They legitimize their place on the basis of competence rather than democracy as such but the scientific quality of their knowledge provides no protection from political earthquakes.' The more a political position masks as a scientific claim, Castellani adds, the greater the ruin will be for the technocratic powers when political events go against them. In short, the technocratic class finds itself subject to the same pressures of turnover and rejuvenation that are present within the political class, but it is particularly ill-suited to this Schumpeterian circulation of elites.

This is one aspect of what happened to Mario Monti's government when he was installed in power in late 2011, under the pressure and guidance of the EU and its leading member states (Anderson 2014). Monti's legitimacy rested heavily on his appeal as a competent technocrat, and yet the highly politicized context of his arrival at the Palazzo Chigi tarnished from the outset this crucial dimension of his legitimacy. When he ran for office with his own political party, *Scelta Civica*, in the 2013 national elections, he failed to make any political inroads. His party came a very distant fourth, with 8.3 per cent of the vote. In the case of the M5S, when its candidates were elected into local office, they were often unable to rely on the local bureaucracies that had long been captured by the dominant political parties, right or left. In Rome, Virginia Raggi entered the Palazzo Senatorio in 2016, accompanied by a long trail of experts who she relied on as her closest advisors. As Lorenzo Castellani (2018) observed, none of these advisors were elected local councillors. They included lawyers, like Raggi herself, university professors, and high-ranking civil servants.

In France, Emmanuel Macron appointed technocrats to key ministerial posts (e.g. health, public education) in his first government after the 2017 presidential and legislative elections. Part of the reason for doing so was that his movement, *En Marche!*, was so new that he had very few political allies to turn to in making up his government. He drew on those from the political left and right to make up his government, plus a large number of independent experts. Later in his presidency, he took time to replace ministers after incumbent resignations simply because there was no one within his own political movement to take their place. When the long-time Socialist mayor of Lyon, Gérard Collomb, resigned as Minister of the Interior in October 2018, Macron was forced to fill the post with a trusted insider, Christophe Castaner. Castaner was a safe choice for Macron but lacked the political weight usually associated with appointments to the interior ministry at the Place Beauvau.[5] What we are seeing here is not the transfer of political power to independent experts but the implantation of experts directly into the political domain, *qua* political actors.

A consequence of this has been to make 'expertise' or *techne* a standalone subject of political debate and controversy; and to subject it—as Castellani observes—to the highs and lows of political fortune. Macron's reliance upon

---

[5] Castaner himself was a socialist politician before joining Macron's *En Marche!* movement in 2016.

outside experts to make his early governments was well received, a sign that he was delivering on his promise to do politics differently and was seeking out as ministers figures who were not part of the much-maligned political class. But as Macron's own political fortunes waned, so opinion about his technocratic style of government changed. Indeed, over time, the adjective *téchnocratique* has become in France a shorthand term to capture the sense in which the President and his government are out of touch and unable to connect properly with voters. There is even a sense in which 'technocratic' as a label is synonymous with a cold rationality that fails to take into account some elementary human sentiments.[6]

The impact of politicization on the legitimacy of expertise is compounded by the stark contrast between the technopopulist orientation towards 'getting things done' and the *necessarily* insubstantial nature of the technopopulist political offer, which we have discussed in detail in chapter 4. Technopopulism as a political logic thrives around rival claims to action, efficacy, and competence. In the 2016 US presidential election, both Clinton and Trump sought to outshine each other in this regard. Clinton emphasized her experience and put herself forward as a trusted and safe pair of hands. Trump argued that only he could break through the political logjam, by 'draining the swap' and by being beholding to neither funders nor the Republic Party machine. In 2017, when Emmanuel Macron and Marine Le Pen faced each other in the second round of the French presidential election, a turning point was her poor performance in a second televised debate. Running for over two hours, Le Pen failed spectacularly in the debate, raising questions about her suitability as party leader. The principle criticism made of Le Pen was that she was unprepared and consistently made errors in her arguments with Macron. After only ten minutes, Le Pen confused SFR—a French telecoms company—with Alston, an engineering conglomerate. 'One company makes telephones, Madame Le Pen', Macron said, looking genuinely shocked at her mistake. 'The other makes turbines and other forms of industrial equipment. That's not the same thing'. Later in the debate, the two clashed over France's future in the euro. Le Pen argued that France should exit the euro and return to

---

[6] In early 2020, the Macron government found itself mired in a vitriolic debate surrounding its policy towards the rights of parents grieving after the loss of a child (Cordier et al. 2020). The debate was centred on whether the leave given to parents under such circumstances should be extended from five to twelve days. A commission working on this issue had left out this change in the law and when it was reintroduced during a debate in the National Assembly, it was dismissed by the French Minister of Labour, Muriel Pénicaud. In her words, such a change in the law was unacceptable because of the burden it would place on employers, who would have to cover their employees' leave. Following the Minister's intervention, the text was voted down by representatives from Macron's party, LREM. The outcry focused on the lack of understanding and empathy shown by the government and its minister, in particular, for an issue which annually would represent a negligible cost to employers. The actions of Pénicaud and the LREM representatives left an 'impression of coldness, of technocratic stubbornness, and... an absence of political sense' (Mahrane 2020). This response was compounded by the fact that Pénicaud herself was an expert, having spent two decades in the private sector, running human resources for two large French companies—the food giant, Danone, and the aircraft engineering firm, Dassault.

the franc, whilst also suggesting that a dual currency arrangement would permit its central bank and largest companies to continue using the euro. Once again, Macron pressed Le Pen. 'Do you mean France should abandon the euro?' he asked repeatedly, surprised again at the confusion in Le Pen's message. In the reactions to the debate, there was little interest showed in the candidate's policy proposals. Overwhelmingly, the discussion was around Le Pen's confusion and lack of preparedness.

The technocratic dimension of the technopopulist political logic thus struggles both with politicization and with the promise of efficient performance, which is difficult to honour given the disconnect between technopopulism and specific policy platforms. The populist dimension faces its own tension, which also has to do with its appeal to generality. Traditional ideological platforms functioned by translating broad political principles into a series of identifiable policy commitments across all the range of issues in which we expect public authorities to act. At the very heart of the ideological political logic was a creative tension between an appeal to the 'parts' and an appeal to the 'whole'; that is, the ability of a specific group to articulate its interests in a way that connects with some notion of the common good. Modern party politics in democracies is what Weber called the 'politics of interested parties': the movement from the particular to the general and back again is one of the principle dimensions of political life. Articulating specific demands at a level of generality is important in elections, of course, which is reflected in the range of arguments that have been made about how the interests of one section of society—such as the bureaucracy, for Hegel, or the working class for Marx—can also represent the interests of all of society. However, the content of an electoral programme nevertheless stems from the group in society that is being represented. Without a clear sense of *whose* interests are being advanced, it is difficult to know what exactly needs to be done.

Technopopulism combines an appeal to competence and efficiency with an appeal to 'the people' which functions as a critique of the very idea of pursuing specific interests. In making this populist appeal, political actors deprive themselves of the determinate social content that forms the basis of programmes for government. In these circumstances, it can end up being very difficult to act. Whilst Macron was better able to communicate his programme than Le Pen in the later stages of the campaign, he has regularly been criticized for trying to reconcile opposing points of view or opposing interests, out of a desire to avoid framing his political project in dichotomous or conflictual terms, i.e., as a 'part' rather than a 'whole'. His use of the term '*en même temps*' (at the same time) became famous as a signalling device for his belief that opposing sides in any debate should and could be reconciled.

Macron argued that '"at the same time" simply means that we take into account imperatives that seem opposed to each other but that must be reconciled in the interests of a well-functioning society' (cited in Bigorne, Baudry, and Duhamel

2017). His appeal 'to everyone' was successful in the 2017 election, but afterwards he was very quickly dubbed the 'President of the rich' because of the nature of his priorities and policy programme. The *gilets jaunes* mobilizations of 2018–19 introduced a territorial and spatial dimension to this critique, accusing Macron of representing the narrow interests of those inhabitants of France's largest cities, at the expense of those who inhabit its suburbs and its vast countryside. The Macron government responded to this attack on his populist appeal by emphasizing the technocratic dimension of its discourse: the reforms are the 'right things for France' in spite of their uneven social consequences. As we have seen above, this response has generated its own backlash against Macron's technocratic approach to politics.

The technopopulist political offer is socially deracinated, meaning that it can be weak as a way of legitimizing political action. This may also be a reason for its endurance as a political logic, however. We must not forget that the origins of technopopulism lie in the weakness of organized interests and the fragmentation and individuation that prevails across the social body. This also means that opposition within the technopopulist field may be quick to form but relatively evanescent and lacking the organizational solidity needed to derail governmental plans entirely. In this respect, Macron has been more successful than some of his predecessors in reforming French society and economy, particularly with regards changes to the French labour market. The *gilets jaunes* protests were dramatic and devastating in some respect, but they fell short of putting an end to Macron's presidency. Their political legacy remains uncertain.

Overall, we can see the manifest internal tensions within the technopopulist political logic. It puts the emphasis on action and efficiency, but the separation of the political domain from organized social groups deprives political actors of clear ideas about what they should be doing and who they are doing it for. An important test for the endurance of the technopopulist political logic will come when governments such as Emmanuel Macron's in France, or Johnson's 'people's government' in the UK, stand for re-election. What are the electoral consequences of failing to deliver on promises when the appeal of the political movement in the first place was its ability to deliver where traditional political actors could not?

Scenarios for the Future

Thinking about possible evolutionary routes *beyond* technopopulism, we identity three scenarios for the future that develop and make concrete the arguments above regarding the internal tensions of this political logic. As this book was finished under the conditions of the lockdowns imposed across much of the globe over the late winter/early spring of 2020 and again in the autumn of the same year, we explore below how the ongoing global coronavirus crisis provides an illustration of these scenarios for the future. It is too early to tell whether this crisis will introduce the sort of fundamental change that philosophers such as John Gray (2020) and others have been attributing to it. However, it has served as a catalyst for thinking about the pressures exercised upon—and also the endurance of—the technopopulist political logic.

Our first scenario is that the coronavirus crisis leads to an exacerbation of the technopopulist logic, proving its enduring relevance in contemporary democratic politics. Our second scenario is that the coronavirus crisis leads to a break with democratic politics *tout court*, which would eliminate this logic which we specifically situate within democratic political procedures. The third is that the crisis leads to a return of ideology, again taking us beyond technopopulism.

An Exacerbation of Technopopulism

> *The coronavirus epidemic... is a major test of citizenship. In the days ahead, each one of us should choose to trust scientific data and healthcare experts over unfounded conspiracy theories and self-serving politicians* (Harari 2020).

In one of the first attempts to sketch out the implications of the coronavirus crisis, the writer Yuval Noah Harari argued that the answers to two questions would shape the world 'after coronavirus'. We could either opt for 'totalitarian surveillance' or for 'citizen empowerment' in the realm of our relationship to technology. This, in turn, poses the question: will governments respond by building 'solidarity' with one another or preferring 'nationalist isolation' (Harari 2020)?

Harari's attempt to address these questions reproduces the technopopulist logic. On the one hand, he argues that the only way to avoid empowering existing democratic governments in potentially totalitarian ways is to embrace the notion of scientific truth. In his words, 'when people are told the scientific facts, and when people trust public authorities to tell them these facts, citizens can do the right thing even without Big Brother watching over their shoulders.' Harari then goes on to establish a stark opposition between scientific expertise and populist misinformation. 'Over the past few years', he observes, 'irresponsible politicians have deliberately undermined trust in science, in public authorities and the media.' The coronavirus has thus taken us to a crossroads, 'a major test of citizenship' in Harari's words: 'each one of us should choose to trust scientific data and healthcare experts over unfounded conspiracy theories and self-serving politicians.'

Harari's argument is here built around an implicit opposition between technocracy and populism. His account of 'science' is explicitly technocratic, in so far as he conceives of it as a domain regulated by the discovery of a single 'truth'. There is never any sense that scientific data and healthcare experts might disagree about what policies to adopt in the face of the crisis, or that there may be political and ethical decisions to be made in the space that lies between a scientific model and a public authority that has to implement a decision. At the same time, Harari's notion of citizen empowerment through technology has echoes of the Five Star Movement's celebration of the power of new technology to disrupt ordinary political life.

Harari argues that there is a liberating and bottom-up dimension to this new embrace of scientific facts and of the information new technologies can provide. Data about personal health 'should enable me to make more informed personal choices and also to hold government accountable for its decisions'. In language that chimes with technopopulist attitudes towards new technology, Harari reminds us that 'whenever people talk about surveillance, remember that the same surveillance technology can usually be used not only be governments to monitor individuals—but also by individuals to monitor governments.'

Other commentary mobilizes the same technopopulist logic. Jan-Werner Müller has written about the way the coronavirus has exacerbated a long-standing 'systematic denigration of professionalism'. He argues that what right-wing populists dislike most of all are not elites as such but rather experts, i.e. 'professionals who claim authority on the basis of education and special licensing—think lawyers, doctors and professors' (Müller 2020). This denigration has its roots in developments prior to the pandemic, but the tension between the populist and the expert has been exacerbated by it, according to Müller.

Rather than simply asserting that need for more trust in expertise, however, Müller reminds us that 'professionalism has its place' as well. In this respect, he distinguishes 'proper professionals' from technocrats and argues that there is a danger if the coronavirus crisis shifts power too much away from the populist politicians to the technocrats. In Müller's words, 'the assumption that there is only one right way is perversely shared by populists and technocrats: populists claim that there is only one authentic popular will... [T]he technocratic stance... holds that there is only one rational answer to policy challenges.' As a result, disagreeing with a populist means being 'declared a traitor to the people', whilst disagreement with a technocrat means that 'you'll be told politely that you're not smart enough.'

Müller's understanding of this logic is in terms of anti-science populists and anti-pluralist technocrats, who oppose each other but have in common their vision of politics as being about the pursuit of 'the right way'. In practice, we have seen the complementarity between populism and technocracy at work in the pandemic, often in unexpected ways. The British government is a case in point. The British Prime Minister, Boris Johnson, had a place in the public imagination—nationally and globally—as a clown. He is widely known for his stunt of riding down a zip line in an East London park during the London 2012 Olympics, only to find himself stuck and unable to get down, 'like a damp towel slung over a washing line on a soggy day' (Addley 2019). Johnson's victory in the

2019 general election confirmed his status as a successful politician but one marked above all by his populist style and willingness to gamble on three-word slogans devised by the same advisers who coined the winning slogan of 'Take Back Control' in the 2016 vote on EU membership.

At the beginning of the coronavirus outbreak in the UK, these impressions of Johnson were challenged by the approach the government took, which appeared to steer as closely as possible to scientific advice. One bemused political reporter wrote that the '"Populist" PM takes non-populist approach when it comes to pandemics' (Rigby 2020). A profile of the UK's Chief Medical Office, Chris Whitty, described Whitty as 'an unlikely hero for anxious times'. It noted that whereas one of Johnson's allies in the Brexit campaign argued that people 'have had enough of experts', Johnson himself in the midst of the coronavirus crisis had 'repeatedly deferred to a member of that disdained breed who was standing alongside him' (Neville 2020). For those accustomed to assuming an unwavering conflict between populists and experts, the development of the UK government's response to the pandemic has been confusingly dictated by the evolution of scientific debate. The government refused initially to introduce lockdown measures of the kind being observed in Italy and France. It dubbed such measures as 'populist' but ineffective, designed to satisfy an expectation from citizens for dramatic action. Johnson instead argued that the scientific advice was to achieve some degree of 'herd immunity' across the population and to try to shift the peak of the outbreak closer towards the period between Easter and Summer, when the country's health service would be better able to cope. Whilst most countries have opted for the lockdown approach, Sweden for instance maintained for some time a different approach which it claimed was equally rooted in the scientific evidence.

The change in the UK government's position occurred in the third week of March, on the back of a new study by a team of epidemiologists at Imperial College London. The study found that any efforts at flattening the morbidity curve, which implied a much higher number of infections, would lead to a prohibitively large number of deaths: 250,000 in the UK and up to 1.2 million in the US. The message of the study was that only a suppression-based approach, with associated lockdown strategies, could work. The UK government promptly changed tack, shutting schools and all non-essential retail outlets and asking people to stay at home. Competition between scientific models has framed British public debate almost entirely: the Imperial College London study recommending suppression is pitted against the University of Oxford study that argued that many more people were already infected and developing immunity than we imagined. Some of the most prominent figures to have emerged from the public debate so far include Neil Ferguson, Imperial College's leading epidemiologist (Clark 2020). Writing about the British experience, *The Atlantic* commented that 'even populists need experts, it turns out' (McTague 2020).

Situating the crisis within the technopopulist logic helps us understand why populists will quickly embrace an approach that frames decisions as 'purely guided by the science'. This is not an aberration but an expression of the technopopulist logic at work in our democratic systems. Those offering a technopopulist synthesis have often, though not always, been viewed in a positive light. This is what figures such as Andrew Cuomo, governor of New York, have achieved, whose reputation and standing have grown throughout the crisis. Explaining his unexpected emergence as 'father of the nation', emphasis is placed on Cuomo's 'ability to communicate empathy while ruthlessly delivering policy'—a description that captures well the technopopulist synthesis of a personal relationship to voters alongside a commitment to efficiency and getting 'the job done'. Cuomo describes himself in ways that highlight the personalized way in which he views political representation: 'I take my job very seriously. I don't make excuses. If I fail, I fail. If something breaks or doesn't work—that's on me. I see the number of deaths every day and I take that personally' (Chaffin 2020). In Germany, Angela Merkel has responded to the crisis in a way that fits well with the technopopulist logic, hence her success and returning popularity. At the end of March, Merkel addressed the German population directly on television. Notwithstanding the brief and uninspired New Year's addresses, this was something she had never done in her fourteen years as Chancellor (Chaffin 2020). Merkel's intervention combined her trademark calm and measured tone, explaining to Germans the measures that had been taken, with a more personal dimension that made it possible for viewers to connect with her. After a steady decline in popularity, Merkel's status as the mother (*mutti*) of the nation is back, something that combines a sense of protection with a personalized and direct relation to the Chancellor. In one journalist's words,

> No one had seen Merkel speak to the nation on TV...Few had seen her show such empathy and emotion. The impact was correspondingly huge: some 30 million people watched the 12 minute speech. They knew they were in the safe hands of Europe's most experienced crisis manager (Chaffin 2020).

Even in Italy, where the coronavirus has had the most devastating effects for an ageing population and its stretched healthcare system, the government led by Giuseppe Conte has seen a dramatic upswing in public opinion polls, from the high 40s at the end of 2019 and early 2020 to over 70 per cent by March 2020. Some of this popularity has its roots in a general 'rally around the flag' effect that we see in national crises, but the technopopulism of Conte's government has played its part.[7]

---

[7] On the technopopulism of the first Conte government (the alliance between the *Lega* and the M5S), see Volpicelli 2018. For a more recent comment on the success of Conte, see Lazar 2020.

Exit from Democracy

> *You can tell how many politicians are relieved they can just listen to and enact what the technocrats tell them to do. Fed up and tired of governing. Once things go back to normal the reality of representation will be hard to handle* (Jäger 2020).

Whilst the technopopulist logic entails a politicization of expertise, classical technocracy is more about the depoliticization of politics, replacing it with a form of expert rule. Much of the discussion around the coronavirus has stemmed from a concern—as well as enthusiasm, as Jäger and others have noted—that it has enfranchised scientific experts at the expense of rule by politicians. We argue that this movement towards pure technocracy is possible but unlikely as a route beyond technopopulism. A departure from democracy *tout court* may be a consequence of the coronavirus crisis in some places but appears scarcely probable in those political systems most marked by technopopulism.

Lorenzo Castellani observes that the epidemic will lead—as did the end of the Second World War—to an explosion in 'technocratic structures', from universities and think tanks tasked with basic research in pandemics and in investigating policy responses. New specialized agencies will be created to deal with the fallout from the crisis (Castellani 2020). The state will emerge reinforced and any lingering fears about bureaucratic domination will give way to the imperative to save lives. As we argued in chapter 1, a feature of technopopulism is that the technocratic component refers to something different from the *techne* in traditional understandings of technocracy. To the extent that responses to the coronavirus signal a fundamental shift towards more direct forms of rule by expert bodies, we may be seeing a movement beyond technopopulism towards technocracy proper. The coronavirus crisis is far from having run its course, but a worry has already emerged that the legacy of the crisis will be less freedom and more direct control by unelected authorities who act in the name of science.

The role of science—and scientific experts—has become a central feature of the coronavirus crisis. Politicians not known for their love of officialdom or experts have surrounded themselves with experts when giving speeches or press briefings. This should not be surprising: a key feature of technopopulism is its orientation towards means rather than ends, and the consequent importance of being seen to be doing something, whatever that something may be. During the coronavirus crisis, scientific advisors and experts have provided the framework within which the politician can act. This is not a return to classical forms of technocracy where power is invested in the experts themselves but rather a testimony to the way in which we tend to look at crises through technocratic lens: the pros and cons of Eurobonds in the Eurozone crisis, suppression vs herd immunity in the coronavirus crisis. Scientific advisors rarely believe that there is only one 'right way' out of the coronavirus crisis. In fact, as we have seen, there are competing accounts and competing models. However, the technocratic dimension of the coronavirus crisis is manifest in the way that debates and disagreements are framed in terms of rival claims about relevant facts—from the way the virus spreads to the difficulties in putting together morbidity figures. Rather than taking us in the direction of pure technocracy, the crisis has accelerated the 'sciencization' of our politics.

What really threatens the technopopulist logic is not direct rule by experts but rather more simply the lasting suspension of democratic procedures. The crisis has provided governments with great scope for increasing authoritarianism: through more intrusive monitoring of citizen behaviour, a concentration of power in executives, and a decline in the power of legislators to hold governments to account. National parliaments thus far have shown a limited appetite to transfer their activities online, leaving a deficit in accountability. As David Runciman (2020) observed,

> In recent years, it has sometimes appeared that global politics is simply a choice between rival forms of technocracy. In China, it is a government of engineers backed up by a one-party state. In the West, it is the rule of economists and central bankers, operating within the constraints of a democratic system...But in the last few weeks, another reality has pushed through. The ultimate judgements are about how to use coercive power. These aren't simply technical questions. Some arbitrariness is unavoidable. And the contest in that exercise of power between democratic adaptability and autocratic ruthlessness will shape all of our futures.

So far, the evidence of an authoritarian turn in those cases that we associate with the emergence of a technopopulist logic is modest. It has been most pronounced in countries where governments were already challenging some basic liberal constitutional norms. In Hungary, the national parliament passed a bill at the end of March, extending the state of emergency in a way that placed relatively few constraints upon the executive. Ending the Orbán government's rule by decree is in the hands of the parliament, and the country's Constitutional Court has the power to review the legality of government decisions. However, both institutions contain enough government supporters to make these limitations merely academic (Hopkins 2020). Governments across Europe have certainly used draconian powers in responding to the crisis: in Spain, a state of emergency was declared and extended in order to enable the government to intervene directly in the economy and in society at large. However, the responses of democratic states remain different from authoritarian states and the difference in political regime has been noticeable and enduring. If what really takes us beyond technopopulism is the definite shift from democracy to authoritarianism in existing democracies, then there is limited evidence to suggest that this will be a consequence of the coronavirus crisis.

The Return of Ideology

There are various ways in which the coronavirus crisis could also introduce a more substantive set of political debates that lay the conditions for a return of ideology in advanced democracies. One is the dramatic manner in which national governments have intervened to support troubled economies. The economic costs of the virus remain incalculable, but figures suggest that national economies will experience long and painful recessions. The International Labour Organization estimated that by Easter 2020 around 195 million workers will have left the labour force (Strauss 2020). In the United States, almost 10 million workers had submitted jobless claims and almost three quarters of US citizens had their income cut in the first months of the crisis. In order to counteract the economic effects of such developments, governments have socialized large parts of the economy. Some have likened the economic fallout to the profound changes in national economies that came with the Second World War: the emergence of large nationalized industries, the entrance of women in the labour market, the creation of national educational and health services. As Gray notes, the economic responses to the virus so far in the UK have been quite different: 'they have been the opposite of what was done [during the Second World War], when the British population was mobilized as never before, and unemployment fell dramatically. Today, aside from those in essential services, Britain's workers have been demobilized.' (Gray 2020) This demobilization of the labour force has been made possibly only by taking over large parts of the wage bill by taxpayers.

These interventions are already generating important debates about the new balance between state and market. As Gray put it, 'liberal capitalism is bust' (Gray 2020). Devalued jobs and social services have revealed themselves as the essential components of economic and social life. Socialism through the backdoor has become a cause for concern in some quarters and celebration in others. The distributive effects of some policies are generating debates about class inequalities. It is unlikely that normality will return after the coronavirus crisis has passed but it is significant that these policy interventions are justified in the name of an economic emergency rather than any new ideology as such.

However sweeping the changes, their relationship to particular claims about how society should be ordered or 'the good life' is unclear. In fact, what is perhaps most striking about the manner in which governments have introduced radical economic measures is the distinctively non-ideological flavour to these interventions: they were passed with bipartisan and cross-party support in most instances. In many cases, parties ostensibly on the ideological right—the Republicans in the US, the Conservatives in the UK, the Christian Democrats in Germany—have been the agents driving the implementation of 'socialistic' policies. This reversal of political roles itself tells us how separate policy programmes are from ideological political families and specific social groups or classes in society.

What has characterized the policy interventions thus far has been their top-down quality, not the sign that they are rebuilding the sorts of 'communities of fate' that characterized an age of ideological politics. New instances of solidarity and collective action have begun to emerge out of the crisis, in the form of the proliferation of mutual aid groups that serve to deliver food to the elderly and more isolated members of a street or *quartier* (Jones 2020). News bonds are being forged between welfare states and national citizens who realize their importance. However, it is unlikely that such developments constitute a fundamental move towards the return of organized interests within society of the kind that can mediate between particular and general interests in the manner of the ideologies of old. Nor are we seeing the thickening of citizenship of the kind that T. H. Marshall observed in the wake of the Second World War (Marshall 1992 [orig. 1950]).

Some have looked to the European Union for a sign that the coronavirus may signal a final push towards building a shared European identity but the evidence points toward a continuation of the European Union's more incremental approach to dealing with crises. Others have declared peremptorily that this sort of regional governance is dead, giving way to a new wave of nationalism. In fact, the same divisions that existed between member states during the Eurozone crisis have reappeared, as have attempts to find some compromise between different points of view.

Rather than any definitive move towards Europeanism or nationalism, we see the same gap between national attitudes and pan-European policymaking. Disagreement about the need for debt mutualization continues to shape the relations between member states, and the EU continues to be pulled in different directions, making it necessary to find some sort of compromise. An agreement on a form of regional debt financing that would not just add to the national debt of member states was a historically significant outcome of the corona crisis. Nevertheless, fighting between northern and southern member states, as well as disagreements between east and west, have prevented any quick form of EU-wide financial assistance. At the time of writing, the Eurozone is facing the prospect of a double-dip recession due to a second wave of the virus, with money from the dedicated corona crisis find still tied up in intergovernmental negotiations. At the same time, the legacy of the disputes between hard-hit southern countries at the outbreak of the crisis – Italy in particular, but also Spain – and northern member states who were facing far lower levels of hospitalisation will remain for some time to come. It raises doubts about the capacity of member states to act in solidarity with one another when faced with national emergencies (Boffey et al 2020).

A final way in which we might move towards a more explicitly ideological sort of politics is if the ethical questions raised by the coronavirus serve as the building blocks for new ways of thinking about social life, community, and the obligations of citizens towards each other. The potential for such debates is certainly there, as the virus has made it necessary to make very consequential decisions relating to the costs and benefits of different approaches. For instance, generational divisions are stark: younger generations are far less likely to fall ill or die from the coronavirus than those over sixty-five. And yet the economic costs of saving the lives of the elderly generation fall entirely on the current and future generations of taxpayers. When we add to this the already existing wealth disparities between older and younger generations, which favours enormously the property-owning and final salary pension receiving over-sixty-fives, then we can see how the virus is raising deep ethical questions (Bickerton 2018: 22).[8]

There has been some discussion of this so far, but mainly about whether the economic cost of the measures being taken is sustainable. What is missing so far is a debate that goes to the heart of political philosophy, namely the difference between the interests of every single living member of a community and what Rousseau called the 'general will' of society. There was never any doubt in Rousseau's mind that there was an important difference between the 'will of all' and the 'general will'. Thus far, we have tended to frame this fundamental ethical question as a matter of rival scientific strategies—suppression versus herd immunity. Those dealing with these ethical dilemmas on a daily basis have been doctors and nurses in hospitals who have had to develop a rule of thumb for allocating scarce medical resources to patients. Testimonies suggest that they have roughly followed the age rule, privileging younger patients who are sick over the more elderly. These have been decisions taken in an ad hoc fashion in a variety of different circumstances rather than the following of any clear societal consensus.

Movement beyond technopopulism is possible because of its own internal tensions. We have sketched out some future scenarios through a discussion of the dimensions of the coronavirus epidemic. There is nothing permanent about the technopopulist political logic, but we find that technopopulism is both an enduring feature of our politics and it has shaped in multiple ways our experience thus far of the pandemic. Before considering democratic life beyond technopopulism, the imperative remains to understand how these appeals to 'the people' and to expertise structure our politics and shape our experience of democracy today and for some time into the future.

---

[8] Of the £2.7 trillion increase in wealth in the UK since 2008, two thirds of this has accrued to those over sixty-five, divided up between pension and housing-related wealth gains. Those aged between sixteen and thirty-four have seen their wealth decline by 10 per cent over the same period. For details, see Bickerton 2018 and Haldane 2016.

Bibliography

Abramowitz, Alan and Saunders, Kyle. 2008. 'Is Polarization a Myth?', *Journal of Politics*, 70: 2.
Abromeit, John, Norman, York, Marotta, Gary, and Chesterton, Bridget M. (eds.) 2015. *Transformations of Populism in Europe and the Americas: History and Recent Tendencies*. New York: Bloomsbury.
Abromeit, John. 2017. 'A Critical Review of Recent Literature on Populism', *Politics and Governance*, 5:4, 177–186.
Addley, Esther. 2019. 'Like a damp towel on a line: the day Boris Johnson got stuck on a zip line'. *The Guardian*, 16 July.
Akin, William E. 1977. *Technocracy and the American Dream. The Technocrat Movement, 1900–1941*, Berkely: University of California Press.
Albertazzi, Daniele, Giovannini, Arianna, and Seddone, Antonella. 2018. 'No regionalism please, we are Leghisti. The transformation of the Italian Lega Nord under the leadership of Matteo Salvini', *Regional and Federal Studies*, 28: 5.
Alexander, Michelle. 2010. *The New Jim Crow: Mass Incarceration in the Age of Colorblindness*, New York: The New Press.
Alexiadou, Despina and Gunaydin, Hakan. 2019. 'Commitment or Expertise? Technocratic Appointments as Political Responses to Economic Crises', *European Journal of Political Research*, 58: 3.
Anderson, Perry. 2002. 'Internationalism: A Breviary', *New Left Review*, 14: 5–25.
Anderson, Perry. 2014. 'The Italian Disaster', *London Review of Books*, 36 (22 May): 10.
Andeweg, Rudy. 2019. 'Consociationalism in the Low Countries: Comparing the Dutch and Belgian Experience', *Swiss Political Science Review*, 25:4, 408–25.
Arditi, Benjamin. 2005. 'Populism as an Internal Periphery of Democratic Politics', in Francisco Panizza (ed.), *Populism and The Mirror of Democracy*, London: Verso.
Baccaro, Lucio and Howell, Chris. 2011. 'A Common Neoliberal Trajectory: The Transformation of Industrial Relations in Advanced Capitalism', *Politics & Society*, 39: 4.
Baccaro, Lucio and Pontusson, Jonas. 2016. 'Rethinking Comparative Political Economy: The Growth Model Perspective', *Politics and Society*, 44: 2, 175–207.
Badiou, Alain. 2009. *De Quoi Sarkozy Est-Il Le Nom?*, Paris: Editions Lignes.
Balandier, Georges. 1980. *Le Pouvoir Sur Scènes*, Paris: Baland.
Balfour, Rosa, Emmanouilidis, Janis A., Grabbe, Heather, Lochocki, Timo, Mudde, Cas, Schmidt, Juliane, Fieschi, Catherine, Hill, Christopher, Mendras, Marie, Niemi, Mari K., and Stratulat, Corina. 2016. *Europe's Troublemakers: The Populist Challenge to Foreign Policy*, Brussels: European Policy Centre.
Balme, Richard. 2006. 'Convergence, Fragmentation and Majority-Cycling in French Public Opinion', in P. Culpepper, P. Hall, and B. Palier (eds.), *Changing France: The Politics that Markets Make*. Basingstoke: Palgrave, 244–75.
Barbagallo, Francesco. 2004. 'Enrico Berlinguer, il Compromesso Storico e l'Alternativa Democratica', *Studi Storici*, 45: 4.
Barker, Alex and Parker, George. 2020. 'Johnson's Cromwell takes aim at Britain's core institutions'. *Financial Times*, 8/9 February.

Barker, Vanessa. 2013. 'Prison and the Public Sphere: Toward a Democratic Theory of the Penal Order', in David Scott (ed.), *Why Prison?*, Cambridge: Cambridge University Press.

Barr, Robert. 2009. 'Populists, Outsiders, and Anti-Establishment Politics', *Party Politics*, 15: 1.

Bartlett, Jamie. 2018. *The People Vs Tech: How the internet is killing democracy (and how we save it)*, London: Penguin.

Bauchard, Philippe. 1986. *La Guerre des Deux Roses: Du rêve a la réalite, 1981–1985*. Paris: Grasset.

Beck, Ulrich and Beck-Gernsheim, Elizabeth. 2001. *Individualization. Institutionalized Individualism and its Social and Political Consequences*, London: Sage.

Beckett, Andy. 2018. 'The Death of Consensus: How Conflict Came Back to Politics'. *The Guardian*, 20 September, available at: https://www.theguardian.com/politics/2018/sep/20/the-death-of-consensus-how-conflict-came-back-to-politics

Beetsma, R. et al. 2019. 'Independent Fiscal Councils: Recent Trends and Performance', *European Journal of Political Economy*, 57: 53–69.

Bellamy, Richard. 2018. 'Was the Brexit Referendum Legitimate, and would a Second one be so?', *European Political Science*, 18: 126–33.

Bellamy, Richard and Palumbo, Antonino (eds.). 2010. *From Government to Governance*, London: Ashgate.

Benewick, Robert. 1972. *The Fascist Movement in Britain*, London: Allen Lane.

Berger, Peter. 1967. *The Sacred Canopy. Elements of a Sociological Theory of Religion*, New York: Doubleday.

Berger, Peter (ed.). 1999. *The Desecularization of the World. Resurgent Religion and World Politics*, Grand Rapids: Eedermans.

Berger, Peter, Davie, Grace, and Fokas, Effie (eds.). 2008. *Religious America, Secular Europe? A Theme and Variations*, London: Ashgate.

Berger, Suzanne D. (ed.). 1983. *Organizing Interests in Western Europe: Pluralism, corporatism, and the transformation of politics*, Cambridge: Cambridge University Press.

Berger, Suzanne. 2006. 'Representation in trouble', in P. Culpepper, P. Hall, and B. Palier (Eds.) *Changing France: The Politics that Markets Make*. Basingstoke: Palgrave, 276–91.

Berman, Sheri. 2017. 'Populism is a Problem. Elitist Technocrats Aren't the Solution', *Foreign Policy*, 20 December.

Bernard, Matthias. 2015. *Les Années Mitterrand: Du Changement Socialiste au Tournant Libéral*, Paris: Belin.

Bertsou, Eri and Caramani, Daniele (eds.). 2020. *The Technocratic Challenge to Democracy*, London: Routledge.

Bevir, Mark. 2006. 'Democratic Governance: Systems and Radical Perspectives', *Public Administration Review*, May–June.

Bevir, Mark, Rhodes, Rod, and Weller, Patrick. 2003. 'Comparative Governance: Prospects and Lessons', *Public Administration*, 81(1): 191–210.

Bickerton, Christopher. 2012. *European Integration. From Nation-States to Member-States*, Oxford: Oxford University Press.

Bickerton, Christopher. 2017. 'An anti-system President in France?', *Juncture*, 23: 4, 271–4.

Bickerton, Christopher. 2018. *Brexit and the British Growth Model: Towards a New Social Settlement*, London: Policy Exchange.

Bickerton, Christopher. 2019. 'How will the EU change over the next five years?', in *The European Elections and Brexit*, London: The UK in a Changing Europe.

Bickerton, Christopher. 2020a. 'Member states in European Integration', in S. Bulmer and C. Lequesne (eds.), *The Member States of the European Union, Third Edition*, Oxford: Oxford University Press.
Bickerton, Christopher. 2020b. 'Pourqui le Labour a perdu', *Le Monde Diplomatique*, February.
Bickerton, Christopher, Hodson, Dermot, and Puetter, Uwe. 2015. *The New Intergovernmentalism. States and Supra-National Actors in the Post-Maastricht Era*, Oxford: Oxford University Press.
Bickerton, Christopher and Invernizzi Accetti, Carlo. 2014. 'Democracy Without Parties? Italy After Berlusconi', *Political Quarterly*, 85: 1.
Bickerton, Christopher and Invernizzi Accetti, Carlo. 2015a. 'Populism and Technocracy: Opposites or Complements?', *Critical Review of International Social and Political Philosophy*, 20: 2.
Bickerton, Christopher and Invernizzi Accetti, Carlo. 2015b. 'Matteo Renzi: The Limits of Doing'. *Le Monde Diplomatique*, 17 February.
Bickerton, Christopher and Invernizzi Accetti, Carlo. 2017. 'Populism and technocracy', in C. Rovira Kaltwasser, P. Taggart, P. Ochoa Espejo, and P. Ostiguy (eds.), *The Oxford Handbook of Populism*, Oxford: Oxford University Press.
Bickerton, Christopher and Invernizzi Accetti, Carlo. 2018. 'Technopopulism as a New Party Family: the case of the M5S and Podemos', *Contemporary Italian Politics*, 10: 2.
Bickerton, Christopher and Invernizzi Accetti, Carlo. 2020. 'Technocracy and Political Theory', in Eri Bertsou and Daniele Caramani (eds.), *The Technocratic Challenge to Democracy*, London: Routledge.
Bickford, Susan. 1997. 'Anti-Anti-Identity Politics: Feminism, Democracy, and the Complexities of Citizenship', *Hypatia*, 12: 4.
Biorcio, Roberto and Natale, Paolo. 2013. *Politica a Cinque Stelle: Idee, Storia e Strategie del Movimento di Grillo*, Milan: Feltrinelli.
Blair, Tony. 1998. *The Third Way: New Politics for the New Century*, London: Fabian Society.
Blair, Tony and Schroder, Gerhard. 1998. *The Third Way/Die Neue Mitte*, document available at: https://web.archive.org/web/19990819090124/http://www.labour.org.uk/views/items/00000053.html
Boatright, Robert (ed.). 2018. *The Routledge Handbook of Primary Elections*, New York: Routledge.
Bobbio, Norberto. 1997. *Left and Right. The Significance of a Political Distinction*, London: Verso.
Bock, Jan-Jonathan. 2017. 'The Five Star Movement in Rome: Utopian Politics and the Eternal City', unpublished manuscript.
Boffey, Daniel, Shoen, Celine, Stockton, Ben and Margottini, Laura. 2020. 'Italy's call for urgent help was ignored as coronavirus swept through Europe', *The Guardian*, 15 July.
Bolton, Matt and Pitts, Frederick Harry. 2018. *Corbynism: A Critical Approach*, London: Emerald.
Bonotti, Matteo. 2017. *Partisanship and Political Liberalism in Diverse Societies*, Oxford: Oxford University Press.
Bordignon, Fabio. 2017. 'In and Out: Emanuel Macron's anti-populist populism'. LSE Europp blog, 28 April, available at: https://blogs.lse.ac.uk/europpblog/2017/04/28/macron-anti-populist-populism/
Bordignon, Fabio. 2016. '5 Stelle: Il Cortocircuito Tecnocratico', *il Mattino*, 2 October, available at: http://incroci-mattinopadova.blogautore.repubblica.it/2016/10/02/5-stelle-il-cortocircuito-tecnocratico/?refresh_ce

Bordignon, Fabio. 2017. 'In and Out- Emmanuel Macron's Anti-Populist Populism', *EUROPP LSE Blog*, available at: https://blogs.lse.ac.uk/europpblog/2017/04/28/macron-anti-populist-populism/

Bordignon, Federico and Ceccarini, Luigi. 2013. 'Five Stars and a Cricket. Beppe Grillo Shakes Italian Politics', *South European Society and Politics*, 18: 4.

Bordignon, Fabio and Ceccarini, Luigi. 2015. 'The Five-Star Movement: A Hybrid Actor in the Net of State Institutions', *Journal of Modern Italian Studies*, 20: 4.

Bordignon, Fabio and Ceccarini, Luigi. 2018. 'Towards the 5 Star Party', *Contemporary Italian Politics*, 10: 4.

Borges, Walt, Clarke, Harold, Stewart, Marianne, Sanders, David, and Whiteley, Paul. 2013. 'The Emerging Political Economy of Austerity in Britain', *Electoral Studies*, 32: 3.

Borriello, Arthur. 2018. *Quand On N'a Que L'Austerité. Abolition et Permanence du Politique dans les Discours de Crise en Italie et en Espagne*, Bruxelles: Pressed de l'Université Librte de Bruxelles.

Borriello, Arthur and Mazzolini, Samuele. 2019. 'European populism(s) as a counter-hegemonic discourse? The Rise of Podemos and M5S in the wake of the crisis', in Jan Zienkowski and Ruth Breeze (eds.), *Imagining the People's of Europe: Populist Discourse across the Political Spectrum*, Amsterdam: John Benjamins, 73–100.

Bottoms, Anthony. 1995. 'The Philosophy and Politics of Punishment and Sentencing', in Chris Clarkson and Rod Morgan (eds.), *The Politics of Sentencing Reform*, Oxford: Clarendon.

Boy, David and Mayer, Nonna. 1997. *Les Modèles Explicatifs du Vote*, Paris: L'Harmattan.

Boyanska, Ivana. 2018. 'The Appeal of Donald Trump's Political Rhetoric: A Critical Discourse Analysis', dissertation defended at the *Universitat Autonoma de Barcelona*, available at: https://ddd.uab.cat/record/196006

Brady, David and Cain, Bruce. 2018. 'Are Our Parties Realigning?', *National Affairs* (Fall).

Brinkbäumer, Klaus, Heyer, Julia Amalia, and Sandberg, Britta. 2018. 'Emannuel Macron: We Need to Develop Political Heroism'. *Der Spiegel*, 13 October, available at: https://www.spiegel.de/international/europe/interview-with-french-president-emmanuel-macron-a-1172745.html

Brody, David. 2020. 'How the Italian Left defied the Far Right in Emilia Romagna'. *New Statesman*, 27 January.

Bromwich, David. 2010. 'The Fastidious President'. *London Review of Books*, 32: 22.

Brownstein, Ronald. 2016. 'Donald Trump and the Populist Wave in Europe'. *The Atlantic*, 8 December.

Bucur, Cristina. 2017. 'A Mould-Breaking Cabinet? Changes and Continuities in the Formation of the 2017 French Government', *French Politics*, 15: 340–59.

Burnham, Peter. 2001. 'New Labour and the Politics of Depoliticisation', *British Journal of Politics and International Relations*, 3: 2.

Buštíková, Lenka and Guasti, Petra. 2019. 'The State as a Firm: Understanding the Autocratic Roots of Technocratic Populism', *East European Politics and Societies and Cultures*, earlyview.

Butler, David and Stokes, Donald. 1969. *Political Change in Britain: Forces Shaping Electoral Choice*. London: Macmillan.

Buzzi, Emanuele. 2013. 'La squadra di Grillo: Una mamma con tre figli al ministero delle finanze'. *Corriere della Sera*, 16 January, available at: http://www.corriere.it/politica/13_gennaio_16/squadra-grillo-mamma-tre-figli-ministro-finanze-buzzi_6bdef200-5fa7-11e2-9e33-1d7fb906e25e.shtml

Calise, Mauro. 2013. *Il Partito del Capo*, Santarcangelo di Romagna: Maggioli.

Calmfors, Lars and Wren-Lewis, Simon. 2011. 'What should fiscal councils do?', *OECD Working Paper*, 1–55.
Calvano, Roberta. 2017. 'Le Primarie e Altri Falsi Antidoti alla Crisi dei Partiti in Italia', *Costituzionalismo*, 2: 3.
Canovan, Margaret. 1999. 'Trust the People! Populism and the Two Faces of Democracy', *Political Studies*, XLVII, 2–16.
Caramani, Daniele. 2017. 'Will vs. Reason. The Populist and Technocratic Forms of Political Representation and Their Critique to Party Government', *American Political Science Review*, 111: 1.
Carty, Kenneth. 2013. 'Are Political Parties Meant to be Internally Democratic?', in William Cross and Richard Katz (eds.), *The Challenges of Intra-Party Democracy*, Oxford: Oxford University Press.
Casaleggio, Gianroberto. 2004. *Web Ergo Sum*, Milano: Sperling & Kupfer.
Casanova, José. 1994. *Public Religions in the Modern World*. Cambridge: MIT Press.
Castellani, Lorenzo. 2016. *The Rise of Managerial Bureaucracy. Reforming the British Civil Service*, London: Palgrave.
Castellani, Lorenzo. 2018. 'L'ère du technopopulisme'. *Le Grand Continent*, 16 March.
Castellani, Lorenzo. 2020. 'Les nouveaux technopopulistes'. *Le Grand Continent*, 31 March.
Cassirer, Ernst. 1923. Substance and Function and Einstein's Theory of Relativity, Chicago: Open Court Publishing.
Centeno, Miguel. 1993. 'The New Leviathan. The Dynamics and Limits of Technocracy', *Theory and Society*: 22.
Cento Bull, Anna and Gilbert, Martin. 2001. *The Lega Nord and the Northern Question in Italian Politics*. Palgrave: Basingstoke.
Chaffin, Joshua. 2020. 'A governor grabs national attention'. *Financial Times*, 4/5 April.
Chakrabortty, Aditya. 2014. 'Narendra Modi: is a hi-tech populist the best India can hope for?' *The Guardian*, 19 May.
Chazan, Guy. 2020. 'Person in the News: Angela Merkel. Germany's crisis manager is back'. *Financial Times*, 27 March.
Chua, Amy. 2018. *Political Tribes: Group Instinct and the Fate of Nations*, London: Bloomsbury.
Clark, Pitilla. 2020. 'Person in the news: Neil Ferguson. A virus modeler sounds the alarm'. *Financial Times*, 21/22 March.
Clarke, Harold, Goodwin, Matthew, and Whiteley, Paul. 2017. *Brexit. Why Britain Voted to Leave the European Union*, Cambridge: Cambridge University Press.
Clegg, Nick. 2016. *Politics: Between the Extremes*. London: Bodley Head.
Cohen, Michael. 2019. 'Ramaphosa's Economic Plans Undermined by Foes in South Africa's ANC'. *Bloomberg News*, 11 March.
Cole, Alistair. 1993. 'The Presidential Party and the Fifth Republic', *West European Politics*, 16: 2.
Collins, Lauren. 2019. 'Can Emmanuel Macron Stem the Populist Tide?'. *New Yorker*, 1 July.
Colonelli, Alessio. 2020. 'Death of a movement', *Open Democracy*, 3 February.
Cook, Chris. 1976. *A Short History of the Liberal Party: The Road Back to Power*, London: Macmillan.
Cordier, Solène, Lemarié, Alexandre, and Bissuel, Bertrand. 2020. 'Congé pour le décès d'un enfant: le gouvernement fait marchine arrière'. *Le Monde*, 3 February.
Cottone, Nicoletta. 2018. 'Nuovi Ministri: La Lista Completa dell'Esecutivo Lega-M5S'. *Il Sole 24 Ore*, 31 May.

Crines, Andrew. 2015. 'Reforming the Labour Party. The Leadership of Jeremy Corbyn'. *Political Insight*, December.
Cross, William and Katz, Richard (eds.). 2013. *The Challenges of Intra-Party Democracy*, Oxford: Oxford University Press.
Crouch, Colin. 1999. *Social Change in Western Europe*, Oxford: Oxford University Press.
Crouch, Colin. 2003. *Post-Democracy*, Cambridge: Polity Press.
Cruddas, Jon. 2019. 'The Left's New Urbanism', *The Political Quarterly*, 90(1): 15–22.
Cummings, Dominic. 2020. 'Two hands are a lot—we're hiring data scientists, project managers, policy experts, assorted weirdos', Dominic Cummings blog, 2 January, available at: https://dominiccummings.com/2020/01/02/two-hands-are-a-lot-were-hiring-data-scientists-project-managers-policy-experts-assorted-weirdos/
Curtice, John and Susan, Holmberg. 2005. 'Party leaders and party choice', in J. Thomassen (ed.), *The European voter. A comparative study of modern democracies*. Oxford, United Kingdom: Oxford University Press.
Dalton, Russel. 1984. 'Cognitive Mobilization and Partisan Dealignment in Advanced Industrial Democracies', *The Journal of Politics*, 46: 1.
Dalton, Russell. 2013. *The Apartisan American: Dealignment and Changing Electoral Politics*, Thousand Oaks: CQ Press.
Dalton, Russel, Flanagan, Scott, and Allen Beck, Paul. 1985. *Electoral Change in Advanced Industrial Democracies. Dealignment or Realignment?*, Princeton: Princeton University Press.
Dalton, Russell and Wattenberg, Martin. 2002. *Parties without Partisans. Political Change in Advanced Industrial Societies*, Oxford: Oxford University Press.
Davet, Gérard and Lhomme, Fabrice. 2016. *'Un Président ne deverait pas dire ça'... Les secrets d'un quinquennat*. Paris: Stock.
Davie, Grace. 1994. *Religion in Britain since 1945: Believing Without Belonging*, Oxford: Blackwell.
De Azua, Felix. 2014. 'Podemos: Un Partido de Profesores'. *El Pais*, 1 December.
Dean, Jonathan and Maiguashca, Bice. 2017. 'Corbyn's Labour and the populism Question', *Renewal*, 25: 3–4.
De Blasio, Emiliana and Sorice, Michele. 2018. 'Populism Between Direct Democracy and Technological Myth', *Palgrave Communications*, 4: 15.
Debord, Guy. 1967. *The Society of the Spectacle*, London: Rebel Press [1983].
De Grauwe, Paul. 2009. 'The Politics of the Maastricht Convergence Criteria'. *Vox*, 15 April.
De La Torre, Carlos. 2013. 'El Tecnopopulismo de Correa', *Latin American Research Review*, 48: 1.
De La Torre, Carlos. 2019. *Routledge Handbook of Global Populism*, London: Routledge.
De la Torrre, Carlo. 2020. 'Rafael Correa's Technopopulism in Comparative Perspective', in Francisco Sánchez and Simón Pachano (eds.), *Assessing the Left Turn in Ecuador*, Basingstoke: Palgrave.
De Royer, Solenn. 2017. 'Emmanuel Macron, La Téchnocratie Au Pouvoir'. *Le Monde*, 6 November.
Deseriis, Marco. 2018. 'Technopopulism: The Emergence of a Discursive Formation', *Communication, Capitalism & Critique*, 15: 2.
Develey, Alice. 2018. 'Emmanuel Macron ne converse pas avec le peuple, il le met à distance'. *Le Figaro*, 11 December.
Diamanti, Giovanni and Pregliasco, Lorenzo. 2019. *Fenomeno Salvini. Chi è, come comunica, perché lo votano*, Roma: Lit Edizioni.
Diamanti, Ilvo. 2010. 'L'Ideologia del Fare'. *La Repubblica*, 21 February.

Diamanti, Ilvo. 2014. 'The Five Star Movement. A Political Laboratory', *Contemporary Italian Politics*, 6: 1.
Diamanti, Ilvo and Lazar, Marc. 2018. *Popolocrazia. La Metamorfosi delle Nostre Democrazie*, Bari: Laterza.
Di Pasquale, Chris. 2017. 'Election Highlights Political Polarisation in France', *RedFlag*, 24 April.
Dobbelaere, Karel. 2002. *Secularization: An Analysis at Three Levels*, Brussels: PIE-Peter Lang.
Donadio, Rachel. 2020. 'An Italian Flash Mob Just Pushed Back Europe's Populist Tide'. *The Atlantic*, 27 January.
Douthat, Ross. 2019. 'Social Media and the Populist Moment'. *New York Times*, 23 November.
Downs, Anthony. 1957. *An Economic Theory of Democracy*, New York: Harper.
Drochon, Hugo. 2017. 'Emmanuel Macron's parliamentary victory marks the return of the experts'. *New Statesman*, 12 June.
Drutman, Lee. 2017. 'We need political parties. But their rabid partisanship could destroy American democracy', *Vox*, 5th September.
Duggan, Christopher. 2014. *A Concise History of Italy, Second Edition*, Cambridge: Cambridge University Press.
Duhamel, Olivier. 2012. *Portraits Souvenir—50 ans de vie politique*, Paris: Perrin.
Duverger, Maurice. 1954. *Political Parties*, Oxford: Wiley.
Dunkel, Frieder. 2016. 'The Rise and Fall of Prison Population rates in Europe', *Newsletter of the European Society of Criminology*, available at: https://escnewsletter.org/newsletter/2016-2/rise-and-fall-prison-population-rates-europe
Dyson, Kenneth and Featherstone, Kevin. 1999. *The Road to Maastricht: Negotiating Economic and Monetary Union*, Oxford: Oxford University Press.
Economist, The. 2018. 'Corbynomics would change Britain—but not in the way most people think'. *The Economist*, 17 May.
Edgerton, David. 2018. *The Rise and Fall of the British Nation: A Twentieth Century History*, London: Allen Lane.
Elgie, Robert. 2018. 'The election of Emmanuel Macron and the new French party system: a return to the éternel marais?', *Modern & Contemporary France*, 26: 1.
Elster, Jon. 1981. 'Snobs', *London Review of Books*, 3: 20.
Errejon, Iñigo. 2014. 'Que Es Podemos?', *Le Monde Diplomatique en Español*, July.
Errejon, Iñigo and Mouffe, Chantal. 2016. *Podemos: In the Name of the People*, London: Lawrence and Wishart.
Esmark, Anders. 2020. *The New Technocracy*, Bristol: Bristol University Press.
Estlund, David. 2008. *Democratic Authority. A Philosophical Framework*, Princeton: Princeton University Press.
Eurostat. 2016. *Crime Statistics*, available at: https://ec.europa.eu/eurostat/statistics-explained/index.php?title=Crime_statistics
Falciola, Luca. 2015. *Il Movimento del 1977 in Italia*, Roma: Carocci.
Faris, Stephan and Bibbona, Marina. 2013. 'Italy's Beppe Grillo: Meet the Rogue Comedian Turned Kingmaker', *Time Magazine*, 7 March, available at: http://world.time.com/2013/03/07/italys-beppe-grillo-meet-the-rogue-comedian-turned-kingmaker/
FBI (Federal Bureau of Investigation). 2017. *Crime in the United States*, available at: https://ucr.fbi.gov/crime-in-the-u.s/2017/crime-in-the-u.s.-2017/topic-pages/tables/table-1
Ferguson, Euan. 2010. 'Interview: The secret of Clegg's success: he listens'. *The Guardian*, 25 April.

Ferrari, Domenico. 2016. *Jeremy Corbyn. La Rivoluzione Gentile*, Roma: Lit.
Finchelstein, Federico. 2017. 'Populists vs. Technocrats? A Historical View', paper presented at Philomathia Forum Workshop on *Populism and Technocracy: Open Antagonisms, Hidden Affinities*, University of Cambridge, 25 September.
Finlayson, Alan. 2004. 'The Interpretive Approach in Political Science: A Symposium', *The British Journal of Politics and International Relations*, 6: 2.
Fiorina, Morris, with Samuel Abrams and Jeremy Pope. 2006. *Culture War? The Myth of a Polarized America*, New York: Pearson Longman.
Fischer, Frank. 1990. *Technocracy and the Politics of Expertise*, London: Sage.
Fittipaldi, Emiliano. 2019. 'Così i poteri forti salgono sulla ruspa del vincitore Matteo Salvini'. *L'Espresso*, 4 June.
Foa, Roberto and Mounk, Yascha. 2016. 'The Danger of Deconsolidation: The Democratic Disconnect', *Journal of Democracy*, 27: 3.
Foa, Roberto, Klassen, A, Slade, M., Rand, A., and Collins, R. 2020. *The Global Satisfaction with Democracy Report 2020*, Cambridge, UK: Centre for the Future of Democracy.
Fottorino, Eric. 2017. *Macron par Macron*, Paris: Editions de L'Aube.
Freeden, Michael. 1995. *Ideologies and Political Theory*, Oxford: Oxford University Press.
Freeden, Michael, Stears, Marc, and Sargent, Lyman Tower. 2013. *Oxford Handbook of Political Ideologies*, Oxford: Oxford University Press.
Fukuyama, Francis. 1989. 'The End of History?, *National Interest*, 16: Summer.
Fukuyama, Francis. 1992. *The End of History and the Last Man*, New York: Free Press.
Fukuyama, Francis. 2018. *Identity: The Demand for Dignity and the Politics of Resentment*, New York: Farrar, Straus and Giroux.
Furet, François. 1995. *The Passing of an Illusion. The Idea of Communism in the 20th Century*, Chicago: Chicago University Press [2000].
Gallo, Zelia. 2015. 'Punishment, Authority and Political Economy: Italian Challenges to Western Punitiveness', *Punishment and Society*, 17: 5.
Gallo, Zelia. 2018. 'The penal implications of austerity: Italian punishment in the wake of the Eurozone crisis', *European Journal of Criminology*, forthcoming.
Galli, Giorgio. 1967. *Il Bipolarismo Imperfetto*, Bologna: il Mulino.
Galli, Giorgio. 2004. *I Partiti Politici Italiani 1943-2004*, Milano: Biblioteca Universale Rizzoli.
Galston, William. 2017. 'The 2016 US Election: the Populist Moment', *Journal of Democracy*, 28: 2.
Gamble, Andrew. 1988. *The Free Economy and the Strong State: The Politics of Thatcherism*, London: MacMillan.
Gamble, Andrew. 2010. 'New Labour and Political Change', *Parliamentary Affairs*, 63: 4.
Gamble, Andrew. 2012. 'Inside New Labour', *British Journal of Politics and International Relations*, 14: 4.
Ganesh, Janan. 2020. 'Vindication of the state does not spell Democratic victory'. *Financial Times*, 9 April.
Ganser, Daniele. 2004. *NATO's Secret Armies: Operation Gladio and Terrorism in Western Europe*, London: Routledge.
Garland, David. 2001. *The Culture of Control*, Chicago: University of Chicago Press.
Garnham, Nicholas and Williams, Raymond. 1980. 'Pierre Bourdieu and the sociology of culture: an introduction', *Media, Culture and Society*, 2: 209–23.
Garrigues, Jean. 2012. *Les Hommes Providentiels: Histoire d'une Fascination Française*, Seuil: Paris.
Garzia, Diego. 2014. *Personalization of Politics and Electoral Change*, London: Palgrave.

Gauchet, Marcel. 1996. 'Right and Left', in Pierre Nora (ed.), *Realms of Memory*, New York: Columbia University Press.
Gauchet, Marcel and Raynaud, Philippe. 2018. 'Macron, An I: un échange', *Le Débat*, 201: 4.
Gauja, Anika. 2015. 'The Individualisation of Party Politics: The Impact of Changing Internal Decision-Making Processes on Policy Development and Citizen Engagement.' *British Journal of Politics and International Relations*, 17: 1.
Geddes, Andrew and Scholten, Peter. 2016. *The Politics of Migration and Immigration in Europe*, London: Sage.
Geertz, Clifford. 1973. *The Interpretation of Cultures*. New York: Basic Books.
Geertz, Clifford. 1975. 'Common Sense as a Cultural System', *The Antioch Review*, 33: 1.
Gentile, Emilio. 2002. *Fascismo. Storia e Interpretazione*, Bari: Laterza.
Gerth, H.H. and Mills, C. Wright. 1970. *Max Weber: Essays in Sociology*, London: Routledge.
Giddens, Anthony. 1990. *The Consequences of Modernity*, Cambridge: Polity.
Giddens, Anthony. 1998. *The Third Way. The Renewal of Social Democracy*, London: Polity.
Ginsborg, Paul. 2003. *Italy and Its Discontents, 1980–2001: Family, Civil Society, State*, London: Penguin.
Gitlin, Todd. 1993. 'The Rise of Identity Politics. An Examination and Critique', *Dissent*, Spring.
Glover, Julian. 2000. 'The five tests'. *The Guardian*, 29 September.
Goldthorpe, John. 1980. *Social Mobility and Class Structure in Modern Britain*, Oxford: Clarendon Press.
Goodhart, David. 2018. *The Road to Somewhere: The new Tribes Shaping British Politics*, London: Penguin.
Goold, Benjamin. 2004. *CCTV and Policing: Public Area Surveillance and Police Practices in Britain*, Oxford: Oxford University Press.
Goulard, Sylvie and Monti, Mario. 2012. *De la Démocratie en Europe*, Paris: Flammarion.
Gould, Philip. 2011. *The Unfinished Revolution. How New Labour Changed British Politics Forever*, London: Abacus.
Graham, Mary. 2002. *Democracy by Disclosure. The Rise of Technopopulism*, Washington DC: Brookings Institution Press.
Gramsci, Antonio. 1922–33. *Prison Notebooks*, New York: Columbia University Press [1992].
Gray, John. 2020. 'Why this crisis is a turning point in history'. *New Statesman*, 1 April.
Green, Adam Isiah. 2008. 'The Social Organization of Desire: The Sexual Fields Approach', *Sociological Theory*, 26(1): 25–50.
Green, Adam Isiah. (ed.). 2013. *Sexual Fields: Towards a Sociology of Collective Sexual Life*, Chicago: University of Chicago Press.
Green, Jane. 2007. 'When Voters and Parties Agree: Valence Issues and Party Competition', *Political Studies*, 55: 3.
Grillo, Beppe. 2018. 'Solo una Rivoluzione ci Salverà', 16 April, available at: http://www.beppegrillo.it/solo-una-rivoluzione-ci-salvera/.
Grillo, Beppe and Casaleggio, Gianroberto. 2011. *Siamo in Guerra. Per una nuova politica*, Milano: Chiarelettere.
Guessier, Léa. 2018. 'La haute administration, véritable parti présidentiel'. *Le Monde*, 22 February.
Habermas, Jurgen. 1994a. *Between Facts and Norms*, Cambridge: MIT Press.
Habermas, Jurgen. 1994b. 'Three Normative Models of Democracy', 1: 1.

Hackett, Joseph. 2017. 'Nobody Wants You Back Tony'. *The Commentator*, 10 May, available at: http://www.thecommentator.com/article/6577/nobody_wants_you_back_tony
Hagemann, Sara. 2018. 'The Brexit Context', *Parliamentary Affairs*, 71: 1.
Haldane, Andrew. 2016. 'Whose recovery?' Speech at Port Talbot, Wales, 30 June.
Hall, Ben. 2019. 'Europe shaken by splintering of traditional political systems', *Financial Times*, 11 January.
Hall, Stuart. 1980. 'Thatcherism—A New Stage?'. *Marxism Today*, February.
Harari, Yuval Noah. 2020. 'After coronavirus'. *Financial Times*, 4/5 April.
Harcourt, Bernard. 2010. 'Neoliberal Penality. A Brief Genealogy', *Theoretical Criminology*, 14: 1.
Hariman, Robert. 2010. *Political Style. The Artistry of Power*, Chicago: University of Chicago Press.
Harvey, David. 2005. *A Brief History of Neoliberalism*. Oxford: Oxford University Press.
Havlik, Vlastimil. 2018. 'Technocratic populism and political illiberalism in Central Europe: the case of ANO in the Czech Republic', paper presented at the *ECPR General Conference* in Hamburg, 22-5 August.
Hawkins, Kirk A., Read, Madeleine, and Pauwels, Teun. 2017. 'Populism and Its causes', in C. R. Kaltwasser, P. A. Taggart, P. O. Espejo, and P. Ostiguy (eds.) *The Oxford Handbook of Populism*. Oxford: Oxford University Press.
Hay, Colin. 2002. *Political Analysis: A Critical Introduction*, Basingstoke: Palgrave.
Hegel, Georg Wilhelm Friedrich. 1821. *Elements of the Philosophy of Right*, Cambridge: Cambridge University Press [1991].
Heilbrunn, John R. 2005. 'Oil and water? Elite politicians and corruption in France', *Comparative Politics*, 37: 3, 277–96.
Hermet, Guy. 2007. *L'Hiver de la Démocratie*, Paris: Armand Colin.
Hershey, Marjorie. 2017. *Party Politics in America*, New York: Routledge.
Hix, Simon. 1998. 'The Study of the European Union II: the "new governance" agenda and its rival', *Journal of European Public Policy*, 5(1): 38–65.
Hobolt, Sara, Leeper, Thomas, and Tilley, James. 2018. 'Divided by the Vote: Affective Polarization in the Wake of Brexit', paper presented at the *Durham University Political Science Colloquium*, 30 April, available at: https://www.dur.ac.uk/sgia/about/pastevents/?eventno=38490
Hobsbawm, Eric. 1992. *Nations and Nationalism since 1780, Second Edition*, Cambridge: Cambridge University Press.
Hobsbawm, Eric. 1994. *Age of Extremes: The Short Twentieth Century, 1914–1991*, London: Abacus.
Holtz-Bacha Christina and Stromback, Jesper. 2012. *Opinion Polls and the Media. Reflecting and Shaping Public Opinion*, London: Palgrave.
Hopkin, Jonathan. 2001. 'Bringing the Members Back In? Democratizing Candidate Selection in Britain and Spain', *Party Politics*, 7: 3.
Hopkins, Valerie. 2020. 'Orban handed power to rule by decree'. *Financial Times*, 31 March.
Hough, Andrew. 2010. 'David Cameron becomes youngest prime minister in almost 200 years', *Daily Telegraph*, 11 May 2020.
Houllebecq, Michel. 1994. *Extension du Domaine de la Lutte*, Paris: Editions Maurice Nadeau.
iFRAP. 2018. 'Macronometre: l'Observatoire des Réformes du Gouvernement', available at: http://www.macronometre.fr
Iglesias, Pablo. 2014. 'The Left Can Win', *Jacobin*, 9 December.

Iglesias, Pablo. 2015. *Politics in a Time of Crisis. Podemos and the Future of Democratic Europe*, London: Verso.
Ignatieff, Michael. 2017. 'Enemies vs. Adversaries'. *The New York Times*, 16 October, available at: https://www.nytimes.com/2013/10/17/opinion/enemies-vs-adversaries.html
Ignazi, Piero. 2003. *Extreme Right Parties in Western Europe*. Oxford: Oxford University Press.
Ignazi, Piero. 2018. *Party and Democracy*, Oxford: Oxford University Press.
Inglehart, Ronald. 1970. 'Cognitive Mobilization and European Identity', *Comparative Politics* (October).
Inglehart, Ronald. 1977. *The Silent Revolution*, Princeton: Princeton University Press.
Inglehart, Ronald. 1990. *Culture Shift in Advanced Industrial Society*, Princeton: Princeton University Press.
Inglehart, Ronald and Christian, Welzel. 2005. *Modernization, Cultural Change, and Democracy*, Cambridge: Cambridge University Press.
Invernizzi Accetti, Carlo. 2016. 'America's Choice in November is Between a Populist and a Technocrat'. *The Guardian*, 5 October.
Invernizzi Accetti, Carlo. 2019. *What is Christian Democracy? Politics, Religion, Ideology*, Cambridge: Cambridge University Press.
Invernizzi Accetti, Carlo and Wolkenstein, Fabio. 2017. 'The Crisis of Party Democracy, Cognitive Mobilization and the Case for Making Parties More Deliberative', *American Political Science Review*, 111: 1.
Ivaldi, Gilles, Lanzone, Maria Elisabetta, and Woods, Dwayne. 2017. 'Varieties of Populism across a Left-Right Spectrum: The Case of the Front National, the Northern League, Podemos and Five Star Movement', *Swiss Political Science Review*, 23: 4.
Iyengar, Shanto and Westwood, Sean. 2015. 'Fear and Loathing Across Party Lines: New Evidence on Group Polarization', *American Journal of Political Science*, 59: 3.
Jacoby, Russell. 1999. *The End of Utopia*, New York: Basic Books.
Jäger, Anton. 2019. 'We Bet the House on Left Populism—And Lost'. *Jacobin Magazine*, 25 November.
Jäger, Anton. 2020. Twitter, 7 April.
Jäger, Anton and Borriello, Arthur. 2019. 'Is Left Populism the Solution?' *Jacobin Magazine*, 31 March.
Jameson, Fredric. 2009. *Ideologies of Theory*, London: Verso.
Jessop, Bob, Bonnett, Kevin, Bromley, Simon, and Ling, Tom. 1984. 'Authoritarian Populism, Two Nations, and Thatcherism', *New Left Review*, 1/147 (Sept–Oct).
Johnson, Miles. 2020. 'Salvini's comeback bid'. *Financial Times*, 14 January.
Jori, Francesco. 2009. *Dalla Liga alla Lega. Storia, Movimenti, Protagonisti*, Venezia: Marsilio.
Jouyet, Jean-Pierre. 2020. *L'Envers du Décor*. Paris: Albin Michel.
Jublin, Mathieu. 2018. 'Emmanuel Macron se désigne désormais comme "populiste"'. La Chaine Info, 22 November, available at: https://www.lci.fr/politique/emmanuel-macron-se-designe-desormais-comme-populiste-comment-s-y-retrouver-parmi-tous-les-populismes-2105364.html
Judis, John. 2016. *The Populist Explosion: How the Great Recession Transformed American and European Politics*, New York: Columbia Global Reports.
Judt, Tony. 2005. *Post-War*, London: Penguin.
Judt, Tony. 2010. *Ill Fares the Land*, London: Penguin.
Kadish, Sharman. 1987. 'Jewish Bolshevism and the Red Scare in Britain', *Jewish Quarterly*, 34: 4.

Kalyvas, Stathis. 1996. *The Rise of Christian Democracy in Europe*, Ithaca: Cornell University Press.
Katz, Richard. 2013. 'Should we believe that improved intra-party democracy would arrest party decline?', in William Cross and Richard Katz (eds.), *The Challenges of Intra-Party Democracy*, Oxford: Oxford University Press.
Katz, Richard and Mair, Peter. 1995. 'Changing Models of Party Organization and Party Democracy, *Party Politics*, 1: 1.
Katz, Richard and Mair, Peter. 2009. 'The Cartel Party Thesis: A Restatement', *Perspectives on Politics*, 7: 4.
Katz, Richard and Mair, Peter. 2018. *Democracy and the Cartelization of Political Parties*, Oxford: Oxford University Press.
Kazin, Michael. 2013. *The Populist Persuasion: An American History*, Ithaca: Cornell University Press.
Kelley, Colleen. 2018. *A Rhetoric of Divisive Partisanship. The 2016 Presidential Campaign Discourse of Donald Trump and Bernie Sanders*, New York: Lexington.
Kellner, Douglas. 2017. 'Guy Debord, Donald Trump, and the Politics of the Spectacle', in Marco Briziarelli and Emiliana Armano (eds.), *The Spectacle 2.0: Reading Debord in the Context of Digital Capitalism*, London: University of Westminster Press.
Kelsen, Hans. 1929. *The Essence and Value of Democracy*, New York: Rowman and Littlefield [2013].
Kelsen, Hans. 1949. *General Theory of Law and State*, New Brunswick: Transaction Publishers [2005].
Khanna, Parag. 2018. *Technocracy in America. The Rise of the Info-State*, New York: CreateSpace.
King, Michael. 2005. 'Epistemic Communities and the Diffusion of Ideas: Central Bank Reform in the UK', *West European Politics*, 28: 1.
Kircheimer, Otto. 1966. 'Germany: The Vanishing Opposition', in Robert Dahl (ed.), *Political Oppositions in Western Democracies*, New Haven: Yale University Press.
Kirchheimer, Otto. 1969. 'The Transformation of the Western European Party System', in F. S. Burin and K. L. Shell (eds.), *Politics, Law and Social Change: Selected Essays of Otto Kirchheimer*, New York: Columbia University Press.
Kioupkiolis, Alexandros. 2016. 'Podemos: the ambiguous promises of left-wing populism in contemporary Spain', *Journal of Political Ideologies*, 21: 2.
Kioupkiolis, Alexandros and Perez, Francisco Seoane. 2019. 'Reflexive Technopopulism: Podemos and the Search for a New Left-Wing Hegemony', *European Political Science*, 18: 24–36.
Kitschelt, Herbert. 1989. 'The Internal Politics of Parties: The Law of Curvilinear Disparity Revisited', *Political Studies*, 37: 3.
Kitschelt, Herbet and McGann, Anthony. 1995. *The Radical Right in Western Europe: A Comparative Analysis*, Ann Arbor: University of Michigan Press.
Khalaf, Roula and Mallet, Vincent. 2020. 'Emmanuel Macron Says Its Time to Think the Unthinkable', *Financial Times*, 16 April.
Kling, Robert (ed.). 1996. *Computerization and Controversy. Value Conflicts and Social Choices*, New York: Academic Press.
Koiman, Jan. 2003. *Governing as Governance*, London: Sage.
Krastev, Ivan. 2007. 'The Populist Moment', *Eurozine*, 18 September.
Krastev, Ivan. 2014. *Democracy Disrupted: The Politics of Global Protest*. Philadelphia: University of Pennsylvania Press.

Krastev, Ivan and Holmes, Stephen. 2020. *The Light that Failed: Why the West Is Losing the Fight for Democracy*, New York: Penguin.
Kriesi, Hanspeter. 1998. 'The transformation of cleavage politics: The 1997 Stein Rokkan lecture', *European Journal of Political Research*, 33: 165–85.
Kriesi, Hanspeter. 2010. 'Restructuration of Partisan Politics and the Emergence of a New Cleavage Based on Values', *West European Politics*, 33(3): 673–85.
Kriesi, Hanspeter, Edgar Grande, Martin Dolezal, Marc Helblin, Paul Statham, and Hans-Jörg Trenz. 2012. *Political Conflict in Western Europe*, Cambridge: Cambridge University Press.
Kriesi, Hanspeter, and Pappas, Takis S. (eds.) 2015. *European Populism in the Shadow of the Great Recession*. Colchester: ECPR Press.
Kundnani, Hans. 2020. 'The Future of Democracy in Europe: Technology and the Evolution of Representation'. *Chatham House Research Paper*, 3 March.
Kyle, Jordan and Gultchin, Limor. 2018. 'Populists in Power Around the World', Tony Blair Institute for Global Change, available at: https://institute.global/sites/default/files/articles/Populists-in-Power-Around-the-World-pdf
Laclau, Ernesto. 1977. *Politics and Ideology in Marxist Theory. Capitalism, Fascism, Populism*, London: Verso.
Laclau, Ernesto. 2005a. *On Populist Reason*, London: Verso.
Laclau, Ernesto. 2005b. 'Populism: What's in a Name?', in Francisco Panizza (ed.), *Populism and The Mirror of Democracy*, London: Verso.
Landemore, Hélène. 2013. *Democratic Reason: Politics, Collective Intelligence and the Rule of Many*, Princeton: Princeton University Press.
Lasch, Christopher. 1996. *The Revolt of the Elites and the Betrayal of Democracy*, New York: Norton.
Laski, Harald. 1931. 'The Limitations of the Expert', *Fabian Tract No.235*, London: The Fabian Society.
Lassman, Peter and Speirs, Ronald (eds.). 1994. *Weber: Political Writings*, Cambridge: Cambridge University Press.
Lazar, Marc. 2018. 'De quoi le macronisme est-il le nom ?', in R. Brizzi and M. Lazar (eds.), *La France d'Emmanuel Macron*, Presse Universitaire de Rennes: Rennes.
Lazar, Marc. 2020. 'The curious Giuseppe Conte', *Institut Montaigne blog*, 1 September.
Lazar, Marc and Diamanti, Ilvo. 2018. *Popolocrazia. La Metamorfosi delle Nostre Democrazie*, Bari: Laterza.
Leach, Edmund. 1962. 'On Certain Unconsidered Aspects of Double Descent Systems', *Man*, 62: 1.
Leavy, Edward Harrison. 2018. 'Technopopulism: Movimento Cinque Stelle, Podemos and the Rise of Digital Direct Democracy', thesis submitted to the faculty of the University of North Carolina at Chapel Hill, available at: https://cdr.lib.unc.edu/indexablecontent/uuid:5f262282-f714-4cb3-9093-139d47fdc248?dl=true
Lee, Jasmine and Quealy, Kevin. 2018. 'The 551 People, Places and Things Donald Trump Has Insulted on Twitter: A Complete List'. *The New York Times*, 28 December.
Legrand, Thomas. 2010. *Ce N'est Rien*, Paris: Stock.
Leibovich, Mark. 2016. 'I'm the Last Thing Standing Between You and The Apocalypse. Inside the Final Weeks of the Clinton Campaign'. *New York Times*, 11 October.
Leonard, Mark. 2012. 'The dark-flipside of European technocracy', European Council on Foreign Relations, 1 June, available at: https://www.ecfr.eu/article/commentary_the_dark_flip-side_of_european_technocracy34594

Leonard, Mark. 2017. 'The Macron Method', Commentary, *European Council on Foreign Relations*, 30 May, available at: https://www.ecfr.eu/article/commentary_the_macron_method_7298

Levi Martin, John. 2003. 'What is Field Theory?' *American Journal of Sociology*, 109(1): 1–49.

Levitsky, Steven and Ziblatt, Daniel. 2018. *How Democracies Die*, New York: Penguin.

Lewis, Paul, Barr, Caelainn, Clarke, Sean, Voce, Antonio, Levett, Cath, and Gutiérrez, Pablo. 2019. 'Revealed: the rise and rise of populist rhetoric', *The Guardian*, 8 March, available at: https://www.theguardian.com/world/ng-interactive/2019/mar/06/revealed-the-rise-and-rise-of-populist-rhetoric

Lijphart, Arend. 1968. *The Politics of Accommodation: Pluralism and Democracy in the Netherlands*, Berkley and Los Angeles: University of California Press.

Linz, Juan. 1996. 'Toward Consolidated Democracies', *Journal of Democracy*, 7: 2.

Lipow, Arthur and Seyd, Patrick. 1995. 'Political Parties and the Challenge to Democracy: from Steam Engines to Technopopulism', *New Political Science*, 17: 1–2.

Lipset, Seymour Martin. 1964. (Abridged modern edition of Ostrogorski, Moisey) *Democracy and the Organization of Political Parties*, Garden City: Doubleday-Anchor.

Lipset, Seymour Martin and Rokkan, Stein. 1967. *Party Systems and Voter Alignments: Cross-National Perspectives*, New York: Free Press.

Lorimer, Marta. 2019. 'Ni droite, Ni gauche, Français! Far right populism and the future of Left/Right politics', in Lise Herman and James Muldoon (eds.), *Trumping the Mainstream: The Conquest of Mainstream Democratic Politics by Far-right Populism*, London: Routledge.

Lorwin, Val R. 1971. 'Segmented Pluralism: Ideological Cleavages and Political Cohesion in the Smaller European Democracies', *Comparative Politics*, 3: 2, 141–75.

Loucaides, Darren. 2019. 'The anti-Semitism crisis tearing the UK Labour Party apart, explained', *Vox*, 8th March.

Luckmann, Thomas. 1967. *The Invisible Religion: The Problem of Religion in Modern Society*, New York: Macmillan.

LREM (*La République En Marche*). 2017. *Le Programme d'Emmanuel Macron*, available at: https://en-marche.fr/emmanuel-macron/le-programme

Lynch, Thomas. 2017. 'President Donald Trump: A Case Study of Spectacular Power', *The Political Quarterly*, 88: 4.

Lyon, David. 2001. *Surveillance Society. Monitoring Everyday Life*, Buckingham: Open University Press.

Mack Smith, Dennis. 1997. *Modern Italy: A Political History*, Ann Arbor: University of Michigan Press.

Macron, Emmanuel. 2016. *Revolution*, London: Scribe [2017].

Macron, Emmanuel. 2017. 'Discours au Louvre', available at: https://en-marche.fr/articles/discours/emmanuel-macron-president-louvre-carrousel-discours

Maddison, Angus. 1991. *Dynamic Forces in Capitalist Development: A Long-Run Comparative View*, Oxford: Oxford University Press.

Mahrane, Saïd. 2020. 'Congé après le déces d'un enfant: ce que révèlent les débatsà l'Assemblée'. *Le Point*, 5 February.

Maier, Charles S. 1975. *Recasting Bourgeois Europe: Stabilisation in France, Germany and Italy in the Decade After World War One*, Princeton: Princeton University Press.

Maier, Charles S. 1983. '"Fictitious bonds . . . of wealth and law": on the theory and practice of interest representation', in Suzanne D. Berger (ed.), *Organizing Interests in Western*

Europe: Pluralism, corporatism, and the transformation of politics, Cambridge: Cambridge University Press.
Mair, Peter. 1992. 'The Myth of Electoral Change and the Survival of Traditional Parties', in Ingrid Van Biezen (ed.), On Parties, Party Systems and Democracy. Selected Writing by Peter Mair, Essex: ECPR Press.
Mair, Peter. 1997. *Party System Change*, Oxford: Clarendon Press.
Mair, Peter. 2000. 'Partyless Democracy: Solving the Paradox of New Labour', *New Left Review*, March–April.
Mair, Peter. 2002. 'Populist Democracy vs. Party Democracy', in Ingrid Van Biezen (ed.), *On Parties, Party Systems and Democracy. Selected Writing by Peter Mair*, Essex: ECPR Press.
Mair, Peter. 2013. *Ruling the Void: The Hollowing Out of Western Democracy*, London: Verso.
Majone, Giandomenico. 1994. 'The rise of the regulatory state in Europe', *West European Politics*, 17(3): 77–101.
Majone, Giandomenico. 1997. 'From the Positive to the Regulatory State: Causes and Consequences of Changes in the Mode of Governance', *Journal of Public Policy*, 17(2): 139–67.
Majone, Giandomenico. 1999. 'The Regulatory State and Its Legitimacy Problems', *West European Politics*, 22: 1.
Mallet, Victor and Khalaf, Roula. 2020. 'Macron: coronavirus is Europe's moment of truth'. *Financial Times*, 16 April.
Mance, Henry. 2016. 'Britain has had enough of experts, says Gove'. *Financial Times*, 3 June.
Mance, Henry. 2016. 'Britain Has Had Enough of Experts, Says Gove'. *Financial Times*, 4 June.
Manent, Aline-Florence. 2017. 'Emmanuel Macron's Political Revolution in France', H-Diplo ISSF, 17 November, available at: https://issforum.org/roundtables/policy/2-2-macron
Manin, Bernard. 1998. *The Principles of Representative Government*. Cambridge: Cambridge University Press.
Manucci, Luca and Amsler, Michi. 2018. 'Where the wind blows: Five Star Movement's populism, direct democracy and ideological flexibility', *Italian Political Science Review*, 48(1): 109–132.
March, Luke. 2017. 'Left and Right Populism Compared. The British Case', *British Journal of Politics and International Relations*, 19: 2.
Marcussen, Martin. 2005. 'Central banks on the move', *Journal of European Public Policy*, 12(5): 903–23.
Margetts, Helen, John, Peter, Hale, Scott, and Yasseri, Taha (eds.). 2016. *Political Turbulence: How Social Media Shape Collective Action*, Princeton, NJ: Princeton University Press.
Marglin, Stephen and Schor, Juliet (eds.). 1990. *The Golden Age of Capitalism: Reinterpreting the Postwar Experience*, Oxford: Clarendon Press.
Marini, Margaret and Singer, Burton. 1988. 'Causality in the Social Sciences', *Sociological Methodology*, 18: 1.
Marquand, David. 1962. 'State of the nation: book review of Anthony Sampson's Anatomy of Britain'. *The Guardian*, 20 July.
Marquand, David. 1999. 'Progressive or Populist? The Blair Paradox', in *The Progressive Dilemma*, London: Phoenix House.

Marshall, T. H. 1992. *Citizenship and Social Class*, London: Pluto.
Mathieu, Isabelle. 2019. 'Le Grand Débat National: La Tentation Populiste d'Emmanuel Macron', *The Conversation*, available at: https://theconversation.com/grand-debat-national-la-tentation-populiste-demmanuel-macron-109777
Matthews, Roger and Young, Jack (eds). 2003. *The New Politics of Crime and Punishment*, London: Routledge.
Mauger, Gérard. 2019. 'The Gilets Jaunes', *Savoir/Agir*, 1: 1.
Mauduit, Laurent. 2018. *La Caste: Enquête sur cette haute fonction publique qui a pris le pouvoir*, La Découverte: Paris.
May, John. 1973. 'Opinion Structures Within Political Parties: The Special Law of Curvilinear Disparity', *Political Studies*, 21: 2.
Mayeur, Jean-Marie. 1980. *Des Partis Catholiques à la Démocratie Chrétienne*, Paris: Armand Colin.
Mazzoleni, Gianpietro. 2008. 'Mediatization of Politics', in *The International Encyclopedia of Communication*, Oxford: Wiley.
Mazzoleni, Gianpietro and Schulz, Winfried. 1999. 'Mediatization of Politics: A Challenge for Democracy?', *Political Communication*, 16: 3.
McAllister, Ian. 2007. 'The Personalization of Politics', in Russell Dalton and Hans-Dieter Klingemann (eds.), *The Oxford Handbook of Political Behaviour*, Oxford: Oxford University Press.
McDevitt, Johnny. 2019. 'Dominic Cummings honed strategy in 2004 vote, video reveals', *The Guardian*, 12 November.
McDonnell, Duncan and Valbruzzi, Marco. 2014. 'Defining and classifying technocrat-led and technocratic governments'. *European Journal of Political Research*, 53:4, 654–71.
McDonnell, Duncan and Werner, Annika. 2019. *International Populism: The Radical Right in the European Parliament*, London: Hurst.
McGuire, Patrick. 2020. 'Keir Starmer: The Sensible Radical'. *New Statesman*, 31 March.
McKenzie, Robert. 1963. *British Political Parties: The Distribution of Power within the Conservative and Labour Parties, Second Edition*. London: Heinemann.
McKibbin, Ross. 2014. 'Labour Vanishes', *London Review of Books*, November.
McLaughlin, Eugene, Muncie, John, and Hughes, Gordon. 2001. 'The Permanent Revolution: New Labour, New Public Management and the Modernization of Criminal Justice', *Criminology and Criminal Justice*, 1: 3.
McNay, Lois. 1999. 'Gender, Habitus and the Field: Pierre Bourdieu and the Limits of Reflexivity', *Theory, Culture and Society*, 16(1): 95–117.
McTague, Tom. 2020. 'The Coronavirus is more than just a health crisis'. *The Atlantic*, 5 March.
Meek, James. 2019. 'The Dreamings of Dominic Cummings', *London Review of Books*, 41 (24 October): 20.
Menand, Louis. 2005. 'Everybody's an expert: Putting predictions to the test'. *The New Yorker*, 28 November.
Mendras, Henri. 1988. *La Seconde Révolution Française. 1965–1984*, Paris: Gallimard.
Mendras, Henri and Cole, Alastair. 1991. *Social Change in Modern France: Towards a cultural anthropology of the Fifth Republic*, Cambridge: Cambridge University Press.
Meynaud, Jean. 1969. *Technocracy*, New York: Free Press.
Michels, Roberto. 1911. *Political Parties. A Sociological Study of the Oligarchic Tendencies of Modern Democracy*, London: Transaction [2009].
Mietzner, Marcus. 2015. *Reinventing Asian Populism: Jokowi's Rise, Democracy and Political Contestation in Indonesia*, Honolulu: East-West Centre.

Moffit, Benjamin. 2020. *Populism*, Cambridge: Polity.
Monedero, Juan Carlos. 2019. 'Snipers in the Kitchen: State Theory and Latin America's Left Cycle', *New Left Review*, 120: 5–32.
Monti, Mario and Goulard, Sylvie. 2012. *De la Démocratie en Europe. Voir Plus Loin*, Paris: Flammarion.
Moran, Michael. 1999. 'Estates, Classes and Interests', in Ian Holliday, Andrew Gamble, and Geraint Parry (eds.), *Fundamentals in British Politics*, London: MacMillan.
Morozov, Evgeny. 2014. *To Save Everything, Click Here: The Folly of Technological Solutionism*, New York: Public Affairs.
Mouffe, Chantal. 2018. *For A Left Populism*, London: Verso.
Mouffe, Chantel. 2019. *For A Left Populism*. London: Verso.
Mosca, Lorenzo. 2014. 'The Five Star Movement: Exception or Vanguard in Europe?', *The International Spectator*, 49(1): 36–52.
Mosca, Lorenzo. 2018, 'Democratic vision and online participatory spaces in the Italian Movimento 5 Stelle', *Acta Politica*, 55, 1–18.
Mounk, Yascha. 2018. *The People vs. Democracy*, Cambridge: Harvard University Press.
Mudde, Cas. 2004. 'The Populist Zeitgeist', *Government and Opposition*, 39: 4.
Mudde, Cas. 2007. *Populist Radical Right Parties in Europe*, Cambridge: Cambridge University Press.
Mudde, Cas. 2017. 'Populism: An Ideational Approach', in Cristobal Rovira Kaltwasser, Paul Taggart, Paulina Ochoa Espejo, and Pierre Ostiguy (eds.), *The Oxford Handbook of Populism*, Oxford: Oxford University Press.
Muirhead, Russel. 2014. *The Promise of Partisanship in a Polarized Age*, Cambridge: Harvard University Press.
Muirhead, Russel and Rosenblum, Nancy. 2019. *A Lot of People Are Saying. The new Conspiracism and the Assault on Democracy*, Princeton: Princeton University Press.
Müller, Jan-Werner. 2013. *Contesting Democracy. Political Ideas in Twentieth-Century Europe*, New Haven: Yale University Press.
Müller, Jan-Werner. 2016. *What is Populism?*, Philadelphia: University of Pennsylvania Press.
Müller, Jan-Werner. 2018. 'Can Movement Politics Renew European Democracy?'. *Project Syndicate*, 3 January.
Müller, Jan-Werner. 2018. 'Angela Merkel Failed'. *Foreign Policy*, 31 October.
Müller, Jan-Werner. 2020. 'Why do rightwing populist leaders oppose experts?'. *The Guardian*, 26 March.
Musella, Fortunato and Webb, Paul. 2015. 'The Revolution of Personal Leaders', *Rivista Italiana di Scienza Politica*, 45: 03.
Musso, Massimilano. 2019. 'Il tradimento di Beppe Grillo e del Movimento 5 Stelle è cominciato con la finta battaglia contro l'euro', *Il Popolo Sovrano*, 10 September.
Musso, Pierre. 2008. *Le Sarkoberlusconisme*, Paris: Aube.
Musso, Pierre. 2019a. *Le temps de L'État-Entreprise*, Paris: Fayard.
Musso, Pierre. 2019b. 'L'ère de l'État-entreprise'. *Le Monde Diplomatique*, May 2019.
Natale, Simone and Ballatore, Andrea. 2014. 'The web will kill them all: new media, digital utopia, and political struggle in the Italian 5-Star Movement', *Media, Culture and Society*, 36(1): 105–21.
Neville, Sarah. 2020. 'Person in the news: Chris Whitty. A very diplomatic expert in disease'. *Financial Times*, 14/15 March.
Norris, Pippa. 1995. 'May's Law of Curvilinear Disparity Revisited', *Party Politics* 1: 1.

Norris, Pippa. 2002. *Democratic Phoenix. Reinventing Political Activism*, Cambridge: Cambridge University Press.
NRC (National Research Council). 2014. 'The Growth of Incarceration in the United States: Exploring Causes and Consequences', Washington: National Academies Press.
Ostiguy, Pierre. 2017. 'Populism: A Socio-Cultural Approach', in Cristobal Rovira Kaltwasser, Paul Taggart, Paulina Ochoa Espejo, and Pierre Ostiguy (eds.), *The Oxford Handbook of Political Science*, Oxford: Oxford University Press.
Packer, George. 2013. *The Unwinding: An Inner History of the New America*, London: Faber and Faber.
Pakulski, Jan and Waters, Malcolm. 1997. *The Death of Class*, London: Sage.
Pakulski, Jan. 2005. 'Foundations of a Post-Class Analysis', in Erik Olin Wright (ed.), *Approaches to Class Analysis*, Cambridge: Cambridge University Press.
Papadopoulos, Yannis. 2013. *Democracy in Crisis? Politics, Governance and Policy*, London: Palgrave.
Papini, Roberto. 1978. *Quelle Identité Pour la Démocratie Chrétienne?*, Rome: Institut International Démocrate Chrétien d'Etudes.
Pardos-Prado, Sergi. 2012. 'Valence beyond Consensus: Party Competence and Policy Dispersion from a Comparative Perspective', *Electoral Studies*, 31: 2.
Pasquino, Gianfranco. 2014. 'The 2013 Elections and the Italian Political System', *Journal of Modern Italian Studies*, 19: 4.
Passarelli, Gianluca and Tuorto, Dario. 2018. *La Lega di Salvini. Estrema Destra di Governo*, Bologna: il Mulino.
Passarelli, Gianluca, Tronconi, Filippo, and Tuorto, Dario. 2013. 'Inside the Movement: organization, activists and programmes', in Piergiorgio Corbetta and Elisabetta Gualmini (eds.), *Il partito di Grillo*, Bologna: il Mulino.
Pearl, Judea. 2000. *Causality*, Cambridge: Cambridge University Press.
Pedder, Sophie. 2018. *Revolution Française: Emmanuel Macron and the Quest to Reinvent a Nation*, Bloomsbury: London.
Phoganpaichit, Pasuk and Baker, Chris. 2007. 'Thaksin's Populism', *Journal of Contemporary Asia*, 38: 1.
Pinçon, Michel and Pinçon-Charlot, Monique. 2019. *Le Président des Ultra-Riches*, Paris: Zones.
Plato. 2000. *The Republic*, Cambridge: Cambridge University Press.
Plowright, Adam. 2017. *The French Exception, Emmanuel Macron: The Extraordinary Rise and Risk*, Icon: London.
Poggioli, Sylvia. 2019. 'Fed Up with Far Right, Italy's 'Sardines' Protests Call for Civility and Equality', *NPR*, 17 December.
Porter, Theodore M. 1995. *Trust in Numbers: The Pursuit of Objectivity in Science and Public Life*. Princeton, New Jersey: Princeton University Press.
Poussielgue, Grégoire. 2017. 'Emmanuel Macron se pose en Protecteur de la démocratie et de la République', *Les Echos*, 1 May.
Pratt, John. 2007. *Penal Populism*, New York: Routledge.
Proctor, Kate. 2019. 'Five Reasons Why Labour Lost the Election', *The Guardian*, 13 December.
Przeworski, Adam. 2019. *Crises of Democracy*, Cambridge: Cambridge University Press.
Pucciarelli, Matteo. 2019. 'Salvini Ascendant'. *New Left Review*, 116/7, 9–30.
Pugh, Martin. 2011. *Speak For Britain! A New History of the Labour Party*, London: Vintage.
Putnam, Robert. 1977. 'Elite Transformation in Advanced Industrial Societies: An Empirical Assessment of the Theory of Technocracy', *Comparative Political Studies*, 10: 3, 383–412.

Putnam, Robert. 2000. *Bowling Alone. The Collapse and Revival of American Community*, New York: Simon and Schuster.
Quinn, Thomas. 2016. 'The British Labour Party's leadership election of 2015', *The British Journal of Politics and International Relations*, 18: 4.
Quito, Anne and Yanofsky, David. 2017. 'Emmanuel Macron's official portrait is a symbolic celebration of centrism'. *Quartz*, 30 June.
Ramsay, Peter. 2008. 'Vulnerability, Sovereignty and Police Power in the ASBO', in M. Dubber and M. Valverde (eds.), *Police and the Liberal State*, Stanford: Stanford University Press.
Ramsay, Peter. 2012. *The Insecurity State: Vulnerable Autonomy and the Right to Security in the Criminal Law*, Oxford: Oxford University Press.
Ramsay, Peter. 2016. 'A Democratic Theory of Imprisonment', in Albert Dzur, Ian Loader, and Richard Sparks (eds.), *Democratic Theory and Mass Incarceration*, Oxford: Oxford University Press.
Rawnsley, Andrew. 2000. *Servants of the People: The Inside Story of New Labour*, London: Penguin.
Rawnsley, Andrew. 2010. *The End of the Party: The Rise and Fall of New Labour*, London: Penguin.
Reeves, Rachel. 2018. *The Everyday Economy*. Self-published.
Rentoul, John. 2013. *Tony Blair. Prime Minister*, London: Faber.
Reus-Smit, Christian. 2009. *The Moral Purpose of the State: Culture, Social Identity and Institutional Rationality in International Relations*, Princeton, NJ: Princeton University Press.
Rhodes, Roderick. 1996. 'The New Governance: Governing Without Government', *Political Studies*, 44: 3.
Richardson, Dick and Rootes, Chris. 1995. *The Green Challenge. The Development of Green Parties in Europe*, London: Routledge.
Rigby, Beth. 2020. 'Coronavirus: "Populist" PM takes non-populist approach when it comes to pandemics'. *Sky News*, 20 March.
Rioux, Jean-Pierre. 2005. 'Les Gouvernements de Gauche sous la IV République', in Jean-Jacques Becker and Gilles Becker (eds.), *Histoire des Gauches en France*, Paris: La Découverte.
Roberts, Julian, Stalans, Loretta, Indermaur, David, and Hough, Mike. 2003. *Penal Populism and Public Opinion*, New York: Oxford University Press.
Roberts, Kenneth. 2006. 'Do Parties Matter? Lessons from the Fujimori Experience', in Carrión, Julio F. (ed.), *The Fujimori Legacy: The Rise of Electoral Authoritarianism in Peru*, Pennsylvania: Pennsylvania State University Press.
Robin, Corey. 2011. *The Reactionary Mind. Conservatism from Edmund Burke to Sarah Palin*, Oxford: Oxford University Press.
Rosanvallon, Pierre. 2008. *Counter-Democracy. Politics in an Age of Distrust*, Cambridge: Cambridge University Press.
Rosanvallon, Pierre. 2011. *Democratic Legitimacy. Impartiality. Reflexivity. Proximity*, Princeton: Princeton University Press.
Rosanvallon, Pierre. 2020. *Le Siècle du populisme: Histoire, théorie, critique*, Paris: Seuil.
Rosenau, James and Czempiel, Ernst-Otto (eds.). 1992. *Governance without Government: Order and Change in World Politics*, Cambridge: Cambridge University Press.
Rosenblum, Nancy. 2008. *On the Side of the Angels. An Appreciation of Parties and Partisanship*, Princeton: Princeton University Press.
Rosenfeld, Sofia. 2019. *Democracy and Truth: A Short History*, Philadelphia: University of Pennsylvania Press.

Rostowski, Jacek. 2016. 'Why Today's Politics Do Not Mirror Those of The 1930s'. *Financial Times*, 28 July.

Rouban, Luc. 2019. 'Le Grand Débat National: Des Demandes Contradictoires sur un Arrière-fond Populiste et Moralisateur'. *The Conversation*, 25 March, available at: https://theconversation.com/le-grand-debat-national-des-demandes-contradictoires-sur-un-arriere-fond-populiste-et-moralisateur-114241

Rousseau, Jean-Jacques. 1762. 'The Social Contract', in *The Social Contract and Other Later Political Writings*, Cambridge: Cambridge University Press [1997].

Rovira, Kaltwasser, Cristobal, Paul Taggart, Paulina Ochoa Espejo, and Pierre Ostiguy (eds.). 2017. *The Oxford Handbook of Populism*, Oxford: Oxford University Press.

Rucht, Dieter. 2007. 'Protest Politics', in Russell Dalton and Hans-Dieter Klingemann (eds.), *The Oxford Handbook of Political Behaviour*, Oxford: Oxford University Press.

Rummens, Stefan. 2017. 'Populism as a Threat to Liberal Democracy', in Cristobal Rovira Kaltwasser, Paul Taggart, Paulina Ochoa Espejo, and Pierre Ostiguy (eds.), *The Oxford Handbook of Populism*, Oxford: Oxford University Press.

Runciman, David. 2016. 'Politics by Nick Clegg review – a painful read', *The Guardian*, 8 September.

Runciman, David. 2017. 'Do your homework', *London Review of Books*, 39: 6.

Runciman, David. 2018. *How Democracy Ends*, London: Basic Books.

Runciman, David. 2020. 'Coronavirus has not suspended politics—it has revealed the nature of power'. *The Guardian*, 27 March.

Salvini, Matteo. 2016. *Secondo Matteo. Follia e Coraggio per Cambiare il Paese*, Milano: Rizzoli.

Sartori, Giovanni. 1970. 'Concept Misformation in Comparative Politics', *American Political Science Review*, 64: 4.

Sartori, Giovanni. 1976. *Parties and Party Systems*, Cambridge: Cambridge University Press.

Sartori, Giovanni. 2000. *Homo videns: Televisione e post-penisero*, Rome: Laterza.

Sayer, Andrew. 2010. *Method in Social Science*, New York: Routledge.

Scarrow, Susan. 2015. *Beyond Party Members. Changing Approaches to Party Membership*, Oxford: Oxford University Press.

Schattschneider, Eric. 1960. *The Semi-Sovereign People. A Realist's View of Democracy in America*, Boston: Wadsworth.

Schmidt, Eric and Cohen, Jared. 2013. *The New Digital Age: Reshaping the Future of People, Nations and Business*, London: John Murray.

Schmitt, Carl. 1921. *The Concept of the Political*, Chicago: University of Chicago Press [2007].

Schmitter, Philippe. 1974. 'Still the century of corporatism?' *The Review of Politics*, 36: 1, 85–131.

Schmitter, Philippe. 1985. 'Neo-Corporatism and the state', in W. Grant (ed.), *The Political Economy of Corporatism*. Basingstoke: Palgrave, 32–62.

Schmitter, Philippe. 1994. 'Interests, Associations and Intermediation in a Reformed Post-Liberal Democracy', *Politische Vierteljahresschrift*, 35: 2.

Schumpeter, Joseph. 1942. *Capitalism, Socialism and Democracy*, New York: Routledge [2003].

Scicluna, Nicole and Auer, Stefan. 2019. 'From the rule of law to the rule of rules: technocracy and the crisis of EU governance'. *West European Politics*, 42(7): 1420–42.

Scoppola, Pietro. 1996. *La Repubblica dei Partiti*, Bologna: il Mulino.

Segal, Howard. 1985. *Technological Utopianism in American Culture*, Syracuse: Syracuse University Press.
Seisselberg, Jörg. 1996. 'Conditions of success and political problems of a 'media-mediated personality-party': The case of Forza Italia', *West European Politics*, 19: 4, 715–43.
Séville, Astrid. 2017a. 'From one right way to one ruinous way? Discursive shifts in TINA', *European Political Science Review*, 9: 3.
Séville, Astrid. 2017b. *'There is No Alternative'. Politik zwischen Demokratie und Sachzwang*, Berlin: Campus Verlag.
Seyd, Patrick. 1987. *The Rise and Fall of the Labour Left*, London: MacMillan.
Seyd, Patrick. 1999. 'New Parties/New Politics? A Case Study of the British Labour Party', *Party Politics*, 5: 3.
Seymour, Richard. 2017. *Jeremy Corbyn: The Strange Rebirth of Radical Politics*, London: Verso.
Smith, Nicholas Rush. 2019. *Contradictions of Democracy*, Oxford: Oxford University Press.
Sola, Jorge and Rendueles, Cesar. 2017. 'Podemos, the upheaval of Spanish politics and the challenge of populism', *Journal of Contemporary European Studies*, 26: 1.
Stafford, James. 2016. 'The Corbyn Experiment', *Dissent*, 63: 1.
Stanig, Piero. 2011. 'Measuring Political Polarization in Comparative Perspective', APSA 2011 Annual Meeting Paper, available at: https://papers.ssrn.com/sol3/papers.cfm?abstract_id=1903475
Stanley, Ben. 2017. 'Populism in Central and Eastern Europe', in Cristobal Rovira Kaltwasser, Paul Taggart, Paulina Ochoa Espejo, and Pierre Ostiguy (eds.), *The Oxford Handbook of Populism*, Oxford: Oxford University Press.
Stokes, David. 1985. 'The Paradox of Campaign Appeals and Election Mandates', *Proceedings of the American Philosophical Society*, 129: 1.
Stokes, David. 1992. 'Valence Politics', in Dennis Kavanagh (ed.), *Electoral Politics*, Oxford: Clarendon Press.
Strauss, Delphine. 2020. 'Global job losses rise sharply as corona virus lockdowns are extended', *Financial Times*, April 29.
Taguieff, Pierre-André. 2017. *Macron: Miracle our Mirage?*, Editions de l'Observatoire: Paris.
Tarchi, Marco. 2008. 'Italy: A Country of Many Populisms', in D. Albertazzi and D. McDonnell (eds.), *Twenty-First Century Populism: The Spectre of Western Democracy*. Basingstoke: Palgrave, 84–99.
Taylor, Charles. 2007. *A Secular Age*, Cambridge: Harvard University Press.
Teorell, Jan. 1999. 'A Deliberative Defense of Intra-Party Democracy', *Party Politics* 5: 3.
Tetlock, Philip. 2005. *Expert Political Judgement: How Good Is It? How Can We Know?*, Princeton, NJ: Princeton University Press.
Thiel, Peter. 2014. *Zero to One: Notes on Startups, or How to Build the Future*, New York: Penguin.
Thomassen, Jacques. 2005. *The European Voter*, Oxford: Oxford University Press.
Tooze, Adam. 2018. *Crashed! How a Decade of Financial Crisis Changed the World*, London: Viking.
Travaglio, Mario. 2012. 'Monti Lavora da Candidato: Pronta la Campagna Elettorale', *Il Fatto Quotidiano*, 20 December.
Trocino, Alessandro. 2019. 'Decreto Sicurezza: I Tormenti del M5S', *Corriere della Sera*, 7 July.

Tronconi, Filippo. 2015. *Beppe Grillo's Five Star Movement: Organisation, Communication and Ideology*, London: Routledge.
Tronconi, Filippo. 2018. 'The Italian Five Star Movement during the Crisis: Towards Normalisation?', *South European Society and Politics*, 23: 1.
Turner, Fred. 2006. *From Counterculture to Cyberculture: Steward Brand, the Whole Earth Network and the Rise of Digital Utopianism*, Chicago: University of Chicago Press.
Urbinati, Nadia. 2014. *Democracy Disfigured. Opinion, Truth and the People*, Cambridge: Harvard University Press.
Urbinati, Nadia. 2015. 'A Revolt Against Intermediary Bodies', *Constellations*, 22: 4.
Urbinati, Nadia. 2017. 'Populism and Majority Rule', in Cristobal Rovira Kaltwasser, Paul Taggart, Paulina Ochoa Espejo, and Pierre Ostiguy (eds.), *The Oxford Handbook of Populism*, Oxford: Oxford University Press.
Urbinati, Nadia. 2019. *Me the People. How Populism Transforms Democracy*, Cambridge: Harvard University Press.
Urbinati, Nadia and Saffon, Maria-Paula. 2013. 'Procedural Equality, the Bulwark of Political Liberty', *Political Theory*, 26: 1.
Van Holsteyn, Joop, Den Ridder, Josye, and Koole, Ruud. 2015. 'From May's Laws to May's legacy: On the Opinion Structure Within Political Parties', *Party Politics*, 23: 5.
Vecchio, Concetto. 2018. 'Di Maio Contro Pd e Fi: Terrorismo Mediatico per far Schizzare lo Spread'. *La Repubblica*, 30 September.
Vibert, Frank. 2007. *The Rise of the Unelected: Democracy and the New Separation of Powers*, Cambridge: Cambridge University Press.
Vignati, Rinaldo. 2015. 'Beppe Grillo and the Movimento 5 Stelle. A Brief History of "Leaderist" Movement with a Leaderless Ideology', in Filippo Tronconi (ed.), *Beppe Grillo's Five Star Movement: Organisation, Communication and Ideology*, London: Routledge.
Vittori, Davide. 2017. 'Podemos and the Five Stars Movement: Divergent Trajectories in a Similar Crisis', *Constellations*, 24: 3.
Volpicelli, Gian. 2018. 'Italy's weird technopopulism could be the new normal'. *Wired Magazine*, 10 June.
Wacquant, Loic. 2009. *Prisons of Poverty*, Minneapolis: University of Minnesota Press.
Wagner. 1994. *A Sociology of Modernity: Liberty and Discipline*, London: Routledge.
Walzer, Michael. 1965. *The Revolution of the Saints. A Study in the Origins of Radical Politics*, Cambridge: Harvard University Press.
Watt, Nicholas. 2010. 'David Cameron reveals "big society" vision—and denies it is just cost-cutting'. *The Guardian*, 19 July.
Wattenberg, Martin. 1998. *The Decline of American Political Parties*, Cambridge: Harvard University Press.
Watts, Duncan and Pilkington, Colin. 2005. *Britain in the European Union Today*, Manchester: Manchester University Press.
Watts, Jake and Bale, Tim. 2018. 'Populism as an Intra-Party Phenomenon. The Case of the British Labour Party under Jeremy Corbyn', *British Journal of Politics and International Relations*, 21: 1.
Weedon, Chris. 1987. *Feminist Practice and Post-Structuralist Theory*. Oxford: Blackwell.
Wells, Marc. 2020. 'The significance of Italy's Sardines movement. International Committee of the Fourth International, 25 January.
Weyland, Kurt. 1996. 'Neopopulism and Neoliberalism in Latin America: Unexpected Affinities', *Studies in Comparative International Development*, 31: 3.

Weyland, Kurt. 2001. 'Clarifying a Contexted Concept: Populism in the Study of Latin American Politics', *Comparative Politics*, 34: 1.
Weyland, Kurt. 2017. 'Populism: A Political-Strategic Approach', in Cristobal Rovira Kaltwasser, Paul Taggart, Paulina Ochoa Espejo, and Pierre Ostiguy (eds.), *The Oxford Handbook of Populism*, Oxford: Oxford University Press.
Whelan, Ella. 2016. 'Triggering Article 50: the precondition of a new politics'. *Spiked online*, 26 July.
White, Jonathan. 2020. *Politics of Last Resort. Governing by Emergency in the European Union*, Oxford: Oxford University Press.
White, Jonathan and Ypi, Lea. 2016. *The Meaning of Partisanship*, Oxford: Oxford University Press.
Wilson, Bryan. 1966. *Religion in Secular Society*, Oxford: Oxford University Press.
Wolin, Sheldon. 2004. *Politics and Vision: Continuity and Innovation in Western Political Thought*, Princeton, NJ: Princeton University Press.
Wolkenstein, Fabio. 2016. 'A Deliberative Model of Intra-party Democracy.' *Journal of Political Philosophy*, 24: 3.
Wolkenstein, Fabio. 2019. *Rethinking Party Reform*, Oxford: Oxford University Press.
Zampano, Giada. 2019. 'Italy's "Sardines" movement threatens Salvini's dominance'. *Agence France Press*, 29 November.
Zanker, Francisca. 2018. 'Liberia', in *Africa Yearbook*, 14.
Zarzalejos, Javier. 2016. 'Populism in Spain: an analysis of Podemos', *European View*, 15.
Zielonka, Jan. 2018. *Counter-Revolution: Liberal Retreat in Europe*, Oxford: Oxford University Press.
Zulianello, Mattia. 2018. 'Anti-System Parties Revisited: Concept Formation and Guidelines for Empirical Research', *Government and Opposition*, 53: 4.

Index

For the benefit of digital users, indexed terms that span two pages (e.g., 52–53) may, on occasion, appear on only one of those pages.

Anti-establishment 23, 41, 50–1, 61, 67n.6, 125, 140–1, 151, 179–80, 191, 198, 202–3
Anti-pluralism 26, 211–12
Anti-system 51, 78, 128–9, 132–3, 165, 172
Austria 101
Authoritarianism 13, 158–64, 173n.1, 193–4, 215

Belgium 94
Berlusconi, Silvio 53, 79, 82–3, 127–32, 136, 151, 204n.4
Blair, Tony 41–50, 130–1, 137–43, 162–3, 167, 192
Brown, Gordon 41, 46, 137–40, 200

Cartel Party 9–10, 93–4, 112–21, 174, 179–80
Casaleggio, Gianroberto 4, 50, 53, 57–8, 156
Catch-all party 50–1, 89n.1, 92, 100
Christian Democracy 7, 10, 78, 95, 101–2, 106, 122–3, 216
Citizen Expert 4–6, 58–9
Class
 - dealignment 104–6
 - structure 7, 33, 97–9, 133
Cleavages 1, 8–9, 33–4, 94–5, 106, 108, 133, 158, 191
Cognitive mobilization 9, 35, 92–4, 102, 107–8, 189, 195
Collective Intelligence 5–6, 57–8, 59n.5, 67, 75–7
Common Sense 6, 71n.7, 76–7, 85–6
Consensus 101, 137, 144–5, 191–2, 218
Corbyn, Jeremy 41, 141–2, 167, 187n.4, 200
Corporatism 62, 98, 102, 113
Coronavirus 198, 209–15
Correa, Rafael 18–19
Crouch, Colin 1, 47, 90n.2, 99, 149
Cummings, Dominic 30–1, 201

Democracy
 - crisis 1–2, 12–13, 171–2, 193–4
Democratic Discontent 12–13, 154–8
Democratization
 - of political parties 170, 182–4
Depoliticisation 30, 45–7, 92, 169–72, 214
Desubstantialization 140, 148–54, 174–5
Di Maio, Luigi 51–2, 146, 199

Duverger, Maurice 7, 33–4, 95–6, 181–2

Epistemic democracy 45n.1, 73, 203–4
European integration 43, 119–20
Expertise 4–5, 8, 28–33, 73–4, 77, 147, 152–3, 169, 171–2, 177, 205–7

First World War 98
Fischer, Frank 29, 152, 171–2
France 5, 59–69, 96–7, 103, 109–10, 115–16, 155–6, 172–3, 206, 208–9
Freezing Hypothesis 9–10, 108, 110
Front National 133
Fukuyama, Francis 123, 166–7

Goal Differentiation 15–16, 22, 36, 117, 181, 184–5
Grillo, Beppe 4, 50–9, 146, 156–8

Hollande, François 22, 27, 60, 67–8, 136–7, 157–8

Incarceration 13, 158–63, 162n.7
Ideal types 28n.1, 33n.4, 34, 202
Identity Politics 164–8
Ideology 2, 8–9, 33–8, 94–102, 145, 152, 170, 188n.5, 190, 198
Individualization 26, 35, 102
Industrial relations 96, 114
Intermediary bodies 12–13, 25–8, 35, 61, 134, 155–6, 183–4
Italy 4, 50–9, 97–8, 100–1, 108–9, 111, 117–18, 126–32, 155, 162, 191–2, 213

Johnson, Boris 200–1, 211–12
Judt, Tony 12, 95n.8, 101, 102n.10, 111–12, 148–9, 154, 165

Kelsen, Hans 157
Kircheimer, Otto 22, 36, 100–1, 117
Kriesi, Hanspeter 125, 145, 191

Labour Party 3–4, 36–7, 41–50, 95, 100–1, 110, 137–43, 187n.4, 193n.6, 200–2
La République En Marche 5, 59–69, 82–3, 172–3, 206–7

Le Pen, Jean-Marie 133
Le Pen, Marine 23, 59–60, 192, 207–8
Lega (*see also:* Lega Nord) 4, 70, 78–87, 155, 163, 199, 199n.1, 202
Lipow, Arthur 18, 20
Lipset, Seymour Martin 25, 33, 35, 94–5, 100, 108, 110

Macron, Emmanuel 5–6, 11, 23, 59–69, 135–6, 146–7, 151–2, 156, 163, 191–2, 200–2, 206, 208–9
Mair, Peter 1, 4–6, 9, 42–4, 48, 90–1, 99, 102n.10, 110, 116–19, 123–4, 154–5, 174–6, 179–83
Mass party 7–9, 15, 33–5, 47–9, 78, 82, 89n.1, 95–6, 100, 127, 130–1, 143, 182–4, 189–90, 198
May, Theresa 141
Mediation 8–9, 12–15, 27, 59n.5, 88, 94, 155–7, 162–4, 166, 168, 182
Meynaud, Jean 29–30
Michels, Roberto 181–2, 182n.3
Mitterrand, François 109–10, 115–16, 118–19, 118n.18, 119, 132n.28, 136
Modernization 105–6, 191
Monti, Mario 23, 53, 55–6, 125–6, 146, 177–8, 206
Mounk, Yascha 154–5, 172, 173n.1, 193–5, 195n.7, 196
Mudde, Cas 25–6, 42, 52–3, 92–3, 147–8
Muller, Jan Werner 19, 25–6, 44, 148, 152, 171, 194, 211

Netherlands 145, 159
Northern League 78

Organized interests 10, 90, 90n.2, 91, 93–4, 96, 102, 113–14, 121–2, 143, 189, 209, 217

Pablo Iglesias 6, 70, 71n.7, 72–6, 82–3, 85–6
Pandemic 211–12, 214, 218
Partisanship 15, 45–7, 170, 181, 184, 188–94, 196
Partito Democratico (PD) 41, 50, 127, 130–1, 199–200
Party democracy 1, 3, 14–15, 34, 89n.1, 99–100, 121, 170, 178–81, 183, 187–9, 193–4
Party system 1, 6, 9, 22, 88, 93–4, 100, 108–12, 123–4, 126–7, 139–40, 145, 184
Personalization 5, 11–12, 63, 82–3, 149–51, 153, 157–8
Pillarization 90n.2, 101, 102n.10
Podemos 6–7, 19, 69–78, 154n.4
Polarization 11, 21, 45, 90, 145–7, 190, 196–7
Political parties 3–4, 7–10, 12–13, 18, 26–8, 39–41, 47, 52–3, 60–2, 69, 81–2, 88–90, 92, 94, 96–7, 99–102, 104–6, 108–11, 115–19, 124, 127, 132n.28, 134, 140–1, 145–7, 154n.4, 156–8, 170, 179–93, 195–6, 198, 206
Political competition 1–2, 20–3, 34–7, 46–7, 49, 55–6, 64, 70, 89–90, 97–8, 100–3, 114–15, 127, 138–9, 144–5, 150, 150n.2, 152–3, 175, 185–7, 191–2, 196–7, 204–5, 204n.4, 205
Political logic 3–4, 7–10, 14–15, 17, 19–24, 32–41, 49, 51–2, 69, 71–4, 77, 85, 87–91, 94, 100, 106, 110–13, 121–7, 129–30, 133, 138–41, 143, 146–7, 164–7, 169–70, 172–4, 180, 182–3, 186–7, 196–7, 199–200, 202, 204–10, 211
Political opposition 22, 98, 147, 174–5, 191–2
Populism
 - definitions 25–8
 - as a mode of political action 25, 28
 - as an ideology 25–7
 - as a political strategy 26–7
Protest Politics 155
Punitive Turn 160–3, 192

Rassemblement National (RN) 51
Renzi, Matteo 41, 53, 86, 130–6, 146, 191–2
Revolutionary Horizon 164–7
Rosenblum, Nancy 3, 26–7, 34, 178–81
Rokkan, Stein 8–9, 33, 35, 94–5, 108, 110

Salvini, Matteo 50, 70, 78–87, 163, 192, 199, 199n.1, 202
Sarkozy, Nicolas 134–7, 151–2
Sartori, Giovanni 128–9
Schattschneider, Eric 1, 21–2, 36–7, 173–5
Secularization 9, 105–7, 106n.12
Second World War 7, 78, 89–90, 98–102, 108–9, 113, 187, 214, 216–17
Seyd, Patrick 18–20, 44
Social democracy 89n.1, 116
Socialism 26, 71n.7, 115–16, 152, 216
Spectacularization of Politics 11–12, 149, 151, 153
Starmer, Keir 200

Technocracy
 - definition 28–33
 - history 29, 29n.2, 93
 - in political theory 28
 - and democracy 28
 - and technology 18, 57–9, 67, 201, 210–11
 - and techne 28, 30–1, 55–6, 206–7, 214
Third Way 41–5, 47, 177
Trade Unions 8–9, 12–13, 15, 94, 96, 114, 134, 157
Trump, Donald 178–9, 190, 204n.4

United Kingdom 99, 109, 114, 172–3, 200
United Kingdom Independence Party (UKIP) 41, 51
Urbinati, Nadia 27